KOSHA

KOSHA

OR

DICTIONARY

OF THE

SANSKRIT LANGUAGE

BY

UMURA SINGHA.

TRANSLATED BY

H. T. COLEBROOKE, ESQ.

GYAN

Published by

GYAN

Gyan Publishing House
5, Ansari Road
Daryaganj, New Delhi-110002
Phone: 011-47034999, 9811692060
E-mail: books@gyanbooks.com

Distribution Network
gyanbooks.com
India, USA, Canada, UK, Australia

ISBN: 978-81-212-7073-1 (PB)
First Published, 1891

2nd Impression 2024

Printed at: Gyan Press, Delhi.

KOSHA
Author: UMURA SINGHA, Translator: H. T. COLEBROOKE

KOSHA

OR

DICTIONARY

OF THE

SANSKRIT LANGUAGE

BY

UMURA SINGHA.

With an English Interpretation and Annotations.

BY

H. T. COLEBROOKE, ESQ.,

Late of the Bengal Civil Service.

Calcutta :

PRINTED BY NUNDO MOHUN BANERJEE & CO.,
AT THE FULL MOON PRINTING WORKS,
24, BEADON STREET, E. C.

1891.

PREFACE.

THE compilation of a Sanskrit Dictionary having been undertaken early after the institution of the College of Fort William, it was at the same time thought advisable to print, in Sanskrit and English, the work which has been chosen for the basis of that compilation ; as well for the sake of exhibiting an original authority to which reference will be frequently necessary, as with the view of furnishing an useful vocabulary which might serve until an ampler dictionary could be prepared and published.

The celebrated *Umura Kósha*, or Vocabulary of Sanskrit by UMURA SINGHA, is, by the unanimous suffrage of the learned, the best guide to the acceptations of nouns in Sanskrit. The work of PA'N'INI on etymology is rivalled by other grammars, some of which have even obtained the preference in the opinion of the learned of particular provinces : but UMURA's vocabulary has prevailed wherever the Sanskrit language is cultivated ; and the numerous other vocabularies, which remain, are consulted only where UMURA's is either silent or defective. It has employed the industry of innumerable commentators, while none of the others (with the single exception of HE'MACHANDRA's) have been interpreted even by one annotator. Such decided preference for the *Umura Kósha*, and the consequent frequency of quotations from it, determined the selection of this as the basis of an alphabetical dictionary, and suggested the expediency of also publishing the original text with an English interpretation.

Like other vocabularies of Sanskrit, that of UMURA is in metre; and a considerable degree of knowledge of the language becomes requisite to discriminate the words from their interpretations and to separate them from contiguous terms which affect their initials and finals. On this account, and to adapt the work to the use of the English student, the words, of which the sense is exhibited, are disjoined from their interpretation (which is included between crotchets); and the close of each word is marked by a Italic letter over it indicating the gender of the noun. Where a letter has been permuted according to the Sanskrit system of orthography, a dot is placed under the line to intimate that a letter is there altered or omitted: and a marginal note is added, exhibiting the radical final of the noun, or its initial, in every instance where either of them is so far disguised by permutation as not to be easily recognized upon a slight knowledge of the rudiments of the language, and of its orthography. An explanation in English is given in the margin, and completed, when necessary, at the foot of the page. The different interpretations proposed by the several commentators, and the variations in orthography remarked by them, are also specified in the same place.

According to the original plan of the present publication, the variations in the reading of the text (for which a careful collation has been made of several copies and of numerous commentaries) are noticed only where they affect the interpretation of a word or its orthography. It was not at first intended to insert those differences which are remarked by commentators upon other authority, and not upon the ground of any variation in the text itself. However, the utility of indicating such differences was afterwards thought to counterbalance any inconvenience attending it: and after some progress had been made at the press, this* and other additions to the original design were admitted, which have rendered a supplement necessary to supply omissions in the first chapters and complete the work upon an uniform plan.

To avoid too great an increase of the volume, the various readings and interpretations are rather hinted than fully set

* These additions are incorporated with the text in the present edition.

forth: it has been judged sufficient to state the result, as the notes would have been too much lengthened, if the ground of disagreement had been everywhere exhibited and explained. For the same reason, authorities have not been cited by name. The mention of the particular commentator in each instance would have enlarged the notes, with very little advantage, as the means of verifying authorities are as effectually furnished by an enumeration of the works which have been employed and consulted. They are as follow:—

I. The text of the *Umura Kósha*:

This vocabulary comprised in three books, is frequently cited under the title of *Trika´nda*;* sometimes under the denomination of *Abhid'ha´na* (nouns), from its subject; often under that of *Umura Ko´sha*, from the name of the author. The commentators are indeed unanimous in ascribing it to UMURA SINGHA. He appears to have belonged to the sect of *Budd'ha*, (though this be denied by some of his scholiasts;) and is reputed to have lived in the reign of VIKRAMA´DITYA; and he is expressly named among the ornaments of the Court of RA´JA´ BHO´JA,† one of the many princes to whom that title has been assigned. If this mention of him be accurate, he must have lived not more than eight hundred years ago; for a poem entitled *Suba´hshita ratna sando´ha*, by a *Jaina* author named AMITAKATI, is dated in the year 1050 from the death of VIKRAMA´DITYA, and in the reign of MUNJA who was uncle and predecessor of RA´JA´ BHO´JA. It, however, appears inconsistent with the inscription at *Budd'ha-gaya´* which is dated in the year 1005 of the era of VIKRAMA´DITYA, and in which mention is made of UMURA DE´VA, probably the same with the author of the vocabulary. From the frequent instances of anachronism both in sacred and profane story as

---

* i. e. The three books. But that name properly appertains to a more ancient vocabulary, which is mentioned by the commentaries on the *Umura Kosha* among the works from which this is supposed to have been compiled.

† In the *Bho´ja Praband'ha*.

current among the *Hindus*, more confidence seems due to the inscription, than to any popular tales concerning RA´JA´ BHO´JA; and the *Umura Ko´sha* may be considered as at least nine hundred years old ; and possibly more ancient.

It is intimated in the author's own preface that the work was compiled from more ancient vocabularies : his commentators instance the *Trika´nda,** *Utpa´lini*, RABHASA and KA´TYA´YANA as furnishing information on the nouns; and VYA´DI and VA´RARUCHI on the genders. The last mentioned of these authors is reputed contemporary with VIKRAMA´DITYA and consequently with UMURA SINGHA himself.

The copies of the original, which have been employed in the correction of the text, in the present publication, are,

1st. A transcript made for my use from an ancient corrected copy in the *Tirhutíya* character, and collated by me with a copy in *Dévanágarí*, which had been carefully examined by SIR WILLIAM JONES. He had inserted in it an English interpretation; of which also I reserved a copy and have derived great assistance from it in the present publication.

2d. A transcript in *Dévana´garí* character, with a commentary and notes in the *Ka´na´ra´* dialect. It contains numerous passages, which are unnoticed in the most approved commentaries, and which are accordingly omitted in the present edition.

3rd. Another copy in the *Dévana´garí* character, with a brief and imperfect interpretation in *Hindí*.

4th. A copy in the Bengali character with marginal notes explanatory of the text.

5th. A copy in duplicate, accompanied by a Sanskrit commentary, which will be forthwith mentioned (that of RA´MA´SRA´MA). It contains a few passages not noticed by most of the commentators. They have been, however, retained on the au-

---

* See a preceding note.

thority of this scholiast. A like remark is applicable to certain other passages expounded in some commentaries but not in others. All such have been retained, where the authority itself has been deemed good.

6th. Recourse has been occasionally had to other copies of the text in the possession of natives, whenever it has been thought any ways requisite.

II. Commentaries on the *Umura Kósha.*

1. At the head of the commentaries which have been used, must be placed that of RA´YA MUKUT´A, (or VRIHASPATI surnamed RA´YA MUKUT´A MAN´I.) This work entitled *Padachandriká,* was compiled, as the author himself informs us, from sixteen earlier commentaries, to many of which he rapeatedly refers : especially those of KSHI´RA SWA´MI´, SUBHU´TI, HA´DD´A CHANDRA, KALINGA, KO´NKAT´A, SARVADHARA, and the *Vyák'hya´mrĭta Ţíkasarvasva,* &c.*

Its age is ascertained from the incidental mention of a date : viz. 1353 *Saka,* or 4532 of the *Kaliyuga,* corresponding to A.D. 1431.

Though the derivations in MUKUT´A's commentary be often inaccurate, and other errors also have been remarked by later compilers, its authority is in general great ; and, accordingly, it has been carefully consulted under every article of the present work.

2. Among the earlier commentaries named by RA´YA MUKUT´A, that of KSHI´RA SWA´MI´ is the only one, which has been examined

---

* The following names may be selected from MUKUT´A's quotations, to complete the number of sixteen : *Mád'havi, Mad'huma´d'havi, Sarva´nanda, Abhinanda,* RA´JA´DE´VA, GO´VERD'HANA, DRA´VI`DA, BHO´JARA´JA. But some of these appear to be separate works, rather than commentaries on the *Umura Ko´sha.* MUKUT´A occasionally cites the most celebrated grammarians as PA´N´INI, JAYA´DITYA, JINE´NDRA, MAITRE´YA, RAKSHITA, PURUSHOTTAMA, MA´D'HAVA, &c.

in the progress of this compilation. It is a work of considerable merit; and is still in general use in some provinces of India, although the interpretations not unfrequently differ from those commonly received.

3. The *Vyá'k'hyásud'há*, a modern commentary by RÁ'MA'S'RA'MA or by BHA'NUDI'KSHITA (for copies differ as to the name of the author) is the work of a grammarian of the school of Benares. He continually refers to RA'YA MUKUT'A and to SA'MI'; and his work serves to confirm their scholia where accurate, and to correct them where erroneous. It has been consulted at every line.

4. The *Vyá'k'hyá Pradípa* by ACHYUTA UPA'D'HYA'YA is a concise and accurate exposition of the text: but adds little to the information furnished by the works above-mentioned. It has been, however, occasionally consulted.

In these four commentaries, the derivations are given according to PA'N'INI'S system. In others, which are next to be enumerated, various popular grammars are followed for the etymologies. But, as the derivations of the words are not included in the plan of the present work, being reserved for a place in the intended alphabetical dictionary of Sanskrit, those commentaries have not been the less useful in regard to the information which was sought in them.

5. The commentary of BHARATA MALLA (entitled *Mugdhabód'hini*) has been as regularly consulted as those of MUKUT'A and RA'MA'S'RA'MA. It is indeed a very excellent work; copious and clear, and particularly full upon the variations of orthography according to different readings or different authorities; the etymologies are given conformably with VO'PADE'VA'S system of grammar. The author flourished in the middle of last century.

6. The *Sárá Sundarí* by MAT'HURE'S'A has been much used. It is perspicuous and abounds in quotations from other commentaries; and is therefore a copious source of information on the various interpretations and readings of the text. The

Supadma is the grammar followed in the derivations stated by this commentator. MAT'HURES'A is author likewise of a vocabulary in verse entitled *Sabdaratna'vali*, arranged in the same order with the *Umura Kósha*, and which might serve therefore as a commentary on that work. It was compiled under the patronage of a Mussulman Chieftain *Mureh'ha Khán*, whose name is prefixed to it. The author wrote not more than 150 years ago.*

7. The *Padárt'ha Kaumudí* by NA'RA'YANA CHAKRAVARTI' is another commentary of considerable merit, which has been frequently consulted. The *Kalápa* is the grammar followed in the etymologies here exhibited.

8. A commentary by RA'MA'NA'T'HA VIDYA'VACHASPATI, entiled *Trika'ndavivéka*, is peculiarly copious on the variations of orthography, and is otherwise a work affording much useful information.

9. Another commentary which has been constantly employed, is that by NI'LAKANT'HA. It is full and satisfactory on most points for which reference is usually made to the expositors of the *Umura Kósha*.

10. The commentary of RAMA TARKAVA'GI'SA has been uniformly consulted throughout the work. It was recommended for its accuracy; but has furnished little information; being busied chiefly with etymology. This, like the preceding, follows the grammar entitled *Kalápa*.

Other commentaries were also collected for occasional reference in the progress of this work; but have not been employed, being found to contain no information which was not also furnished, and that more amply, by the scholiasts

* His work contains the date 1588 Saka or A. D. 1666.

above mentioned. The list of them, contained in the subjoined note, may therefore suffice.*

III. Sanskrit dictionaries and vocabularies by other authors. Throughout the numerous commentaries on the *Umura Ko'sha*, the text itself is corrected or confirmed, and the interpretation and remarks of the Commentators supported, by references to other Sanskrit vocabularies. They are often cited by the scholiasts for the emendation of the text in regard to the gender of a noun, and not less frequently for a variation of orthography, or for a difference of interpretation. The authority quoted has been in general consulted before any use has been made of the quotations; or, where the original work cannot now be procured, the agreement of commentators has been admitted as authenticating the passage. This has been particularly attended to, in the chapter containing homonymous words; it having been judged useful to introduce into that chapter, the numerous additional acceptations stated in other Dictionaries, and understood to be alluded to in the *Umura Kósha.*

The dictionaries, which have been consulted, are 1st. The *Médini*, an alphabetical dictionary of homonymous terms by MEDINIKARA. 2nd. The *Viswaprakása* by MAHE'S'WARA VAIDYA, a similar dictionary, bnt less accurate and not so well arranged. It is the ground-work of the *Médini* which is an improved and corrected work of great authority. Both are very frequently cited by the Commentators.

---

* *Kaumudi* by NAYANA'NANDA; *Trikánd'a chinta'mani* by RAG'HUNA'THA CHAKRAVARTI'; both according to PA'NINI's system of etmology. *Vaishamya kaumudi* by RA'MAPRASA'DA TARKALANKA'RA; *Padamanjari* by LO'KANA'T'HA; both following the grammatical system of the *Kalapa*. *Pradipamanjari* by RA'MA-S'RAMA, a jejune interpretation of the text. *Vrihat Haravali* by RA'MES'WARA. Also commentaries, by KRISHNADA'SA, TRILOCHANA DA'SA, SUNDARA'NANDA, VANADI'YABHAT'T'A, VISWANAT'HA, GOPA'L CHACRAVARTI, GOVINDA'NANDA, RA'MA'NDA BHOLA'NATHA, &c.

3. The *Haima*, a dictionary by HE´MA CHANDRA, in two parts ; one containing synonymous words arranged in six chapters ; the other containing homonymous terms in alphabetical order. Both are works of great excellence.

4. The *Abhid'hána Ratnamálá*, a vocabulary by HALA´-YUD'HA in five chapters ; the last of which relates to words having many acceptations. It is too concise for general use ; but is sometimes quoted.

5. The *D'haraní*, a vocabulary of words bearing many senses. It is less copious than the *Médiní* and *Haima* : but being frequently cited by Commentators, has been necessarily consulted.

6. The *Trika´ndasésha*, or supplement to the *Umura Kósha* by PURUSHO´TTAMA DE´VA.

6. The *Ha´rávalí* of the same author.

The last of these two supplements to *Umura*, being a collection of nncommon words, has not been much employed for the present publication. The other has been more used. Both are of considerable authority.

The reader will find in the notes a list of other dictionaries quoted by the Commentators, but the quotations of which have not been verified by reference to the originals, as these have not been procurable. *

Works under the title of *Varn´adés´ana´*,*Dwiru´pa* and *Unádi* have indeed been procured : but not the same with the books cited ; many different compilations being current under those titles. The first relates to words the orthography of which is likely to be mistaken from a confusion of similar letters ; the second exhibits words which are spelt in more than one way ; the third relates to a certain class of derivatives, separately noticed by grammarians.

* *Umuramálá*, UMURA DATTA, *Sabdárn´ava*, *Sás´wata*, *Varn´adés´aná*, *Dwirúpa*, *Una´dikósha*, *Ratna ko´sha*, *Ratnamálá*, RANTIDE´VA, RUDRA, VYA´DI, RABHASA, VOPA´LI´TA, BHA´GURI, AJAYA, VA´CHASPATI, TA´RA´PA´LA, ARUNADATTA.

IV. Grammatical works.

Grammar is so intimately connected with the subject of this publication, that it has been of course necessary to advert to the works of Grammarians. But as they are regularly cited by the commentators, it is needless to name them as authorities, since nothing will be found to have been taken from this source, which is not countenanced by some passage in the commentaries on the *Umura Kósha.*

V. Treatises on the roots of Sanskrit.

Verbs not being exhibited in the *Umura Kósha*, which is a vocabulary of nouns only, the treatises of MAITRE´YA, MA´D'HAVA, and others on Sanskrit roots, though furnishing important materials towards a complete dictionary of the language, have been very little employed in the present work ; and a particular reference to them was unnecesssary, as authority will be found in the commentaries on UMURA, for any thing which may have been taken from those treatises.

VI. The Scholia of classic writings.

Passages from the works of celebrated writers are cited by the commentators on the *Umura Kósha* ; and the scholiasts of classic poems frequently quote dictionaries in support of their interpretation of difficult passages. In the compilation of a copious Sanskrit dictionary an ample use may be made of the Scholia. They have been employed for the present publication so far only as they are expressly cited by the principal commentaries on the *Umura Kósha* itself.

Should the reader be desirous of verifying the authorities, upon which the interpretation and notes are grounded, he will in general find the information sought by him in some one of the ten commentaries of UMURA, which have been before named ; and will rarely have occasion to proceed beyond those which have been specified as the works regularly consulted.

In regard to plants and animals and other objects of natural history, noticed in different chapters of this vocabulary, and especially in the 4th, 5th and 9th chapters of the 2nd book, it is proper to observe, that the ascertainment of them generally depends on the correctness of the corresponding vernacular names. The commentators seldom furnish any description or other means of ascertainment besides the current denomination in a provincial language. A view of the animal, or an examination of the plant, known to the vulgar under that denomination, enables a person conversant with natural history to determine its name according to the received nomenclature of European Botany and Zoology: but neither my inquiries, nor those of other Gentlemen, who have liberally communicated the information collected by them,* nor the previous researches of SIR WILLIAM JONES, have yet discovered all the plants and animals, of which the names are mentioned by the Commentaries on the *Umura Kósha*; and even in regard to those which have been seen by us, a source of error remains in the inaccuracy of the Commentators themselves, as is proved by the circumstance of their frequent disagreement. It must be, therefore, understood, that the correspondence of the Sanskrit names with the generic and specific names in Natural History is in many instances doubtful. When the uncertainty is great, it has usually been so expressed; but errors may exist where none have been apprehended.

It is necessary likewise to inform the reader that many of the plants, and some animals (especially fish), have not been described in any work yet published. Of such, the names have been taken from the manuscripts of DR. ROXBURGH and DR. F. BUCHANAN.

Having explained the plan and design of this edition of the *Umura Kósha*, I have only further to state, that the delay which has arisen since it was commenced (now more than five years) has been partly occasioned by my distance from the press (the

* Drs. Roxburgh, F. Buchanan, and W. Hunter, and Mr. William Carey.

work being printed by MR. CAREY at Serampoor),and partly by avocations which have retarded the progress of collating the different copies of the text and commentaries : a task the labour of which may be judged by those who have been engaged in similar undertakings.

H. T. COLEBROOKE.

CALCUTTA, *Dec.* 1807.

CONTENTS.

CHAPTER III.

CHAPTER IV.

CHAPTER V.

CHAPTER VI.

CHAPTER VII.

CHAPTER VIII.

CHAPTER V.

CHAPTER VI.

Genders.

अमरकोषः ।

यस्य ज्ञानदयासिन्धोरगाधस्यानघा गुणाः ।
सेव्यतामक्षयो धीराः स श्रिये चामृताय च ॥
समाहृत्यान्यतन्त्राणि संक्षिप्तैः प्रतिसंस्कृतैः ।
सम्पूर्णमुच्यते वर्गैर्नामलिङ्गानुशासनम् ॥
प्रायशो रूपभेदेन साहचर्य्याच्च कुत्रचित् ।
स्त्रीपुंनपुंसकं ज्ञेयं तद्विशेषविधेः क्वचित् ॥
भेदाख्यानाय न द्वन्द्वो नैकशेषो न सङ्करः ।
कृतोऽत्र भिन्नलिङ्गानामनुक्तानां क्रमादृते ॥
त्रिलिङ्ग्यां त्रिष्विति पदं मिथुने च द्वयोरिति ।
निषिद्धलिङ्गं शेषार्थं त्वन्ताथादि न पूर्वभाक् ॥

BOOK I.

CHAP. I. SECT. I.

1. स्वर्[i] (अव्ययं) स्वर्ग[m] नाक[m] त्रिदिव[m] त्रिदशालयाः[1 m] — Heaven.
सुरलोको[2 m] द्यो[f] दिवौ[f] (द्वे स्त्रियौ)[a] (क्लीबे) त्रिविष्टपं[n b]

2. अमरा[m] निर्जरा[m] देवास्[m] त्रिदशा[m] विबुधाः[m] सुराः[m] — Gods or deities. c
सुपर्वाणः[3 m] सुमनसस्[4 m] त्रिदिवेशा[m] दिवौकसः[5 m d]

1—य. 2—क. 3—र्वन्. 4—नस्. 5—कस्.

[a] द्यो and दिव् both fem. also neut. दिवं. [b] Or त्रिपिष्टपं, and त्रिविष्टपं. [c] A god, sing. अमरः. pl. अमराः. [d] दिवौकाः or दिवौकाः (स्).

m 1 m a m m

3. आदितेया दिविषदो लेखा अदितिनन्दनाः

m 2 m b m m 3 m

आदित्या ऋभवोऽस्वप्ना अमर्त्या अमृतान्धसः

m c 4 m m 5 m

4. बर्हिर्मुखाः क्रतुभुजो गीर्वाणा दानवारयः

m 6 m. n d f

वृन्दारका दैवतानि (पुंसि वा) देवता (स्त्रियाम्)

m m f 7 m m 8 m 9 m

Sets of divinities. e — 5. आदित्या विश्व वसवस् तुषिताभास्वरानिलाः

m g m m

महाराजिक साध्याश्(च) रुद्राश्(च गणदेवताः)

m 10 f m i 11 n m m

Demi-gods, & nymphs. h — 6. विद्याधरोऽप्सरो यक्ष रक्षो गन्धर्व किन्नराः

m j m m m m

पिशाचो गुह्यकः सिद्धो भूतो (ऽमी देवयोनयः)

m m m m 12 m m

Giants or Titans. k — 7. असुरा दैत्य दैतेय दनुजेन्द्रारि दानवाः

m m m 13 m

शुक्रशिष्या दितिसुताः पूर्वदेवाः सुरद्विषः

m m m l 14 m m

A *Jina* or *Buddha*. — 8. सर्वज्ञः सुगतो बुद्धो धर्मराजस् तथागतः

1—षद्. 2 ऋभु. 3—धस्. 4—भुज्. 5—रि. 6—क. 7 वसु. 8 भा—. 9 अ—. 10 अप्सरस्. 11—क्षस्. 12 इ—. 13—द्विट्. 14—राज.

[a] दिविषत् or द्युसद् and द्युसत् (द्यु). [b] ऋभुः or ऋभूः. [c] बर्हिर्मुखः or बर्हिर्मुखाः. [d] Masc. or neut. [e] Each consists of a specified number (see their names in other dictonaries.) *Adityas* 12. *Viswadévas* 10. *Vasus* 8. *Tushitas* 36. *A'bháswáras* 64. *Anilas* 49. *Mahárájikas* 220. *S'ad'hyás* 12. *Rudras* 11. [f] Pl. विश्वे i.e. विश्वेदेवाः. [g] Also महाराजकाः. [h] Of various classes and denominations, as *Vidyád'haras* &c. [i] Likewise यक्षः, fem. यक्षी and यक्षिणी. [j] Also पैशाचः. [k] A demon, sing. असुरः, pl. असुराः. Likewise आसुरः. [l] Also बुधः.

m 1 m m m m

समन्तभद्रो भगवान् मारजित् लोकजित् जिनः

m m 2 m m

9. षडभिज्ञो दशबलोऽद्वयवादी विनायकः

m m 3 m a m

मुनीन्द्रः श्रीघनः शास्ता मुनिः

4 m

शाक्यमुनिस् (तु यः)

m c m d 5 m

10. (स)शाक्यसिंहः सर्वार्थसिद्धः शौद्धोदनिश्(च सः) BUDD'HA. b

6 m 7 m 8 m

गौतमश्(चा)ऽर्कबन्धुश्(च)मायादेवीसुतश्(च सः)

9 m f 10 m m 11 m m

11. ब्रह्मात्मभूः सुरज्येष्ठः परमेष्ठी पितामहः BRAHMA'. e

m m 12 m m

हिरण्यगर्भो लोकेशः स्वयम्भुश् चतुराननः

13 m 14 m 15 m g m h m

12. धाताब्जयोनि र्द्रुहिणो विरिञ्चिः कमलासनः

16 m m 17 m 18 m 19 m m

स्रष्टा प्रजापतिर्वेधा विधाता विश्वसृड् विधिः

m 20 m j m m 21 m

13. विष्णुर्नारायणः कृष्णो वैकुण्ठो विष्टरश्रवाः VISHN'U. i

m m m m m

दामोदरो हृषीकेशः केशवो माधवः स्वभूः

1—भत्. 2—दिश्. 3 शास्तृ. 4—मुनि. 5—दनि. 6—तम. 7—बन्धु. 8—सुत. 9—त्मन्. 10 ब्रा—. 11—शिन्. 12—म्भु. 13 धातृ. 14 ब्ज—. 15 द्रु—. 16 स्रष्टृ. 17 वेधस्. 18—तृ. 19—सृज्. 20 ना—. 21—वस्.

[a] Likewise शासिता (तृ). [b] The founder of the religion named from him. [c] Also शाक्यः. [d] Likewise सर्वार्थः, and सिद्धार्थः. [e] Providence, or the Creator. [f] Also ब्रह्मा. [g] Likewise द्रुघणः, and द्रुघनः. [h] विरिञ्चः, विरञ्चिः, विरञ्चः and विरञ्चनः. [i] The pervader and preserver; identified by Hindu mythology with the hero *Krishn'a* son of *Vasudéva.* [j] Likewise नरायणः.

m m m m
14. दैत्यारिः पुण्डरीकाक्षो गोविन्दो गरुडध्वजः
m m 1m m a m
पीताम्बरोऽच्युतः शार्ङ्गी विष्वक्सेनो जनार्दनः
m 2m 3m m
15. उपेन्द्र इन्द्रावरजश्चक्रपाणिश्चतुर्भुजः
m b m 4m c m
पद्मनाभो मधुरिपुर्वासुदेवस्त्रिविक्रमः
m d m e m m
16. देवकीनन्दनः शौरिः श्रीपतिः पुरुषोत्तमः
5m 6m f m 7m
वनमाली बलिध्वंसी कंसारातिरधोक्षजः
m 8m m m g
17. विश्वम्भरः कैटभजिद् विधुः श्रीवत्सलाञ्छनः
m m i
VASUDE'VA.h वसुदेवो (ऽस्य जनकः स एव) आनकदुन्दुभिः
m k m m m
BALARA'MA.j 18. बलभद्रः प्रलम्बघ्नो बलदेवोऽच्युताग्रजः
m m m m
रेवतीरमणो रामः कामपालो हलायुधः
m 9m m 10m l 11m
19. नीलाम्बरो रौहिणेयस्तालाङ्को मुसली हली
m m m m m
संकर्षणः सीरपाणिः कालिन्दीभेदनो बलः

---

1 शार्ङ्गिन्. 2—रज. 3—षि. 4 वा—. 5—लिन्. 6—सिन्. 7 अधोक्षज. 8—जित्. 9—ण. 10—लिन्. 11 हलिन्.

[a] Also विश्वक्सेनः. [b] Likewise पद्मनाभिः. [c] Also वासुदेवः, वासुः. [d] Likewise दैवकीनन्दनः. [e] Or सौरिः. [f] Also बलिध्वंसी. [g] Likewise श्रीवत्सः. [h] Father of *Krishn'a*, and son of *Anacadundubha.* [i] Also आनकदुन्दुभिः. And दुन्दुः. [j] Brother of *Krishn'a.* [k] Likewise बलभद्रः. And भद्रबलः. [l] Also मुसली or मुशली. [m] Likewise बलः.

m m m m m
20. मदनो मन्मथो मारः प्रद्युम्नो मीनकेतनः — KA'MADE'VA. a

m m m m m m
कन्दर्पो दर्पको ऽनङ्गः कामः पञ्चशरः स्मरः

m b 1 m c m 2 m
21. शम्बरारिर्मनसिजः कुसुमेषुरनन्यजः

3 m d m m m
पुष्पधन्वा रतिपतिर्मकरध्वज आत्मभूः

m f 4 m g m m h
22. ब्रह्मसूर्विश्वकेतुः (स्याद्) ऽनिरुद्ध उषापतिः — ANIRUD'DHA. e

f f f f f f
लक्ष्मीः पद्मालया पद्मा कमला श्रीर्हरिप्रिया — Lakshmi. i

f 5 f f f f
23. इन्दिरा लोकमाता मा क्षीराब्धितनया रमा

m
(शंखो लक्ष्मीपतेः) पाञ्चजन्यश् — *Krsihn'a's* conch.

m
(चक्रं) सुदर्शनः — His discus & missile weapon.

f j
24. कौमुदकी (गदा) — His mace.

m
(खड्गो) नन्दकः — His sword.

m
कौस्तुभो (मणिः) — His jewel.

6 m 7 m m m m
गरुत्मान् गरुडस् तार्क्ष्यो वैनतेयः खगेश्वरः — The vehicle of *Vishn'u*. k

m m m m
25. नागान्तको विष्णुरथः सुपर्णः पन्नगाशनः

---

1 म—. 2 मनन्यज. 3 —त्मभू. 4 वि—. 5 —मातृ. 6 —त्मन्. 7 —ड.

a Love or Cupid; son of *Krishn'a.* b Also शम्बरारिः, and सम्बरारिः, or संवरारिः. c Likewise मनोजः. d Also पुष्पधनुः (स). e Son of *Pradyumna* and husband of *Ushá.* f This and the following terms are titles both of *Kámadéva* and *Anirudd'ha.* g Likewise ब्रह्मकेतुः or ऋष्यकेतुः, and रिश्यकेतुः, or रिष्यकेतुः—रिष्यकेतनः. h Also उषापतिः. i The wife of *Vishn'u*, and goddess of prosperity. j Likewise कौमादी, and कौमोदकी. k Variously described as a gigantic crane, a vulture, or an eagle.

Siva.[a] शंभुरीशः[m][b] पशुपतिः[m] शिवः[m] शूली[1][m] महेश्वरः[m]

26. ईश्वरः[m] सर्व[m][c] ईशानः[m] शङ्करश्[2][m] चन्द्रशेखरः[m]

भूतेशः[m] खण्डपरशुर्[m][d] गिरीशो[m] गिरिशो[m] मृडः[m]

27. मृत्युञ्जयः[m] कृत्तिवासाः[3][m][e] पिनाकी[4][m] प्रमथाधिपः[m]

उग्रः[m] कपर्दी[5][m] श्रीकण्ठः[m] शितिकण्ठः[m] कपालभृत्[m]

28. वामदेवो[m] महादेवो[m] विरूपाक्षस्[6][m] त्रिलोचनः[m]

कृशानुरेताः[7][m] सर्वज्ञो[m] धूर्जटिर्[m] नीललोहितः[m]

29. हरः[m][f] स्मरहरो[m] भर्गस्[8][m][g] त्र्यम्बकस्[9][m] त्रिपुरान्तकः[m]

गङ्गाधरो[m] ऽन्धकरिपुः[m] क्रतुध्वंसी[10][m] वृषध्वजः[m]

30. व्योमकेशो[m] भवो[m] भीमः[m] स्थाणू[11][m] रुद्र[m] उमापतिः[m]

His braided hair.[h] कपर्दो[m] ऽस्य जटाजूटः)

His bow. पिनाको[m] ऽजगवं[n][i] (धनुः)

His attendants. 31. प्रमथाः[m][j] (स्युः[k] पारिषदाः)

The divine mothers.[l] ब्राह्मी[m] त्याद्यास्तु[f] मातरः)

1—शिन्. 2—कर. 3—सस्. 4—किन्. 5—दिन्. 6—स. 7—सस्. 8 भर्ग. 9—म्बक. 10—णिन्. 11—स्थाण.

[a] The destroyer and reproducer. [b] Also शम्भुः. [c] Likewise शर्वः. [d] Also खण्डपर्शुः. [e] Likewise कृत्तिवासः (स). [f] Also हीरः. [g] Likewise भर्ग्यः. [h] Rolled on his head. [i] Also आजकवं, आजगवं, आजगावं, आजकावं, and अजीकवं. [j] Sing. प्रमथः. [k] This, which is likewise a name of Siva's attendants, is variously written. Sing. पारिषदः पार्षदः, or पार्षद्यः. [l] Or energies of the gods, viz. *Bráhmí*, *Mahéswarí*, *Aindri*, *Varáhí*, *Vaishnaví*, *Kaumárí*, *Kauvérí* or *Chámundá*, and *Charchicá*. [m] Also ब्रह्माणी.

f f b n
विभूति र्भूतिरैश्वर्यम् (अणिमादिकमष्टधा) Superhuman power. a

f f f d f e f 1 f f
32. उमा कात्यायनी गौरी काली हैमवतीश्वरी BHA´WANI´. c

f g f f f f
शिवा भवानी रुद्राणी शर्वाणी सर्वमङ्गला

f f f f f h 2 f i
33. अपर्णा पार्वती दुर्गा मृडानी चण्डिकाम्बिका

3 m m m m
विनायको विघ्नराज द्वैमातुर गणाधिपाः GAN´E´SA. j

4 m m m m
34. (अप्ये) कदन्त हेरम्ब लम्बोदर गजाननाः

m m 5 m l m
कार्त्तिकेयो महासेनः शरजन्मा षडाननः KA´RTI´KEYA. k

m m m m m
35. पार्वतीनन्दनः स्कन्दः सेनानीरग्निभूर्गुहः

6 m m m m m
बाहुलेयस् तारकजित् विशाखः शिखिवाहनः

m m m m n
36. षाण्मातुरः शक्तिधरः कुमारः क्रौञ्चदारणः

m 7 m 8 m p 9 m q m
इन्द्रो मरुत्वान् मघवा बिडौजाः पाकशासनः INDRA. o

---

1 ई—. 2 अ—. 3—क. 4 ए—. 5—जन्. 6—लेय. 7—त्वत्. 8—वन्. 9—जस्.

a Consisting in preternatural faculties of eight sorts (see the enumeration in other dictionaries), such as the power of assuming an imperceptible form &c. b This and the preceding term (विभूतिः) are by some considered to be here intended for names of ashes rubbed on the person of SIVA. c The wife of *Siva* and goddess of destruction. d Likewise गौरा. e Also काला. f Likewise ईश्वरा. g Also शिवी. h Likewise चण्डिः, चण्डी or चण्डा. i Also अम्बा. j The obviator of difficulties. k The god of war. l Likewise शरजन्मा. m Also बाहुलेय. n Likewise क्रौञ्चदारणः. o Regent of the sky. p Also मघवान् (वत्); some add मघवन्. q Likewise बिडौजाः.

1 *m* a *m* b *m* *m*

37. वृद्धश्रवाः सुनासीरः पुरुहूतः पुरन्दरः

m *m* *m* *m* *m*

जिष्णुर्लेखर्षभः शक्रः शतमन्युर्दिवस्पतिः

2 *m* c *m* 3 *m* *m* 4 *m* 5 *m*

38. सुत्रामा गोत्रभिद् वज्री वासवो वृत्रहा वृषा

m d *m* *m* *m*

वास्तोष्पतिः सुरपतिर्बलारातिः शचीपतिः

6 *m* *m* 7 *m* *m*

39. जम्भभेदी हरिहयः स्वाराण् नमुचिसूदनः

m 8 *m* 9 *m* *m*

संक्रन्दनो दुश्च्यवनस् तुराषाण् मेघवाहनः

m *m* 10 *m*

40. आखण्डलः सहस्राक्ष ऋभुक्षास्

(तस्य तु प्रिया)

f *f* f 11 *f*

SACHI. e — पुलोमजा शची न्द्राणी

12 *f* g

Indra's City. — (नगरी त्व्) मरावती

13 *m* h

His horse. — 41. (हय) उच्चैःश्रवाः

m

His charioteer. — (सूतो) मातलि

n

His grove or garden. — नन्दनं (वनं)

m

His palace. — (स्यात् प्रासादो) वैजयन्तो

m *m*

JAYANTA. i — जयन्तः पाकशासनिः

1—वस्. 2—मन्. 3—जिन्. 4—हन्. 5—वन्. 6—दिन्. 7—राज्. 8—वन. 9—साह्. 10—वह्. 11 इ—. 12 अ—. 13— वस्.

[a] Also वृषश्रवाः. [b] Likewise शुनासीरः and शुनाशीरः. [c] Also सूत्रामा. [d] Some add वास्तोष्पतिः. [e] The wife of *Indra*. [f] Likewise शचिः, and सची, or सचिः. [g] Also अमरा. [h] Likewise उच्चैःश्रवस् (स्). [i] Son of *Indra*.

m 1m 2m 3m

42. ऐरावतोऽभ्रमातङ्गैरावणाभ्रमुवल्लभाः — *Indra's* elephant.

f mn mna nb m

ह्रादिनी वज्रम् (अस्त्री स्यात्) कुलिशं भिदुरं पविः — His thunderbolt.

m mc md m 4mfe

43. शतकोटिः स्वरुः शम्बो दम्भोलिरशनिर् (द्वयोः)

n mn

व्योमयानं विमानोऽ(स्त्री) — The car of *Indra*. f.

5m

(नारदाद्याः) सुरर्षयः — A divine sage. g.

6f f

44. (स्यात्) सुधर्मा देवसभा — The council of the gods.

ni 7n f

पीयूषममृतं सुधा — The food of the gods. h.

f f fk f

मन्दाकिनी वियद्गङ्गा स्वर्णदी सुरदीर्घिका — The river of heaven. j.

m m 8m m m

45. मेरुः सुमेरुर्हेमाद्री रत्नसानुः सुरालयः — The mountain *Sumeru*. l

m m

(पञ्चैते देवतरवो) मन्दारः पारिजातकः — Five celestial trees. m.

m 9m . mn

46. सन्तानः कल्पवृक्षश्च् (च पुंसि वा) हरिचन्दनं

---

1 ष—. 2 ऐ—. 3 ष—. 4 ष—. 5—र्षिं. 6—र्म्मा. 7 ष—. 8—द्रिः. 9—क्ष.

[a] Also कुलीशं. [b] Likewise भिदिरं and भिदुः. [c] Also स्वरुः (रु). [d] Likewise शम्बः. And सम्बः or संवः. [e] Also अशनी, and वज्राशनिः. [f] Or of any god. [g] As *Nárada*, &c. [h] Ambrosia and Nectar; or the food and drink which confer immortality. [i] Likewise पेयूषं and पैयूषं. [j] The Ganges of the sky, suggested probably by the milky-way. [k] Also स्वर्गंदी. [l] The extremity of the world's axis; where the gods abide. [m] Severally named in the text.

SANATKUMARA. a

mb mc

सनत्कुमारो वैधात्रः

The Aswini. d

m 1m

स्वर्वैद्यावश्विनीसुतौ

me 2m m 3m

47. नासत्यावश्विनौ दस्रावाश्विनेयौ (च तावुभौ)

Nymphs. f

4f fg h

(स्त्रियां बहुष्व्) अप्सरसः स्वर्वेश्या (उर्वशीमुखाः)

Celestial musicians. i

mj 5mk 6ml

48. (हाहा हूहूश्चैवमाद्या) गन्धर्व्वास् (त्रिदिवौकसः)

Fire.

mm m m m m

अग्निर्वैश्वानरो वह्निर्वीतिहोत्रो धनञ्जयः

m m 7m 8mn

49. कृपीटयोनिर्ज्वलनो जातवेदास् तनूनपात्

9m 10mo 11m m m

बर्हिः शुष्मा कृष्णवर्त्मा शोचिष्केश उषर्बुधः

---

1 च—. 2 अश्विन. 3 धा—. 4 अप्सरस्. 5—हू. 6—र्वं. 7—दस्. 8—पाद्. Or—पात्. 9 बर्हि Or बर्हिस्. 10—न्. 11—र्त्मन्.

a The son of *Brahmá*, and eldest of the progenitors of mankind. b Likewise सनत्सुजात. c Also वैधात्रकः. d Physicians of heaven, and twin sons of the sun by his wife *Sanjnyá* in the shape of a mare, or children of the constellation *Aswiní*. One of the twins is named *Násatya*, and the other *Dásra*; but these terms, in the dual, designate both of them. Their patronymics are used in the singular, when either is singly intended. e Likewise नासिक्यौ. f Celestial courtesans, as *Urvasí*, *Rambhā*, *Ménacá*, *Ghritáchi*, *Tilóttamá*, &c. g Likewise स्वर्वेश्या. h Also उर्वशी and उर्व्वशी. Quiristers of heaven, as *Háhá*, *Húhú*, *Tumbura*, *Viswávasu*, *Chitrarat'ha*, &c. j Likewise हाहा; and हाहाः (स्). And Indec. हाहाः. k Also हूहूः and हाहाहूहूः. And Indec. हूहूः. l Sing. गन्धर्वः. Also गन्धर्वः and गान्धर्वः. m One commentator makes the plural of this word विश्वानराः, but erroneously say others. n Or, according to a different etymology, तनूनपाद् (द्). And तनूनपाः (पा). o शुष्मन्, or बर्हिःशुष्मन्. Also शुष्मः (स्).

m a m m b m m

50. आश्रयाशो बृहद्भानुः कृशानुः पावकोऽनलः

m 1 m 2 m 3 m

रोहिताश्वो वायुसखा शिखावानाशुशुक्षणिः

4 m 5 m m m

51. हिरण्यरेता हुतभुग् दहनो हव्यवाहनः

6 m c 7 m d 8 m m m

सप्तार्चिर्दमुनाः शुक्रश् चित्रभानुर्विभावसुः

m 9 n

52. शुचिरप्पित्तं

10 m m m

और्वस् (तु) वाडवो वडवानलः — Submarine fire. c

m f m f g 11 f h f f

(वह्नेर्द्वयो) र्ज्वालकीलावर्चिर्हेतिः शिखा (स्त्रियां) — Flame. f

m f n i m

53. (त्रिषु) स्फुलिङ्गोऽग्निकणः — A spark.

m m

सन्तापः संज्वरः (समौ) — A burn.

m m 12 m 13 m

धर्म्मराजः पितृपतिः समवर्त्ती परेतराट् — YAMA. j

m 14 m m 15 m m

54. कृतान्तो यमुनाभ्राता शमनो यमराड् यमः

m m k m m m

कालो दण्डधरः श्राद्धदेवो वैवस्वतोऽन्तकः

1—खि, Or —ख. 2—वत्. 3 आ—. 4—तस्. 5—भुज्. 6—स्. EX. —र्चिस्. 7—नस्. 8—क्र. 9 अ—. 10—र्व: 11 अर्चि. 12—र्त्तिन् 13— राज्. 14 —तृ. 15—राज्.

a Likewie आशयाशयः. b Also कृषानु. c Likewise सप्तार्चिः (र्चि). d Also दमूनाः. e A being consisting of flame, but with a mare's head, sprung from the thighs of *Urva*, and was received by the ocean. f Masc. ज्वालः, fem. ज्वाला. g Fem. कीला. h Also f. n. अर्चिः, (स्). i Fem. स्फुलिङ्गा, neut.—ङ्गं. j The regent of worlds below; or death, and judge of departed souls. Likewise दण्डधारः.

A giant or ghost.

55. राक्षसः कौणपः क्रव्यात् क्रव्यादो ऽस्रप आशरः

रात्रिञ्चरो रात्रिचरः कर्बुरो निकषात्मजः

59. यातुधानः पुण्यजनो नैर्ऋतो यातु रक्षसी

VARUNA.[f]

प्रचेता वरुणः पाशी यादसांपतिरप्पतिः

Air or wind.

57. श्वसन स्पर्शनो वायुर्मातरिश्वा सदागतिः

पृषदश्वो गन्धवहो गन्धवाहा निलाशुगाः

58. समीर मारुत मरुज् जगत्प्राण समीरणाः

नभस्वद् वात पवन पवमान प्रभञ्जनाः

Air inhaled.[m]

59. प्राणो ऽपानः समानश्(चो)दान व्यानौ(च वायवः

शरीरस्था इमे)

Speed or velocity.

रंहस् तरसी (तु) रयः स्यदः

---

1 क्रव्याद्. 2 रक्षस्. 3—तस्. 4 पाशिन्. 5 अप्—. 6—श्वन्. 7 पृ—. 8 आ—. 9—त्. 10—त्. 11—न. 12 उ—. 13 तरस्.

[a] Or अस्रपः. [b] Or आशिरः. [c] Likewise कर्बूरः. and कर्वरः. [d] Or जातुधानः. [e] Also नैरृतिः. [f] Or the regent of water. [g] Likewise वरणः. [h] Also अपांपतिः. [i] Or पृषताश्व. [j] Likewise मरुतः. [k] Also जगत् (du. जगती; or जगन्तौ;) and प्राणः. [l] Likewise वातिः. [m] Five breaths, or air inhaled or emitted several ways, as breath, deglutition, &c. [n] Also रंहः.

1 m a n n n n 2 n c n

60. जवो (ऽथ) शीघ्रं त्वरितं लघु क्षिप्रमरं द्रुतं — Quick, or swiftly. b

n n n 3 n 4 n d

सत्वरं चपलं तूर्णमविलम्बितमाशु (च)

n f n 5 n n 6 n 7 n g

61. सतते ऽनारताश्रान्त सन्तताविरतानिशं — Eternal, or continually. e

n 8 n 9 n h

नित्यानवरताजस्रम् (ऽप्य)

m m j

(ऽथा) ऽतिशयो भरः — Much or excessive. i

n n 10 n 11 n 12 n n

62. अतिवेल भृशात्यर्थातिमात्रोद्गाढ निर्भरं

13 n 14 n 15 n n n k 16 n

तीव्रैकान्तनितान्तानि गाढ बाढ दृढानि (च)

l m

63. (क्लीबे) शीघ्राद्यसत्वे स्यात् त्रिष्वेषां भेद्यगामि यत्

---

1 जव. 2 अर. 3 अ—. 4 आ—. 5 अ—. 6 अ—. 7 आ—. 8 अ—. 9 अ—. 10 अ—. 11 अ—. 12 उ—. 13 तीव्र. 14 ए—. 15 —न्त. 16 दृढ.

a Likewise जवनः. b These terms, used adverbially, are neuter; but as adjectives, they agree in gender with the subject. Masc. शीघ्रः, fem. शीघ्रा, neut. शीघ्रं. c Also Indec. अरं. d Except this term, which properly should not be used as an adjective. e These likewise are neuter as adverbs, but vary as adjectives. f This is reckoned among indeclinables. g Except this, which properly should not be used as an adjective. h Except this also, which is never used as an adjective. This is also reckoned among indeclinables. i These likewise are neuter as adverbs, but vary as adjectives. j Except these two, which are invariably masculine; but they are used adverbially in the second singular neuter. k This is indeclinable according to some. l They are neuter when used not as nouns; consequently, as adverbs. m A various reading is भेद्यगामि, (used as an epithet or discriminative) instead of सत्वगामि, (used as a noun; i.e. as an adjective.)

1 m m 2 m m

KUVE´RA. a — कुबेरस् त्र्यम्बकसखो यक्षराड् गुह्यकेश्वरः

3 m m m m

64. मनुष्यधर्मा धनदो राजराजो धनाधिपः

m m m m

किन्नरेशो वैश्रवणः पौलस्त्यो नरवाहनः

4 m b 5 m c 6 m d m 7 m

65. यक्षैकपिङ्गैलविल श्रीद पुण्यजनेश्वराः

n

The garden of *Kuvéra*. — (अस्योद्यानं) चैत्ररथं

m f

Nalakúvara. e — (पुत्रस्तु) नलकूबरः

m

Kailasa. g. — 66. कैलासः (स्थानं)

f

Kuvéra's city. — अलका (पूर्)

m n

His throne and vehicle. — (विमानं तु) पुष्पकं

m 8 m m m

His attendants. — (स्यात्) किन्नरः किंपुरुषस् तुरंगवदनो मयुः

m m h

His treasure. — 67. निधि (र्ना) शेवधि

n n

Auriferous gems. i — (भेदाः पद्मशङ्खादयो निधेः)

1—र. 2—राज्. 3—र्मन्. 4 यक्ष. 5 ए—. 6 ए—. 7—र. 8—ष.

[a] The god of riches. [b] Also यक्षेश्वरः. [c] Likewise एकपिङ्गलः. [d] Also ऐलविलः, or ऐडविडः, and ऐडबिड. [e] Son of *Kuvéra*. [f] The same term, in the dual, designates both the sons of KUVE´RA; named NALAKU´VARA, and MANI´GRI´VA. [g] A bode of *Kuvéra*. [h] Also सेवधिः [i] See an enumeration of the other seven (for there are nine such fabulous gems) in other dictionaries.

SECTION II.

f f a 1 n b 2 n n 3 n

1. द्यो दिवौ (द्वे स्त्रियाव्) अभ्रं व्योम पुष्करम् अम्बरं — The sky or atmosphere.

4 n c n d n n 5 n n

नभो ऽन्तरीक्षं गगनम् अनन्तं सुरवर्त्म खं

6 n n 7 m n 8 m n e

2. वियद् विष्णुपदं (वा तु पुंस्या) काश विहायसी

9 f 10 f g f 11 f 12 f

दिशस् (तु) ककुभः काष्ठा आशाश् (च) हरितश् (च ताः) — Space, region or quarters. f

13 f 14 f i 15 f

3. प्राच्य् अवाची प्रतीच्यस् (ताः पूर्व्व दक्षिण पश्चिमाः) — The several quarters. h

f

(उत्तरा दिग्) उदीची (स्याद्)

m f n

दिश्यं (तु त्रिषु दिग्भवे) — Situated or bearing. j

m m m m m m

4. इन्द्रो वह्निः पितृपति नैर्ऋतो वरुणो मरुत् — The regents of quarters and points. k

m m

कुबेर ईशः (पतयः पूर्व्वादीनां दिशां क्रमात्)

---

1 अ—. 2 —अन्. 3 अं—. 4 —अस्. 5 —त्मन्. 6 —त्.
7 आ—. 8 —यस्. 9 दिश्. 10 ककुभ्. 11 आशा. 12 हरित्.
13 प्राची—. 14 अ—. 15 —ची.

[a] See § i. v. 4. [b] Or अभ्रं. [c] Likewise नभं (अ.) [d] Or अन्तरीक्षं. [e] Masc. विहायाः. Neut. विहायः. Also विहायसः—स; and indec. विहायसा. [f] A tract or quarter of the world; sing. दिक्, pl. दिशः. Or with the feminine termination दिशा, pl. दिशाः. [g] Nom. ककुप्. Also with the feminine termination ककुभाः. [h] In their order: namely, East, South, West, North. [i] Some read अपाची for the South; restricting अवाची to the region below. [j] Ex. पूर्वदिश्यः eastern; fem—श्या: neut.—श्यं. [k] In their order: E., S. E., S., S. W., W., N. W., N., N. E. Thus fire S. E. *Nairita* S. W. Air N. W. *Síva* N. E. From the regents, the points are denominated: as ऐन्द्र, East; आग्नेयी, South-east; याम्या, South; &c.

Elephants, at the points. a

5. ऐरावतः[m] पुण्डरीको[m] वामनः[m] कुमुदो[m] ऽञ्जनः[1m]

पुष्पदन्तः[m] सार्वभौमः[m] सुप्रतीकश्[2m] (च दिग्गजाः)

Their females b

6. (करिण्यो) ऽभ्रमु[fc] कपिला[f] पिङ्गलानुपमाः[f] (क्रमात्)[3f]

ताम्रकर्णी[f] शुभ्रदन्ती[fd] (चा) ऽङ्गना[fe] (चा) ऽञ्जनावती[f]

Intermediate point. f

7. (क्लीबाव्ययं त्व) ऽपदिशं[n] दिशोर्मध्ये विदिक्[fg] (स्त्रियां)

Included space.

अभ्यन्तरं[n] (त्व) ऽन्तरालं[n]

The sensible horizon. h

चक्रवालं[mi] (तु) मण्डलं[m]

A cloud.

8. अभ्रं[mj] मेघो[m] वारिवाहः[m] स्तनयित्नु[m] र्बलाहकः[m]

धाराधरो[m] जलधरस्[4m] तडित्वान्[5m] वारिदो[mk] ऽम्बुभृत्[m]

9. घन[m] जीमूत[m] मुदिर[m] जलमुग्[6ml] धूमयोनयः[7mm]

A succession of clouds.

कादम्बिनी[f] मेघमाला[f]

Belonging to clouds.

(त्रिषु मेघभवे) ऽभ्रियं[mfn]

---

1 अंजन. 2—द. 3 च—. 4—धर. 5—स्वत्. 6—मुच्. 7—नि.

[a] Belonging to the several regents of them, respectively. [b] In the same order. [c] Also अभ्रमुः. [d] Likewise शुभदन्ती. [e] Also अङ्गना. [f] Or half quarter, as S. E. &c. [g] Likewise प्रदिक्. [h] Or any orb and circumference. [i] Or चक्रवाडं. [j] Or अभ्र. [k] Also वारिधरः. [l] Likewise जलमुक्, जलद, &c. [m] Properly this signifies a cloud of smoke : and जीमूतः is a visible exhalation.

n *n* *n* 1 *n* b

10. स्तनितं गर्जितं मेघनिर्घोषे रसिता (दि च) — The rattling of thunder. a

f c *f* 2 *f* 3 *f* *f*

शंपा शतह्रदा ह्रादिन्यैरावत्यः क्षणप्रभा — Lightning.

f *f* d *f* *f* *f*

11. तड़ित् सौदामिनी विद्युत् चञ्चला चपला (ऽपि च)

m f g

स्फूर्जथु (र्वज्रनिर्घोषः) — A clap of thunder. e

m 4 *m*

मेघज्योतिर् इरम्मदः — A flesh of lightning. h

n 5 *n*

12. इन्द्रायुधं शक्रधनुस् — A rainbow.

n

(तदेव ऋजु) रोहितं — INDRA's bow unbent. i

f *n* j

वृष्टिर्वर्षं — Rain.

m 6 *m*

(तद्विघाते) ऽवग्राहावग्रहौ (समौ) — Drought.

m *m*

13. धारासम्पात् आसारः — A hard shower.

m k l

शीकरो (ऽम्बुकणाः स्मृताः) — Thin rain.

1—त. 2—नी: 3 ई—ती. 4 इ—. 5—ष्. EX.—चप्. 6 ग्र—.

a Or the grumbling of clouds. b Including other synonyms, as ध्वनितं, &c. c Also झम्पा. d Better सौदामनी; Likewise सौदाम्नी. e The noise attending a fall of thunder or stroke of lightning. f Also स्फूर्जथुः. and विस्फूर्जथुः, or विस्फूर्जथः. g Or वज्रनिर्घोषः. h Or the fire attending a stroke of lightning. i When his bow is bent, its shadow appears as a rainbow ; when unbent, it is invisible to mortals. Some of the commentators have approached towards a true explanation of the rainbow ; saying that it proceeds from the rays of the sun, which are of various colours, and being dispersed by the air, appear in the sky. j Likewise वर्षा. k Or सीकरः. l Or स्मृताः.

1m mf

Hail. वर्षोपलस् (तु) करका

n

A cloudy day. a (मेघाच्छन्ने ऽह्नि) दुर्दिनं

f f m 2n

Covering or disappearance. b 14. अन्तर्द्धा व्यवधा (पुंसि तु) त्वन्तर्द्धिरपवारणं

n n nc 3n

अपिधान तिरोधान पिधानाच्छादनानि (च)

4m 5md me m mf

The moon. 15. हिमांशुश् चन्द्रमाश् चन्द्र इन्दुः कुमुदबान्धवः

m m m 6m m

विधुः सुधांशुः शुभ्रांशुरोषधीशो निशापतिः

m m mg m m m

16. अब्जो जैवातृकः सोमो ग्लौर्मृगाङ्कः कलानिधिः

m mh m m

द्विजराजः शशधरो नक्षत्रेशः क्षपाकरः

f

A digit. i 17. कला (तु षोडशो भागो)

mnj mfn

The disk of the sun or moon. बिम्बो (ऽस्त्री) मण्डलं (त्रिषु)

n mn mn m

A part. भित्तं शकल खण्डे (वा पुंस्य) ऽर्द्धो

n

Half. ऽर्द्धं (समे ऽंशके)

1—स. 2 अ—. 3 आ—न. 4—शु. 5—अस्. 6 ओ—.

[a] Or obscured by clouds. [b] Or anything, which hides and withholds from sight. [c] Also छादनं. and छदनं. [d] Likewise मा:, (अस्.) [e] Also चन्द्र:. [f] Likewise कुमुदबन्धुः. [g] Also सोमा, (नृ.) [h] Likewise शशाङ्कः, शशलाञ्छनः, and शशी, (नृ.) [i] Or the sixteenth part of the moon's diameter [j] One author makes this fem. Also बिम्बी.

f a *f* *f*
18. चन्द्रिका कौमुदी ज्योत्स्ना — Moonlight.

1 *m* *f*
प्रसादस् (तु) प्रसन्नता — Purity or brightness.

m 2 *m* *n* *n* 3 *n* *n* b
कलङ्काङ्कौ लाञ्छनं (च) चिह्नं लक्ष्म (च) लक्षणं — A spot or mark.

f
19. सुषमा (परमा शोभा) — Exquisite beauty.

f *f* c 4 *f* *f*
शोभा कान्तिर्द्युतिश् छविः — Beauty or splendour.

5 *m* 6 *m* 7 *m* *n* *n*
अवश्यायस् (तु) नीहारस् तुषारस् तुहिनं हिमं — Frost.

n *f* d
20. प्रालेयं मिहिका (च)

f *f*
(अथ) हिमानी हिमसंहतिः — Ice and snow.

n
शीतं (गुणे) — Cold or chilness.

m f n c *m f n* *m f n*
(तद्वदर्थाः) सुषीमः शिशिरो जडः — Cold or frigid.

m f n *m f n* *m f n* *m f n*
21. तुषारः शीतलः शीतो हिमः (सप्तान्यलिङ्गकाः)

m *m*
ध्रुव औत्तानपादिः (स्याद्) — The polar star. f

m h *m*
अगस्त्यः कुम्भसम्भवः — AGASTYA. g

1—द. 2 अङ्क. 3—च्छन्. 4—ति. 5—य. 6—हार. 7—षार.

[a] Also चन्द्रिमा. [b] Likewise लक्ष्मणं. [c] Also द्युती, and छवी. [d] Or महिका. [e] Likewise सुषीमः, and सुसीमः. [f] Or the north pole itself. In mythology, *Dhruva* is son of *Uttánapáda*, and consequently grandson of the first *Manu*. In Astronomy, *Uttánapáda*, is β Ursæ minoris. [g] *Agastya* is regent of the star Canopus. [h] Also अगस्तिः.

1 *m* a
22. मैत्रावरुणिः

f
His consort. (अस्यैव) लोपामुद्रा (सधर्मिणी)

n b 2*n* *n* *f* *f n* c 3*f n* d
A star. नक्षत्रमृक्षं भं तारा तारका (अप्यु) उडु (वा स्त्रियां)

Asterisms. c 23. दाक्षायण्यो (ऽश्विनीत्यादि तारा)

4*f* 5*f*
The head of Aries. अश्वयुगश्विनी

f *f* f
Stars in the Southern scale. राधा विशाखा

m *m* *m*
Stars in Cancer. पुष्ये (तु) सिध्य तिष्यौ

6*f*
The Dolphin. श्रविष्ठया

f
24. (समा) धनिष्ठा

f *f* g
The wing of Pegasus. (स्युः) प्रोष्ठपदा भाद्रपदाः (स्त्रियः)

n h *n* 7*f*
Orion. मृगशीर्षं मृगशिरस् (तस्मिन्नेवा) अग्रहायणी

8*f* i
Stars in his head. 25. इल्वलास् (तच्छिरोदेशे तारका निवसन्ति याः)

m *m* *m* k 9*m* *m*
The planet Jupiter. j बृहस्पतिः सुराचार्यो गीष्पतिर्धिषणो गुरुः

1—णि. 2 ऋक्ष. 3 उडु. 4—युज्. 5 अ—. 6—ष्ठा.
7 आ—. 8—ला. 9 धि—.

[a] Likewise वरुणिः. [b] Also नक्षत्रं. [c] Neut. तारकं. Likewise masc. तारः, and तारकः. [d] Neut. उडु, fem. उडुः or उडूी. [e] *As'wini* and others, the longitude of which regulates the divisions of the zodiac. In mythology, they are nymphs, and daughters of *Daksha.* [f] Properly dual, as indicating two stars, which compose this constellation according to ancient authors. But astronomers now recken four. [g] Also भद्रपदाः. [h] Likewise masc. मृगशीर्षः, and fem. मृगशिराः (स्). Also masc. मृगः. [i] Also इल्वकाः. [j] *Vrihaspati,* the preceptor of the gods, son of *Angiras.* [k] Likewise गीर्पतिः, गीःपतिः, and गीष्पतिः.

m ma 1m m
26. जीव् आङ्गिरसो वाचस्पतिश् चित्रशिखण्डिजः

m m m 2mc md m
शुक्रो दैत्यगुरुः काव्य् उशना भार्गवः कविः — Venus. b

m m m m m
27. अङ्गारकः कुजो भौमो लोहिताङ्गो महीसुतः — Mars. e

m m m
रौहिणेयो बुधः सौम्यः — Mercury. f

mh mi
(समौ) सौरि शनैश्चरौ — Saturn. g

nk m m m m
28. तमस् (तु) राहुः स्वर्भानुः सैंहिकेयो विधुन्तुदः — The ascending node. j

m
(सप्तर्षयो मरीच्यत्रिमुखास्) चित्रशिखण्डिनः — Ursa major. l

n
29. (राशीनामुदयो) लग्नं — Ascension. m

(ते तु मेषवृषादयः) — Signs of the Zodiac. n

mo m 3m 4m 5m 6m
सूर सूर्यार्यमादित्य द्वादशात्म दिवाकराः — The Sun

1—ति. 2—नस्. 3 श—नृ. 4 शा—. 5—त्मन्. 6—र.

[a] The patronymic in the plural, reverts to the original form अङ्गिरसः. [b] *S'ukra* or *U'sanas,* the preceptor of the giants, son of *Bhrigu* and regent of the planet Venus. [c] In the vocative sing. उशनः(स्) उशनन्, or उशनः. [d] Likewise भृगुः. This and the patronymic, in the plural, make भृगवः. [e] According to mythology, the son of the earth. [f] *Bud'ha,* son of *Sóma,* (or the moon) by *Róhinï* (or the Hyades). [g] *Saní,* the offspring of the sun by *Ch'háyá.* [h] Or more properly, सौरिः. Also सौरः [i] Likewise अगिः [j] *Ráhú,* son of *Sinhiki.* [k] Also masc. तमाः, (स.) [l] The seven principal stars in Ursa major are the seven sages ; *Marichi, Atri, Angiras, Pulastya, Pulaha, Kratu* and *Vasisht'ha.* [m] The rising of the signs. [n] The sign (*Rás'i*) are Aries, Taurus, &c. [o] Likewise सूरः.

m 1m m m

30. भास्कराहस्कर ब्रध्न प्रभाकर विभाकराः

2m m m m 3m

भास्वद् विवस्वत् सप्ताश्व हरिदश्वोष्णरश्मयः

m 4m ma mb 5m 6m

31. विकर्त्तनार्क मार्त्तण्ड मिहिरारुण पूषणः

7m m 8m m m

द्युमणिस् तरणिर्मित्रश् चित्रभानुर्विरोचनः

m 9m m 10mc

32. विभावसुर्ग्रहपतिस् त्विषांपतिरहर्पतिः

m m 11m md 12m m

भानुर्हंसः सहस्रांशुस् तपनः सविता रविः

m m 13m

Three of the sun's attendants. e — 33. माठरः पिङ्गलो दण्डश् (चण्डांशोः पारिपार्श्विकाः)

m m m mg m

The dawn. f — सूरसूतोऽरुणोऽनूरुः काश्यपिर्गरुडाग्रजः

14mh m 15n n

Halo. — 34. परिवेषस् (तु) परिधिरुपसूर्य्यक मण्डले

m16m m17m mf m 18mi

A ray. — किरणोस्र मयूखांशु गभस्ति घृणि घृष्णयः

m m mf f

35. भानुःकरोमरीचिः(स्त्रीपुंसयोः)दीधितिः(स्त्रियाम्)

---

1 अह—. 2—त्. 3 स—श्व. 4 अ—. 5 अ—. 6 पूषन्.
7—णि. 8—त्र. 9—ति. 10 अह—. 11—शु. 12—तृ.
13—ण्ड. 14—ष. 15 उ—. 16 उस्र. 17 अंशु. 18 घृणि.

[a] Also मार्त्ताण्ड, [b] Likewise मिहरः. [c] Also अहःपतिः. [d] Likewise तापनः. [e] Severally named in the text. They are INDRA, YAMA, and FIRE, under other names: one placed on the left of the sun; the two others on his right. [f] The charioteer of the sun. [g] Likewise काश्यपः. [h] Also परिवेषः. [i] Some read भस्त्रि.

f 1f f 2ffa 3ff f 4f

(स्युः)प्रभा रुग्‌रुचि त्विड्भा भाश्छवि द्युतिदीप्तयः Light.

5n 6n

36. रोचिः शोचि (उभे क्लीबे)

m m m

प्रकाशो द्योत आतपः Sunshine. b

n n n n d

कोष्णं कवोष्णं मन्दोष्णं कदुष्णं (त्रिषु तद्वति) Warmth. c

n n n f

37. तिग्मं तीक्ष्णं खरं (तद्वत्) Heat. e

f f

मृगतृष्णा मरीचिका Sultry vapour. g

---

1 रुच्. 2 त्विष्. 3 भास्. 4 दीप्ति. 5 रोचिस्. 6 शोचिस्.

[a] Also masc. भाः (स्) or भासः, (स). [b] Or any lustre and heat. Some interpret this, the converse of darkness. Others make the three terms of this article synonymous with the preceding eleven, as signifying light and illuminatien. They are distinguished from the article which precedes, as not immediately issuing from the sun. [c] Or warm. [d] When used as adjectives they vary with the gender. [e] Or hot. [f] These also, when employed as adjectives, vary with the gender. [g] Appearing at a distance like a sheet of water. The phenomenon called Mirage.

SECTION III.

m m 1 m m
Time. 1. कालो दिष्टो (ऽप्य्) नेहा (पि) समयो (ऽप्य्)

f b
First lunar day. a (ऽथ) पक्षतिः

2 f c
प्रतिपद् (द्वे इमे स्त्रीत्वे)

3 m f d
A lunar day. (तदाद्यास्) तिथयो (द्वयोः)

m n 4 n m n m n e
A day. 2. घस्रो दिनाहनी (वा तु क्लीबे) दिवस वासरौ

m n n f 5 n g 6 n h
Morning. प्रत्यूषो ऽहर्मुखं कल्यमुषः प्रत्यूषसी (अपि)

n i
3. प्रभातं (च)

f k
Eve. j (दिनान्ते तु) सायं

f l f
Twilight. सन्ध्या पितृप्रसूः

---

1 अनेहस्. 2—पद्. 3 तिथि. 4 अहन्. 5 उषस्. 6—षस्.

[a] The beginning of the moon's increase or wane. [b] Or पक्षती. [c] The thirtieth part of a lunation. [d] Also fem. तिथी. [e] Some write वाशरः, erroneously. [f] Likewise काल्यं. [g] Also masc. उषः (सु.) and fem. उषा. [h] Likewise masc. प्रत्युषः (ष) and neut. प्रत्युषः (स.) [i] Also भातं and विभातं. [j] Or the close of the day. [k] Masc. सायः. Indec. सायं. [l] Likewise सन्ध्यां.

प्राह्णा[m]पराह्ण[1m]मध्याह्नास्[2m] (त्रिसन्ध्यम्)	Periods of the day.[a]
(अथ) शर्वरी[f b]	Night.
4. निशा[f] निशीथिनी[f] रात्रिस्[3f c] त्रियामा[f] क्षणदा[f] क्षपा[f d]	
विभावरी[f] तमस्विन्यौ[4f e] रजनी[f f] यामिनी[f g] तमी[f h]	
5. तमिस्रा[f] तामसी[f i] (रात्रिः)	A dark night.
ज्योत्स्नी[f j] (चन्द्रिकयान्विता)	A moon-light night.
(आगामिवर्त्तमानाहर्युक्तायां निशि) पक्षिणी[f]	A night and two days.[k]
6. गणरात्रं[n] (निशाव्रजः)	A multitude of nights.
प्रदोषो[m] रजनीमुखम्[n]	Evening.[l]
अर्द्धरात्र[m] निशीथौ[m] (द्वौ)	Midnight.
(द्वौ) याम[m] प्रहरौ[m] (समौ)	A watch.[m]

---

[1] अप—. [2]—ह्न. [3]—त्रि. [4]—नी.

[a] Forenoon, afternoon, and mid-day. The three turns of the day are collectively called त्रिसन्ध्य, n. or त्रिसन्ध्या, f. [b] Also शार्वरी. [c] Also रात्री. [d] Likewise क्षिपा. [e] Also तमस्वती. [f] Likewise रजनिः. [g] Also यामवती. [h] Likewise तमिः, or तमा and तामी. [i] Some make this a part of the explanation. But it is one of the terms exhibited, according to others. It also signifies night in general. [j] This is interpreted by one author the night of full moon. [k] Or a day and two nights. [l] The beginning of night. The two first hours *(g'hatis)* after sunset. [m] The eighth part of the day.

The full and change of the moon.[a]	7. (स) पर्वसन्धिः[m b] (प्रतिपत्पञ्चदश्योर्यदन्तरम्)
Last day of the half month.	पक्षान्तौ[f] (पञ्चदश्यौ द्वे)
Day of full moon.	पौर्णमासी[f] (तु) पूर्णिमा[f c]
Moon a little gibbous.[d]	8. (कलाहीने सा) ऽनुमतिः[f]
Moon quite full.[e]	(पूर्णे) राका[f] (निशाकरे)
Day of new moon.	अमावास्या[f f] (त्व्) मावस्या[1 f] दर्शः[m g] सूर्येन्दुसङ्गमः[m]
Moon a little horned.[h]	9. (सा दृष्टेन्दुः) सिनीवाली[f]
Moon exactly new.[i]	(सा नष्टेन्दुकला) कुहूः[f j]
An eclipse.	उपरागो[m] ग्रहो[m]
Eclipsed.	(राहुग्रस्ते त्विन्दौ च पुष्णि च)

---

1 च—.

[a] The junction of the 15th and 1st of a half month, or the precise moment of the full or change of the moon. [b] Also पर्व and संधिः. [c] Likewise पूर्णिमा, पूर्णिमासी, पूर्णमासी and पौर्णमी. [d] That is, a fifteenth day of the moon's age, on which she rises one digit ($\frac{1}{16}$th.) less than full. [e] A similar day; but on which she rises quite full. [f] Also अमावासी, अमावसी, अमामासी, अमामसी, and अमा. [g] Some add अदर्शः. [h] That is, a thirtieth day of the moon's age, on which she rises visible. Or sets visible; the first lunar day having commenced, or the fourteenth of the dark half month being unfinished. [i] A similar day, but on which she rises invisible. [j] Also कुहुः.

10. सोपप्लवोपरक्तौ (द्वौ)[m, 1m]	
ऽग्न्युत्पात उपाहितः[m, m]	A meteor. a
(एकयोक्त्या) पुष्पवन्तौ (दिवाकर निशाकरौ)[2m]	Sun & moon.
(अष्टादश निमेषास्तु) काष्ठा[f]	Sixteen thirds. b
(त्रिंशत्तु ताः) कलाः	Eight seconds. c
(तास्तु त्रिंशत्) क्षणः[m]	Four minutes. d
(ते तु) मुहूर्त्तो (द्वादशास्त्रियाम्)[m n]	An hour. e
12. (ते तु त्रिंशद्) अहोरात्रः[3 m g]	A day. f
पक्ष (स्ते दशपञ्च च)[m]	A fortnight. h
(पक्षौ पूर्व्वापरौ) शुक्ल कृष्णौ[m, m]	Light & dark fortnights. i
मास (स्तु तावुभौ)[m k]	A month. j

---

1 उ—. 2—वत्, or वन्त. 3 अ—.

[a] As a falling star, &c. also a comet. [b] Or thirtieth part of a *Kalá* and measured by eighteen twinklings. [c] Or thirtieth part of a *Kshańa*. [d] The three hundred and sixtieth part of the day. [e] The thirtieth part of the day; containing twelve *Kshanas*. [f] A nycthemeron, containing thirty *Muhúrtas*. [g] Some make this neuter: but erroneously. [h] Half a month, comprising fifteen days. [i] Respectively, from new moon to full, and from the opposition to the conjunction. [j] The twelfth part of a year; comprising two *pakshas*, or thirty days. This is according to lunar time. But the same name is applicable to the solar and sidereal months. [k] Likewise माः (स्).

A season. a — 13. (द्वौ द्वौ माघादिमासौ स्यात्) ऋतु[m]

A half year. b — (तै[1 n]) रयनं (त्रिभिः)

A year. c — (अयने द्वे गतिरुदग् दक्षिणार्कस्य) वत्सरः[m]

Equinox. — 14. (समरात्रिंदिवे काले) विषुवद्[2 n] विषुवं[n d] (च तत्)

A'grahâyana. e — मार्गशीर्षे[m] सहा[3 m f] मार्ग[m] आग्रहायणिक[m g] (श्च सः)

Pausha. h — 15. पौषे[m] तैष[m] सहस्यौ[m] (द्वौ)

Mágha. i — तपा[4 m j] माघे[m]

Phâlguna. k — (ऽथ) फाल्गुने[m]

(स्यात्) तपस्यः[m] फाल्गुनिकः[m]

Chaitra. m — (स्यात्) चैत्रे[m] चैत्रिको[m] मधुः[m]

---

1 ऋ—. 2—वत्. 3 सहस्. 4 तपस्.

a The sixth part of a year, comprising two months, as *Mágha* and *Phálgun'a*. Properly the season consists of two solar months: but the term is also applicable to lunar time. b Or the sun's alternate journies towards the tropics, measured by three seasons. c Consisting of the northern and southern tracts of the sun. d Also masc. विषुवान्, and विषुपः. And विषुवः or विषुपः. e Month in which the moon is full, nearly in the longitude of Orion's head. f Likewise सहः (स्.) g Also आग्रहायणः. h Near γ and δ of Cancer. i Near the lion's heart. j Some add तपः (—प). k Near the lion's tail. l Also फाल्गुनः. m Near the virgin's spike.

16. वैशाखे माधवो राधो — *Vais'ák'ha.* a

ज्यैष्ठे शुक्रः — *Jyaisht'ha.* b

शुचि (स्त्वयम्) — *A'shád'ha.* d

आषाढे

श्रावणे (तु स्यान्) नभाः श्रावणिक (श्च सः) — *Srávan'a.* f

17. (स्यु) र्नभस्य प्रौष्ठपद भाद्र भाद्रपदाः (समाः) — *Bhad'ra.* g

(स्यादा) श्विन इषो (ऽप्या) श्वयुजो (ऽपि) — *A's'wina.* h

(स्यात्तु) कार्त्तिके — *Kárttika.* k

18. बाहुलोर्जौ कार्त्तिकिको

हेमन्तः — winter. l

शिशिरो (ऽस्त्रियाम्) — Cold season. n

वसन्ते पुष्पसमयः सुरभिर् — Spring. o

ग्रीष्म ऊष्मकः — Hot season. p

---

1 नभस्. 2 आ—. 3 आ—. 4 ऊर्ज. 5—षि.

a Month in which the moon is full near the southern scale. b Near the scorpion. c Likewise ज्येष्ठः. d Near the bow of Sagittarius. e Also अषाढः, आषाढकः. and आषाढः. f Nearly in the longitude of the eagle. g Nearly in the longitude of the wing of Pegasus. h Near the head of Aries. i Likewise ईषः j Also अश्वयुजः. k Near the Pleiades. l Comprising *A'grahayan'a* and *Pausha.* m Likewise हेमा and (पु). n Including *Mágha* and *Phálgun'a.* o Consisting of *Chaitra* and *Vaisák'ha.* p Comprehending *Jyaisht'ha* and *A'shád'ha.* q Or ऊष्मकः. Also उष्मा, or ऊष्मा (पु).

19. निदाघ् उष्णोपगम् उष्ण् ऊष्मागमस् तपः[m] [m] [m] [1 m a] [m b]

Rains. c — (स्त्रियां) प्रावृट्[2 f d] (स्त्रियां भूम्नि) वर्षा[f e]

Sultry season. f — (अथ) शरत्[3 f g] (स्त्रियाम्)

20. (षडमी ऋतवः[4 m] पुंसि मार्गादीनां युगैः क्रमात्)[h]

A year. — संवत्सरो[m i] वत्सरो[m j] ऽब्दो[5 m] हायनो[m n] (ऽस्त्री) शरत्[6 f k] समाः[f l]

A patriarchal day. m — 21. (मासेन स्याद्) ऽहोरात्रः पैत्रो

A day of the gods. n — (वर्षेण) दैवतः

A day of *Brahmá*. o — (दैवे युगसहस्रे द्वे) ब्राह्मः

A kalpa. p — कल्पौ[7 m] (तु तौ नृणाम्)

A manwantara. q — 22. मन्वन्तरं[n] (तु दिव्यानां युगानामेकसप्ततिः)

A destruction of the world. — संवर्त्तः[m r] प्रलयः[m] कल्पः[m s] क्षयः[m] कल्पान्त[n] (इत्यपि)

1—ष. 2—वृ. 3—दु. 4 ऋतु. 5 अब्द. 6—दु. 7 कल्प.

[a] Likewise ऊष्णोपगमः, ऊष्णः, and ऊष्मागमः. Or उष्मोगमः, &c. and ऊष्मोगमः, &c. [b] Also तपः (स्). [c] Containing *S'rávan'a* and *Bhádra*. [d] Likewise प्रावृषा. [e] Restricted to the plural. [f] Answering to *A's'wina* and *Kárttika*. [g] Also शरदा. [h] These six seasons severally correspend to two months each, in the same order. [i] Also संवत्सरः. [j] Likewise परिवत्सरः, and अनुवत्सरः. But in the quinquennial cycle these are names of different years. [k] Also शारदः. [l] Some restrict this to the plural. [m] Or a month of mortals. [n] Or year of mortals. [o] Or 2000 *yugas* of the gods: that is, 1000 *yugas* constitute *Brahma's* day, and his night contains as many. [p] The same grand period, or 432,000,000, years of mortals, measuring the duration of the world; and as many, the interval until its renovation. [q] Or a grand period containing seventy-one *yugas* of the gods. [r] Also संव र्तः. Likewise परिवर्तः. [s] Also विवर्त.

SECTION IV.

m n 1 m n a n n

1. (अस्त्री) पङ्कं(पुमान्)पाप्मा पापं किल्बिष कल्मषम् Sin.

n n 2n 3n 4n n n

कलुषं वृजिनैनोऽघमंहो दुरित दुष्कृतम्

m n n b 5n n m

2. (स्याद्) धर्म्म (मस्त्रियां) पुण्य श्रेयसी सुकृतं वृषः Virtue or moral merit.

6 f d f m m m 7 m m

मुत् प्रीतिः प्रमदो हर्षः प्रमोदामोद संमदाः Joy, or pleasure. c

8 m 9 m e 10 n n f g n h

3. (स्यादा) नन्दथुरानन्द शर्म्म सात सुखानि (च)

n n n n i n n

श्वःश्रेयसं शिवं भद्रं कल्याणं मङ्गलं शुभम् Happy, well, or right.

n n n n j m n

4. भावुकं भविकं भव्यं कुशलं क्षेम (मस्त्रियाम्)

n k

शस्तं (च।)

1

(अथ त्रिषु द्रव्ये पाप पुण्य सुखादि च)

---

1 पाप्मन्. 2 एनस्. 3 अघ. 4 अंहस्. or अंहस्. 5 श्रेयस्.
6 मुद्. 7 आ—. 8 आ—. 9 आ—. 10 शर्म्मन्.

a Used as an epithet, this word varies with the gender of the subject. b As an adjective, this likewise varies with gender of the subject. c Some restrict the seven terms in the first line, as signifying the actual sensation or mental affection of pleasure; and the other five, as importing pleasure in the abstract. d Likewise मुदा and मुदिता. e Also आनन्दिः and नन्दिः. f Also सातं. g Likewise सौख्यं. h Used as epithets, this and the following words vary with the gender of the subject. i Fem. कल्याणी. j Also कुषलं. and कुसलं. k These adjectives are restricted to the genders stated in the text, when employed as substantives to denote the abstract quality. l The three nouns here specified, with those which follow them respectively, or with such only as follow the last of them, being used as adjectives, agree in gender with the subject.

f f mn 1m ma

Excellence, or happiness. 5. मतल्लिका मचर्चिका प्रकाण्डमुद्धतल्लजौ (प्रशस्तवाचकान्यमूनि)

2 m

Good luck, or favourable fortune. ऽयः (शुभावहो विधिः)

m n b m m m f m

Destiny, or luck. 6. दैवं दिष्टं भागधेयं भाग्यं (स्त्री) नियतिर्विधिः

m n c n

A cause. हेतु (र्ना) कारणं बीजं

n 3 n

A primary cause. (निदानं त्वा) दिकारणं

n 4 m m d

The soul. 7. क्षेत्रज्ञ आत्मा पुरुषः

n f

Nature. e प्रधानं प्रकृतिः (स्त्रियाम्)

f

State or condition. f (विशेषः कालिको) ऽवस्था

f n h 5 n i 6 n j

Qualities of nature. g (गुणाः) सत्वं रजस् तमः

7 n n n k f l 8 f 9 m

Birth or production. 8. जनुर्जनन जन्मानि जनिरुत्पत्तिरुद्भवः

---

1 उ—. 2 अय 3 भा—. 4 आत्मन्. 5 रजस्. 6 तमस्.
7 —स्. 8 उ—. 9 उ—.

[a] In apposition, even as epithets, these do not vary in their gender [b] Also दैव्यं. [c] Likewise करणं. [d] Also पूरुषः. [e] The cause of the material world, or secondly the natural state of anything. [f] Any particular state, varying with the progress of time ; as youth, &c. [g] Severally named in the text ; first, the principle of existence or truth ; secondly, that of foulness or passion ; thirdly, that of darkness. The first enlightens, constitutes knowledge, and is the cause of truth. The second occasions coveting, and is the cause of pain. The third overspreads, and is the cause of error and illusion. These attributes and essential qualities of nature are according to the *Sank'hya* philosophy. [h] Likewise सत्वः [i] Also masc. रजः (रजस्). [j] Likewise masc. तमः (तमस्). [k] Sing. जन्म or जन्मं. Also masc. जन्मः. [l] Or, जनीः. Also masc. जनि.

प्राणी[1m] (तु) चेतनो[m] जन्मी[2m] जन्तु[m] जन्यु[m] शरीरिणः[3m] — An animal or sentient being.

9. जातिर्[f] जातं[n] (च) सामान्यं[n] — Kind or sort.

व्यक्तिस्[f] (तु) पृथगात्मिका[f] — Individuality.

चित्तं[n] (तु) चेतो[4n] हृदयं[n] स्वान्तं[n] हृन्[5n] मानसं[n] मनः[na] — The mind or faculty of reson.

10. बुद्धिर्[f] मनीषा[f] धिषणा[f] धीः[f] प्रज्ञा[fc] शेमुषी[fd] मतिः[f] — Understanding or intellect.[b]

प्रेक्षो[f]पलब्धिश्[6f] चित्[7f] सम्वित्[8f] प्रतिपज्[9f] ज्ञप्ति चेतनाः[f]

11. (धीर्धारणावती) मेधा[f] — Retentive intellect.

संकल्पः[me] (कर्म्ममानसम्) — A resolve or act of determination.

चित्ताभोगो[m] मनस्कारश्[mg] — Consciousness of pleasure or pain.[f]

चर्चा[fi] संख्या[f] विचारणा[f] — Reflection or consideration.[h]

12. अध्याहारस्[10m] तर्क[m] ऊहो[11mj] — Reasoning.

विचिकित्सा[f] (तु) संशयः[f] — Doubt or uncertainty.

---

1 प्राणिन्. 2 जन्मिन्. 3—रिन्. 4 चेतस्. 5 हृद्.
6 श—ब्धि. 7—त्. 8—द्. 9—द्. 10—र. 11—क.

[a] Some make this masc. and neut. [b] Or the terms in the first line signify intellect and the faculty of understanding ; and those in the second line signify comprehension, or the exercise of that faculty. [c] Also प्रज्ञा. [d] Likewise शेमुषी. [e] Also विकल्प. [f] The attention of the mind to its own sensations. Fixed attention and profound meditation, keeping the mind to one object, or continually returning to it ; and calling up a particular thought. For the terms are variously interpreted by the different commentators. [g] Likewise मनसिकारः. [h] The act of a mind on a subject present to the thoughts ; the exercise of judgment. Or trying a thing by the test of proof [i] Also चर्चनं, संख्यानं, and विचारः. [j] Likewise ऊहा.

m m
संदेह द्वापरौ (च।

Cartainty or ascertainment. — m m
(ऽथ समौ) निर्णय निश्चयौ

Heterodox or heresy. a — f f
13. मिथ्यादृष्टिर्नास्तिकता

An injurious design. b — m n
व्यापादो द्रोहचिन्तनम्

A demonstrated truth. — m m
(समौ) सिद्धांत राद्धांतौ

Error or mistake. — f f m
भ्रान्तिर्मिथ्यामति र्भ्रमः

An agreement. — 1 f 2 f c n m 3 m m
14 संविदागूः प्रतिज्ञानं नियमाश्रव संश्रवाः

m 4 m m 5 m
अङ्गीकाराभ्युपगम प्रतिश्रव समाधयः

True knowledge. d — n e
15. (मोक्षेधी) र्ज्ञानं

Knowledge of arts. f — n
(अन्यत्र) विज्ञानं (शिल्पशास्त्रयोः)

Beatitude. g — f n n 6 n n 7 n
मुक्तिः कैवल्य निर्वाणं श्रेयोनिःश्रेयसामृतम्

1—द्. 2 आगू or आगुर. 3 आ—. 4 अ—. 5—धि.
6 श्रेयस. 7 अ—.

[a] The disbelief of heaven or a future world, or the denial of a God. [b] The meditating of harm, or wishing ill to another ; or the attempt to injure. [c] According to different etymologies, (the termination being either derivative or radical,) 2d. sing. and pl· आगूः or आग्व, and आगूम् or आग्वम्. But आगुः (र्), आगुरं. [d] Or that which tends to exempt the soul from further transmigration. [e] Some make this interpretation, and धीः the word exhibited. [f] Or any knowledge, but that of theology. [g] The delivery of the soul from body, and its exemption from further transmigration.

16. मोक्षो[m]ऽपवर्गो[m]

(ऽथा) अज्ञानम्[1 n]अविद्या[2 f]ऽहंमतिः[3 f] (स्त्रियाम्) — Spiritual ignorance.[a]

रूपं[n] शब्दो[m] गन्ध[m] रस[m] स्पर्शाश्[4 m] (च) — Five objects of sense.[b]

विषया[m] (अमी) — An object of sense.[c]

17. गोचरा[m] इन्द्रियार्थाश्[5 m] (च)

हृषीकं[n] विषयीन्द्रियम्[6 n][7 n] — An organ of sense.

कर्मेन्द्रियं[n] (तु पाय्वादि)[d] — An organ of action.[d]

(मनोनेत्रादि) धीन्द्रियम्[n] — An intellectual organ.[e]

18. तुवरस्[8 m n f] (तु) कषायो[m n] (ऽस्त्री) — An astringent taste.

मधुरो[m] लवणः[m] कटुः[m h] — Five other tastes.[g]

तिक्तो[m]ऽम्लश्[9 m i] (च) रसाः (पुंसि)

(तद्वत्सु षडमी त्रिषु)[j]

---

1 अ—. 2 अ—. 3 अ—. 4 स्पर्श. 5—र्थ. 6—यिन्. 7 हृ—. 8—र. 9 अम्ल.

[a] Or belief of external appearances. [b] Severally named in the text; viz. colour, sound, odour, flavour, and contact. [c] Sing. विषयः [d] Viz. the hand, the foot, the voice, the organ of generation, and the organ of excretion. [e] Viz. the mind, the eye, the ear, the nose, the tongue, and the skin. [f] Also तूवरः or तुबरः. [g] Severally stated in the text; viz. sweet, salt, pungent, bitter and sour. [h] Fem. कटुः or कट्वी. [i] Also अम्लू. [j] All these terms, signifying particular tastes, vary with the gender of the subject, when they are used as adjectives.

A pleasing scent. a	19. (विमर्दोत्थे) परिमलो (गन्धे जनमनोहरे) [m]
A fragrancy or perfume. b	आमोदः (सोऽतिनिर्हारी) [m]
	(वाच्यलिङ्गत्वमागुणात्) [c]
A scent spreading far.	20. समाकर्षी [1 m] (तु) निर्हारी [2 m]
A perfume or fragrant substance. d	सुरभिर्घ्राणतर्पणः [m e] [m]
	इष्टगन्धः [m] सुगन्धिः [m f] (स्यात्)
A perfume for the mouth. g	आमोदी [3 m] मुखवासनः [m h]
An ill smelling substance.	21. पूतिगन्धिस्(तु) [4 m] दुर्गन्धो [5 m i]
A smell like that of raw meat. j	विस्रं [m k] (स्यादा) मगन्धि [6 n] (यत्)
White. l	22. शुक्ल [m] शुभ्र [m] शुचि [m] श्वेत [m m] विशद [m*] श्येत [m m] पाण्डुराः [m]

1—र्षिन्. 2—रिन्. 3—दिन्. 4—न्धि. 5—न्ध. 6 आ—.

[a] Such as is extracted by rubbing fragrant substances. Ex. Blossoms of the Mimusops elengi. [b] A very delightful odour, and strong smell. Ex. Musk. [c] Used as adjectives, they agree in gender with the subject. This extends to the close of the section. [d] Ex. the flower of the Michelia champa. Some restrict the two first terms, others the two last, to signify a fragrant substance; and the remaining terms, fragrancy. [e] Fem. सुरभी. [f] Fem. सुगन्धी. [g] Usually prepared in the form of a pill; or any fragrant drug so employed. Ex. Camphor. [h] Also मुखभासनः. [i] Also दुर्गन्धी (न्). [j] Or, according to some, like the smoke of a funeral pile. [k] Likewise विश्रं. [l] These and the following names of colours, when used as adjectives, agree in gender with the subject. [m] Fem. श्वेता and श्येता or श्येनी. [*] Also विषदः.

m m a m m b m m
अवदातः सितो गौरो वलक्षो धवलो ऽर्जुनः

m m 1 m
23. हरिणः पाण्डुरः पाण्डुर् — Yellowish white.

m
(ईषत्पाण्डुस्तु) धूसरः — Grey.

m m c 2 m m m m m
कृष्णो नीलासित श्याम काल श्यामल मेचकाः — Black or dark blue.

m m m
24. पीतो गौरो हरिद्राभः — Yellow.

m d m e m
पलाशो हरितो हरित् — Green.

m f m m g
रोहितो लोहितो रक्तः — Red.

m i n
शोणः कोकनदच्छविः — Crimson. h

3 m
25. (अव्यक्तरागस्तु) अरुणः — Dark red. j

m
(श्वेतरक्तस्तु) पाटलः — Pale red or pink. k

m m
श्यावः (स्यात्) कपिशो — Brown. l

m m m
धूम्र धूमलौ कृष्णलोहिते — Purple. m

1—ण्डुः. 2 च—. 3 च—.

[a] Fem. सिता. [b] Likewise अवलक्षः. [c] Fem. नीला. [d] Also पालाशः. [e] Fem. हरिता, or हरिणी. [f] Fem. रोहिता or रोहिणी, and लोहिता or लोहिनी. [g] Fem. रक्ता. [h] The colour of the red lotus. [i] Fem. शोणा or शोणी. [j] The colour of the dawn, or of madder. [k] The colour of carthamus. [l] Compounded of black and yellow ; the colour of an ape. [m] Compounded of black and red ; the colour of smoke.

m m m m a m b m c

Tawny. कडारः कपिलः पिङ्ग पिशंगौ कद्रु पिङ्गलौ

m n m d m m l m e m f

Variegated. 26. चित्रं किर्मीर कल्माष शबलैता (च) कर्बुरे

g

(गुणे शुक्लादयः पुंसि गुणिलिङ्गास्तु तद्वति)

SECTION V.

f f f 2 f i 3 f j f k f

The goddess of speech. h 1. ब्राह्मी(तु)भारती भाषा गीर्वाग् वाणी सरस्वती

m f n n n 4 n

Voice or speech. व्याहार् उक्तिर् लपितं भाषितं वचनं वचः

m l m

Ungrammatical language. 2. अपभ्रंशो ऽपशब्दः (स्याच्)

m m

A word. (शास्त्रे) शब्द (स्तु) वाचकः

---

1 एत. 2 गिर्. 3 वाच्. 4—स्.

a Fem. पिशंगी. b Some read कडुः. c Fem. पिंगला. d Also कर्मीरः. e Fem. एता or एनी. f Also कर्बुरः. g The foregoing names of colours vary with the gender of the subject, when they are used as adjectives. h The same words are also synonymous with the following as denoting speech. i Likewise गिरा. j Also वाचा. k Likewise वाणिः. l Some add अपभ्रंशः.

3. (तिङ्सुबन्तचयो) वाक्यं[n] (क्रिया वा कारकान्विता)	A sentence.
श्रुतिः[f] (स्त्री) वेद[m] आम्नायस्[m]	The *Védas*, or any one of them. a
त्रयीधर्म्म[m c] (स्तु तद्विधिः)	The duty enjoined by them. b
4. (स्त्रियां) ऋक्[1 f] साम[2 n] यजुषी[3 n]	Three *Védas*. d
(इति वेदास्त्रयः) त्रयी[f]	The aggregate of them.
(शिक्षेत्यादि श्रुतेर्) अङ्गम्[4 n]	A *Védánga*. e
ओङ्कार[m] प्रणवौ[m] (समौ)	The sacred name of GOD. f
5. इतिहासः[m] पुरावृत्तं[n]	History. g
(उदात्ताद्यास्त्रय) स्वराः[m]	An accent. h
आन्वीक्षिकी[f] दण्डनीति[f] (स्तर्कविद्यार्थशास्त्रयोः)	Logic and ethics. i
6. आख्यायिको[5 f] (पलब्धार्था)	A tale. j
पुराणं[n] पञ्चलक्षणं[n]	A *Pura'n'a.* k

1 ऋच्. 2 सामन्. 3 यजुस्. 4 अंग. 5 —का.

[a] The Indian scriptures and holy writ. [b] Chiefly the performance of sacrifices in the manner directed by the *Védas*. [c] Or धर्म्मं, for the preceding term may belong to the synonyms of *Véda*. [d] Severally named in the text. [e] A science appendant on the *Védas;* viz. pronunciation, grammar, prosody, explanation of obscure terms, religious rites, or astronomy. [f] The syllable *O'm*. [g] Or a work recording former transactions, and containing traditions : heroic history. [h] Acute, grave, or circumflex. Sing. स्वरः. Pl. स्वराः. [i] Severally named in the text, and explained in the same order. Logic includes the *Nyáya*, *Vais'éshika* and other schools of reasoning. [j] A true, or a probable story. [k] Or theogony, comprising past and future events, under five heads : the creation; the destruction and renovation of worlds; genealogy of gods and heroes; the reigns of *Manus;* and the transactions of their descendants.

A feigned story. a	(प्रबन्धकल्पना) कथा [f]
A riddle. b	प्रवह्लिका [f c] प्रहेलिका [f d]
A code of laws.	7. स्मृति [f] (स्तु) धर्म्मसंहिता [f]
A compilation and abridgment.	समाहृति [f] (स्तु) संग्रहः [m]
A part of a stanza. e	समस्या [f] (तु) समासार्था [f f]
A rumour. g	किंवदन्ती [f h] जनश्रुतिः [f]
Tidings or intelligence.	8. वार्त्ता [f] प्रवृत्ति [f] र्वृत्तान्त [m] उदन्तः [m] (स्याद्)
A name or appellation.	(अथा) ह्वयः [1 m]
	आख्या [f] ह्वे [2 f] (अ) भिधानं [3 n i] (च) नामधेयं [n] (च) नाम [4 n] (च)
A call or summons.	9. हूति [5 f j] राकारणा [6 n k] ह्वानं [7 n]
Clamour. l	संहूति [f] (र्बहुभिः कृता)
A contest or law suit.	विवादो [m] व्यवहारः [m m] (स्याद्)
The exordium.	उपन्यास [m] (स्तु) वाङ्मुखम् [n]

1 आ—. 2 आह्वा. 3 अ—. 4 —नू. 5—ति. 6 आ—. 7 आ—.

[a] Whether founded in fact or not; for example, the poem entitled *Kádambari*. [b] Or intricate question. [c] Also प्रवह्लुका and प्रवह्लि or प्रवह्ली [d] Likewise प्रहेलिः. [e] Proposed as a trial of skill, to be completed. Or rather the verse or verses by which the stanza is completed. [f] Also समस्यार्था and असमप्रार्था. [g] Whether true or false. [h] Also किंवदन्तिः. [i] Likewise fem. अभिधा, अभिख्या, संज्ञा, &c. [j] Also आकृतिः. [k] Likewise fem. आकरणा. and आकारणा. [l] Or citation by many at once. [m] Also व्यवहरणं.

m m a
10. उपोद्घात् उदाहारः — An example or apposite argument.

n b m
शपनं शपथः (पुमान्) — An oath.

m c m f
प्रश्नो ऽनुयोगः पृच्छा (च) — A question.

n d 1 n
प्रतिवाक्योत्तरे (समे) — An answer.

m n
11. मिथ्याभियोगो ऽभ्याख्यानम् — A groundless demand.

n
(अथ) मिथ्याभिशंसनम् — A false accusation.

m e
अभिशापः

m f
प्रणादः (तु शब्दः स्यादनुरागजः) — A sound indicating affection and satisfaction.

2 n f g f h
12. यशः कीर्त्तिः समाज्ञा (च) — Fame and reputation.

m n f f
स्तवः स्तोत्रं स्तुतिर्नुतिः — Praise.

n
आम्रेडितं (द्विस्त्रिरुक्तम्) — Repetition.[i]

n f
उच्चैर्घुष्टं (तु) घोषणा — Making a loud noise.

f
13. काकुः (स्त्रियां विकारो यः शोकभीत्यादिभिर्ध्वनेः) — Change of voice in grief, fear, &c.

m 3 m m m 4 m
अवर्णाक्षेपनिर्वाद परीवादापवाद (वत्) — Censure, blame, or contempt.

m f f f n
14. उपक्रोशो जुगुप्सा (च) कुत्सा निन्दा (च) गर्हणे

---

1 उ—. 2—स्. 3 आ—. 4 अ—.

[a] Likewise उदाहरणं. [b] Also शपः. [c] Likewise प्रच्छनं. [d] Also प्रतिवचनं. [e] Likewise अभिशपनं. [f] Also प्रणदनं. [g] Likewise कीर्त्तिः and कीर्त्तना. [h] Also समज्ञा, समज्या and समाख्या. [i] A sound uttered twice or thrice, or oftener.

Opprobrious or unfriendly speech. पारुष्यम्[n] अतिवादः[1 m] (स्यात्)

Reproach or menace. भर्त्सनं[n] (त्व) पकारगीः[2 f]

Reproof attended with insult or disparagement. 15. (यः सनिन्द उपालम्भस् तत्र स्यात्) परिभाषणम्[n]

An imputation of adultery. (तत्र त्वा) क्षारणा[3 n f a] (यः स्यादाक्रोशो मैथुनं प्रति)

Address, or speaking to. 16. (स्याद्) आभाषणम्[4 n] आलापः[5 m]

Incoherent speech. प्रलापो[m] (ऽनर्थकं वचः)

Tautology. अनुलापो[m] मुहुर्भाषा[f]

Lamentation. विलापः[m] परिदेवनम्[n]

Quarrel, or mutual contradiction. 17. विप्रलापो[m] विरोधोक्तिः[f]

Conversation. संलापो[m] (भाषणं मिथः)

Speaking well, or elegant discourse. सुप्रलापः[m] सुवचनं[n]

Denial, or concealment of knowledge. अपलाप[m] (स्तु) निह्नवः[m]

Declaration. 18. संदेशवाग्[6 m f] वाचिकं[n] (स्याद्)

(वाग्भेदास्तु त्रिषूत्तरे)[b]

Unauspicious discourse. रुशती[m f c] (वागकल्याणी)

Good and auspicious discourse. (स्यात्) कल्या[f d] (तु शुभात्मिका)

---

1 अ—. 2 अ—र्. 3 आ—. 4 आ—. 5 आ—. 6 —ष्.

[a] Also आक्षारणा. [b] The following terms vary with the gender of the subject. [c] Masc. रुशन्. Fem. रुशती. Neut. रुशत्. Also रुषती. Masc. रुषन्. &c. [d] Likewise काल्या.

19. (अत्यर्थमधुरं) सान्त्वं[n]	Very sweet and conciliating.
संगतं[n] हृदयंगमम्[n]	Apposite and proper.
निष्ठुरं[n] परुषं[n]	Harsh, and contumelious.
ग्राम्यम्[n] अश्लीलं[1n]	Rustic and homely.
सूनृतं[n] (प्रिये	Pleasing, but true.
20. सत्ये)	
(इथ) संकुल[n] क्लिष्टे[n] परस्परपराहते[n]	Inconsistent, and contradictory.
(लुप्तवर्णपदं) ग्रस्तं[n]	Imperfectly pronounced, or slurred.[a]
निरस्तं[n] त्वरितोदितम्[n]	Spoken fast, hurried.
21. (अम्बूकृतं) सनिष्ठीवं[n c]	Sputtered.[b]
अबद्धं[n d] (स्याद्) अनर्थकम्[2 n]	Unmeaning or nonsensical discourse.
अनक्षरम्[n] अवाच्यं[3 n] (स्याद्)	Unfit to be uttered.[e]
आहतं[n] (तु) मृषार्थकम्[n]	An impossibility.
22. (अथ) म्लिष्टम्[n] अविस्पष्टं[4 n]	An indistinct speech.
वितथं[n] (तु) अनृतं[5 n] (वचः)	False.
सत्यं[n] तथ्यम्[n] ऋतं[6 n] सम्यक्[7 n f]	Truth ; or true.
(अमूनि त्रिषु तद्वति)[g]	

---

1 अ—. 2 अ—. 3 अ—. 4 अ—. 5 अ—. 6 ऋत. 7 सम्यच्.

[a] By omitting a letter or syllable. [b] Spoken with emission of saliva. [c] Or सनिष्ठीवं. [d] Or अबद्धं. [e] Blamable discourse. [f] Masc. सम्यङ्. Fem. समीची. Neut. सम्यक्. [g] The foregoing likewise agree in gender with the subject, when metaphorically used as epithets of the speaker instead of the speech.

SECTION VI.

Sound.

1. शब्दे[m a] निनाद[m] निनद[m] ध्वनि[m] ध्वान[m] रव[m b] स्वनाः[m]

स्वान[m] निर्घोष[m] निर्ह्राद[m] नाद[m] निस्वान[m] निस्वनाः[m]

2. आरवाराव[m l m] संराव[m] विरावा[m]

Rustling.[c] (अथ) मर्मरः[m]

(स्वनिते वस्त्रपर्णानां)

The tinkling of ornaments. (भूषणानां तु) शिञ्जितम्[n d]

A tone, or musical sound. 3. निक्वाणो[m] निक्वणः[m] क्वाणः[m] क्वणः[m] क्वणन[n] (मित्यपि)

The sound of a lute. (वीणायाः क्वणिते प्रादेः) प्रक्वाण[m] प्रक्वणा[m] (दयः)[e]

A confused or mingled sound.[f] 4. कोलाहलः[m] कलकलस्[m]

The cry of birds, &c. (तिरश्चां) वाशितं[n g] रुतं[n]

An echo. (स्त्री) प्रतिश्रुत्[f] प्रतिध्वाने[m h]

A song or singing. गीतं[n] गानम्[n] (इमे समे)

---

1 च—.

[a] Also शब्दनं. [b] Likewise रावः. [c] Of clothes or dry leaves. [d] Also शिञ्जा. [e] Including उपक्वणः, संक्वणः, &c. [f] Or a noise made by many. [g] Also वासितं. [h] Likewise प्रतिस्वनः.

SECTION VII.

1. [m b]निषाद[1 m]र्षभ [m]गांधार [m]षड्ज [m]मध्यम [2 m]धैवताः — The seven musical notes. a

[3 m]पञ्चमश् (चेत्यमी सप्त तंत्रीकण्ठोत्थिताः स्वराः)

2. [f d]काकली (तु कले सूक्ष्मे) — Minute tone. c

(ध्वनौ तु मधुरास्फुटे) — An inarticulate, but pleasing tone.

[4 m c]कलो!

[m g]मन्द्र (स्तु गंभीरे) — A base or low tone. f

[m]तारो! (ऽत्युच्चैस्) — A high tone.

(त्रय स्त्रिषु)[h]

3. (समन्वितलयस्त्वे) [5 m j]कतालो! — Harmony. i

[f]वीणा (तु) [f]वल्लकी — A lute.

[f]विपंची

(सा तु तंत्रीभिः सप्तभिः) [f]परिवादिनी — A lute with seven strings.

---

1 ऋ—. 2—म. 3—श्. 4 कल. 5 ए—.

[a] Severally named in the text. They are so called respectively, whether produced by the voice, or by a musical instrument. [b] Also निषदः. [c] As the chirping, of birds ; inarticulate and sweet. [d] Likewise काकलिः. [e] Or, as an adjective, it agrees in gender with the subject ; and so do the two following [f] Ex. the grumbling of clouds. [g] Likewise मन्द्रः. [h] The three last nouns vary with the gender when used as adjectives. [i] Or proper union of song, dance and instrumental music, keeping time together. See *v.* 10. [j] Also एकतालः.

Any stringed instrument.	4. ततं[n] (वीणादिकं वाद्यं)
A drum or tympan.	आनद्धं[n a] (मुरजादिकम्)
A wind instrument	(वंशादिकं तु) सुषिरं[n b]
A cymbal, bell, &c.	(कांस्यतालादिकं) घनम्[n]
A musical instrument.	5. (चतुर्विधमिदं) वाद्यं[n] वादित्रातोद्य[n 1m] (नामकम्)
Drums and tabours.	मृदङ्गा[m c] मुरजा[m]
Three sorts of drums. d	(भेदास्तु) अङ्क्या[2m]लिङ्ग्यो[3m]र्ध्वका[4m e] (स्त्रयः)
A double drum. f	6. (स्याद्) यशः[5m] पटहो[m] ढक्का[f]
A kettle drum. g	भेरी[f h] (स्त्री) दुन्दुभिः[m i] (पुमान्)
A large kettle drum.	आनकः[m] पटहो[m n] (ऽस्त्री स्यात्)
The quill, or bow. j	कोणो[m] (वीणादिवादनम्)
The neck of a lute.	7. वीणादण्डः[m] प्रवालः[m] (स्यात्)
The belly below the neck. k	ककुभ[m] (स्तु) प्रसेवकः[m l]

1 वा—. 2 अंक्य. 3 आ—. 4 ऊ—. 5 य—.

[a] Likewise आनहं. [b] Also शुषिरं. [c] Sing. मृदंगः and मुरजः. [d] Severally named in the text. They vary in size and shape, and are borne differently. See the descriptions in other dictionaries. [e] Likewise अंक्यौ, आलिंग and ऊर्ध्वकं. [f] In Hindi a *D'hōl*. [g] A large *D'hōl*. [h] Likewise भेरिः. [i] Also on a different reading of the text, आनकः[m], आनकदुन्दुभिः[m], and आनकदुन्दुभी[f]. [j] Or any thing with which a musical instrument is struck. [k] A wooden vessel covered with leather, placed under the neck to render the sound deeper; or a crooked piece of wood at the extremity of the lute. [l] Also प्रसेवः.

कोलम्बक (स्तु) कायो (ऽस्या)	The body of the lute. a
उपनाहो निबंधनम्	The tie. b
8. (वाद्यप्रभेदा डमरु मडु डिंडिम झर्झराः मर्दलः पणवो (ऽन्ये च)	Other instruments. c
नर्तकी लासिके (समे)	A female dancer. f
9. (विलम्बितं द्रुतं मध्यं) तत्वमोघोघनं (क्रमात्)	Slow, quick, and mean, time. g
तालः (कालक्रियामानम्)	Beating time.
लयः (साम्यम्)	Equal time in music and dance.
(अथास्त्रियाम्)	
10. ताण्डवं नटनं नाट्यं लास्यं नृत्यं (च) नर्तने	Dancing.
तौर्य्यत्रिकं (नृत्यगीतवाद्यं) नाट्य (मिदं त्रयम्)	Symphony. j
11. भ्रकुंस (श्च) भ्रुकुंस (श्च) भ्रूकुंस (श्चे) ति नर्तकः	A male dancer in woman's apparel.

1—का. 2 घोष.

[a] Complete, excepting the wires ; including, therefore, the gourd, neck, and belly. [b] Or lower part of the tail-piece where the wires are fixed. [c] Of divers sorts ; severally mentioned in the text : besides others, as गोमुखः, कुडुक्क, &c. See descriptions in various dictionaries. [d] Likewise neut. डमरुकं. [e] Also प्रणवः. [f] So, नर्त्तकः. or लासकः, a male dancer. [g] Severally stated, in their order. [h] Also तत्त्व°, and ततृत्व°. [i] Also नृत्तं, [j] Or union of song, dance, and instrumental music. [k] Also भ्रुकुंसः, भ्रूकुंस.

कौविमधारी पुरुषो)

A courtesan. a — (गण्योक्तौ गणिका) ऽज्जुका *f*

A sister's husband — 12. (भगिनीपतिरा) वुत्तो[1] *m*

A learned man. — भावो (विद्वान्) *m*

(अथा) वुकः[2] *m*

A father. — (जनको)

A prince. b — (युवराजस्तु) कुमारो *m* भर्तृदारकः *m*

A king. — 13. (राजा) भट्टारको *m* देवस् *m*

A princess. — (तत्सुता) भर्तृदारिका *f* c

A queen. d — देवी *f* (कृताभिषेकायां)

Any wife of a king. — (इतरासु च) भट्टिनी *f* e

Sacred. f — 14. अब्रह्मण्य *n* g (मवध्योक्तौ)

A king's brother-in-law. — (राजश्यालस्तु) राष्ट्रियः *m*

A mother. — अम्बा *f* (माता)

A young girl. — (ऽथ बाला स्याद्) वासू *f*

A venerable person. — (आर्यस्तु) मारिषः *m* h

---

1 आ—. 2 आ—.

a This, and the terms exhibited in the three following couplets, are used in theatrical language ; and some are forms of address employed only by certain descriptions of persons. See other dictionariés. b Designated as successor, and associated to the empire. c Some add भर्तृदारिका. d Consecrated with the king. e One commentary reads भाविनी. f Implying, according to some, a request to spare the thing in question. g Likewise अब्रह्मण्यं. h Also मार्षः and मार्षकः

f a

15. अन्तिका (भगिनी ज्येष्ठा) An eldest sister.

f *n* c

निष्ठा निर्वहणे (समे) The catastrophe. b

i *i* *i*

हण्डे हञ्जे हला (ह्वानं नीचं चेटीं सखीं प्रति) Appropriate vocatives. d

n e *m*

16. अङ्गहारोऽङ्गविक्षेपो Gesture.

m 1 *m*

व्यञ्जकाभिनयौ (समौ) Indication of a passion.

2 *m f n* *m f n*

(निर्वृत्ते त्वङ्गसत्त्वाभ्यां द्वे त्रिष्वा) ङ्गिक सात्त्विके Two sorts of tokens. f

17. (शृङ्गार वीर करुणाद्भुत हास्य भयानकाः Taste, or sentiment. g

m h

बीभत्स रौद्रौ च) रसाः

m 3 *m* 4 *m*

शृङ्गारः शुचिरुज्ज्वलः Love.

m *m*

18. उत्साहवर्द्धनो वीरः Heroism.

n *f* *f*

कारुण्यं करुणा घृणा Tenderness.

f *f* 5 *f* 6 *m*

कृपा दयानुकम्पा (स्याद्) अनुक्रोशो (ऽप्य)

m

(ऽथो) हसः Laughter.

---

1 व्य—. 2 वा— 3 —वि. 4 उ—. 5 व—. 6 व—.

[a] Also अत्तिका or अन्तिका. [b] Or conclusion of the fable. [c] Some add निर्वहणं. [d] Addressed, respectively, to a low woman, a slave girl, or a female friend. These vocative particles and the preceding terms, from the close of v. 11. are in general restricted to theatrical language. [e] Also अंगहारिः. [f] First corporeal, as an assumed posture ; second sincere, as a blush or change of colour. Besides other sorts ; by speech, &c. [g] In dramatic poetry the *tastes*, or sentiments, in which the audience sympathizes, are reckoned eight : as here enumerated. To which some add शान्तः, devotion and resignation. Others वात्सल्यं, parental affection. [h] Sing. रसः.

m n
19. हासो हास्यं (च)

Disgust.
mfn mfn b
बीभत्सं विकृतं (त्रिष्विदं द्वयम्)

Surprise, or wonderful.
m n c 1 n n
विस्मयोऽद्भुतमाश्चर्यं चित्रम् (अप्य्)

Horror, or terrific.
n d
(अथ) भैरवम्

m n n n n n
20. दारुणं भीषणं भीष्मं घोरं भीमं भयानकम्

n n
भयङ्करं प्रतिभयं

Wrath, or angry.
n 2 n
रौद्रं (तू) ग्रं

(अमी त्रिषु

e
21. चतुर्दश)

Fear, or terror.
mn mf f f g n n
दर त्रासो भीतिर्भीः साध्वसं भयम्

Sentiment or passion.
m
(विकारो मानसो) भावो

Indication of it.
m
ऽनुभावो (भावबोधकः)

Pride.
m m m
22. गर्वो ऽभिमानो ऽहंकारो

Arrogance. h
m 3 f
मानश्चित्तसमुन्नतिः

Disrespect.
m m m i 4 f
अनादरः परिभवः परिभावस्तिरस्क्रिया

---

1 का—. 2 उ—. 3 चि—. 4 ति—.

[a] Also fem. हासिका. [b] Likewise वैकृतं. [c] This and the following admit the three genders when employed as adjectives. [d] Masc. भैरवः. Fem.—वी. [e] The last fourteen terms, used adjectively, admit the three genders. *Ex.* Fem. रौद्री. [f] Also संत्रासः, उत्त्रासः, वित्रासः. [g] Likewise भीतं, भिया, भयः. [h] Some, not improperly, reckon these terms to be synonymous with the preceding. [i] Also परीभावः.

f 1 f a 2 f n b 3 n c

23. रीढा ऽवमानना ऽवज्ञा अवहेलनमसूक्षणम्

n d f 4 f m f e f f

मन्दाक्षं ह्रीस्त्रपा व्रीडा लज्जा — Modesty or shame.

f

(सा) ऽपत्रपा (ऽन्यतः) — Bashfulness.

f 5 f

24. क्षान्तिस्तितिक्षा — Patience, forbearance.

f

ऽभिध्या (तु परस्वविषये स्पृहा) — Coveting another's property.

f 6 f

अक्षान्तिरीर्ष्या — Envy. g

f

ऽसूया (तु दोषारोपो गुणेष्वपि) — Detraction.

n m m h

25. वैरं विरोधो विद्वेषो — Enmity.

n 7 m 8 f

मन्यु शोकौ (तु) शुक् (स्त्रियाम्) — Grief or sorrow.

m m m i

पश्चात्तापो ऽनुताप (श्च) विप्रतीसार (इत्यपि) — Repentance.

m m m j m 9 m 10 f 11 f k

26. कोप क्रोधा ऽमर्ष रोष प्रतिघा रुट्क्रुधौ (स्त्रियाम्) — Wrath, or rage.

n

(शुचौ तु चरिते) शीलं — Good conduct.

m 12 m

उन्माद चित्तविभ्रमः — Madness.

---

1 अ—. 2 अ—. 3 अ—. 4 त्र—. 5 ति—. 6 ई—. 7 शोक. 8 शुच्. 9—ष. 10 रुष्. 11 क्रुध्. 12 चि—.

[a] Also विमानना. [b] Likewise अवहेला, and हेला. [c] Also असुक्षणं, असूर्क्षणं, असुर्क्षणं, and संसूर्क्षणं. [d] Likewise मन्दास्यं. [e] Also ह्रीणं, and ह्रीतं. [f] Likewise लज्या. [g] Or impatience of another's excellence or success. [h] Also द्वेषः. [i] Or विप्रतिसारः. [j] अमर्षः or आमर्षः. [k] Also रुषा, and क्रुधा.

Affection or kindness.

1 *m* *f* *n* 2*n* a *m*

27. प्रेमा (ना) प्रियता हार्दं प्रेम स्नेहो

Desire or longing. b

m n c

(ऽथ) दोहदम्

Wish or desire.

f 3*f* d *f* 4*f* 5*f* *f* e *f* *m*

इच्छाकांक्षा स्पृहेहातृड्वाञ्छा लिप्सा मनोरथः

m *m* f 6*m*

28. कामोऽभिलाषस्तर्षं (च)

Ardent desire.

m f g

(स मशाल्) लालसा (द्वयोः)

Virtuous reflexion.

m *f*

उपाधि (र्ना) धर्म्मचिन्ता

Anxiety. h

m i

(पुंस्या) धि (र्मानसी व्यथा)

Recollection.

f j *f* 7*n* k

29. (स्याच्) चिन्ता स्मृतिराध्यानं

Missing. l

f 8*f*

उत्कंठोत्कलिके (समे)

Perseverance.

m *m*

उत्साहोऽध्यवसायः (स्यात्)

Fortitude.

n m

(स) वीर्य्यं (मतिशक्तिभाक्)

Deceit, or fraud.

m n *m* *m* 9*m* 10*n* *n*

30. कपटो (ऽस्त्री) व्याज दम्भोपधयश्छद्मकैतवे

1—मृ. 2—मृ. 3 का—. 4 स्पृहा. 5 तृष्. 6 त—. 7 चा—. 8 उ—का. 9 उपधि. 10 छ—मृ.

a Also प्रेम. b As a pregnant woman's. c The term is also synonymous with the following. d Likewise कांक्षा. e Likewise तृषा. f Or अभिलाषः. g Some add लालसा, but erroneously. h Or mental pain. i आधिः or अधिः. j Also चिन्तिया, and m. चिन्तः. k This term is by some connected with the next article. It signifies recollection accompanied with regret. Likewise आध्या. l Remembering with regret, affection, or desire. m Or fem. वीर्य्या.

f 1f n
कुसृतिर्निकृतिः शाठ्यं — Wickedness. a

m f b
प्रमादोऽनवधानता — Inadvertency or mistake.

31. कौतूहलं कौतुकं (च) कुतुकं (च) कुतूहलम् — Eagerness. c

(स्त्रीणां विलास बिब्बोक विभ्रमा ललितं तथा — Dalliance, or blandishment. d

2 m
32. हेला लीले(त्यमी)हावाः (क्रियाः शृङ्गारभावजाः)

m m f e m f f f 3 n
द्रव केलि परीहासाः क्रीडा लीला (च) नर्म (च) — Sport or amusement.

m m n g
33. व्याजोऽपदेशो लक्ष्यं (च) — Disguise.

f f n i
क्रीडाखेला (च) कूर्दनम् — A play or game. h

---

1 नि—. 2 लीला. 3—र्मृ.

a Synonymous with the preceding, according to some ; but others interpret these, mischievousness or fraudulency ; and the preceding, imposition or trick. b Also अनवधानं. c Or vehemence in seeking a proper thing ; or else impetuosity in action, with disregard of consequences. d The instance of feminine actions proceeding from love, which are stated in the text, are thus explained. विलासः, change of place, posture, gait, or look, on the approach of the lover. बिब्बोकः, affection of indifference. विभ्रमः, wantonness of youth : caprice. ललितं, languid gestures, and signs. हेला, lasciviousness. लीला, imitation of the lover's manner to beguile the time in his absence. e Also fem. केली. f Also परिहासः. g Likewise लक्ष्यं. h Such as playing at ball, &c. i Some read कुर्दनं ; but improperly.

Sweat. [a] — m m mb
घर्म्मो निदाघः स्वेदः (स्यात्)

Fainting. — m f
प्रलयो नष्टचेष्टता

Dissimulation. — f c 1 m
34. अवहित्थाकारगुप्ति

Hurry. — m d m
(समौ) सम्वेग सम्भ्रमौ

A horse-laugh. — 2 n e
(स्यादा) च्छुरितकं (हासः सोत्प्रासः)

A smile. — n
(स मनाक्) स्मितम्

A laugh. — n
35. (मध्यमः स्याद्) विहसितं

Horripilation. — m f n
रोमाञ्चो लोमहर्षणम्

Weeping. — n g n n
क्रन्दितं रुदितं क्रुष्टं

Gaping. — m f n h n
जृम्भ (स्तु त्रिषु) जृम्भणम्

Disappointing. [i] — m j m
36. विप्रलम्भो विसम्वादो

Creeding or tumbling. [k] — n l n
रिङ्गणं स्खलने (समे)

Sleep. [m] — f n m n m m
(स्यान्) निद्रा शयनं स्वापः स्वप्नः सम्वेश (इत्यपि)

---

1 आ—. 2 आ—.

[a] Or else heat, occasioning perspiration. [b] Also प्रस्वेद. [c] Likewise neut. अवहित्थं, and आहित्थं. [d] Also आवेगः. [e] Likewise अपच्छुरितं. [f] Also रोमहर्षः, रोमविक्रिया, रोमोद्गमः, रोमोद्भेदः. [g] Likewise क्रन्दनं, and रोदनं. [h] Fem. जृम्भा. [i] Deceiving by a false affirmation; or not effecting a promise. [j] Also विप्रलापः. [k] Creeping, as infants, on all fours; or else, falling as on slippery ground; or deviating from duty &c. [l] Likewise रिंखणं. [m] Or else a mistake occasioned by sleep; a dream. [n] Also सुप्तिः.

f a *f*
37. तन्द्री प्रमीला — Lassitude.

f 1*f* *f* b
भ्रकुटि र्भ्रुकुटी भ्रूकुटिः (स्त्रियः) — A frown.

f
अदृष्टिः (स्यादसौम्ये ऽक्ष्णि) — A look of displeasure.

f 2*f*
संसिद्धि प्रकृती (त्विमे) — The natural state.

n c *m* *m*
38. स्वरूपं (च) स्वभाव (श्) निसर्ग (श्चा)

m
(ऽथ) वेपथुः — A tremour.

m d
कम्पो

m *m* *m* e *m* *m*
(ऽथ) क्षण उद्धर्षो मह उद्धव उत्सवः — A festival.

1—टि. 2—ति.

[a] And तन्द्रि or तन्द्रीः. But this last mode of inflection is censured. Likewise तन्द्रा. [b] Also भ्रुकुटिः. Some make these terms synonymous with the following. Also भ्रकूटी, भ्रुकुटी, भ्रूकुटी, and भ्रुकुटी. [c] Also रूपं [d] Likewise कम्पनं, and कम्पितं. [e] Also क्षणः. See Book III, Ch. IV.

CHAPTER II.

SECTION I.

The infernal region. [a]

n b n 1 n 2 n

1. अधोभुवन पाताल बलिसद्म रसातलम्

3 m

नागलोको

A hole or vacuity.

n n c n n

(ऽथ) कुहरं शुषिरं विवरं बिलम्

n n n d n n e f f i

2. छिद्रं निर्व्यथनं रोकं रन्ध्रं श्वभ्रं वपा शुषिः

m f 4 m g

A hole in the ground.

गर्त्ता ऽवटौ (भुवि श्वभ्रे)

m f n

Perforated, or full of holes.

(सरन्ध्रे) शुषिरं (त्रिषु)

m n m n n n 5 n h

Darkness.

3. अन्धकारो (ऽस्त्रियां) ध्वान्तं तमिस्रं तिमिरं तमः

n i

Great darkness.

(ध्वान्ते गाढे) ऽन्धतमसं

n

Imperfect darkness.

(क्षीणे) ऽवतमसं

Universal darkness.

(तमः

n

4. विष्वक्) सन्तमसं

m m

The Nagas. [j]

नागाः काद्रवेयास्

Their chief.

(तदीश्वराः)

1—सू. 2—स. 3—अ. 4—ट. 5—स.

[a] Abode of Bali and of the *Nágas*, under the earth. [b] Also अधः, (स) m. अधोलोकः, &c. [c] Likewise सुषिरं. [d] Also निर्व्यधनं. [e] Or सभ्रं. [f] Also शुषी and सुषिः. Or सुषिः. [g] Likewise अवटिः. [h] Also तमसं. And तमः, तमा, तमं. [i] Likewise अन्धातमसं. [j] Demigods, in the human shape with a serpent's tail, and dilated neck, like the Koluber *Naga*. Sing. नागः. They are Children of Kadru', the wife of *Kas'yapa*.

m m
शेषो ऽनंतो

m b m
वासुकि (स्तु) सर्पराजो — King of serpents. [a]

m c
(ऽथ) गोनसे — Sort of snake.

m
5. तिलित्सः (स्याद्)

m m 1 m
अजगरे शयुर्वाहस (इत्युभौ) — A Boa, or large serpent. [d]

m e m
अलगर्दो जलव्यालः — A water snake.

m m f
(समौ) राजिल डुण्डुभौ — Amphisbæna.

m g m
6. मालुधानो मातुलाहिर् — A variegated serpent.

m m
निर्मुक्तो मुक्तकंचुकः — A snake, that has cast his slough.

m h 2 m 3 m m m 3 m
सर्पः पृदाकुर्भुजगो भुजंगो ऽहिर्भुजंगमः — A snake or serpent.

m m 4 m m i m j
7. आशीविषो विषधरश्चक्री व्यालः सरीसृपः

---

1 वा—. 2 —कू. 3 भु—. 4 चक्रिन्.

[a] Son of VASUKA, and often confounded with the preceding; as are the other chiefs of the *Nágas*, TAKSHAKA, SANK'HA, MAHAPADMA, &c. [b] Also वासुकिः. [c] Or गोनासः. Vulg. *Bòr.* [d] Boa Constrictor; &c. [e] Or अलगर्दः. But some read अलगर्द्धः, others अलिगर्दः. Vulg. *Alád'h.* [f] डुण्डुभः or दुण्डुभः. And डुडुभः. Vulg, *Dhònrá.* But generally described as a harmless double-headed snake. There is a great disagreement among commentators respecting the correspondent vulgar names of the snakes mentioned in the text. [g] One commentator describes this as a four-footed serpent with a large body and long tail; intending perhaps some species of Iguana; unless a fabulous creature be meant. [h] Fem. सर्पी, and सर्पिणी. Likewise व्याडः. [j] Some add सरिसृपः.

1*m* 2*m*a 3*m* *m* 4*m*

कुण्डली गूढपाच्चक्षुःश्रवाः काकोदरः फणी

m *m* *m* *m*b

8. दर्वीकरो दीर्घपृष्ठो दन्दशूको बिलेशयः

*m*c *m* 5*m* *m* *m*

उरगः पन्नगो भोगी जिह्मगः पवनाशनः

*mfn*d

Belonging to a snake. 9. (त्रिष्वा) हेयं (विषास्थ्यादि)

*mf*e *mf*f

His expanded head. स्फटायां (तु) फणा (द्वयोः)

m *m*

His skin. (समौ) कंचुक निर्मोकौ

m *n* *mn*

His venom. क्ष्वेड (स्तु) गरलं विषं

mn *mn* *mn*h

Nine sorts of fixed poison. g 10. (पुंसि क्लीबे च) काकोल कालकूट हलाहलाः

*m*i *m* *m* *m*

सौराष्ट्रिकः शौक्लिकेयो ब्रह्मपुत्त्रः प्रदीपनः

m *m*

11. दारदो वत्सनाभ (श्च विषभेदा अमी नव)

m *m*k

A dealer in antidotes. j विषवैद्यो जाङ्गुलिको

6*m*l *m*m

A snake-catcher. व्यालग्राह्यहितुण्डिकः

1—नृ. 2—पाद्. 3 च—क्षु. 4—नृ. 5—नृ. 6—हिन्.

[a] Also गूढपदः, and गूढपात्, (द). [b] Likewise बिलशयः. [c] Also उरंगः, and उरंगमः. [d] Fem. आहेयी. [e] स्फटा or फटा. [f] Masc. फणः. Likewise neut. फणं. [g] Severally named in the text; some mineral, others vegetable. [h] हलाहलः, and हालाहलः, or हालहलः. Also हाहलः. [i] Likewise सौराष्ट्रिकः. [j] Or a conjurer, using charms against poison. [k] Likewise जांगलिकः. [l] Also व्यालग्राहः. [m] आहितुण्डिकः. or अहितुण्डिकः.

SECTION II.

1. (स्यान्) नारक[m] (स्तु) नरको[m] निरयो[m] दुर्गति:[f] (स्त्रियाम्) Hell.

(तद्भेदास्) तपना[m] [1] वीचि[m f] महारौरव[m] रौरवा:[m] Various hells. [a]

2. संहार:[m b] कालसूत्रं[n] (चेत्याद्या:)

(सत्त्वास्तु) नारका:[m] Departed souls.

प्रेता[m c]

वैतरणी[f d] (सिंधुः) The river of hell.

(स्याद्) अलक्ष्मी[f] (स्तु) निर्ऋति:[f] Misfortune or misery.

3. विष्टि[f] राजू:[f e] Unpaid labour. [e]

कारणा[f g] (तु) यातना[f h] तीव्रवेदना[f] Agony, or sharp pain.

पीडा[f] बाधा[f i] व्यथा[f] दुःखम्[n] आमनस्यं[n j] प्रसूतिजम्[n k] Pain.

---

[1] च—.

[a] Severally named in the text; besides others. as *Támisra, And'hatámisra, Sálmalí, Asipatravana,* &c. [b] Or संघात:. [c] Likewise परेता:. [d] Also वैतरणि:. [e] Or else, casting into hell; or, in astrology, the period (*karan'a*) called *bhadrá*. Compulsory and unrewarded labour, being the occasion of pain, is placed under the present head. The terms, as by some explained, signify the person executing such labour, [f] आजू or आजुर्. [g] Also कारिका. [h] Likewise यामना. [i] Or आबाधा. [j] Likewise अमानस्यं and आमानस्यं. [k] These two last terms are, by some, separated from the rest; as signifying mental distress. Others, on the contrary, make these and the preceding four, synonymous with the three following words,

n n 1n

Corporeal pain. 4. (स्यात्) कष्टं कृच्छ्रमाभीलं

a

(त्रिष्वेषां भेद्यगामि यत्)

SECTION III.

m m 2mb mc

The sea or ocean. 1. समुद्रोऽब्धिरकूपारः पारावारः सरित्पतिः

3m 4m m 5m m m

उदन्वानुदधिः सिन्धुः सरस्वान् सागरोऽर्णवः

m m 6m 7m

2. रत्नाकरो जलनिधिर्यादःपतिरपांपतिः

m m

Particular seas. d (तस्य प्रभेदाः) क्षीरोदो लवणोद (स्तथापरे)

f pl. e 8*fn* n nf n ng

Water. 3. आपः (स्त्री भूम्नि) वार्वारि सलिलं कमलं जलम्

9n n 10n nh n n

पयः कीलालममृतं जीवनं भुवनं वनम्

ni 11nj 12n n n

4. कबन्धमुदकं पाथः पुष्करं सर्वतोमुखम्

---

1 आ—. 2 स—. 3—न्वत्. 4 उ—. 5—स्वत्. 6 या—. 7 अ—. 8—र्. 9—स्. 10 अ—. 11 उ—. 12—स्.

a Such of the foregoing, as are used as adjectives, vary with the gender. b Also आकूपारः, कूपारः, and कूवारः, c Or पारापारः. Likewise अवारपारः. d That of milk, and of salt water; besides five others, as the sea of fresh water, spirituous liquor, butter, curds, and the juice of sugar-cane; apparently designations of gulfs or divisions of the ocean, e अप्. Also neut. आपस्. f And सरिलं or सर्लं. g Also जडं. h Also जीवनीयं. i Or, according to another reading, (वनकबन्धं), two words are here exhibited, वं and कबन्धं. Or a single word वनकबन्धं. j Also उदं. And दकः.

1*n* 2*n* 3*n* *n* *n*a *n* 4*n* *n*b
अंभो ऽर्णस्तोय पानीय नीर क्षीरांबु शंबरम्

n *mn*
5. मेघपुष्पं घनरसस्

mfn *mfn*d
(त्रिषु द्वे) आप्यमम्मयम् — watery, or consisting of water.[c]

m 5*m* *mf*e 6*mf*f
भङ्गस्तरङ्ग ऊर्मि (र्वा स्त्रियां) वीचिर — A wave.

(थोर्मिषु)

7*m* *m*
6. महत्सूल्लोल कल्लोलौ — A surge or billow.

8*m*
(स्याद) वर्त्तो (ऽम्भसां भ्रमः) — A whirlpool.

*m*h *m* *m*i 9*f*j
पृषंति बिन्दु पृषताः (पुमांसो) विप्रुषः (स्त्रियः) — A drop of water.[g]

*n*l *m*
7. चक्राणि पुटभेदाः (स्युर्) — A winding descent of water.[k]

m *m*
भ्रमा (श्च) जलनिर्गमाः — A drain.[m]

n 10*n*n *n* *n* *mf*no
कूलं रोध (श्च) तीरं (च) प्रतीरं (च) तटं (त्रिषु) — A shore or bank.

1—स्. 2—स्. 3 तोव. 4 च—. 5 त—.
6—पि. 7 उ—. 8 वा—. 9—प्. 10—स्.

[a] Also नारं. [b] Or संवरं. [c] As froth, &c. [d] Fem. आप्या, and अम्मयी. [e] Also fem. ऊर्मी. [f] Likewise विचिः, and fem. वीची, or विची. [g] Or of any other liquid. [h] Sing. पृषत् or पृषंति. [i] Sing. पृषतः. [j] Sing. विप्रुट्. Also विप्रुड् (—ष्). [k] A winding course. Some say a reach of the river. Others Eddy water. [l] Sing. चक्रं. Also चक्रः. [m] Or pipe along the wall of an edifice. But some make these and the two preceding terms synonymous. Sing. भ्रमः. Some explain them bubbling up of water. Others surf. [n] Also Masc. रोधः (रोध.) [o] Fem. तटी.

The opposite, and the near bank. a
n l m n
8. पारावारे (परार्वाची तीरे)

The channel.
n
पात्रं (तदंतरम्)

An island.
m n 2 m n
द्वीपो (ऽस्त्रियाम्) न्तरीपं (यदंतर्वारिणस्तटम्)

One formed by alluvion. b
n
9. (तोयोत्थितं तत्) पुलिनं

A sand bank. c
n n
सैकतं सिकतामयम्

Mud or clay.
m m m n m m
निषद्वर (स्तु) जंबालः पङ्को (ऽस्त्री) शाद कर्दमौ

Inundation. d
m m e
10. जलोच्छ्वासाः परीवाहाः

A temporary well. f
m m
कूपका (स्तु विदारकाः)

Navigable.
m f n g
नाव्यं (त्रिलिंगं नौतार्ये)

A boat.
f h 3 f f i
(स्त्रियां) नौस्तरणिस्तरिः

A raft or float. j
m n k n m
11. उडुपं (तु) प्लवः कोलः

A natural stream. l
4 m n
स्रोतो (ऽम्बुसरणं स्वतः)

---

1 अ—. 2 अ—. 3 त—. 4—सृ.

a Respectively, viz. पारं, the opposite bank or shore, अवारं, the contiguous bank or shore, b Or any island, or one with the steep banks. c Or an island with sandy shores. d Or else a water pipe, or channel, for carrying off an excess of water. e Sing. परीवाहः. Also परिवाहः. f Or hole dug for water in the dry bed of a rivulet; or else, a rock, or tree, dividing the stream of a river. Sing. कूपकः. g Fem. नाव्या. h Also नौका. Also तरणी and तरी. i Made of grass's, &c. k Likewise उडूपं. l Or a rapid one. m Likewise स्रोतं.

m a 1*n* आतरस्तरपण्यं (स्यात्)	Fare, or freight.
f c *f* द्रोणी काष्ठाम्बुवाहिनी	An oval basin. b
m 2*m* 12. सांयात्रिकः पोतवणिक्	A voyaging merchant.
m *m* कर्णधारस्तु नाविकः	The pilot or helmsman.
m e *m* नियामकाः पोतवाहाः	The crew. d
m *m* f कूपको गुणवृक्षकः	The mast.
m *f* g 13. नौकादण्डः क्षेपणिः (स्यात्)	The oar.
n *m* अरित्रं केनिपातकः	The rudder.
f h *m* i अभ्रिः (स्त्री) काष्ठकुद्दालः	A scraper or shovel.
n *n* सेकपात्रं (तु) सेचनम्	A bucket. j
n 14. (क्लीबे) ऽर्धनावं (नावोऽर्धे)	The boat's half.
m f n k (अतीत नौके) ऽतिनु (त्रिषु)	Landed from a boat.

1 त—. 2—ज्.

[a] Also आतारः, and उत्तरः. [b] Shaped like a boat, with an aperture in front, and used for pouring water. It is made of wood, stone, or other materials. [c] Or द्रोणिः and द्रुणिः, or द्रुणी. According to another reading द्रोणिका, and अम्बुवाहिनी. Also अम्बुसेचनी. [d] Variously explained; as the steersman, or rower, or as one employed in dragging the boat, or in watching from the mast-head. Sing. नियामकः, पोतवाहः. [e] Likewise नियाम. [f] Some explain this a post to which a boat is made fast. [g] Or क्षेपणी. Also क्षिपणिः. And क्षिपणी. [h] Or अभ्री. Also अवभ्रिः. [i] Likewise कूद्दालः, and कुदालः. [j] Or vessel for lading water out of the boat. [k] Masc. or Fem. अतिनौः.

[a]
(त्रिष्वागाधात्)

Clear, transparent. — *m f n*[b] *m f n*[c] प्रसन्नो ऽच्छः

Turbid water. — *m f n* *m f n* *m f n* कलुषे ऽनच्छ, आविलः

Deep. — 15. *m f n* *m f n* *m f n* निम्नं गभीरं गंभीरं

Shallow. — *m f n* उत्तानं (तद्विपर्य्यये)

Very deep, — *m f n*[d] [1]*m f n* अगाधमतलस्पर्शं

A fisherman. — *m* *m*[e] *m*[f] कैवर्त्तो दाश धीवरौ

A net. — 16. *m* *n* आनायः (पुंसि) जालं (स्यात्)

Pack-thread.[g] — *n*[h] *n* शणसूत्रं पवित्रकम्

A fish basket. — *f* *f*[i] मत्स्याधानी कुवेणी (स्याद्)

A fish hook. — *n*[j] *n*[k] बडिशं मत्स्यवेधनम्

---

[1] अ—.

[a] The following are adjectives. [b] Fem. प्रसन्ना. [c] Also स्वच्छः. [d] Likewise आगाधं. [e] Or दाशः [f] Fem. धीवरी [g] Made of rushy Crotaloria ; or, according to different interpretations, a net made of such pack-thread ; or, generally, the rope of a net. [h] Also सणसूत्रं and सनसूत्रं. [i] Likewise कुवेणा. And कुवेणिः. Also कुपिनी. [j] Or Fem. बडिशा, or बडिशी. Likewise बलिशं, बलिशी. [k] Or Fem. मत्स्यवेधनी.

1*m* *m*a *m*b *m* *m*c *m*

17. पृथुरोमा झषो मत्स्यो मीनो वैसारिणोऽण्डजः A fish.

m 2*m*d

विसारः शकली (चा)

m *m*

(ऽथ) गडकः शकुलार्भकः Sort of gilt head. e

m *m*

18. सहस्रदंष्ट्रः पाठीन A sheat-fish. f

3*m*h *m*

उलूपी शिशुकः (समौ) A porpoise. g

*m*j 4*m*k

नलमीनश्चिलिचिमः Sort of sprat. i

m/*f*m 5*m*/*f*n

प्रोष्ठी (तु) शफरी (द्वयोः) A sort of carp. l

m *n*

19. क्षुद्राण्डमत्स्यसंघातः पोताधानम् Small fry.

(अथो झषाः) Various sorts of fish. o

*m*p *m* *m*q *m* *m*r *m*s

रोहितो मद्गुरः शालो राजीवः शकुलस्तिमिः

1—मन्. 2—नृ. 3—नृ. 4 चि—. 5—रः.

[a] Likewise झषः. [b] Fem. मत्सी. Also masc. मत्सः, मत्स्यरः, मच्छः. [c] Also विसारी (न्). [d] Likewise शकली (न्). [e] Sparus emarginatus, B. Mss. [f] Silurus Pelorius, B. Mss. [g] But, according to some interpretations, another sort of fish shaped like a porpoise. [h] Also अलूपी, उलुपी, उ'लुपी, उलपी, and चुलूपी. [i] Clupea Cultrata (B. Mss.)? Three several explanations are given by different authors; but they agree that the fish, here meant, frequents flags and reeds. [j] Or तलमीनः. And नडमीनः. [k] Also चिलीचिमिः, चिलिचीमः. or चिलीचिमः. And चिलिचिमिः. चिलीमः, चिलिमीनकः. [l] Cyprinus chrysoparcius, B. Mss. [m] Masc. प्रोष्ठः. [n] Masc. शफरः. Some add सफरी —रः. [o] Severally named in the text, viz. a carp (Cyprinus denticulatus, B.); a sheat-fish (Silurus Batrachus, L.); a gilt-head (Sparus spilotus, B.) &c. [p] Also रोहित्, and लोहितः. [q] Or सालः. [r] Some add शकुलः. [s] This is a fabulous sea-fish of prodigious size.

20. तिमिङ्गिला[1 m] (दयश्च ते)[a]

Aquatic animals. b (ऽथ) यादांसि[2 n] जलजन्तवः[3 m]

Various sorts. c (तद्भेदाः) शिशुमारो[m]द्र[4 m] शङ्कवो[5 m] मकरा[6 m] (दयः)

A crab. 21. (स्यात्) कुलीरः[m] कर्कटकः[m d]

A turtle or tortoise. कूर्मे[m] कमठ[m] कच्छपौ[m]

A shark. e ग्राहो[m] ऽवहारो[m]

A crocodile. नक्र[m] (स्तु) कुम्भीरो[m f]

A worm. (ऽथ) महीलता[f]

22. गण्डूपदः[m] किंचुलुको[m g]

A gangetic alligator. h निहाका[f] गोधिका[f] (समे)

A leech. रक्तपा[f] (तु) जलौकायां[f i] (स्त्रियां भूम्नि) जलौकसः[7 f j]

1—स. 2—स्. 3—द. 4 उद्र. 5 शंकु. 6—र. 7—कस्.

[a] Besides many sorts noticed in other dictionaries. [b] Especially amphibious kinds. [c] Severally named in the text, viz. the porpoise, otter, scate, and marine monster (a whale ? or a seal ?), besides the following, and other, sorts. [d] Or कर्कंटः. [e] Interpretations differ : one terms this a water-elephant ; (perhaps the hippopotamus may be meant :) others make it the gangetic alligator. [f] Also कुंभीलः. [g] Likewise किंचिलिकः. And किंचलुकः, or किंचलुः. [h] Some make this to be the *Iguana* : distinguishing, however, another sort from the aquatic one. Book II. Ch. 5. [i] जलोका or जलौका, and जलूका, जलायुका, जलालुका, जलालोका, जलजंतुका, जलसूपी, जलोरगी, जलिकावेणी. [j] Or जलौकसी. Also जलौकसः, masc. and जलौकसं, neut. Pl. with the sense of the sing. f. जलौकसः. Also sing. जलौकाः.

23. मुक्तास्फोटः [m] (स्त्रियां) शुक्तिः [f]	A pearl oyster.
शंखः [m n] (स्यात्) कंबु [m n] (र्स्त्रियाम्)	A conch.
क्षुद्रशंखाः [m a] शंखनखाः [m b]	A small shell.
शंबूकाः [m f c] जलशुक्तयः [1 f]	A bivalve shell.
24. भेके [2 m] मण्डूक [m] वर्षाभू [m d] शालूर [m e] प्लव [m] दर्दुराः [3 m]	A frog.
शिली [f] गण्डूपदी [f]	A small worm. f
भेकी [f] वर्षाभ्वी [f]	A female frog. g
कमठी [f] डुलिः [f i]	A female turtle. h
25. (मद्गुरस्य [k] प्रिया) शृङ्गी [f l]	Sort of sheat-fish. j
दुर्नामा [f m] दीर्घकोशिका [f n]	A cockle.
जलाशया [m] जलाधारास् [m p]	A lake or pond. o
(तत्रागाधजलो) ह्रदः [m q]	A deep lake.

1—क्ति. 2 भेक. 3—र.

[a] Sing. क्षुद्रशंखः. [b] Sing. शंखनखः. Also शंखनकः. [c] Masc. शंबूकः. Also शंबुकः, शंबुः and शाबकः. Or शांबूकः. [d] Also हरिभूः. [e] Or शालूरः. [f] Some say, a female worm. [g] Or any small frog. [h] Or any small tortoise or turtle. [i] Or डुली. Also डुलिः. And डुडिः. [j] Silurus Pungentisimus, B. Mss. [k] Or, according to some commentators, two synonyma, मद्गुरसी, f. अप्रिया, f. [l] Also शृङ्गिः. [m] Also दुर्नामन् and—म्नी. [n] Or दीर्घकोषिका. [o] Or a reservoir; or any piece of water. [p] Sing. जलाशयः, and जलाधारः. [q] Likewise ह्रदः.

A trough near a well. a — 26. आहाव (स्तु) निपानं (स्यादुपकूप जलाशये)

A well. — (पुंस्येवा) न्धु प्रही कूप उदपानं (तु पुंसि वा)

The wooden frame for the rope. b — 27. नेमिस्त्रिका (ऽस्य)

The cover or facing of a well — वीनाहो (मुखबंधनमस्य यत्)

A square, or a large pond. — पुष्करिण्यां (तु) खातं (स्यात्)

A natural pond. d — अखातं देवखातकम्

One deep enough for the lotus. — 28. पद्माकरस्तडागो (ऽस्त्री)

Any pond or pool. g — कासारः सरसी सरः

A basin. h — वेशंतः पल्वलं (चा) ऽल्पसरो

A large and oblong pond. — वापी (तु) दीर्घिका

A moat, or ditch. — 29. खेयं (तु) परिखा

A dike. — आधार (स्त्वम्भसां यत्र धारणम्)

A basin round the foot of a tree. — (स्याद्) आलवालमावालमावापो

A river. — (ऽथ) नदी सरित्

1 धं—. 2—न्हि. 3—णी. 4 त—. 5—स्. 6—स्. 7 वा—. 8—वा.

a Filled from the well, and intended for watering cattle. b A triangular frame. Some interpret it the wooden frame at the bottom of the well, on which the masonry rests. Others the cover of the well. Or the frame at its mouth. c Some add विनाहः. d Or else one in front of a temple. e Also अखोत. f Also तडाकः. And तटाकः. g These terms are synonymous with the preceding according to some interpretations : or they are restricted to such a factitious pond, according to others. h Or small pond ; or one, which, in the hot season, is either shallow or quite dry. i Or वापिः. j Also अलवालं.

30. तरंगिणी[f] शैवलिनी[f] तटिनी[f] ह्रादिनी[f,a] धुनी[f,b]
स्रोतस्विनी[f,c] द्वीपवती[f] स्रवंती[f] निम्नगा[f]पगा[1,f]

31. गंगा[f] विष्णुपदी[f] जह्नुतनया[f] सुरनिम्नगा[f] — The *Ganges.*
भागीरथी[f] त्रिपथगा[f] त्रिस्रोता[2,f] भीष्मसू[f] (रपि)

32. कालिंदी[f] सूर्यतनया[f] यमुना[f,e] शमनस्वसा[3,f] — The *Yamuná.* d
रेवा[f] (तु) नर्मदा[f] सोमोद्भवा[f] मेकलकन्यका[f,g] — The *Narmadá.* f

33. करतोया[f] सदानीरा[f] — The *Karatóyá.* h
बाहुदा[f] सैतवाहिनी[f] — The *Báhudá.*
शतद्रु[f,j] (स्तु) शतद्रुः[f] (स्याद्) — The *Satadru.* i
विपाशा[f] (तु) विपाट्[4,f] (स्त्रियाम्) — The *Vipásá.* k

34. शोणो[m] हिरण्यबाहुः[m,m] (स्यात्) — The *Sóna.* l
कुल्या[f] (ल्पा कृत्रिमा सरित्) — A canal. n
शरावती[f] वेत्रवती[f] चन्द्रभागा[f,p] सरस्वती — Various rivers. o

---

1 स्र—, or स्रा—. 2—स्रत्. 3—स्व. 4—श.

a Also ह्लादिनी. b Likewise धुनिः and धूनी. c Likewise स्रोतस्वती and स्रोतोवहा. d Vulgarly *Jamuna* or *Juwun*. It joins the Ganges near *Prayág*. e Also यमी. f Vulgarly *Narbadá*. g Likewise मेखलकन्यका. h A river in the north of Bengal. i Vulgarly *S'atlaj*; in the *Punjáb*. j Also शुतद्रिः. k Another river of the *Punjáb*. l This joins the Ganges above Patna. m Or हिरण्यवाहः. n A channel for irrigation: or a rivulet in general. o Severally named in the text. Besides others, as the *Kausikí, Gandak'i, Gódávar'i, Charm'anvat'i, Tápi* or *Tapati, Sarayu, Gautamí,* &c. p Or चंद्रभागी. Also चांद्रभागा, or—गी.

35. कावेरी[f] (सरितोऽन्याश्च)

The mouth of a river. a — संभेदः[m] सिन्धुसंगमः[m]

An issue from a pond. b — (द्वयोः) प्रणाली[m f c] (पयसः पदव्यां)

Belonging to certain Rivers. d — (त्रिषु तूत्तरौ

36. देविकायां सरय्वां च भवे) दाविक[m f n] सारवौ[m f n]

A white water-lily. e — सौगन्धिकं[n] (तु) कल्हारं[n f]

A red one. g — हल्लकं[n] रक्तसंध्यकम्[n]

Any water-lily. — 37. (स्याद्) उत्पलं[n] कुवलयं[n h]

A blue one. i — (अथ) नीलाम्बुजन्म[1 n] (च)

इन्दीवरं[n j] (च नीले ऽस्मिन्)

The esculent white sort. k — (सिते) कुमुद[n l] कैरवे[n]

The root of a water-lily. m — 38. शालूक[n n] (मेषां कंदः स्याद्)

Pistia stratiotes. — वारिपर्णी[f o] (तु) कुंभिका[f]

1—न्.

[a] The confluence of two rivers; or the junction of a river with the sea. [b] Or a drain of an edifice. [c] Masc. प्रणालः. [d] To the *Dévikâ* (or *Déwâ*), and *Sarayu* (or *Sarju*), respectively. In these two instances, the adjective is irregular. [e] Nymphæa Lotus. [f] These, and the two following words, are names of four different plants, according to some interpreters. [g] Nymphæa rubra. [h] Also कुवलं and कुवं. And कुवेलं. [i] Nymphæa cœrulea and stellata; [j] Or इंदीवारं. [k] Nymphæa esculenta. [l] Also कुमुत्, (—द्). [m] The esculent root of any of the preceding sorts. [n] Likewise शालूकं. [o] Or वारिपूर्णी. Also पर्णी.

जलनीली (तु) शैवालं शैवलो[b] — Vallisneria.[a]

(ऽथ) कुमुद्वती[c]

39. कुमुदिन्यां[1] — A place abounding in water-lilies.[d]

नलिन्यां (तु) बिसिनी पद्मिनी (मुखाः)[2] — An assemblage of lotus flowers.[e]

(वा पुंसि) पद्मं नलिनमरविन्दं महोत्पलम्[3] — A lotus.[f]

40. सहस्रपत्रं कमलं शतपत्रं कुशेशयम्

पंकेरुहं तामरसं सारसं सरसीरुहम्[g]

41. बिसप्रसून[h] राजीव पुष्कराम्भोरुहाणि[4][i] (च)

पुण्डरीकं सिताम्भोजं — A white lotus.

(अथ) रक्तसरोरुहे — A red lotus.

42. रक्तोत्पलं कोकनदं

नालानालं[j] — The stalk of a water-lily. The film or fibres attendant on it.

(अथास्त्रियाम्)

1—नी. 2—नी. 3 च—. 4 च—ह.

[a] Comprehending several sorts found in stagnant waters. [b] Likewise शेवलं. Also शेवालं and शेवालः. But different copies further disagree in the genders assigned to these various readings. Also m. n. शेपालः, and शेवालः. [c] Likewise कुमुदवती. [d] Or, as some interpret it the flexible stalk of a water-lily; or, according to others a plant, viz. Menyanthes Indica or Cristata. [e] Besides other synonyma, as उत्पलिनी, कमलिनी, पुटकिनी, &c. [f] Nelumbium speciosum or Nymphæa Nelumbo. [g] Also सरसिरुहं. [h] Likewise बिसप्रसून॰, and बिसप्रसून॰. [i] Also अम्भोरुह, (च ह). [j] Also नाली. Likewise masc. नालः.

m n a *n* b
मृणालं बिसं

An assemblage of water-lilies. *m n* c
(अब्जादि कदंबे) षण्ड (मस्त्रियाम्)

The root of a water-lily. *m* *m n* d
43. करहाटः शिफाकंदं

A filament. *m* *m n* e
किंजल्कः केशरो (ऽस्त्रियाम्)

A new leaf of a water-lily. *f* f *n*
संवर्त्तिका नवदलं

The seed of the lotus. g *m* h *m*
बीजकोशो वराटकः

44. (उक्तं स्वर्व्योम दिक्कालधीशब्दादिसनाट्यकम्
पातालभोगि नरकं वारि चैषां च संगतम्)

---

[a] And मृणाली, a small fibre. [b] Also बिशं or विसं. [c] Or षंडं. [d] Likewise शिफा. f. कंदः, m. n. [e] Also केसरः. [f] Or संवर्त्तिः· Also संवर्त्ती. [g] Or the honey-combed pericarp containing it. [h] Or बीजकोषः.

BOOK II.

CHAPTER I.

1. वर्गाः पृथ्वी पुर क्ष्माभृद्वनौषधि मृगादिभिः

नृ ब्रह्म क्षत्र विट् शूद्रैः साङ्गोपाङ्गैरिहोदिताः

f a f b 1f f f f f

2. भूर्भूमिरचलाऽनन्ता रसा विश्वम्भरा स्थिरा — Earth.

f f f f c f f f

धरा धरित्री धरणिः क्षोणी ज्या काश्यपी क्षितिः

f d f 2f 3f f

3. सर्वंसहा वसुमती वसुधोर्वी वसुन्धरा

f f f e f f f f g 4f f h

गोत्रा कुः पृथिवी पृथ्वी क्ष्माऽवनिर्मेदिनी मही

5f i f

4. मृन्मृत्तिका — Soil.

f f

(प्रशस्ता तु) मृत्सा मृत्स्ना (च मृत्तिका) — An excellent soil.

f

उर्वरा (सर्वसस्याढ्या) — Fertile with every crop.

m f

(स्याद्) ऊषः क्षारमृत्तिका — Salt ground.

---

1 च—. 2—धा. 3 उ—. 4 मे—. 5—दु.

[a] Also indec. भूः (र्). [b] Also भूमी. [c] Likewise धरणी and क्षोणिः. Also क्षाणिः, and क्षौणी. [d] Likewise सहा. [e] Also पृथवी. [f] Likewise क्ष्मा. [g] Also अवनी. [h] Likewise महिः. [i] Also मृदा, and मृत्तिः.

1 m f n a 2 m f n

A spot with such soil. 5. ऊषवानूषरौ (द्वावप्यन्यलिंगौ)

n f b

A place, or firm spot — स्थलं स्थली

m 3 m

A region devoid of water. — (समानौ) मरु धन्वानौ

m f n c m f n

Untilled or waste. — (द्वे) खिलाऽप्रहते (समे)

6. (त्रिषु)

f m n d n n

A world. — (ऽथो) जगती लोको विष्टपं भुवनं जगत्

n e

INDIA. — (लोको ऽयं) भारतं (वर्षं)

The eastern region. f — (शरावत्यास्तु यो ऽवधे:

m

7. देश: प्राग्दक्षिण:) प्राच्य

m

The northern region. g — उदीच्य: (पश्चिमोत्तर:)

m m

A country of barbarians. — प्रत्यन्तो म्लेच्छदेश: (स्यान्)

m m

The middle region. h — मध्यदेश (स्तु) मध्यम:

m f

The region of sanctity. i 8. आर्यावर्त्त: पुण्यभूमि (र्मध्यं विंध्यहिमागयो:)

1—षत्. 2 ऊ—. 3 धन्वन्.

[a] Some, varying this reading, write ऊषर:, and अनूषर: [b] Likewise स्थला. [c] Masc. खिल: ; fem. खिला ; and खिलं [d] Also पिष्टपं, or masc. पिष्टप:. [e] Or भरतवर्षं. [f] East, or south of the river *Sarávati*, which flows from N. E. to S. W. [g] North or west of the river *Sarávati*. [h] Between the two ranges of mountains ; from the confluence of the Ganges and Jamuna, to the disappearance of the *Saraswati*. [i] From the eastern to the western sea, and bounded by the two ranges of mountains.

1 *m f* *m*
नीवृज्जनपदो — An inhabited country.

m *m* 2 *m*
देश विषयौ (तु) पवर्त्तनम् — Any country.[a]

b
9. (त्रिष्वागोष्ठात्)

3 *m f n* 4 *m f n*
(नडप्राये) नड्वान्नड्वल (इत्यपि) — One abounding in reeds;[d]

5 *m f n*
कुमुद्वान् (कुमुदप्राये) — —in water-lilies.

6 *m f n*
वेतस्वान् (बहुवेतसे) — —in ratans;

m f n
10. शाद्वलः (शादहरिते) — —in green grass.

m f n
(सजंबाले तु) पंकिलः — Clayey and muddy.

m f n 7 *m f n*
जलप्रायमनूपं (स्यात्) — Watery, or wet.

m d
(पुंसि) कच्छ (स्तथाविधः) — Contiguous to water.[c]

f *m f n* *m f n* 8 *m f n* e
11. (स्त्री) शर्करा शर्करिलः शार्करः शर्करावति — Full of stony or similar nodules.

(देश एवादिमाव्)

9 *m f n* f
(एवमुन्नेयाः) सिकतावति — Sandy.

1—वृ. 2 ब— 3—नड्वत्. 4 न—. 5—द्वत्.
6—स्वत्. 7 ज—. 8—वृ. 9—वृ.

[a] Whether inhabited or uninhabited. But some interpretations make these terms synonymous with the preceding. [b] The following are used as adjectives, and vary with the three genders. [c] Some interpretations make this synonymous with the preceding. [d] Also neut. and, according to some, fem. [e] The two first terms are exclusively applied to a spot abounding in stony nodules, or potsherds, &c. The other two are applicable to anything gritty. [f] The words are here exactly similar to the preceding : thus सिकता, सिकतिलः, sandy, as a country ; सैकतः, सिकतवान् (—वत), sabulous.

Watered (viz. its rice) from a river.

12. (देशो) नद्यंबु वृष्ट्यंबु संपन्नव्रीहिपालितः

m f n

स्यान्) नदीमातृको

m f n

Or by rain.

देवमातृक (श्च यथाक्रमम्)

1 m f n

Ruled by a just king.

13. (सुराज्ञि देशे) राजन्वान्

2 m f n

Governed by a monarch.

(स्यात्ततो ऽन्यत्र) राजवान्

n n

A fold for kine.

गोष्ठं गोष्ठानकं

n

The site of a former one.

(तत्तु) गौष्ठीनं (भूतपूर्वकम्)

f m

Contiguous ground. a

14. पर्य्यन्तभूः परिसरः

3 m 4 f b

सेतुरालौ (स्त्रियां पुमान्)

m m m n d

A hillock. c

वामलूर (श्च) नाकु (श्च) वल्मीकं (पुन्नपुंसकम्)

n 5 n m 6 m m e f f f

A road, path or way.

15. अयनं वर्त्म मार्गाध्व पंथानः पदवी सृतिः

f g f h f f i f j

सरणिः पद्धतिः पद्या वर्त्तन्येकपदी (ति च)

m m m

A good road.

16. अतिपंथाः सुपंथा (श्च) सत्पथ (श्चार्च्चिते ऽध्वनि)

m m m 7 m m k

A bad road.

व्यध्वो दुरध्वो विपथः कदध्वा कापथः (समाः)

---

1 —न्वत्. 2—वत्. 3 सेतुः. 4 आलिः. 5—न्.
6 अध्वन्. 7—न्.

[a] Near the banks of a river, or the skirts of a mountain, &c. [b] Also आली. [c] Thrown up by termes, or by moles, &c. [d] Also वल्मिकं. [e] पथिन्, पथन्, or पथ. [f] Likewise पदविः. [g] Also सरणिः. सरणी, and सारणी. [h] Likewise पद्धती. [i] वर्त्तनी, or वर्त्तनिः. Also वर्त्मनिः, or वर्त्मनी. [j] Also एकपाद्. [k] Likewise कुपथ.

17. अपंथा[1 m] (स्त्व) पथं[2 n] (तुल्ये)	The want of a road.
शृंगाटक[n] चतुष्पथे[n]	Meeting of four roads.
प्रांतरं[n] (दूरशून्योऽध्वा)	A long and lonesome way.
कांतारो[m n] (वर्त्म दुर्गमम्)	A difficult road. a
18. गव्यूतिः[m f] (स्त्री) क्रोशयुगं[n]	A league. b
नल्वः[m] (किष्कुचतुःशतम्)	A furlong. c
घंटापथः[m] संसरणं[n]	A highway.
(तत्पुरस्यो) पनिष्करम्[3 n]	A street.

CHAPTER II.

1. पूः[4 f] (स्त्री) पुरी[f d] नगर्यौ[f n e] (वा) पत्तनं[n f] पुटभेदनम्[n g]	A town or city.
स्थानीयं[n] निगमो[m]	

1—थिन्. 2 अ—. 3 उ—. 4 पुर्.

[a] Or a dangerous one : but some interpretations make this synonymous with the preceding term. [b] Measured by two thousand fathoms. [c] Measured by four hundred cubits. [d] Also पुरिः. [e] Fem. नगरी. Neut. नगरं. Also पुरं. [f] Likewise पट्टनं, or पट्टनी. [g] Also पटभेदनं.

A suburb. — (ऽन्यत्तु यन्मूलं नगरात्पुरम्

1 n

2. तच्च) शाखानगरं

m a m

The abode of harlots. — वेशो वेश्याजनसमाश्रयः

m 2f

A market. — आपणस्तु निषद्यायां

m f c f

A shop. b — विपणिः पण्यवीथिका

f f f

A high street. — 3. रथ्या प्रतोली विशिखा

m m n

A rampart. d — (स्याच्चयो वप्रम् (मस्त्रियाम्)

m m m f

An edifice. e — प्राकारो वरणः शालः

n h

A bound hedge. g — प्राचीरं (प्रांततोवृतिः)

f n i

A wall. — 4. भित्तिः (स्त्री) कुड्यम्

n k

One built with rubbish. j — एडूकं (यदन्तर्न्यस्तकीकसम्)

n m n 3n 4n 5n n

A house. — गृहं गेहोदवसितं वेश्म सद्म निकेतनम्

---

1 या—. 2 —द्या. 3 ह—. 4 —मू. 5 —मू.

[a] Likewise वेषः. [b] Here interpretations differ greatly : some make these terms synonymous with the preceding; others explain them, the street of a market; a stall; a platform on which commodities are exposed for sale; a place of vend without a market, &c. [c] Also विपणी. [d] Interpretations differ greatly. Some explain the terms, a mound of earth raised from the ditch of a fortified town and serving as a foundation for edifices. Others say the foundation of an edifice generally; others again, any mound of earth raised from a ditch. Some likewise the gate of a fortified city. [e] Particularly a surrounding wall of masonry on a rampart or mound of earth. [f] Or सालः. [g] Also a mud-wall or other enclosure. [h] Likewise प्राचीनं. [i] Likewise कुड्यम्. [j] Or else a tomb. [k] Also एडुकं. Or एडोकं.

n *n* a *n* b *n* *n* c *n f*

5. निशांत वस्त्य सदनं भवनागार मंदिरम्

m pl. *m* *m* 1 *m*

गृहाः (पुंसि च भूम्न्येव) निकाय्य निलयालयाः

m *m f* d *f* e *f*

6. वासः कुटो (द्वयोः) शाला सभा

n f

संजवनं (त्विदम्) — A cluster of four houses.

n g

चतुःशालं

2 *f* *m n*

(मुनीनां तु) पर्णशालोटजो (ऽस्त्रियाम्) — A hut made of leaves.

n 3 *n*

7 चैत्यमायतनं (तुल्ये) — An altar. h

f *f*

वाजिशाला (तु) मंदुरा — A stable.

n *f* i

आवेशनं शिल्पिशाला — A working house.

f *f*

प्रपा पानीयशालिका — A place of refreshment. j

m

8. मठ (श्छात्रादिनिलयो) — A college. k

f l *n*

गञ्जा (तु) मदिरागृहम् — A tavern.

---

1 आ—. 2 उ—. 3 आ—.

a Likewise वसतं. b Also सादनं. c अगारं or आगारं. d Masc. or fem. कुटिः. Fem. कुटी. Also neut. कुटीरं, and masc. कुटः. e Likewise शाला. f Likewise संजवनं. g Also fem. चतुःशाली. h Or shed for sacrifices. Some interpret it, a sacred tree. Others explain it; a monument of wood or other materials placed in honour of a deceased person. i Also शिल्पिशाला. And neut. शिल्पशालं, or शिल्पिशालं. j Where water is distributed, k A school of students; or a convent of ascetics, &c. Likewise गुञ्जा.

Middle of a house. — गर्भागारं[n] वासगृहं[n]

A woman's apartment.[a] — अरिष्टं[n] सूतिकागृहम्[n b]

A window or air hole. — 9. वातायनं[n] गवाक्षः[m] (स्यात्)

A temporary hall. — मंडपो[m n c] (ऽस्त्री) जनाश्रयः[m]

The abode of the wealthy.[d] — हर्म्यं[n e] (दि धनिनां वासः)

A temple or palace. — प्रासादो[m] (देवभूभुजाम्)

A royal residence.[f] — 10. सौधो[m n] (ऽस्त्री) राजसदनं[n]

A king's house. — उपकार्योपकारिका[f g][1 f]

Temples of divers holy forms. — स्वस्तिकः[m n] सर्वतोभद्रो[m n] नंद्यावर्त्ता[2 m n h] (दयो ऽपि च)

11. विच्छंदकः[m i] (प्रभेदा हि भवंतीश्वरसद्मनाम्)

The queen's apartments. — (स्त्र्यगारं भूभुजाम्) अंतःपुरं[n] (स्यात्) अवरोधनम्[n]

12. शुद्धांत (श्चा)[m] ऽवरोध (श्च)[m]

An airy room, a top of the house.[j] — (स्यात्) अट्टः[m] क्षौम[m n k] (मस्त्रियाम्)

---

1 उ—. 2—स.

[a] Appropriated to a woman in labour. These and the preceding are synonymous terms, according to some commentaries. [b] Also सूतिकागृहं. [c] Likewise, fem. मंडपा. [d] Any grand edifice of masonry. [e] हर्म्यं, besides other synonymous terms; as अट्टः, &c. [f] Synonymous with the preceding; according to some interpretations. [g] उपकार्या. Also उपकारी. [h] Besides other terms; as रुचकः, &c. [i] Also विच्छर्दकः. [j] Here, and in the two following articles, interpretations differ greatly. The explanations, most generally received are inserted. Other interpretations are; the back of an edifice, a fortified place in front of the building; an apartment on the top of the hall; a building of a particular form. [k] Likewise क्षोमं.

m *m* a *m* b प्रघाण प्रघणा॒लिंदा (बहिर्द्वारप्रकोष्ठके)	A terrace before the house door.
f 1*f* 13. गृहावग्रहणी देहल्य	The threshold.
n c 2*n* *n* ऽङ्गनं चत्वरा॒ऽजिरे	A court or yard.
f d (अधस्ताद्दारुणि) शिला	The lower timber of a door.
f नासा (दारूपरिस्थितम्)	The upper timber.
n 3*n* 14. प्रच्छन्नमन्तर्द्वारं (स्यात्)	A private door within the house.
n *m* पक्षद्वारं (तु) पक्षकः	A back door. e
m *n* *n* f *m* वलीक नीध्रे पटलप्रांते	The edge of the thatch.
n g 4*f* h (ऽथ) पटलं छदिः	The thatch or roof.
f *f* i 15. गोपानसी (तु) वलभी (छादने वक्रदारुणि)	The wood of a thatch.
5*f* *m* *n* कपोतपालिकायां (तु) विटंकं (पुन्नपुंसकम्)	A dovecot, or aviary.
6*f* *n* *m* 16. (स्त्री) द्वार्द्वारं प्रतीहारः	A door, or gate.
f k *f* l (स्याद्) वितर्दि (स्तु) वेदिका	A covered terrace in the yard. j

1—णी. 2—र. 3 प—. 4—छ. 5—का. 6—द्वार.

[a] Also, as some write these words, प्रघानः and प्रघनः. [b] अलिंद, or आलिंदः. [c] Likewise अंगणं. [d] Or शिली. [e] Some make this and the preceding article synonymous. [f] Likewise, according to another reading, नीव्रं. [g] Also पटं, and चालं. [h] Not neuter as erroneously stated by the commentators. [i] Also वडभिः or वडभीः. [j] Here, and in the following article, as in many other places, interpretations differ greatly. A quadrangular resting place made of wood. A place for sitting in a court yard; or one for standing under. A quadrangular spot in the court of a temple or great edifice. A terrace furnished with pillars. A floor on four posts in the middle of a quadrangular house. [k] Likewise वितदी. [l] Also वेदि, and वेदी.

Decoration of the gate-post. [a] — m n … n
तोरणो ऽस्त्री बहिर्द्वारं

A city gate. — n … n
पुरद्वारं (तु) गोपुरम्

A raised place over the gate. — 1 m
17. (कूटं पूर्द्वारि यद्) हस्तिनख (तस्मिन्)
(अथ त्रिषु)

A door. — m f n b, m f n c
कपाटमररं (तुल्ये)

Its bolt or bar. — d, f n e
(तद्विष्कंभे) ऽर्गलं (न ना)

Stairs. — n … n
18. आरोहणं (स्यात्) सोपानं

A ladder. — f f, 2 f g
निःश्रेणि (स्त्व)धिरोहिणी

A broom. — f f
संमार्जनी शोधनी (स्यात्)

Dust, or sweepings. — m h, m
संकरो ऽवकर (स्तथा)

19. (क्षिप्ते)

The entrance of a house. — n n
मुखं निःसरणं

An open space in a town. [i] — m n
संनिवेशो निकर्षणं

---

1 हृ—. 2 ब—.

[a] This is explained as signifying, the ornamented arch of a gateway. Some interpret, the outer gate. [b] Also कवाटः. Fem. कपाटी and कवाटी. [c] Fem. अररी or अररिः. [d] By a variation in the reading, this is made to exhibit a synonymous term, विष्कंभः, or, according to some विष्कंभि (—न्). [e] Fem. अर्गला or अर्गली. [f] Likewise निःश्रेणी. And निश्रयिणिः, or निश्रेणी. [g] Also अधिरोहणी. [h] Likewise संकारः. [i] The passage in, or out of a house, town or market. The road of ingress and egress. The entrance through the house-door.

m *m* (समौ) संवसथ ग्रामौ	A village. a
f 1 *m n* वेश्मभूर्वास्तु (रस्त्रियाम्)	The site of a habitation.
m *n* b 20. ग्रामांत उपशल्यं (स्यात्)	Space near a village, &c.
2*f* 3 *f* सीमसीमे (स्त्रियामुभे)	A boundary or limit.
m *f* c घोष. आभीरपल्ली (स्यात्)	A station of herdsmen.
m n *m* पक्कणः शबरालयः	An abode of the lowest men.

---

1 वास्तु. 2—मन्. 3—मा.

[a] Place for diversion outside of a town, or within it. [b] These two words are synonymous with the following, according to some. [c] Also आभीरपल्लिः.

CHAPTER III.

m a 1 m 2 m 3 m m m

A mountain. 1. महीध्रे शिखरि क्ष्माभृद् हार्य्य धर पर्वताः

m m m 4 m 5 m m m

अद्रि गोत्र गिरि ग्रावाचल शैल शिलोच्चयाः

m 6 m c

A range, surrounding the earth. b 2. लोकालोकश्चक्रवाल

m 7 m

A hill with three peaks. त्रिकूटस्त्रिककुत् (समौ)

m 8 m

The western mountain. d अस्त (स्तु) चरमक्ष्माभृद्

m m

The eastern mountain. e उदयः पूर्व्व पर्व्वतः

9 m m m 10 m 11 m

Divers mountains. f 3. हिमवान्निषधो विंध्यो माल्यवान् पारियात्रकः

n 12 m

गंधमादन (मन्ये) च हेमकूटा (दयो नगाः)

m m 13 m 14 m 15 m f 16 f

A stone or rock. 4. पाषाण प्रस्तर ग्रावोपलाश्मानः शिला दृषत्

m n n n

A peak or summit. कूटो (ऽस्त्री) शिखरं शृंगं

m m g m

A precipice. प्रपात (स्त्व) तटो भृगुः

1—रिन्. 2—त्. 3 च—. 4—वन्. 5 च—. 6 च—. 7 त्रि—द. 8—त्. 9—वत्. 10—वत्. 11 पा—. 12—ट. 13—वन्. 14 उ—. 15 अश्मन्. 16 द्.

[a] Likewise महीधर, and अहिध्रः. [b] The limit of light and darkness. [c] Also चक्रवाडः. [d] Behind which the sun sets. [e] Over which the sun rises. [f] Severally named in the text, viz. the snowy range north of India; the mountain called *Nishad'ha*; the tropical range dividing South from Noth India, &c. Besides others, as *Malaya*, *Chitrakúta*, *Mainâka*, &c. [g] अतटः, or, according to another reading, तटः.

5. कटको[m n] (ऽस्त्री नितम्बो ऽद्रेः) — The side of a mountain.

स्नु[m n]: प्रस्थ[m n]: सानु[m n] (र् स्त्रियां) — Table land.

उत्स[n]: प्रस्रवणं[n a] — A fountain.

(वारिप्रवाहो) निर्झरो[m] झर[m]: — A cascade.

6. दरी[f] (तु) कंदरो[m f b] (वा स्त्री) — An artificial cave.

(देवखात[n] बिले[n c]) गुहा[f] — A natural cave.

गह्वरं[n]

गंडशैला[1 m] (स्तु. च्युता: स्थूलोपला गिरे:) — Rocks fallen from a mountain.

7. खनि[f d]: (स्त्रियाम्) आकर[m]: (स्यात्) — A mine.

पादा[2 m]: प्रत्यन्तपर्व्वता[3 m]: — Hills near a mountain.

उपत्यका[f] (ऽद्रेरासन्ना भूमिर्) — Land near a mountain.

(ऊर्द्ध्वम्) अधित्यका[4 f] — Land on it.

8. धातु[m] (र्मनः शिलाद्यद्रेः) — A fossil, or mineral.

गैरिकं[m] (तु विशेषत:) — Red chalk.

निकुंज[m] कुंजौ[m n] (वा क्लीवे लतादिपिहितोदरे) — A place overgrown with creepers, &c.

1—स्थ. 2 पाद. 3—त. 4 अ—.

[a] Some make these synonymous with the following. [b] Fem. कंदरा or कंदरी. [c] These are synonyma, according to some, instead of being the explanation of the two other terms here exhibited. [d] Also खनी or खानि:.

CHAPTER IV.

SECTION I.

A forest or grove.

f[a] 1n n n n n[b]

1. अटव्यरण्यं विपिनं गहनं काननं वनम्

A large forest.

n 2f

महारण्यमरण्यानी

A grove near a house.

m[c] m

गृहारामा (स्तु) निष्कुटाः

A garden.

m 3n

2. आरामः (स्याद्) उपवनं (कृत्रिमं वनमेव तत्)

One planted by a state minister, &c.

f

(अमात्यगणिकागेहोपवने) वृक्षवाटिका

A royal public one.

4m n n

3. (पुमाना) क्रीड उद्यानं (राज्ञः साधारणं वनं)

A royal pleasure ground.

n[d]

(स्यादे तदे व) प्रमदवन (मं तःपुरोचितम्)

A row or range.

5f 6f 7f f f[e]

4. वीथ्यालिरावलिः पंक्तिः श्रेणी

A continuous line. f

f[g] f[h]

लेखा (स्तु.) राजयः

---

1 अ—. 2 अ—. 3 उ—. 4 आ—. 5—थी. 6 आ—. 7 आ—.

[a] Sing. अटविः. Also अटवी. [b] Likewise, fem. वनी. [c] Sing. गृहारामः. [d] Or प्रमदावनं. [e] Also आली and आवली; वीथिः and श्रेणिः. Some add पंक्ती. [f] Some make these synonymous with the preceding. [g] Likewise रेखा. [h] Sing. राजिः. Also राजी.

f 1 m
वन्या वनसमूहे (स्यात्) — A multitude of groves.

m a 2 m
अंकुरोऽभिनवोद्भिदि — A germin.

m m 3 m 4 m 5 m
5. वृक्षो महीरुहः शाखी विटपी पादपस्तरुः — A tree.

m m b m c 6 m m m 7 m
अनोकहः कुटः सालः पलाशी द्रु द्रुमागमाः

m
6. वानस्पत्यः (फलैः पुष्पात्) — One fructifying from blossoms. d

m
(तैरपुष्पाद्) वनस्पतिः — One without apparent blossoms. e

f g
ओषध्यः (फलपाकान्ताः) — An annual plant. f

8 m f n m f n h
(स्याद्) वंध्यः फलेग्रहिः — Fruitful.

m f n m f n 9 m f n
7. वंध्यो ऽफलोऽवकेशी (च) — Barren.

10 m f n m f n 11 m f n
फलवान् फलिनः फली — Bearing fruit.

m f n 12 m f n m f n i m f n m f n m f n
प्रफुल्लोत्फुल्ल संफुल्ल व्याकोष विकच स्फुटाः — Blown, as a flower.

m f n m f n
8. फुल्ल (श्चैते) विकसिते (स्युर्)

j
(अवंध्यादय स्त्रिषु)

m n m 13 m
स्थाणु (वा ना) ध्रुवः शंकुर् — The trunk of a lopped tree.

m
(ह्रस्वशाखाशिफः) क्षुपः — A small tree. k

1—हः. 2—द्रुः. 3—नुः. 4—नुः. 5 त—. 6—नुः. 7 आगम. 8 च—. 9—नुः. 10—वत्. 11—नुः. 12 स—. 13 शंकुः.

[a] Likewise अंकूरः. [b] Likewise कुटः. [c] Also सालः. [d] As the Mango, Eugenia, &c [e] As the Bread-fruit, &c. [f] Dying after ripening its fruit. [g] Sing. ओषधि. Also ओषधी. [h] Likewise फलेग्रहिः. [i] Likewse व्याकोषः. [j] The preceding admit the three genders, as adjectives. [k] With short branches and roots.

A shrub.	9. (अप्रकाण्डे) स्तंब[m] गुल्मौ[1 m]
A creeper.	वल्ली[f a] (तु) व्रततिर्[f b] लता[2 f]
A spreading one. c	(लता प्रतानिनी) वीरुद्[3 f] गुल्मिन्य्[4 f] उलप[5 m] (इत्यपि)
Height of a tree, hill, &c.	10. (नगाद्यारोह) उच्छ्राय[m] उत्सेध[m] (श्चो) च्छ्रय[6 m] (श्च सः)
The trunk.	(अस्त्री) प्रकाण्डः[m n] स्कंधः[m] (स्यान्मूलाच्छाखावधिस्तरोः)
A branch.	11. (समे) शाखा[f] लते[7 f]
A large branch.	स्कंधशाखा[f] शाले[f]
A fibrous root.	शिफा[f] जटे[f]
From a radicant branch. d	(शाखा शिफा) ऽवरोहः[m] (स्यात्)
Scandent fibres.	(मूलाच्चाग्रं गता) लता[f e]
The top of a tree.	12. शिरो[8 n] ऽग्रं[n] शिखरं[m n] (वा ना)
Its root.	मूलं[n] बुध्नो[m] (ऽङ्घ्रिनामकः)[f]
The pith.	सारो[m] मज्जा[9 m] (समौ)
The bark.	त्वक्[10 f] (स्त्री) वल्कं[n] वल्कलम्[m n] (अस्त्रियाम्)
Wood.	13. काष्ठं[n] दारु[m n]

1—म्बा. 2ल—. 3—ध्. 4गु—मी. 5उ—. 6उ—. 7लता. 8—स्. 9—न्. 10—त्वच्.

[a] Also वल्लिः. [b] Likewise व्रतती and प्रततिः. [c] Some make the explanation to be one of the synonyma; and others, moreover, make these and the preceding bear the same sense. [d] For example, that of the India fig-tree. [e] Some make this a second interpretation of अवरोहः and expound it otherwise; viz. a plant climbing from the root to the top of a tree. [f] Any term signifying a foot.

n 1n n 2m 3f a
इंधनं (त्वे) ध इध्ममेधः समित् (स्त्रियाम्) Fuel.

m m n
निष्कुहः कोटरं (वा ना) The hollow of a tree.

f b f
वल्लरिर्मञ्जरिः (स्त्रियौ) A compound pedicel.

n c n n d n n m
14. पत्रं पलाशं छदनं दलं पर्णं छदः (पुमान्) A leaf.

m n m n
पल्लवो (ऽस्त्री) किसलयं A sprout or shoot. e

m m n
विस्तारो विटपो (ऽस्त्रियाम्) The branch and its shoot. f

n n g
15. (वृक्षादीनां) फलं सस्यं Fruit.

n n
वृन्तं प्रसवबंधनम् The foot stalk. h

m f n
(आमे फले) शलाटुः (स्यात्) Moist. (fruit.)

m f n
(शुष्के) वान (उभे त्रिषु) Dry.

m n
16. क्षारको जालकं (क्लीबे) A bud or a germ.

f i m j
कलिका कोरकः (पुमान्) An unblown flower.

m k m
(स्याद्) गुच्छक (स्तु) स्तबकः A cluster of blossoms.

m n l m n
कुड्मलो मुकुलो (ऽस्त्रियाम्) An opening bud.

---

1 एधस्. 2 एध. 3—ध

[a] Some restrict the two last, others the three last, to signify sacred fuel. [b] Likewise वल्लरी and मञ्जरी. [c] Also पत्त्रं. [d] Likewise छादनं. [e] The extremity of a branch bearing new leaves, &c. [f] Some make this and the preceding synonymous. [g] Likewise शस्यं. [h] Of a leaf or fruit: the petiole or peduncle. [i] Likewise कलिः and कली. [j] And neuter. [k] Also गुलुच्छः. Likewise गुच्छः or गुत्सः. [l] And कुड्मलः.

L

A flower.

17. (स्त्रियः) सुमनसः[1 f a] पुष्पं[n] प्रसूनं[n b] कुसुमं[n] (सुमम्)[c]

Its nectar or honey.

मकरंदः[m] पुष्परसः[m]

Its dust or farina.

परागः[m] सुमनोरजः[2 n]

18. (द्विहीनं प्रसवे सर्व्वं[d] हरीतक्यादयः स्त्रियाम्)[e]

Fruits of certain plants.

आश्वत्थं[n] वैणवं[n] प्लाक्षं[n] नैयग्रोधैङ्गुदं[n 3 n] (फले)[f]

19. बार्हतं[n] (च)

Fruit of the Eugenia.

(फले जंबाः)[f] जंबूः (स्त्री)[n] जंबु जांबवम्[n g]

(पुष्पे जातीप्रभृतयः[h] स्वलिंगा व्रीहयः फले

20. विदार्य्याद्यास्तु मूलेऽपि)

Blossom of the Bignonia.

(पुष्पेक्लीवेऽपि) पाटला[f i]

1—नस्. 2—जस्. 3 ऐ—.

[a] Plural with the sense of the singular, though some make it admit the singular number, and even the neuter gender. Ex. सुमनाः and सुमनः. [b] Likewise सूनं. [c] According to another reading सुमं a flower. [d] Names of plants generally become neuter, to signify the produce of the plant; viz. its blossom and fruit: some add the root, and even the leaf. [e] Except *Harítakí* and certain others, which are feminine denoting the fruit, &c. As *Drákshá*, *Kóshátakí*, &c. [f] In these instances, derivatives are employed to signify the fruit: and, in some other instances likewise; as वैणवं, &c. [g] Here the neuter, the derivative, and the irregular feminine, are all three employed. [h] *Játí* and certain others (as *Yut'hiká*, *Malliká*, &c.) irregularly retain the original genders, to signify the flower of the plant; so do the names of corn and pulse, to signify the seed. And so do *Vidárí*, and others (as *Gambhárí* &c.) to denote tho root, or the blossom: some add the fruit. [i] Here the neuter, and the original feminine gender, are both admissible; and even the masculine.

SECTION II.

m b 1 m m m

1\. बोधिद्रुमश्चलदलः पिप्पलः कुञ्जराशनः — Holy fig-tree a

m

अश्वत्थे

m d m 2 m 3 m

(ऽथ) कपित्थे (स्युर्) दधित्थ ग्राहि मन्मथाः — Elephant, or wood apple. c

m m 4 m

2\. (तस्मिन्) दधिफलः पुष्पफलदंतशठा (वपि)

m f m m m

उडुंबरे जंतुफलो यज्ञाङ्गो हेमदुग्धकः — Glomerous fig-tree. e

m m m m

3\. कोविदारे चमरिकः कुद्दालो युगपत्रकः — Mountain ebony. g

m 5 m f i m

सप्तपर्णो विशालत्वक् शारदी विषमच्छदः — Echites. h

m j m m k m

4\. आरग्वधे राजवृक्ष सम्पाक चतुरङ्गुलाः — Cassia fistula.

m m m m

आरेवत व्याधिघात कृतमाल सुवर्णकाः

m m m m m

5\. (स्युर्) जम्बीरे दंतशठ जंभ जंभीर जंभलाः — A lemon or citron.

m m m 6 m m

वरुणो वरणः सेतुस्तिक्तशाकः कुमारकः — Tapia. l

---

1 श्व—. 2—नू. 3—थ. 4—ठ. 5—ष्. 6 ति—.

[a] Ficus religiosa. [b] Also बोधि. [c] Feronia Elephantium or Cratæva Valanga. [d] Also कपित्थाः. [e] Ficus glomerata, R. [f] Some write उदुंबरः. [g] Bauhinia variegata, and other species. [h] Echites scholaris. [i] Likewise masc. शारदः. [j] Also आरग्वधः and आरग्वधः. [k] Likewise शंपाक and सम्पाक. [l] Cratæva Tapia or Capparis trifoliata.

Punag. [a] — 6. पुन्नागे पुरुषस्तुंगः केसरो देववल्लभः

Coral tree. [c] — पारिभद्रे निंबतरुर्मन्दारः पारिजातकः

Tinis. [d] — 7. तिनिशे स्यन्दनो नेमी रथद्रुरतिमुक्तकः

वञ्जुलश्चित्रकृच् (चा

Spondias. [f] — ऽथ द्वौ) पीतन कपीतनौ

8. आम्रातके

Bassia. [h] — मधूके (तु) गुडपुष्प मधुद्रुमौ

वानप्रस्थ मधुष्ठीलौ

Another sort. [j] — (जलजे ऽत्र) मधूलकः

Pilu. [k] — 9. पीलौ गुडफलः स्रंसी

Walnut. [l] — (तस्मिंस्तु गिरिसंभवे)

अक्षोट कंदरालौ (द्वा)

---

[1] वं—. [2] अ—. [3] चि—त्. [4]—ष्ठ. [5]—तृ.

[a] Probably Rottlera tinctoria, R. Mss. [b] Also केशरः. [c] Erythrina fulgens. But some apply the Sanskrit names to the Melia sempervirens. [d] Dalbergia Oujeinensis, R. Mss. [e] नेमि. Also नेमिनु and fem. नेमी, according to some. [f] Spondias Mangifera. [g] Also आम्रातकः [h] Bassia latifolia. [i] Likewise मधुकः and मधुः. [j] Growing in water; or, according to another reading, on mountainous ground. [k] The name is applied in some provinces to Careya arborea (R. Mss.); in others, to Salvadora Persica (R.) [l] Described as a species of the preceding, growing on mountains: but the corresponding Hindi name belongs to Juglans regia, and also to Croton Moluccanum, or Aleurites Triloba. [m] Likewise अक्षोटः and आक्षोटः. Also कर्परालः.

m m b
अंकोठे (तु) निकोचकः — Alangium. [a]

m m m m
10. पलाशे किंशुकः पर्णो वातपोथे — Butea frondosa.

1 m
(ऽथ) वेतसे — *Bayas*, or *Bént.* [c]

2 m m d m m m m
रथाऽभ्रपुष्प विदुल शीत वानीर वञ्जुलाः

m m f 3 m
11. (द्वौ) परिव्याधविदुलौ नादेयी (चा) ऽम्बुवेतसे — The same growing in water.

m f m m g m h m
शोभाञ्जने शिग्रु तीक्ष्णगंधकाऽक्षीव मोचकाः — Morunga. [e]

m
12. (रक्तो ऽसौ) मधुशिग्रुः (स्यात्) — A red variety of the same.

m j m
अरिष्टः फेनिलः (समौ) — Soap berry. [i]

m m 4 m m 5 m
बिल्वे शाण्डिल्य शैलूषौ मालूर श्रीफला (वपि) — Marmelos. [k]

m m m m
13. प्लक्षो जटी पर्कटी (स्यात्) — Waved leaved fig-tree. [l]

m 6 m 7 m
न्यग्रोधो बहुपाद्वटः — Indian fig-tree. [n]

1—स. 2 रथ. 3 धं—स. 4—म. 5—ख.
6—पाद्. 7 वट.

[a] A hexapetalum. [b] Likewise निकोठकः. [c] The Sanskrit name is by some referred to the Ratan: but a different plant appears to be meant. [d] अभ्रपुष्पः. Also रथाभ्रपुष्पः. [e] Hyperanthera Morunga or Guilandina Morunga. [f] Likewise शोभांजनः or शोभाजनः. [g] तीक्ष्णगंधकः and तीक्ष्णगंधः. [h] अक्षीवः or आक्षीवः, and आक्षीवः. [i] Sapindus Saponaria and other species: but applied also to Mimosa abstergens, R. [j] Also रिष्टः. [k] Ægle Marmelos or Cratæva Marmelos. [l] Ficus venosa. [m] जटिन्. Also fem. जटी, or जटि (Nom. जटिः). So पर्कटिन्; and fem. पर्कटी, or पर्कटि (—टिः). [n] Ficus Indica.

m mb m 1m 2m m

Lod'h. The pale sort. a — गालवः शावरो लोध्रस्तिरीटस्तिल्व मार्ज्जनौ

m 3m m

Mango. c — 14. आम्रश्चूतो रसालो

m

A very fragrant sort of it. — (ऽसौ) सहकारो (ऽतिसौरभः)

n nd m me m

Bdellium. — कुंभोलूखलकं (क्लीबे) कौशिको गुग्गुलुः पुरः

mg m m m m

Sebesten. f — 15. शेलुः श्लेष्मातकः शीत उद्दालो बहुवारकः

ni mj m mk

Piya. h — राजादनं पियालः (स्यात्) सन्नकद्रुर्धनुः पटः

f f m

Gambhari. l — 16. गंभारी सर्व्वतोभद्रा काश्मरी मधुपर्णिका

f f mm

श्रीपर्णी भद्रपर्णी (च) काश्मर्य्यः (चाप्य)

Jujube. n — (ऽथ द्वयोः)

mfo mfp mfq

17. कर्कन्धूर्बदरी कोलिः

n n 4n

The fruit. — कोलं कुवल फेनिले

---

1 ति—. 2 ति—. 3 चूत. 4 —ल.

[a] The lodh is a bark used in dying, of which two sorts are in use. Some restrict the first term to this species, and make the rest common to both. [b] Also शाबरः. [c] Mangifera Indica. [d] कुंभं and उलूखलकं. Also कुम्भोलुः and खलकं. Likewise कुम्भोलूखलकं. [e] Also गुग्गुलु. [f] Cordia myxa. Also Cordia latifolia, R. Mss. [g] Also शेलुः. [h] Chironjia Sapida, R. Mss. But the name is in some places applied to Grewia orientalis and didyma. [i] Likewise राजातनं or—नः. [j] And प्रियालः. Also सन्नः and कद्रुः. [k] Likewise धनुः (धनु of धनुष्) and पटः. [l] Probably Gmelina arborea, R. [m] Also काश्मरी. [n] Zizyphus Jujuba, and other species. [o] Masc. कर्कन्धुः and न्धूः. Fem. कर्कन्धूः. [p] Masc. बदरः. [q] Also, in the fem. कोली and कोला.

n n f a
सौवीरं बदरं घोण्टा (ऽप्य)

m
(ऽथ स्यात्) स्वादुकण्टकः *Bun'chi.* b

m c m m 1 m
18. विकंकतः स्रुवावृक्षो ग्रंथिलो व्याघ्रपाद् (पि)

m m d f f e
ऐरावतो नागरंगो नादेयी भूमिजंबुका Orange.

m g m m m
19. तिंदुकः स्फूर्जकः कालस्कंध (श्च) शितिसारके Sort of ebony. f

m m m m
काकेन्दुः कुलकः काकतिन्दुकः काकपीलुके Another sort. h

m i m m f j 2 m m
20. गोलीढो झाटलो घण्टापाटलिर्मोक्ष मुष्ककौ *Ghantá-pa'tali.*

m m 3 m
तिलकः क्षुरकः श्रीमान् *Tila'.*

m m
(समौ) पिचुल झावुकौ Tamarix. k

f f f m m
21. श्रीपर्णिका कुमुदिका कुंभी कैटर्य्य कट्फलौ *Kayap'hal.*

m f 4 m m
क्रमुकः पट्टिका (ख्यः स्यात्) पट्टी लाक्षाप्रसादनः Red *Lód'h.*

1—द्रु. 2 मोच. 3—वृ. 4—मु.

a Some make the three last, others the two last, signify the wild sort : others again explain the last, as denoting both plant and fruit ; and the rest, as indicating the fruit of the common Jujube. b Flacourtia Sapida, R. c Also वैकंकतः. d Likewise नारंगः or नार्य्यंगः. e Some disjoin the two last as names of a different plant. f Diospyros melanoxylon, (R), and Glutionsa, (Koen.) g Also तिंदुकी. h Diospyros tomentosa, R. i Likewise गोविडः. j Or घंटा and पाटलिः. k T. Indica and Dioeca.

m m m m n

Mulberry.[a] 22 तूद (स्तु) यूपः क्रमुको ब्रह्मण्यो ब्रह्मदारु (च)

n

तूलं (च)

m m m b m

Nauclea orientalis. नीप प्रियक कदंबा (स्तु) हलिप्रिये

m m f m f n d

Marking nut. e 23. वीरवृक्षोऽरुष्करोऽग्निमुखी भल्लातकी (त्रिषु)

m m m m

Parspipal. a गर्दभाण्डे कंदराल कपीतन सुपार्श्वकाः

24. प्लक्ष (श्च)

f f f f g

Tamarind. तिंतिडी चिञ्चाऽम्लिका

m

Asan. h (ऽथ) पीतसारके

m m i m m m

सर्जका ऽसन बंधूकपुष्प प्रियक जीवकाः

m k m m l m m m

Sak'hwa or *Sal* j 25. साले (तु) सर्ज कार्श्या (श्वकर्णकाः सस्यसंवरः

m 1 m 2 m m m

Kahua. n नदीसर्जो वीरतरुरिंद्रद्रुः ककुभोऽर्जुनः

1—न्द्र. 2 द्रु—.

[a] Morus Indica. But some make it the Hibiscus Populneoides. See 23. [b] Likewise कादम्बः. [c] Semecarpus Anacardium. [d] Masc. भल्लातकः. [e] Hibiscus Populneoides, R. Some confound these Sanskrit names with those of the Ficus venosa. [f] Also तिंतिडी and तिंतिडीकः,—का,—कं. [g] Likewise अम्लीका, आम्लिका and आम्लीका. [h] Terminalia Alata tomentosa, R. [i] Also आसनः and असनः. [j] A common timber tree described (Polyandria monogynia) but not yet named by botanists. [k] Likewise सालः. [l] Also कार्श्यः. [m] Or सस्यसंबरः. [n] Terminalia Alata glabra, R.

m n *n* b 1

26. राजादन फलाध्यक्षो क्षीरिकायां — *Khirani.* [a]

(अथ द्वयोः) — *Inguä.*

m f c *m*

इङ्गुदो तापसतरु

m 2 *m* 3 *m*

भूर्ज चर्मि मृदुत्वचौ — *Bho´jpatr.* [d]

f *f* *f* *m* *m f* f

27. पिच्छिला पूरणो मोचा स्थिरायुः शाल्मलि (द्वयोः) — Silk-cotton. [e]

m

पिच्छा (तु) शाल्मलीवेष्टे — Its gum.

m *m f*

रोचनः कूटशाल्मलिः — Another sort of silk-cotton.

m h *m* *m* *m*

28. चिरबिल्वो नक्तमालः करज (श्च) करञ्जके — *Caranj.* [g]

m *m* *m* j *m*

प्रकीर्यः पूतिकरजः पूतिकः कलिमारकः — Gray Bonduc. [i]

m 4 *f* 5 *f*

29. (करञ्जभेदाः) षड्ग्रंथो मर्कटाङ्गारवल्लरो — Other sorts. [k]

6 *m* *m* m *m* 7 *m*

रोहो रोहितकः प्लीहशत्रुर्दाडिमपुष्पकः — *Rôhin.* [l]

1—का. 2—र्जू. 3—च, and —च्. 4—टी.
5 व—. 6 —हू. 7 दा—.

[a] Perhaps a species of Mimusops. M. Kauki. [b] Also राजादन फलं and अध्यक्षं. [c] Masc. इङ्गुदः. [d] The bark is used. [e] Bombax heptaphyllum. [f] Also fem. शाल्मली. Likewise m. or f. शाल्मलिः. [g] Galedupa Arborea or Robinia mitis. [h] Also चिरिबिल्वः. [i] Cæsalpinia, or Guilandina, Bonduccella. [j] Likewise पूतिकरञ्जः, पूतीकः, and कलिकारकः. [k] Seemingly varieties of the Bonduc. [l] A medicinal plant so called. [m] Also रोहीतकः.

Khayar.[a] 30· गायत्री[f b] बालतनयः[m c] खदिरो[m] दंतधावनः[m]

A fetid Mimosa. अरिमेदो[m] विट्खदिरे[m] ॥

A white sort. कदरः[m] (खदिरे सिते)

31. सोमवल्को[m] (ऽप्य्)

Palma christi.[d] (ऽथ) व्याघ्रपुच्छ[m] गंधर्वहस्तकौ[m]

एरंड[m] उरुबूक[m e] (श्) रुचकश्चित्रक[m f 1 m] (श् सः)

32. चंचुः[m] पंचांगुलो[m] मंड[m g] वर्द्धमान[m] व्यडंबकाः[m h]

A variety of the *S'amí*. (अल्पा शमी) शमीरः[m i] (स्याच्)

S'amí or *saen*.[j] छमी[2 f] सक्तुफला[f k] शिवा[f]

Mayan.[l] 33. पिण्डीतको[m] मरुवकः[m] श्वसनः[m] करहाटकः[m]

शल्य[m] (श्) मदने[m]

Déoda'r.[m] शक्रपादपः[m] पारिभद्रकः[m]

34. भद्रदारु[m n] द्रुकिलिमं[n] पीतदारु[n] (च) दारु[n] (च)

---

1 चि—. 2 शमो.

[a] Mimosa Catechu (Khayar) Linn. [b] Also masc. गायत्रिन् (—त्री) [c] Likewise बालपत्रः and बालदलकः. [d] Ricinus communis. [e] Also उरुबुकः. [f] Likewise वबूकः and रुबुकः or वबुकः. [g] Also चमंडः or चामंडः. [h] Likewise व्यडंबनः. [i] Also शमोरः. [j] Mimosa albida. [k] Or सक्तुफली. [l] Vangueria spinosa, R. But the Sanscrit names are referred also to Gardenia dumetorum. [m] In Bengal, Uvaria longifolia : but properly seems to be a pine or fir.

n [1] *m n*

पूतिकाष्ठ (ष्ठं सप्त स्युर्) देवदारुण्य

(ऽथ द्वयोः) Trumpet flower. [a]

m f [b] *f* *f* [c] *f* [d] *f*

35. पाटलिः पाटला ऽमोघा काचस्थाली फलेरुहा

f *f*

कृष्णवृन्ता कुबेराक्षी

f *f* [e]

श्यामा (तु) महिला (ह्वया) *Priyangu.* [e]

f *f* *f* *f* *f* *f*

36. लता गोवंदनी गुन्द्रा प्रियङ्गुः फलिनी फली

f *f* *f* *m f*

विष्वक्सेना गंधफली कारंभा प्रियक (श्च सा)

m *m* *m* *m* *m*

37. मण्डूकपर्ण पत्रोर्ण नट कट्वङ्ग टुंटुकाः *Són'apat.* [g]

m [h] *m* [2] *m* *m* *m*

स्योनाक शुकनासर्क्ष दीर्घवृंत कुटन्नटाः

m *m* [i]

38. शोणक (श्चा) ऽरलु

f [3] *m f n* [k]

तिष्यफला (त्वा) मलकी (त्रिषु) Emblic myrobalan. [j]

f *f* [l]

अमृता (च) वयस्था (च)

m f n [n]

(त्रिलिङ्ग (स्तु) विभीतकः Beleric myrobalan. [m]

1—रु. 2 शुक. 3 मा—.

[a] Bignonia suave-olens. [b] Also fem. पाटली. [c] अमोघा or मोघा. [d] Likewise काची and स्थाली. [e] A fragrant seed so named. [f] And other synonyma of woman. [g] Bignonia Indica. [h] Also सोनाकः. [i] अरलुः or अरटुः. [j] Phyllanthus. Emblica. [k] Masc. आमलकः. [l] Or पयःस्था. Also कायस्था. [m] Terminalia belerica. [n] Fem. विभीतकी.

m 1m m m m

39. अक्षस्तुषः कर्षफलो भूतवासः कलिद्रुमः

Yellow myrobalan. a

f 2f f fb f f

अभया (त्व्) अव्यथा पथ्या वयस्था पूतनाऽमृता

f f f f f

40. हरीतकी हैमवती चेतकी श्रेयसी शिवा

Sural. c

m m n

पीतद्रुः सरलः पूतिकाष्ठं (चा)

Caniyár. d

m

(ऽथ) द्रुमोत्पलः

m m

41. कर्णिकारः परिव्याधो

Barahal. e

mf m m

लकुचो लिकुचो डहुः

Bread fruit or Jaca tree. g

mh mi

पनसः कंटकिफलो

Hijjal. j

m m mk

निचुलो ऽम्बुजः इज्जलः

Opposite leaved fig-tree. l

f f fm 3f

42. काकोडुंबरिका फल्गुर्मलपूर्जघनेफला

Nimb. n

m m m m

अरिष्टः सर्वतोभद्र हिङ्गुनिर्यास मालकाः

mo m

43. पिचुमर्द (श्च) निम्बे

Sisó. p

f n fq

(ऽ.थ) पिच्छिला ऽगुरु शिंशपा

---

1 लक्ष. 2 च—. 3 ज—.

[a] Terminalia citrina. [b] Also वयःस्था and कायःस्था. [c] A tree which yields a resin. [d] Pterospermum acerifolium or Pentapetes acerifolia. [e] Artocarpus Lokutsha (Lucucha), R. [f] Likewise नकुचः. [g] Artocarpus integrifolia. [h] Also फलसः. [i] And कंटकोफलः. or कंटकफलः. [j] Eugenia acutangula. [k] Likewise हिज्जलः. [l] Ficus oppositifolia, R. [m] मलपूः (पू). Also मलपूः (—र्), and मलयुः (—यु). [n] Nimba Azadaracta (*A'za'dderakht*) or Melia Azadirachta. [o] And पिचुमंदः. [p] Dalbergia Sissoo, R. [q] Or, according to some, अगुरुशिंशपा.

f
कपिला भस्मगर्भा (सा) — Another sort. [a]

m *m*
शिरीष (स्तु.) कपीतन: — *Siris.* [b]

m [c]
44. भण्डिलो (ऽप्य्)

m [1] *m* *m*
(ऽथ) चाम्पेयश्चम्पको हेमपुष्पक: — *Champá.* [d]

f
(एतस्य कलिका) गंधफली (स्याद्) — Its flower.

m [f]
(ऽथ) केसरे — *Mul-sari.* [e]

m
45. बकुलो

m *m*
वञ्जुलो ऽशोके — *Asoc.* [g]

m *m* [h]
(समौ) करक दाडिमौ — Pomegranate.

m *m* *m* [j] [2] *m* [k]
चाम्पेय: केसरो नागकेसर: काञ्चनो (ह्वय:) — *Nágésar.* [i]

f *f* *f* *f* *f*
46. जया जयंती तर्कारी नादेयी वैजयंतिका — *Jainti.* [l]

[n] [3] *m* *f* *f*
श्रीपर्णमग्निमंथ: (स्यात्) कणिका गणिकारिका — *Ganiyári.* [m]

m [n]
47. जयो

---

[1] च—. [2]—न. [3] श्च—.

[a] Some make these terms synonymous with the preceding. [b] Mimosa Seereessa (Siríshá), R. [c] Also भंडिर: and भंडील: or भंडीर:. [d] Michelia Champaca, [e] Mimusops Elengi. [f] Likewise केशर:. [g] Jonesia Asoca, R. [h] And दाडिम:, दाड़िम्ब: or डालिम:. Also fem. दाड़िमी. [i] Mesual ferrea. [j] Likewise केशर: and नाग केशर:. [k] And all synonyma of gold. [l] Æschynomene Sesban. [m] Premna spinosa, and longifolia. [n] Some make these five synonymous with the preceding five, as names of the *Araní* or Premna spinosa.

m b m m f
Coraiya. a (ऽथ) कुटजः शक्रो वत्सको गिरिमल्लिका
m f n 1 m n n
Its seed. (एतस्यै.व) कलिङ्ग.न्द्रयवभद्रयवं (फले)
2 m d * m e m m
Caro'nda. c 48. कृष्णपाकफलाऽविग्न सुषेणाः करमर्दके
m 3 m m g
Tamál. f कालस्कन्धस्तमालः (स्यात्) तापिच्छो (ऽप्य.)
m
Séduári. h (ऽथ) सिंदुकः
m i 4 m j f k 5 f
49. सिन्दुवारेन्द्रसुरसौ निर्गुण्डी.न्द्राणिके. (त्यपि)
f f f m m m
Déótár. l वेणी खरा गरी देवताडो. जीमूत (इत्यपि)
f f
Sirtári. n 50. श्रीहस्तिनी (तु) भूरुण्डी
n!p f
Arabian Jasmin. o तृणशून्यं (तु) मल्लिका
f q
भूपदी शीतभीरु (श्च)

---

1 द्र—. 2—ल. 3 त—. 4 द्र—. 5 द्र—का.

[a] Echites antidysenterica or Nerium antidysentericum. [b] Also कौटजः. [c] Carissa Carandas. Applied also, but erroneously, to the Flacourtia Cataphracta. [d] Also कृष्णपाकः, पाकफलः, कृष्णफलः, पाककृष्णफलः and other combinations of the same terms. [e] Likewise प्राविग्नः. [f] A tree noted for the dark hue of its blossoms. [g] Also तापिञ्जः. [h] Vitex trifolia and Nigundo. Applied also to Buddleia Neemda, B. Mss. [i] Likewise सिंदुकः and सिंधुवारः. [j] Or इन्द्रसुरिसः. [k] Also निर्गुण्डी [l] A plant so called. [m] Likewise वगरी, and खरागरी or गरागरी. [n] Heliotropium Indicum. [o] J. Zambac. [p] Also fem. तृणशून्या. [q] Likewise शतभीरुः.

(सैवा॰) स्फोता (वनोद्भवा) — [1] *f* [a] — A wild variety.

51. शेफालिका (तु) सुवहा निर्गुण्डी नीलिका (च सा) — *f* [c] *f f f* — *Nébari.* [b]

(सितासौ) श्वेतसुरसा भूतवेशी. — *f* [2] *f* — The same white.

(ऽथ) मागधी — *f* — Sort of Jasmin. [d]

52. गणिका[1]यूथिका ऽम्बष्ठा — *f f f*

(सा पीता) हेमपुष्पिका — *f* — Yellow Jasmin.

अतिमुक्तः पुण्ड्रकः (स्याद्) वासन्ती माधवीलता — *m m f f* [f] — *Mâlatî latâ.* [e]

53. सुमना मालती जातिः — *f* [h] *f f* [i] — Great flowered Jasmin. [g]

सप्तला नवमालिका — *f f* — Double Jasmin. [j]

माघ्यं कुन्दं — *m* [n] *m* [n] — Many flowered Jasmin. [k]

रक्तक (स्तु) बन्धूको बन्धुजीवकः — *m m* [m] *m* — *Dop'hariya.*

54. सहा कुमारी तरणिः — *f f* [3] *f* — Aloe. [n]

---

1 आ—. 2—षी. 3 वि—.

[a] आस्फोता or आस्फोटा. [b] Jasminum villosum, R. The sanscrit names are assigned, in Bengal, to the Nyctanthes Arbor tristis. Some apply the two last terms to a distinct sort. [c] Also शेफालिः or शेफाली and शोफालिका. [d] J. Auriculatum. [e] Gærtnera racemosa or Banisteria Bengalensis. [f] Likewise माधवी and लता. [g] J. Grandiflorum. [h] सुमनाः (—नस्) or सुमना. [i] Also जाती. [j] J. Zambac fl. multiplicatis. [k] J. multiflorum or pubescens. [l] Pentapetes phœnicea. The Sanscrit names are by some assigned to the Ixora coccinea. [m] Also बंधुकः. [n] Also perfoliata.

Globe amaranth. [a] — अम्लान[m] (स्तु.) महासहा[f]

The crimson sort. — (तत्र शोणे) कुरवक[m b]

The yellow [or white] variety. — (तत्र पीते) कुरंटकः[m c]

Blue Barleria. [d] — 55. (नीलाझिण्टी द्वयोर्)बाणा[m f e]दासी[f](च)ऽर्त्तगल[m f](श्च सा)

Jhinti. [g] — सैरेयक[m h] (स्तु.) झिण्टी[f] (स्यात्)

A purple sort. — (तस्मिन्) कुरवको[m] (ऽरुणे)

A yellow sort. [i] — 56. (पीता)कुरंटको[m](झिण्टी तस्मिन्)सहचरी[m f j](द्वयोः)

China rose. [k] — ओड्रपुष्पं[n] जवा[f l]

The blossom of sesamum. — वज्रपुष्पं (पुष्पं तिलस्य यत्)

Oleander. [m] — 57. प्रतिहास[m n] शतप्रास[m] चण्डात[m] हयमारकाः[m]

करवीरे[m]

Caril. [o] — करीरे[m] (तु) क्रकर[m p] ग्रंथिला[l m] (वुभौ)

Thorn apple. [q] — 58. उन्मत्तः[m] कितवो[m] धूर्तो[m r] धुस्तूरः कनको[m s] (ह्वयः)

मातुलो[m] मदन[m] (श्च)

1—पा.

[a] Gomphrena globosa. [b] Or कुरबकः. [c] Also कुरंटकः. [d] Barleria cærulea, R. [e] Masc. बाणः. [f] Or आर्तगलः. [g] Barleria cristata. [h] Or सैरेयकः. [i] Barleria Prionitis. [j] Masc. सहचर. Also सहाचरः. [k] Hibiscus Rosa sinensis. [l] Also जपा. [m] Nerium Odorum. [n] Or प्रतीहासः. [o] Described as a thorny plant, of which Camels are fond. [p] Also क्रकचः. [q] Datura Metel and Fastuosa. [r] Likewise धुस्तुरः and धुत्तूरः. [s] Or any other name of gold.

(ऽस्य फले) मातुलपुत्रकः[m] — The fruit

59. फलपूरो[m] बीजपूरो[m] रुचको[m] मातुलुङ्गके[m] — Citron.[a]

समीरणो[m] मरुवकः[m] प्रस्थपुष्पः[m] फणिज्जकः[m] — *Maruā.*[b]

60. जंबीरो[m c] (ऽप्य)

(ऽथ) पर्णासे[m] कठिञ्जर[m] कुठेरकौ[m] — *Parnās.*[d]

(सिते) ऽर्जको[m] (ऽत्र) — The white sort.[e]

पाठी[1 m] (तु) चित्रको[m g] वह्नि[m h] (संज्ञकः) — Lead wort.[f]

61. अर्का[m j] (ह्व) वसुका[m] स्फोत[2 m] गणरूप[m] विकीरणाः[m] — Swallow wort.[i]

मन्दार[m] (श्चा) ऽर्कपर्णो[m]

(ऽत्र शुक्ले) ऽलर्क[m] प्रतापसौ[m] — The white sort.

62. शिवमल्ली[f] पाशुपत[m] एकाष्ठीलो[m l] बुको[m m] वसुः[m n] — *Bacapushpa.*[k]

वन्दा[f p] वृक्षादनी[f] वृक्षरुहा[f] जीवन्तिके[3 f] (त्यपि) — A parasite plant.[o]

---

[1]—नू. [2]धा—. [3]—का.

[a] Citrus medica. Two sorts are here named : but some make the terms synonymous. [b] Marjoram ? The Sanscrit names are also assigned to a species of basil (Ocimum) with small leaves ; and to another sort of citron. [c] Also जंबीरः. [d] Considered by some to be the sacred Basil (Ocimum sanctum). [e] Ocimum gratissimum. [f] Plumbago zeylanica. [g] Or चित्रकः. [h] And other names of fire. [i] Asclepias Gigantea. [j] Or any name of the sun. [k] Confounded by some with Æschynomene grandiflora, but appears to be a different plant. [l] Likewise fem. एकाष्ठीला. [m] Also बुकः. [n] And वसुकः or वस्तुकः. [o] Epidendrum Tesseloides and other species. [p] Likewise वन्दका and वन्दाका.

SECTION III.

Guricha. a

f f fb f f

1. वत्सादनी छिन्नरुहा गुडूची तंत्रिकाऽमृता

f f f 1f

जीवन्तिका सोमवल्ली विशल्या मधुपर्ण्य (ऽपि)

Aletris. c

fd f f f f fe

2. मूर्वा देवी मधुरसा मोरटा तेजनी स्रुवा

f ff f 2f

मधूलिका मधुश्रेणी गोकर्णी पीलुपर्ण्य (ऽपि)

A'cana'di. g

f f fh f f f

3. पाठाऽम्बष्ठा विद्धकर्णी स्थापनी श्रेयसी रसा

f f f f

एकाष्ठीला पापचेली प्राचीना वनतिक्तिका

Catuci. i

f fj fk f

4. कटु कटम्बराऽशोकरोहिणी कटुरोहिणी

f f f f

मत्स्यपित्ता कृष्णभेदी चक्रांगी शकुलादनी

Cawach, or Cowitch. l

f fm fn fo f

5. आत्मगुप्ता जडाऽव्यण्डा कण्डूरा प्रावृषायणी

f fp fq f

ऋष्यप्रोक्ता शूकशिम्बिः कपिकच्छु (श्च) मर्कटी

1—र्णी. 2—र्णी.

a Menispermum glabrum. b Also गुडुची. c Aletris Hyacinthoides or Dracona nervosa. d And मुर्वी. e Likewise स्रवा. f Also मधुःश्रेणी; or मधुः and श्रेणी. g Cissampelos hexandra. h Likewise अविद्धकर्णी and अविद्धकर्णा. i A medicinal plant so called. j Also कटंभरा. k Likewise अशोका and रोहिणी. l Dolichos pruriens. m Also अजडा. n Likewise अव्यथा. o Or कण्डुरा. p And शूकशिम्बी, or शूकशिम्बा. q Also कपिकच्छूः.

f 1f f f fb f

6. चित्रोपचित्रा न्यग्रोधी द्रवन्ती शंबरी वृषा *Musalí.* a

f f f 2f

प्रत्यक्श्रेणी सुतश्रेणी रण्डा मूषिकपर्ण्यपि

m md mc 3m

7. अपामार्गः शैखरिको धामार्गवमयूरकौ *Apáng.* c

ff fg f f

प्रत्यक्पर्णी कीशपर्णी किणिही खरमञ्जरी

f f f f f

8. फञ्जिका ब्राह्मणी पद्मा भार्गी ब्राह्मणयष्टिका *Bamanait'hí.* h

f mi m m

अङ्गारवल्ली बालेयशाकबर्बरवर्धकाः

f fk f f fl

9. मञ्जिष्ठा विकसा जिङ्गी समङ्गा कालमेषिका Madder. j

f fm f 4fn

मण्डूकपर्णी भण्डीरी भण्डी योजनवल्ल्यपि

m mp m mq m

10. यासो यवासो दुःस्पर्शो धन्वयासः कुनाशकः *Jawásá.* o

fr f f f f

रोदनी कच्छुराऽनन्ता समुद्रान्ता दुरालभा

ft f 5f 6f

11. पृश्निपर्णी पृथक्पर्णी चित्रपर्ण्यङ्घ्रिवल्लिका *Cháoulíya.* s

---

[1] च—. [2]—र्णी. [3]—क. [4]—ल्ली. [5]—र्णी. [6] अ°—.

[a] A medicinal plant: probably Anthericum tuberosum, R. Mss. [b] Likewise संवरी. [c] Achyranthes aspera. [d] And शैखरेयः. [e] Also अपामार्गकः. [f] Or प्रत्यक्पुष्पी. [g] And कोशपर्णी. [h] Ovieda verticellata, R. [i] Also बालेयः. [j] Rubia Munjeet (Manjit'h), R. [k] Or विकषा. [l] Also कालमेशिका. [m] And भण्डिरी. [n] Likewise योजनपर्णी. [o] Perhaps Hedysarum Alhagi? or rather, a new species. [p] Likewise यासः, and अपयासः. [q] Also धन्वयवासः and धनुर्यासः. [r] Likewise चोदनी. [s] Explanations differ; the names in both lines being synonymous according to some; but denoting two distinct plants according to others. The first seems to be Hedysarum lagopodioides. [t] Or पृश्निपर्णी.

Ràmvdsac. क्रोष्टुविन्ना[f] सिंहपुच्छी[f] कलशि[f a]र्धावनि[f b]र्गुहा[1 f]

Sort of prickly nightshade. c — 12. निदिग्धिका[f] स्पृशी[f] व्याघ्री[f] बृहती[f] कण्टकारिका[f]
प्रचोदनी[f] कुली[f] क्षुद्रा[f] दुःस्पर्शा[f] राष्ट्रिके.[2 f] (त्यपि)

Indigo. d — 13. नीली[f] काला[f] क्लीतकिका[f] ग्रामीणा[f] मधुपर्णिका[f]
रञ्जनी[f] श्रीफली[f] तुत्था[f] द्रोणी[f e] दोला[f f] (च) नीलिनी[f]

Sòmra'j. g — 14. अवल्गुजः[m] सोमराजी[3 m h] सुवल्लिः[f] सोमवल्लिका[f]
कालमेषी[f i] कृष्णफला[f] बाकुची[f j] पूतिफल्य[4 f] (ऽपि)

Long pepper. — 15. कृष्णो[f]पकुल्या[5 f] वैदेही[f] मागधी[f] चपला[f] कणा[f]
उषणा[f k] पिप्पली[f l] शौण्डी[f] कोला[f]।

Another sort. — (ऽथ) करिपिप्पली[f]

16. कपिवल्ली[f] कोलवल्ली[f] श्रेयसी[f] वशिरः[m m] (पुमान्)

The plant. n — चव्यं[n o] (तु) चविका[f p]

---

[1] शु—. [2] —का. [3] —जिन्. [4] —ली. [5] ष—.

[a] Also कलशी and कलसिः. [b] धावनिः or धावनी. [c] Solanum Jacquini, Willd. [d] Indigofera tinctoria. [e] Some read तूणी, others तूली. [f] Also देला, according to another reading. [g] Conyza (or serratula) anthelmintica. [h] Or fem. सोमराजी (—जी). [i] Likewise कालमेषी. [j] Some write वाकुची. [k] Also ऊषणा. [l] Likewise पिप्पलिः. [m] And वसिरः. [n] Or synonymous with the preceding : or else the name of a different plant ; Tetranthera apetala, R. [o] Also fem. चव्या. [p] Or चवी. Also neut. चविकं.

f 1f f
काकचिञ्ची गुञ्जे (तु) कृष्णला — *Retti.* a

f 2f mf m
17. पलङ्कषा (त्वि) क्षुगन्धा श्वदंष्ट्रा स्वादुकण्टकः — *Go'c'haru.* b

m m m
गोकण्टको गोक्षुरको वनशृङ्गाट (इत्यपि)

f f f f 3f f
18. विश्वा विषा प्रतिविषा ऽतिविषोपविषा ऽरुणा — *Atis.* c

f n
शृङ्गी महौषधं (च)

f f
(ऽथ) क्षीरावी दुग्धिका (समे) — *Dud'hi.* d

f f f 4f f
19. शतमूली बहुसुता ऽभीरुरिन्दीवरी वरी — *S'atávari'.* e

f f ff f
ऋष्यप्रोक्ता भीरुपत्री नारायण्यः शतावरी

f
20. अहेरु (रु)

m mh 5m
(ऽथ) पीतद्रु कालेयक हरिद्रवः — *Da'ru haldi'.* g

f fi f f
दार्वी पचम्पचा दारुहरिद्रा पर्जनी (त्यपि)

f 6f f f f
21. वचोग्रगन्धा षड्ग्रन्था गोलोमी शतपर्विका — Orris root. j

f
(शुक्ला) हैमवती — A white sort. k

---

1 गुञ्जा. 2 ह—. 3 उ—. 4 इ—. 5—द्रु. 6 उ—.

[a] Abrus precatorius. [b] Barleria (or Ruellia) longifolia. The name seems to be also applied to Tribulus Lanuginosus. [c] Betula? As. Res. vol. vi. p. 573. [d] Asclepias rosea, (R.) and other species. [e] Asparagus racemosus, Willd. [f] Sing. नारायणी. [g] Amomum Zanthorhizon, Roxb. [h] Also कालीयकः. [i] Likewise पचंपचा. [j] Iris pseudacorus? [k] Acorus calamus.

Justicia. a — f 1f bf
वैद्यमातृ सिंह्यौ (तु) वाशिका

m c, m d, m, m e, m
22. वृषो ऽटरूषः सिंहास्यो वासको वाजिदन्तकः

f g, f, f, f
Clitoria. f — आस्फोता गिरिकर्णी (स्याद्) विष्णुक्रान्ता ऽपराजिता

f, m, m, 2 m, m
Barleria. h — 23. इक्षुगन्धा (तु) काण्डेक्षु कोकिलाक्षेक्षुरक्षुराः

m j, 3 m, 4 f, f, f k
Anethum. i — शालेयः (स्याच्) छीतशिवश्छत्रा मधुरिका मिशी

24. मिश्रेया (प्य्)

m m, m n, 5 f, f o, f p
Euphorbia. l — (ऽथ) सीहुण्डो वज्रद्रुः स्नुक् स्नुही गुडा

f
समन्तदुग्धा

m n, f r, f
Bàbreng. q — (ऽथो) वेल्लममोघा चित्रतंडुला

m s, m, m t
25. तंडुल (श्) कृमिघ्न (श्) विडंङ्गं (पुन्नपुंसकम्)

f, m
Sida. u — बला वाट्यालको

f, f
Crotalaria. v — घण्टारवा (तु) शणपुष्पिका

1—मषी. 2 ख—. 3 सी—. 4 स—. 5—हू.

[a] Justicia adhatoda & ganderussa. [b] Also वाशा and वाशिका. [c] Or वृषः. [d] And अटरूष. [e] Likewise वासकः [f] Clitoria ternatea. [g] Also आस्फोटा. [h] Barleria Longifolia : but applied also to Capparis spinosa. [i] Anethum Sowa and Pammorium, R. [j] Or शालेय. [k] Also मिशिः, मिसी and मिषिः. [l] Including divers species, as Tirucalli, &c. [m] Also सिहुण्डः and सेहुण्डः. [n] Likewise वज्रः. [o] Or स्नुषा. Also स्नुहिः. [p] And गुडी. Likewise masc. गुडः. [q] The seed is used as a vermifuge. [r] अमोघा and मोघा. [s] Also तंडुलः. [t] This and the two preceding terms admit the three genders, say some. [u] S. cordifolia and Rhombifolia, &c. [v] C. retusa, sericea and some other species.

26. मृद्वीका[f] गोस्तनी[f, a] द्राक्षा[f] स्वाद्वी[f] मधुरसे[1 f]. (ति च) — A grape.

सर्वानुभूतिः[f] सरला[f, b] त्रिपुटा[f, c] त्रिवृता[f] त्रिवृत्[2 f] — *Teórí* : the white sort.

27. त्रिभण्डी[f] रोचनी[f, d]

श्यामा[f] पालिन्द्यौ[f, e] (तु) सुषेणिका[f] — The black sort.

काला[f] मसूरविदला[f] अर्धचन्द्रा[f] कालमेषिका[f]

28. मधुकं[n] क्लीतकं[n] यष्टिमधुका[f] मधुयष्टिका[f, g] — Liquorice.

विदारी[f] क्षीरशुक्ला[f] इक्षुगन्धा[3 f] क्रोष्ट्री[f] (च या सिता)[i] — *Bhuinraon-ra* the dark sort. h.

29. (अन्या) क्षीरविदारी[f] (स्यात्) महाश्वेता[4 f] ऋक्षगन्धिका[5 f] — Another sort (pale).

लाङ्गली[f] शारदी[f] तोयपिप्पली[f] शकुलादनी[f] — *Canchara'*. j

30. खराश्वा[f] कारवी[f] दीप्यः[m, l] मयूरः[m] लोचमस्तकः[m, m] — Celosia. k

---

1—सा. 2—तृ. 3 क्षु—. 4—ता. 5 ऋ—.

[a] Or गोस्तना. [b] Also सरणा, सरसा, and सबला; some read सुवहा. [c] And त्रिपुटी. [d] Likewise रेचनी. [e] पालिंदी. or पालिंधी. [f] Glycyrrhiza glabra? Or Abrus precatorius albus, the root of which is substituted for liquorice. [g] Also यष्टी. [h] Convolvulus paniculatus. [i] Interpretations differ, transposing the distinction of colour. [j] Jussieua repens. [k] C. Cristata. [l] Also दीपकः. [m] Likewise लोचमर्कटः.

Syám-lata'.[a] गोपी श्यामा शारिवा (स्याद्) अनंतोत्पलशारिवा

Ridd'hi. 31. योग्य मृद्धिः सिद्धि लक्ष्मी

Vrida'hi. वृद्धे (र्प्याह्वया इमे)

SECTION IV.

A banana.[d] 1. कदली वारणबुसा रंभा मोचांशुमत्फला

काष्ठीला

Muga'ni. मुद्गपर्णी (तु) काकमुद्गा सहे (त्यपि)

Egg plant.[g] 2. वार्त्ताकी हिंगुली सिंही भण्टाकी दुष्प्रधर्षिणी

Rasan.[j] नाकुली सुरसा रास्ना सुगन्धा गन्धनाकुली

---

1 श्च—. 2 न—. 3 ऋ—. 4 लक्ष्मी. 5 वृधि

6 श्च'—. 7 सहा.

[a] Interpretations differ ; some referring the two last terms, others the whole line, to a different plant. [b] Or गोपा. [c] The same synonyma with the preceding. They are medicinal drugs. [d] Musa sapiantum. [e] Also masc. कदलः. [f] Likewise वारणबुषा. Some write वारबुषा. [g] Solanum melongena. [h] Also वार्त्ता or वार्त्ताकुः ; and masc. वार्त्ताकः,—कु,—की, (—किन्) [i] Likewise दुःप्रधर्षिणी. [j] Uncertain. See As. Res. vol. iv. p. 309. [k] Some read नागसुगंधा. [l] Physicians reckon this a variety of the preceding.

f f f f a

3. नकुलेष्टा भुजङ्गाक्षी छत्राकी सुवहा (च सा)

f c 1f fd f f

विदारीगंधांशुमती सालपर्णी स्थिरा ध्रुवा — *Sa'lparni'.* b

f f mfc 2f

4. तुण्डिकेरी समुद्रान्ता कर्पासी बदरे (ति च) — Cotton.

f

भारद्वाजी (तु सा वन्या) — Wild cotton. f.

fh m m

शृङ्गी (तु) ऋषभो वृषः — *Rishabha.* g

f f f f

5. गाङ्गेरुकी नागबला झषा ह्रस्वगवेधुका — *Górakha.* i

m m

धामार्गवो घोषकः (स्यात्) — *Ghóshá* with white flowers.

fj

महाजाली (स पीतकः) — With yellow flowers.

fl f f

6. ज्योत्स्नी पटोलिका जाली — A small cucumber. k.

f f

नादेयी भूमिजंबुका — *Bhuinjâmb.* m

3f 4f

(स्यात्) लाङ्गलिकाग्निशिखा — *La'ngaliya.*

f f

काकाङ्गी काकनासिका — *Ca'c-janghi.* n

---

1 च'—. 2—रा. 3—की. 4 च—.

a The last line contains names of a different plant, say some. b Hedysarum Gangeticum. c Also विदारी. d Likewise शालपर्णी. e And कार्पासी. f In Bengal, Hibiscus vitifolius is called wild cotton, वनकार्पासः. g A medicinal drug. h Also masc. शृङ्गी (—न्). i Uncertain : many different plants being shown under this name. j Some erroneously make it masc. महाजाली (—लिन्). k Trichosanthes diœca, R. Applied also to Luffa acutangula, (R.) or Cucumis acutangulus. l And ज्योत्स्ना. m Interpretations differ much. Some remark, that the terms are here repeated by mistake. See § 2. 18. n Leea æquata. But, according to other Hindi synonyma, Trichosanthes Cucumerina.

Cissus.[a] 7. गोधापदी (तु) सुवहा

Musal.[b] मुसली तालमूलिका

Méra'sringi'.[d] अजशृङ्गी विषाणी (स्यात्)

Gôgi'.[e] गोजिह्वा दार्विके (समे)

Betel.[g] 8. ताम्बूलवल्ली ताम्बूली नागवल्ल्य् (प्य)

Rénuca'.[h] (ऽथ) द्विजा

हरेणू रेणुका कौन्ती कपिला भस्मगन्धिनी

Ela'ba'luca. 9. एलवालुकमैलेयं सुगन्धि हरिवालुकम्

वालुकं (चा).

Cunduru.[j] (ऽथ) पालंक्यां मुकुन्दः कुन्द कुन्दुरू

Ba'la'.[o] 10. बालं ह्रीवेर बर्हिष्ठो दीच्यं (केशाम्बुनाम च)

1—ल्ली. 2—णु. 3 ऐ—. 4—रू. 5 उ—.

[a] C. pedata, Vahl. [b] Perhaps Anthericum tuberosum. [c] Also सुवली. [d] Described as a milky and thorny plant, with a fruit shaped like a ram's horn; and used as a medicine for the eyes. [e] A potherb wild in corn fields, perhaps Phlomis esculenta. [f] Or दर्विका. [g] Piper betel. [h] This and the five following articles are perfumes of different sorts. [i] Likewise हरिवालुकं. [j] Perhaps the resin of Boswellia serrata. [k] पालंकी and पालंक्या. [l] Also masc. and fem. मुकुन्दुः. [m] Some read कुंदुः. [n] Erroneously कुंदुरः. [o] Perhaps Andropogon schœnanthus. [p] Also ह्रिबेरं. [q] बर्हिष्ठं or बर्हिःष्ठं. [r] All the synonyma of hair and of water.

n 1n n 2n

कालानुसार्य्यं वृद्धा ऽश्मपुष्प शीतशिवानि (तु) — Benzoin.[a]

n

11. शैलेयं

f f f f

तालपर्णी (तु) दैत्या गन्धकुटी मुरा — *Murá.*

f

गंधिनी

fb f fc f

गजभक्ष्या (तु) सुवहा सुरभी रसा — *Salái.*[a]

fd f fe ff

12. महेरणा कुन्दुरुकी शल्लकी, ह्लादिनी, (ति च)

f 3f f fh

अग्निज्वाला सुभिक्षा (तु) धातकी धातुपुष्पिका — Lythrum. g.

f 4f 5f fi 6f

13. एथीका चन्द्रबालैला निष्कुटिर्बहुला — Large Cardamoms.

(ऽथ सा)

7f f f f fj

(सूक्ष्मोऽपि) कुञ्चिका तुत्था कोरंगी त्रिपुटा त्रुटिः — Small Cardamoms.

m n n nl n 8n

14. व्याधिः कुष्ठं पारिभाव्यं व्याप्यं पाकलमुत्पलम् — *Cúr*, or *Cút'h.* k

f f 9f

शङ्खिनी चोरपुष्पी (स्यात्) केशिन्य — *Chór-ca'nta'.* m

m

(ऽथ) वितुन्नकः — *Bhúmi'a'mala'ci'.* n.

---

1 वृद्ध. 2—व. 3—क्षा. 4—ला. 5ए—.

6 ब—. 7 स—. 8 स—. 9—नी.

[a] Boswellia serrata, R. Mss. [b] And गजभक्ता. [c] सुरभिः or सुरभी. Also सुरभिरसा. [d] Likewise महेरणा. [e] Also सल्लकी and सिल्लकी or शिल्लकी. [f] Likewise ह्लादिनी. [g] Lythrum fruticosum, L. or Grislea tomentosa, R. [h] Or धातुपुष्पिका. [i] And निष्कुटी. [j] Or त्रुटी. [k] Perhaps a sort of Costus. [l] And पाप्यं or पाप्यं. [m] Andropogon aciculatum. [n] One Commentator applies the Sanscrit names to Flacourtia cataphracta.

f f[a] f[b] f f f

15. झटा ऽमला ऽज्झटा ताली शिवा तामलकी.(ति च)

n n[d]

Pundariya. [c] प्रपौण्डरीकं पुण्डर्यं

m m

Tunna. [c] (अथ) तुम्बः कुबेरकः

m[f] m m m[g]

16. कुणिः कच्छः कान्तलको नन्दिवृक्षो

f

Cho'r : sort of perfume. (ऽथ) राक्षसी

f f m m m[h]

चण्डा धनहरी क्षेम दुष्पत्र गणहासकाः

n[j] n n n

Nac'hi. [i] 17. व्याडायुधं व्याघ्रनखं करजं चक्रकारकम्

f . 'f f 1f f

Nali. शुषिरा विद्रुमलता कपोताङ्घ्रिर्नटी नली

f[k] 2f[l] 3f

Another perfume. 18. धमन्यञ्जनकेशी (च) हनुर्हट्टविलासिनी

f m m n n[n]

Nac'ht. [m] शुक्तिः शङ्खः खुरः कोलदलं नखं

---

1 न—. 2 ध—. 3 ह—.

[a] Some read झाटा and मला. Also झाटामला. [b] Likewise अमला-ज्झटा. [c] Described as a small herbaceous plant, with leaves like Hedysarum Gangeticum ; used as a remedy for diseased eyes. [d] Or पौण्डर्यं. [e] Cedrela Toona, R. [f] Also तुणिः. [g] Or नन्दीवृक्षः. [h] Likewise गणः. [i] This and the following are perfumes. [j] Also व्यालायुधं. [k] धमनिः or धमनी. [l] Some make both these terms synonymous with the preceding instead of the following. [m] This and the similar article before-mentioned are here stated as vegetable perfumes : but what is sold under this head, appears to be a dried shell-fish. [n] Also any term signifying nails. Likewise fem. नखी. Some make all the terms in the two preceding lines synonymous with this.

1 *f*
(अथा) ढकी — *Túbarí*. a

f *f* *f* b *n* c *n*
19. काक्षी, मृत्स्ना तुवरिका मृत्तालक सुराष्ट्रजे
n *n* d *n* *n* e
कुटन्नटं दाशपुरं वानेयं परिपेलवम् — Cyperus rotundus.
n *n* *n* 2 *n* f
20. प्लव गोपुर गोनर्द कैवर्त्तीमुस्तकानि (च)
n *n* *n* h *n* 3 *n* i
ग्रन्थिपर्णं शुकं बर्हिपुष्पं स्थौणेय कुक्कुरे — *Ga'nt'hala.* g
f k *f* l *f* *f* *f*
21. मरुन्माला (तु) पिशुना स्पृक्का देवी लता लघुः — *Piring* or *Asparac.* j
f *f* *f* m *f* n
समुद्रान्ता वधूः कोटिवर्षा लंकोपिके (त्वपि)
f *f* p *f* *f* *f* q
22. तपस्विनी जटामांसी जटिला लोमशा मिसी — Spikenard. o

---

1 आ—. 2—क्ष. 3—र.

a A fragrant earth. b Also तुबरी or तूबरी, and तुबरिका or तूबरीका. c Likewise मृत्सालकं and मृत् (—द्) and तालकं. d Also दाशपूरं and दशपुरं or दशपूरं. e Or, according to another reading, परिपेलं or पारिपेलं. f Likewise कैवर्त्तमुस्तकं or कैवर्त्तीमुस्तकम्. g Said to be a perfume. h Or बर्हिःपुष्पं. Also बर्हि (—र्) and पुष्पं; likewise बर्ह and शुकबर्ह. i Some add from the next line मरुत्. j Medicago esculenta, R. k Also मरुत् and माला. l Or स्पृक्का. m Also कोटी and वर्षा. n Also लंकापिका or लंकायिका. Likewise वर्षालंकायिका. o Valeriana Jatamansi. p Also जटा and मांसी. q Or मिषिः, मिषिः and मिषी. Some here read आमिषी; but erroneously.

Woody Cassia. a — त्वक्पत्त्रमुत्कटं भृङ्गं त्वचं चोचं वराङ्गकम्

Zerumbet or zedoary. c — 23. कर्चूरको द्राविडकः काल्पको वेधमुख्यकः

SECTION V.

A herb, or deciduous plant. — 1. ओषध्यो (जातिमात्रे स्युर्)

A drug, or simple. — (अजातौ सर्वम्) ओषधम्

Any esculent plant. — शाकं (ख्यं पत्त्र पुष्पादि)

Amaranth. f — तण्डुलीयोऽल्पमारिषः

A sort of potherb. g — 2. विशल्याऽग्निशिखाऽनन्ता फलिनी शक्रपुष्प्य(पि)

Another sort. h — (स्याद्) ऋक्षगन्धा छगलान्त्र्यावेगी वृद्धदारकः

3. जुङ्गो

The moon-plant. l — ब्राह्मी (तु) मत्स्याक्षी वयस्था सोमवल्लरी

1 ष—. 2—ओ. 3—न्त्री. 4 वा—.

[a] Or the three first terms signify Malobathrum; and the three next, the Cassia bark. [b] Also त्वच् (—च्) and पत्रं. [c] Curcuma Zerumbet, R. [d] Or काल्यकः. [e] ओषधिः and ओषधी. [f] Amaranthus polygamus. [g] Not ascertained. [h] Perhaps Convolvulus Argenteus. [i] Or ऋष्यगन्धा. [j] छगलांत्री or छगलांघ्री. Also छगला and चंत्री. [k] Likewise fem. जुङ्गा. [l] Asclepias acida, (R.) or Cynanchum Viminale. But some distinguish this *Bráhmí* from the *Sóma latá.* [m] Or ब्रह्मी. [n] And वयःस्था. [o] Also सोमवल्लरिः and सोमवल्लिका. Likewise synonymous terms; as सोमलता, चन्द्रवल्लरी.

f f f f

पटुपर्णी हैमवती स्वर्णक्षीरी हिमावती — A medicinal sort.[a]

f f f f

4. हयपुच्छी (तु) कांबोजी माषपर्णी महासहा — *Másha'ní'.*

f c f f 1 f

तुण्डिकेरी रक्तफला बिंबिका पीलुपर्ण्य.(ऽपि) — *Téla'cucha'.*[b]

f f• f f f

5. बर्ब्बरा कबरी तुङ्गी खरपुष्पा ऽजगन्धिका — *Barbara'.*[d]

f f f f

एलापर्णी (तु) सुवहा रास्ना युक्तरसा (च सा) — *E'la'ní.*[e]

f f f f f

6. चाङ्गेरी चुक्रिका दन्तशठा ऽम्बष्ठा ऽम्ललोणिका — Wood Sorrel.[f]

2 m m m 3 m

सहस्रवेधी चुक्रो ऽम्लवेतसः शतवेध्य(ऽपि) — Sorrel.[g]

f f i f f

7. नमस्कारी गण्डकाली समङ्गा खदिरी.(त्यपि) — A sensitive plant.[h]

f f k f f f l

जीवन्ती जीवनी जीवा जीवनीया मधु (स्र वा) — *Ji'yati'.*[j]

m m m m m

8. कूर्चशीर्षो मधुरकः शृङ्ग ह्रस्वाङ्ग जीवकाः — *Ji'vaca.*

m m m n

किराततिक्तो भूनिम्बो ऽनार्य्यतिक्तो — Sort of Gentian.[m]

f

(ऽथ) सप्तला — *Charma-gha's.*

1—र्णी. 2—न्. 3—न्.

[a] Stated to be the produce of the snowy mountains. [b] Momordica monadelpha or Bryonia grandis. [c] Or तुण्डकेरी. [d] Ocymum gratissimum ? [e] Mimosa octandra ? [f] Oxalis monadelpha, R. [g] Other interpretations are also stated by commentators. [h] Some make those four and the preceding five terms synonymous, as names of a sensitive plant. Others refer this line to the Lycopodium imbricatum, (R.) [i] Also गंडकारी. [j] Celtis orientalis ? [k] Or जीवना. [l] Also मधुस्रवा and स्रवा. [m] Gentiana Cherayta, R. [n] Likewise चिरातिक्तः.

9. विमला[f] सातला[f a] भूरिफेना[f] चर्मकषे[f b].(त्यपि)

Ca'co'li'. वायसोली[f] स्वादुरसा[f] वयस्था[f c]

D.nti. (ऽथ) मकूलक:[m d]

10. निकुम्भो[m e] दन्तिका[f] प्रत्यक्श्रेण्यु[1 f e]दुम्बरपर्णी[2 f]. (ऽपि)

Carui. f. अजमोदा[f] (तू.) उग्रगन्धा[3 f]

Ajwaen. g. ब्रह्मदर्भा[f] यवानिका[f h]

Costus. i. 11. (मूले) पुष्कर[n] काश्मीर[n] पद्मपत्राणि[4 n j] (पौष्करे)

St'hal'padma' k अव्यथा[f] ऽतिचरा[f] पद्मा[f] चारटी[f] पद्मचारिणी[f]

S'undá-ro'ol-ani. l. 12. काम्पिल्ल:[m m] कर्कशश्चन्द्रो[m] रक्ताङ्गो[5 m] रोचनी[m f n]. (त्यपि)

Cassia. o प्रपुन्नाड[m p] (स्त्वे.) डगजो[6 m] दद्रुघ्नश्चक्रमर्दक:[m 7 m]

13. पद्माट्[m] उरणाख्य[m q] (श्च)

1—णी. 2डु—र्णी. 3ड—. 4—त्र. 5चं—. 6ए—. 7च—.

[a] Or ग्रातला. [b] Also चर्मकषा. [c] And कयस्था or कायस्था. [d] Or मुकूलक. [e] Likewise निकुंभ:. [f] Carum Carui: or, according to some, synonymous with the following. Others confound it with Apium involucratum. [g] Ligusticum Ajwaen, R. [h] Or यवानी. Also यमानी and यमानिका. [i] Costus speciosus? [j] Likewise पद्मपर्णं. [k] Hibiscus mutabilis. [l] Crinum? [m] And कंपिल्ल: or कंपील:. Also कांपिल्य: and कांपिल्ल:. [n] Likewise रेचनी. [o] Cassia Tora or Alata. [p] And प्रपुन्नट: or प्रपुनाड:. [q] According to another reading, any term for a ram.

पलाण्डु[m] (स्तु) सुकन्दकः[m b]	Onion. a
लतार्क[m] दुद्रुमौ[m c] (तत्र हरिते)	A green onion.
(ऽथ) महौषधम्	Garlick.
14. लशुनं[n] गृञ्जना[m]ऽरिष्ट[m] महाकन्द[m] रसोनकाः[m]	
पुनर्नवा[f] (तु) शोथघ्नी[f]	Hogweed. d
वितुन्नं[n] सुनिषण्णकम्[n]	A sort of potherb. e
15. (स्याद्)वातकः[m] शीतलो[m f]ऽपराजिता[f] ऽशनपर्ण्य[1 f g] (ऽपि)	*Asan-parnī.*
पारावताङ्घ्रिः[f] कटभी[f] पण्या[f i] ज्योतिष्मती[f] लता[f]	Heart-pea. h
16. वार्षिकं[n] त्रायमाणा[f] (स्यात्) त्रायन्ती[f] बलभद्रिका[f]	*Trāyamāṅa.*
विष्वक्सेनप्रिया[f] गृष्टि[f k]र्वाराही[2 f] बदरे[3 f] (त्यपि)	*Vārāhī* or *chāmārālu.* j
17. मार्कवो[m m] भृङ्गराजः[m n] (स्यात्)	*Bhringa-rāja.* l
काकमाची[f] (तु) वायसी[f]	A potherb. o

1—र्णी. 2 वा—. 3—रा.

[a] Allium cepa and ascalonicum. [b] Also सुकन्दकः and सुगन्धकः. [c] Likewise दुर्द्रुमः. [d] Boerhavia diffusa alata. [e] Marsilea dentata, R. [f] Also शीतलवातकः. [g] Likewise शणपर्णी. [h] Cardiospermum Halicacabum. [i] Also पिण्या. [j] Dioscorea. [k] Also गृष्टिः. [l] Eclipta or Verbesina prostrata. [m] Likewise मार्करः. [n] Also भृङ्गराजा (—जू); and neut. भृङ्गरजः (—स्). [o] Perhaps Solanum trilobatum.

f b *f* *f* *f* c

Sónph. a — शतपुष्पा सितच्छत्रा ऽतिच्छत्रा मधुरा मिसिः

f *f* d

18. अवाक्पुष्पी कारवी (च)

f t *f*

Gand'ha-bhádáliyá. e — सरणा (तु) प्रसारणी

f *f* 1*f*

(तस्यां) कटम्भरा राजबला भद्रबले(ति च)

f h *f* i *f* j 2*f* 3*f*

Chacawat. g — 19. जनी जतूका रजनी जतुकृच्चक्रवर्त्तिनी

f

संस्पर्शा

f l *f* m 4*f*

Ambahaldí. k — (ऽथ) शटी गन्धमूली षड्ग्रन्थिके (त्यपि)

m n *m*

20. कर्वूरो (ऽपि) पलाशो

m *m*

Momordica charantia. — (ऽथ) कारवेल्लः कटिल्लकः

f o

सुषवी (च)

n q *m* 5*m* *m*

Trichosanthes. p — (ऽथ) कुलकं पटोलस्तिक्तकः पटुः

m s 6*m*

A pumpkin gourd. r — 21. कूष्माण्डक (स्तु) कर्कारु

1—णा. 2—तृ. 3 च—. 4—का. 5 ति—. 6—रु.

[a] Anise; or else Anethum sowa, R. [b] Or शतपुष्पा. [c] And मिशिः or मिषिः. [d] Some refer the two last terms to a different plant. [e] Pæderia fœtida. [f] Also सरणी. [g] A fragrant plant. [h] Or जनिः. [i] Likewise जतुका. [j] Some read जननी. [k] The Hindi name, here taken from medical writings, appertains to a new species of Curcuma. [l] And सटी or षटी. [m] Some read गन्धषटी. [n] or कर्बुरः. Also कर्चूरः. [o] And सुषवी or सुषवी. [p] Trichosanthes dioeca, R. [q] Also कुलकं. [r] Cucurbita Pepo. [s] Or कूष्माण्डकः

m f b *f* c इर्वारुः कर्कटी (स्त्रियौ)	A sort of cucumber. [a]
f *f* इक्ष्वाकुः कटुतुम्बी (स्यात्)	A bitter gourd. [d]
f 1 *f* g तुंब्यलाबू (रुभे समे)	A long gourd. [e]
f *f* *f* 22. चित्रा गवाक्षी गोडुम्बा	Another sort of cucumber. [h]
f 1 *f* विशाला (त्वि) न्द्रवारुणी	Coloquintida. [i]
m *m* k *m* अर्शोघ्नः सूरणः कन्दो	An esculent root. [j]
m *f* गण्डीर (स्तु) समष्ठिला	A potherb. [l]
f n *f* o *m* n *f* 23. कलंब्युपोदिका (स्त्री तु) मूलकं हिलमोचिका *n* p वास्तूकं (शाकभेदाः स्युर्)	Various sorts of potherbs. [m]
f *f* दूर्वा (तु) शतपर्विका.	Bent grass. [q]
f 2 *f* 3 *f* *f* 24. सहस्रवीर्या भार्गव्यौरुहाऽनन्ता (ऽथ सा सिता)	A similar grass with white blossoms. [r]

1 इ—. 2—वी. 3 वा—.

[a] Cucumis Utilatissimus, R. [b] Also ऐर्वारुः, इर्वालुः, उर्वारुः and एर्वारु. [c] Likewise कर्कटिः. [d] It is a variety of the next species. [e] Cucurbita lagenaris. [f] तुम्बी or तुम्बिः. [g] अलाबूः. Also अलाबुः, आलाबुः and लाबुः. [h] Cucumis Madraspatanus. [i] Cucumis Colocynthis. [j] Arum campanulatum, R. [k] Also सूरणः. [l] Described as growing on watery ground. [m] Severally named in the text: 1. Convolvulus repens; 2. Basella rubra or lucida; 3. Radish; 4. Hingtsha (*Hilancha*) repens, R. 5. Chenopodium album, &c. [n] कलम्बी. Also कलम्बूः and कलम्बः. [o] उपोदिका. Also उपोदकी, उत्पादिका and अपोदिका. Likewise पोतकी, पोतिका and पूतिका. [p] Or वास्तुकं. [q] Agrostis linearis, Koen. [r] Agrostis diandra? Some refer two of these terms to one species; and the two remaining, to another.

f f f m
गोलोमी शतवीर्या (च) गण्डाली शकुलाक्षक:

m mb f m n
A fragrant grass. a — 25. कुरुविन्दो मेघ (नामा) मुस्ता मुस्तक (मस्त्रियाम्)

m d f
Another sort. c — (स्याद्) भद्रमुस्तको गुन्द्रा

f f 1 1 f
A different kind. e — चूडाला चक्रलोच्चटा

m m m m m
A bamboo. g — 26. वंशे त्वक्सार कर्मार त्वचिसार तृणध्वजा:

2 m m m m m
शतपर्वा यवफलो वेणु मस्कर तेजना:

m h
The same, rattling or whistling. — 27. (वेणव:) कीचका (स्ते स्युर्ये स्वनन्त्यनिलोद्धता:)

m 3 n n i
A knot or joint. — ग्रन्थि (र्ना) पर्व परुषी

m 4 m m k
Sarahari. j — गुन्द्रस्तेजनक: शर:

m m m m
A reed. l — 28. नड (स्तु) धमन: पोटगलो

m n o
Cás. n — (ऽथ) काश (मस्त्रियाम्)

f m
इक्षुगन्धा पोटगल:

m pl. q
Bugai. p — (पुंसि भूम्नि तु) बल्वजा:

1—ख. 2—वंन्. 3—नृ. 4 ते—.

[a] Cyperus rotundus. [b] And other synonyma of cloud. [c] Cyperus pertenuis, R. [d] Also भद्रं. [e] Interpretations differ : it is a Cyperus, according to some ; but others make it the Zedoary. [f] चक्रला and गुन्द्रला. [g] Bambusa Arundinacea, and other species, R. [h] Sing. कीचक:. [i] Sing. परु: (परुस्). Also masc. परु: (परु). [j] Saccharum Sara, R. [k] Or सर:. [l] Arundo tibialis, R. [m] And नल:. [n] Saccharum spontaneum. [o] Or काश:. Also fem. काशी and काशा. [p] Perhaps Saccharum Cylindricum, Willd. But the Sanscrit name seems to be also applied to Coracanus Indious or Eleusine Indica. [q] Likewise Sing. बल्वज:.

m 1*m*

29. रसाल इक्षुस् | Sugarcane.

m a *m*

(तद्भेदाः) पुण्ड्रकान्तारका (द्यः) | Varieties of the same.

n *n*

(स्यादू) वीरणं वीरतरं | A fragrant grass. b

2*m n c*

(मूलेऽस्यो) शीर (मस्त्रियाम्) | Its root.

n *n* 3*n* *n d* *n*

30. अभयं नलदं सेव्यममृणालं जलाशयम्

n *n e* 4*n f* 5*n g*

लामज्जकं लघुलयमवदाहेष्टकापथे

n 6*f* 7*m*

31. (नडादयस्)तृणं (गर्मुच्छ्यामाकप्रमुखा अपि) | A gramineous plant. h

m n *m* *m*

(अस्त्री) कुशं कुशो दर्भः पवित्रं | Sacrificial grass. i.

n

(अथ) कत्तृणम् | A fragrant grass.

n *n* *n* *n* *n*

32. पौर सौगन्धिक ध्याम देवगन्धक रौहिषम्

f *m* *m*

छत्रा ऽतिच्छत्र पालघ्नौ | A mushroom.

n *n*

मालातृणक भूस्तृणे | Andropogon. j

n k *n*

33. शष्पं बालतृणं | Young grass.

m *m n m*

घासो यवसम् | Meadow grass. l

---

1 इक्षु. 2 उ—. 3 सेव्य. 4 अ—. 5 इ—.
6—त. 7 श्या—.

a Or पौण्ड्रः. b Andropogon muricatum. c उशीरं and उषीरं. d अमृणालं and मृणालं. e Also लघु and लयं. f अवदाहं. Some erroneously add अवदानं. g Likewise इष्ट° and कापथं. h Including reeds, grasses, and corn ; as Panicum frumentaceum, (R.) &c. comprehending the after-mentioned grasses, besides various sorts of grain, as कंगुः, Panicum Italicum, कोद्रवः, Paspalum frumentaceum, &c. i Poa cynosuroides, Koen. j A. schœnanthus. But some make these synonymous with the preceding terms. k And शष्प°. l Such as cattle feed on. m Also यवसः.

Grass in general. — तृणम्[n] अर्जुनम्[1 n]

Abundance of grass. — (तृणानां संहतिस्) तृण्या[f]

Abundance of reeds. — नड्या[f] (तु नडसंहतिः)

Plamyra. a — 34. तृणराजा[2 m] (ह्वयस्) तालो[m b]

Coconut. c — नारिकेर[m d] (स्तु) लाङ्गली[f e]

Faufel. f — घोण्टा[f] (तु) पूगः[m] क्रमुको[m] गुवाकः[m g] खपुरो[m]

Its nut, called Betel-nut. — (ऽस्य तु

35. फलम्) उद्वेगम्[n]

Marshy date tree. h — (एते च) हिन्ताल[m i] (सहितास्त्रयः)

Date. j — खर्जूरः[m]

Pandanus. k — केतकी[m f l]

Corypha. m — ताली[f n]

Wild date tree. o — खर्जूरी[f] (च)

A Palm. — तृणद्रुमाः[m p]

1—ब. 2—ज.

[a] Borassus flabelliformis. [b] Likewise तलः. [c] Cocos nucifera. [d] And नारिकेलः, नालिकेर, नारीकेलः, &c. Also fem. नारिकेली or नारिकेलिः, &c. [e] Likewise masc. लाङ्गली (—न्). But some do not admit this. [f] Areca Faufel (or Catechu). [g] And गूवाकः. [h] Phœnix (or Elate) Paludosa, R. The three before-mentioned, this, and the following, are Palms. [i] Also हीन्तालः. [j] Phœnix (or Elate) Sylvestris. [k] Pandanns odoratissimus. [l] Masc. केतकः. [m] C. Talliera, (R.) or C. umbraculifera. [n] तालिः or ताली and तालिः. [o] Perhaps Phœnix bulbifera, R. [p] Sing. तृणद्रुमः.

CHAPTER V.

m m m m 1 m a m

1. सिंहो मृगेन्द्रः पञ्चास्यो हर्य्यक्षः केसरी हरिः — A lion.

m 2 m b m

शार्दूल द्वीपिनौ व्याघ्रे — A tiger.

m d m

तरक्षु (क्षु.) मृगादनः — A hyena. c

m m e m f m 3 m m g m

2. वराहः सूकरो घृष्टिः कोलः पोत्री किरः किटिः — A hog.

4 m 5 m 6 m m m

दंष्ट्री घोणी स्तब्धरोमा क्रोडो भूदार (इत्यपि)

m m m h m 7 m i

3. कपि प्लवङ्ग प्लवग शाखामृग वलीमुखाः — A monkey or ape.

प m m m 8 m

मर्कटो वानरः कीशो वनौकाः

m j

(अथ) भल्लुके — A bear.

m m k 9 m

4. ऋक्षा ऽच्छभल्ल भाल्लुकाः

m m m l

गण्डके खड्ग खड्गिनौ — A rhinoceros.

1—न्. 2—न्. 3—न्. 4—न्. 5—न्.
6—न्. 7—ख. 8—कस्. 9—क.

[a] Also केशरी (—रिन्). [b] Sing. द्वीपी. This, as a distinct species from the tiger, is the ounce ; or else the panther. [c] Some suppose a leopard to be meant. [d] Also तरक्षः. [e] Likewise शूकरः. [f] And घृष्टिः. [g] Some read किरिः. Fem. किर्याणी. [h] Also प्लवङ्गमः and प्लवङ्गः, or प्लवगः. Some add प्लवङ्गमः. [i] Likewise वलिमुखः. [j] भल्लुकः and भल्लूकः. Also भालुकः. [k] Likewise अच्छः and भल्लः. [l] Sing. खड्गी (—न्).

A buffalo.

m a *m* b 1 *m* 2 *m* *m*

लुलापो महिषो वाहद्विषत्कासर सैरिभाः

A jackal.

f c *m* *m* *m*

5. (स्त्रियां) शिवा भूरिमाय गोमायु मृगधूर्त्तकाः

m d *m* *m* e *m* *m* *m* f

शृगाल वञ्चक क्रोष्टु फेरु फेरव जम्बुकाः

A cat.

m g 3 *m* h *m* *m* 4 *m*

6. ओतुर्विडालो मार्जारो वृषदंशक आखुभुक्

An iguana.

m *m* 5 *m* 6 *m*

(त्रयो) गौधेर गौधार गौधेया गोधिकात्मजे

A porcupine.

7 *m* 8 *m*

7. श्वावित् (तु) शल्यस्

His quills.

f *n* *n*

(तल्लोम्नि) शलली शललं शलम्

A swift antelope.

m i 9 *m*

वातप्रमीर्वातमृगः

A wolf.

m *m* *m*

कोक ईहामृगो वृकः

A deer or antelope.

m *m* *m* 10 *m* 11 *m*

8. मृगे कुरङ्ग वातायु हरिणा ऽजिनयोनयः

Belonging to a doe.

m f n

ऐणेयम् (एण्याश्चर्माद्यम्)

Belonging to a buck.

m f n

(एणस्य) ऐणम् (उभे त्रिषु)

Sorts of deer, of which the hides are used.

f *f* j *m* 12 *m* 13 *m*

9. कदली कन्दली चीनचमूरु प्रियका (अपि)

1—दू. 2 का—. 3 वि—. 4—ज्. 5—ध
6—ज. 7—ध्. 8 शल्य. 9 वा—. 10—च.
11—नि. 12 च—. 13—रु.

[a] And लुलाय:. [b] Fem. महिषी. [c] This is feminine, even when the male animal is meant. [d] Or सृगाल:. [e] Fem. क्रोष्ट्री. [f] Likewise जम्बूक:. [g] The same in the feminine. [h] Also बिराल: and विडाल:. [i] Fem. वातप्रमी: and वातप्रमी. [j] Some consider these to be masculine, and make the radical termination,—विन्.

m
समूरु (श्चेति हरिणा अमी अजिनयोनयः)

mb m m mc md 1 me
10. कृष्णसार रुरु न्यङ्कु रंकु शम्बर रौहिषाः — Various sorts of deer. a

m mf 2m mg mh mi
गोकर्ण पृषतै णर्श्य रोहिताश्चमरो (मृगाः)

k ml m m mm mn
11. गंधर्वः शरभो रामः सृमरो गवयः शशः — Various animals. j

m
(इत्यादयो मृगेन्द्राद्या गवाद्याः) पशु (जातयः) — A beast in general. o

mp mq 3m
12. उन्दुरुर्मूषिको (प्या) खुर् — A rat.

f f
गिरिका बालमूषिका — A mouse, or small rat.

mr ms
सरटः कृकलास (स्यात्) — A lizard, cameleon, &c.

ft fu
मुसली गृहगोधिका — A small house-lizard.

f mv 4mw m
13. लूता (स्त्री) तन्तुवायोर्णनाभ मर्कटकाः (समाः) — A spider.

1—म. 2 एण. 3 आखु. 4 ऊ—.

[a] Severally named in the text, as the black antelope, the stag, &c. But these terms are not all rigidly applied to different species; and some are not of the deer kind. [b] Or कृष्णसारः. [c] The spotted Axis. [d] Also सम्बरः. [e] And रोहिष् (—ष). [f] पृषतः and पृषत् (fem. पृषती); the porcine deer. [g] ऋष्यः. Also ऋश्यः and रिश्यः. The painted or white-footed antelope. [h] Likewise रोहित्. [i] चमरः; though here placed among deer, the Bos grunniens is meant. [j] Severally named in the text. [k] Some make this the musk deer. [l] A fabulous animal with eight legs. [m] Bos Gavœus, As. Res. vol. viii, p. 487. [n] A hare. [o] The preceding, as well as the lion and other wild beasts, and domestic cattle, are so denominated. [p] Also उन्दुरः. [q] Likewise मूषकः, and मूषी. [r] Also शरट् and शरटः. [s] Or कृकुलासः. [t] And मुषली or मुशली. [u] Likewise गृहगोलिका, गृहगोधा and गृहालिका. [v] Also तन्तुवापः. [w] Or ऊर्णनाभिः.

An insect. — नीलङ्गु[m a] (स्तु) क्रमिः[m b]

A centipede. — कर्णजलौका[f c] शतपदी[1 f] (भे)

A caterpillar. — 14. वृश्चिकः[m] शूककीटः[m] (स्यात्)

A scorpion. — अलि[m d] द्रुणौ[m e] (तु) वृश्चिके[m]

A dove or pigeon. — पारावतः[m f] कलरवः[m] कपोतो[m]

A hawk or falcon. — (ऽथ) शशादनः[m]

15. पत्त्री[2 m] श्येनम्[m]

An owl. — उलूके[m g] (तु) वायसाराति[m] पेचकौ[m]

A sky-lark. — व्याघ्राटः[m] (स्यात्) भरद्वाजः[m h]

A wagtail. — खञ्जरीट[m] (स्तु) खञ्जनः[m]

A heron. — 16. लोहपृष्ठ[m] (स्तु) कंकः[m] (स्यात्)

A blue jay. — (अथ) चाषः[m j] किकीदिविः[m k]

The fork-tailed shrike.[l] — कलिङ्ग[m] भृङ्ग[m] धूम्याटा[3 m]

A wood-pecker. — (ऽथ स्यात्) शतपत्रकः[4 m]

17. दार्व्वाघाटो[m]

Pipihá. m — (ऽथ) सारंग[m n] स्तोकक[m o] श्चातकः[5 m] (समाः)

1—दी. 2—त्रु. 3—ट. 4 घ—. 5 चा—.

[a] And नीलाङ्गुः. [b] Likewise क्रिमिः [c] Also कर्णजलौकाः (—कस्) [d] अलिः or अली (—लिन्); also आलिः and आली. [e] द्रुणः or द्रोणः. [f] Likewise पारापतः. [g] Or अलूकः. [h] And भारद्वाजः. [i] Coracias Indica and Bengalensis; or as otherwise explained, a different bird. [j] Or चाषः. [k] Likewise किकिदीविः, किकीदीविः, and किकिदिवि; or किकीदिवः, &c. Also खिखिः and दिविः; or कीविः and दीविः. [l] Lanius Cœrulescens and Corvus Balicassius. [m] Cubulus Radiatus. But it is not certain whether the *Chàtaca* be not a different brid. [n] Or सारङ्गः. And स्तोकः.

कृकवाकुस्ता[1]म्रचूडः कुक्कुटश्च[2]रणायुधः	A gallinaceous fowl.
18. चटकः कलविङ्कः (स्यात्)	A sparrow.
(तस्य स्त्री) चटका	Its female.
(तयोः पुमपत्ये) चाटकेरः (स्त्र्यपत्ये) चटका[3] (एव च)	Their offspring male and female.
19. कर्करेटुः करेटुः (स्यात्)	Numidian crane.
कृकणक्रकरौ[4] (समौ)	Căĕr.[a]
वनप्रियः परभृतः कोकिलः पिकः (इत्यपि)	The black cuckoo.
20. काके[5] (तु) करटाऽरिष्टबलिपुष्टसकृत्प्रजाः[6]	A crow.
ध्वाङ्क्षा[7]त्मघोषपरभृ[8]द्बलिभु[9]ग्वायसा[10] (अपि)	
21. द्रोणकाकः[b] (तु) काकोलः	A raven.
दात्यूहः[c] कालकण्ठकः	A gallinule.
आतापि[d]चिल्लौ[11]	A kite.
दाक्षाय्यगृध्रौ[12]	A vulture.
कीरशुकौ[13][e] (समौ)	A parrot.
22. कुङ्[14]क्रौञ्चः[f]	A curlew.

---

1 ता—. 2 च—. 3 —का. 4 —र. 5 —क. 6 —ज. 7 आ—. 8 —भृत्. 9 —भुज्. 10 वायस. 11 चिल्ल. 12 गृध्र. 13 शुक. 14 कुङ्.

[a] Perhaps Perdix Sylvatica. [b] Also द्रोणः. [c] Or दात्योहः. [d] आतायी (—न्) or आतापी (—न्). [e] Also सुवः. [f] Likewise क्रुञ्चः. Fem. कुचा and क्रौञ्चा.

A crane. — (ऽथ) बकः (m) कह्वः (m)

The Indian crane. — पुष्कराह्व (m a) (स्तु) सारसः (m)

The ruddy goose. — कोकश्[m] चक्रश्[1 m] चक्रवाको[2 m] रथाङ्गा (ह्वयनामकः) (m b)

A drake. — 23. कादम्बः (m) कलहंसः (m) (स्याद्)

An osprey. — उत्क्रोश (m) कुररौ (8 m c) (समौ)

Geese. — हंसा (m d) (स्तु) श्वेतगरुतश्[4 m] चक्राङ्गा[5 m] मानसौकसः (6 m)

Varieties of geese. — 24. राजहंसा (m e) (स्तु ते चञ्चुचरणैर्लोहितैः सिताः)

(मलिनैर्) मल्लिकाक्षा (m f) (स्ते) धार्तराष्ट्राः (m g) (सितेतरैः)

Sarali. h — 25. शरारिर् (f i) आटिर् (7 f) आडि (8 f) (श्च)

A small crane. j — बलाका (f) बिसकण्ठिका (f)

A duck or goose. — (हंसस्य योषिद्) वरटा (f k)

A female Indian crane. — (सारसस्य तु) लक्ष्मणा (f l)

A bat. — 26. जतुका (9 f m) जिनपत्रा (f) (स्यात्)

A cockroach. — परोष्णी (f n) तैलपायिका (f)

---

1 च—. 2 च—. 3—र. 4—वत्. 5 च—. 6—चस्.
7 आ—. 8 आ—. 9—च—.

[a] पुष्करः or any term signifying the lotos. Also पुष्कराह्वः. [b] Any word signifying a wheel. [c] Fem. कुररी. [d] Sing. हंसः. Fem. हंसी. [e] Sing. राजहंसः. A white gander with red legs and bill. [f] Sing. मल्लिकः, with brown legs and bill. Also मल्लिकाख्य. [g] धार्तराष्ट्रः, with black legs and bill. [h] Perhaps Turdus Ginginianus. [i] Also शराटि. or शरालिः [j] Feminine, even when the male bird is intended. [k] Also वरटी. [l] Likewise लक्षणा. [m] Gr जतूका. [n] Also परोष्टी.

	f [a] वर्वणा (मक्षिका नीला)	A blue fly.
	f f सरघा मधुमक्षिका	A bee.
27.	f f पतङ्गिका पुत्तिका (स्याद्)	A small bee.
	f f दंश (स्तु) वनमक्षिका	A gadfly.
	f दंशी (तज्जातिरल्पा स्याद्)	A smaller sort of gad-fly.
	f m f [b] गन्धोली वरटा (द्वयोः)	A wasp.
28.	f f f [c] f भृङ्गारी झीरुका चीरी झिल्लिका (च समा इमाः)	A cricket.
	m m (समौ) पतङ्ग शलभौ	A grass-hopper.
	m m खद्योतो ज्योतिरिङ्गणः	A firefly.
29.	m m 1 m [e] 2 m f 3 m मधुव्रतो मधुकरो मधुलिण्मधुपाऽलिनः	A large black bee. [d]
	m 4 m 5 m m m 6 m द्विरेफ पुष्पलिड्भृङ्ग षट्पद भ्रमराऽलयः	
30.	m m 7 m m 8 m मयूरो बर्हिणो बर्ही नीलकंठो भुजङ्गभुक्	A peacock.
	m 9 m 10 m 11 m शिखावलः शिखीकेकी मेघनादानुलास्य (ऽपि)	
31.	f केका (वाणी मयूरस्य)	His cry.
	m m (समौ) चन्द्रक मेचकौ	The eye of his tail.

1—ह्. 2 म—. 3 —न्. 4 —ह्. 5 भृ—. 6 अलि. 7—न्. 8—भुज्. 9—न्. 10 —न्. 11—नी (—न्).

[a] Some deduce two synonyma from the explanation. मक्षिका and नीला or नीली. [b] Also गंधाली and वरटी. Masc. वरटः. [c] Likewise चीरुका. [d] Or a black beetle. [e] Nom. मधुलिट्, or —ड् (—ह्). Also मधुपायी (—न्).

f f

His crest. शिखा चूडा

m n n a

His tail. शिखण्ड (स्तु) पिच्छ बर्हे (नपुंसके)

m m m m 1 *m* b

A bird in general. 32. खगे विहङ्ग विहग विहङ्गम विहायसः

m 2 *m m m m* 3 *m*

शकुन्ति पक्षि शकुनि शकुन्त शकुन द्विजाः

5 *m m* 6 *m* 7 *m* 8 *m*

33. पतत्रि पत्रि पतग पतत्पत्ररथाण्डजाः

9 *m* 10 *m m m* c *m* 11 *m*

नगौको वाजि विकिर वि विष्किर पतत्रयः

12 *m* 13 *m* d 14 *m m*

34. नीडोद्भवा गरुत्मन्तः पित्सन्तो नभसङ्गमाः

m f *m* g *m* h *m*

Various birds. e (तेषां विशेषा) हारितो मद्गुः कारण्डवः प्लवः

m i *m* j *m* k *m* l 15 *m* m

35. तित्तिरिः कुक्कुभो लावो जीवञ्जीवश्चकोरकः

m 16 *m* n *m f* o

कोयष्टिकष्टिट्टिभको वर्त्तको वर्त्तिका (दयः)

17 *m* m p 18 *m n n n n*

A wing. 36. गरुत्पक्षच्छदाः पत्रं पतत्र (च) तनूरुहम्

1—यस्. 2—न्. 3—ज. 4—न्. 5—न्. 6—न्. 7—ग. 8—ज. 9—कस् and —क. 10—न्. 11—त्रि. 12—व. 13—मत्. 14—त्. 15 प—. 16 टि—. 17—त्. 18 छ—.

a Also masc. बर्हः. b Sing. विहायाः. c Masc. विः, Fem. वी. d Sing. गरुत्मान्. e Severally named in the text; viz. Green pigeon, &c. Besides others, as मत्स्यरङ्कः, a king-fisher, &c. f Also हारितः, (Columba Hurriala, B. Mss). g A shag. h Sort of duck. i Or तित्तिरः. The francoline Partridge. j A wild cock, (Phasianus Gallus.) k Sort of quail, (Perdix Chinensis.) l Perhaps a pheasant. m Sort of partridge, (Perdix rufa, B.) n And टिट्टिभकः, Jacana, Tringa Goensis, (Parra Goensis, &c.) o A quail, and its female. Likewise fem. वर्त्तिका. p Also neut. पक्षं and पक्षः (—क्ष).

f *n* (स्त्री) पक्षतिः पक्षमूलं	Its root.
f a 1*f* b चञ्चुस्त्रोटि (रुभे स्त्रियौ)	The beak.
n 2*n* 3*n* 37. प्रडीनोड्डीन संडीना (न्येताः खगगतिक्रियाः)	Acts of flying. c
f d *mn* e *n* पेशी कोशो (द्विहीने) ऽण्डं	An egg.
m *mn* कुलायो नीड (मस्त्रियाम्)	A nest.
m f *m* g *m* *m* *m* h *m* *m* 38. पोतः पाको ऽर्भको डिम्भः पृथुकः शावकः शिशुः	Young of any animal.
n *n* i (स्त्री पुंसौ) मिथुनं द्वन्द्वं	A couple, male and female.
n *n* *n* युग्मं (तु) युगलं युगम्	A pair or brace.
m *m* *m* *m* *m* *m* 39. समूह निवह व्यूहसन्दोह विसर व्रजाः	A flock or multitude.
m 4*m* *m* *m* *m* *m* *m* स्तोमौघ निकर व्रात वार संघात सञ्चयाः	
m *m* *m* j 5*m* *m* 40. समुदायः समुदयः समवायश्चयो गणः	
f 6*n* *n* *n* (स्त्रियां तु) संहतिर्वृन्दं निकुरम्बं कदम्बकम्	

---

[1] त्रो—. [2] ड—. [3] —न. [4] कोष. [5] च—. [6] ह—.

[a] And चञ्चूः. [b] Or त्रोटी. [c] Severally mentioned: viz. taking flight, soaring, and perching; or otherwise interpreted, whirling, ascending, and alighting. [d] And पेशिः. [e] Or कोषः. Likewise पेशीकोषः. [f] Fem. पोती. [g] Fem. पाका. [h] Also पृथुकः. [i] Some make the last term, others both words synonymous with the following. [j] And समावायः.

A multitude of similar things. — 41. (वृन्दभेदाः समैर्) वर्गः [m]

Of animals. — संघ [m] सार्थौ [1m] (तु जन्तुभिः)

Of homogeneous animals. — (सजातीयैः) कुलं [n]

Of birds and beasts. — यूथं [m n] (तिरश्चां पुन्नपुंसकम्)

Of beasts. — 42. (पशूनां) समजो [m]

Of other beings (men, &c.) — (ऽन्येषां) समाजो [m]

Of persons practising like duties. — (ऽथ सधर्मिणाम् स्यान्) निकायः [m]

A heap of grain, &c. — पुञ्ज [ma] राशी [2mf] (तु) त्करः [3m] कूट [mn] (मस्त्रियाम्)

Flocks of various animals. [b] — 43. कापोत [n] शौक [n] मायूर [n] तैत्तिरा [n] (दीनि तद्गणे)

Domesticated, (a bird or beast). — (गृहासक्ताः पक्षिमृगाश्) छेका [m c] (स्ते) गृह्यका [m] (श्च ते)

---

[1] —र्थं. [2] —शि. [3] उ—.

[a] Also fem. पुञ्जिः. [b] Of doves, parrots, peacocks and francoline partridges: other derivatives are similarly formed, as औलूकं, a flock of owls. [c] sing. छेकः and गृह्यकः.

CHAPTER VI.

SECTION I.

m m a m m m b m

1. मनुष्या मानुषा मर्त्या मनुजा मानवा नराः — Man : mankind.

m d m m m m c

(स्युः) पुमांसः पंचजनाः पुरुषाः पूरुषा नरः — Man ; or male. c.

f 1 f f 2 f f g f f f

2. स्त्री योषिदबला योषा नारी सीमन्तिनी वधूः — A woman ; or female.

f f f f h

प्रतीपदर्शिनी वामा वनिता महिला (तथा)

3 f f j f f

3. (विशेषास्त्व) ङ्गना भीरुः कामिनी वामलोचना — Various descriptions of women. i

f f k f f f

प्रमदा भाविनी कान्ता ललना (च) नितम्बिनी

f f l f m

4. सुन्दरी रमणी रामा

f f

कोपना (सैव) भामिनी — A passionate woman.

f 4 f o 5 f f

वरारोहा मत्तकाशिन्युत्तमा वरवर्णिनी — An excellent woman. n.

---

[1]—तृ. [2] अ—. [3] अ—. [4]—नो. [5] उ—.

[a] Sing. मनुष्यः, मानुषः, &c. (Fem. मनुषी. मानुषी). [b] Also (with an ill sense) मानवः. [c] Both lines contain synonymous terms, according to some. [d] Sing. पुमान् (पुंस्). [e] Sing. ना (नृ). [f] Also योषिता. [g] Likewise जोषा. [h] Or महेला, and महीला. [i] The terms are commendatory ; as well-shaped ; timid ; loving ; having fine eyes, &c. [j] Also भीरुकः, and भीलुः. [k] Another reading exhibits मानिनी. [l] Some write रमणा. [m] Likewise रमा. [n] Handsome, healthy and affectionate. However some make the terms not synonymous, but significant of various descriptions of women. [o] मत्तकासिनी, or मत्तकाषिणी.

A queen.[a] — 5. (कृताभिषेका) महिषी *f*

Other wives of a king. — भोगिन्यो *f*[b] (ऽन्या नृपस्त्रियः)

A wife, or wedded woman.[c] — पत्नी *f* पाणिगृहीती *f* (च) द्वितीया *f* सहधर्मिणी *f*[d]

6. भार्या *f* जाया *f* (ऽथ पुंभूम्नि) दाराः *m pl.*[e]

A matron.[f] — (स्यात्तु) कुटुम्बिनी *f*

पुरंध्री *f*[g]

A virtuous faithful wife. — सुचरित्रा *f* (तु) सती *f* साध्वी *f*[h] पतिव्रता *f*

A superseded wife.[i] — 7. कृतसापत्निका *f*[j] ऽध्यूढा *f* ऽधिविन्ना *f*

A bride choosing her husband. — (ऽथ) स्वयंवरा *f*

पतिंवरा *f* (च) वर्या *f*

A chaste woman. — (ऽथ) कुलस्त्री *f* कुलपालिका *f*[k]

A maiden.[l] — 8. कन्या *f*[m] कुमारी *f*

---

[a] Consecrated as such. Also a king's wife in general. [b] Sing. भोगिनी. [c] Some restrict the two first terms (other the four first) to the particular sense of a wife married with religious rites. [d] Likewise सधर्मिणी. [e] Also fem. Sing. दारा. [f] Or one, who has children and her husband living. [g] Some add पुरंध्रिः. [h] Or साधु. [i] One whose husband has married another wife. [j] And कृतसापत्नका, कृतसापत्नी, कृतसापत्नीका, or कृतसपत्निका. [k] And कुलपाली. [l] The first term denotes a girl nine years old; the second twelve; or, without discriminating the age, both terms signify a virgin. [m] Also कन्यका.

f fb f
गौरी (तु) नग्निका ऽनागतार्त्तवा — A girl. a

fc 1f
(स्यान्) मध्यमा दृष्टरजास् — One arrived at puberty.

fe ff
तरुणी युवतिः (समे) — A young woman. d

f fg fh
9. (समाः) स्नुषा जनी वध्वश् — A daughter-in-law.

fj fk
चिरण्टी (तु) सुवासिनी — A woman staying in her father's house. i.

f f
इच्छावती कामुका (स्याद्) — A woman desirous of any thing. l

f f
वृषस्यंती (तु) कामुकी — One amorous or lustful.

f
10. (कान्तार्थिनी तु या याति संकेतं सा)ऽभिसारिका — One who goes to an assignation.

f fm 2f 3f 4f 5f
पुंश्चली धर्षिणी बन्धक्यसती कुलटेत्वरी — A disloyal or unchaste woman.

f fn
11. स्वैरिणी पांशुला

f
(ऽथ स्याद्) अशिश्वी (शिशुना विना) — A childless woman.

f
अवीरा (निष्पतिसुता) — One who has neither husband nor son.

fo 6f
विश्लस्ता विधवे (समे) — A widow.

1—अस्. 2—की. 3 ब—. 4—टा. 5 इ—. 6—वा.

a Here also, if ages be discriminated, the first is a girl eight years old ; the second, ten : as synonymous terms, they signify a girl who has not menstruated. b And नम्निका. c Likewise मध्या. d Between sixteen and thirty years of age. e Or तलुनी. f Also युवती and यूनी. g जनिः, or जनी. h Sing. वधुः, or वधूः. Likewise वधूटी. i Married or unmarried. j Likewise चिरिण्टी. k Also स्ववासिनी. l Covetous of wealth ; eager for food, &c. m Also धर्षणी. n Likewise पांसुला. o And विश्वस्ता.

A woman's female friend.	12. आलिः[f, a] सखी[f] वयस्या[f] (च)
A woman whose husband is living.	पतिवत्नी[f] सभर्तृका[f]
Old or grey-haired.	वृद्धा[f] पलिक्नी[f, b]
Intelligent.	प्राज्ञी[f] (तु) प्राज्ञा[f]
Wise.	प्रज्ञा[f] (तु) धीमती[f]
The wife of the *Súdra*.[c]	13. शूद्री[f] (शूद्रस्य भार्य्या स्याच्)
A woman of the *Súdra* tribe.	शूद्रा[1 f] (तज्जातिरङ्गना)
A milk-woman.[d]	आभीरी[f] (तु) महाशूद्री[f] (जातिपुंयोगयोः समा)
A woman of the *Vaisya* tribe.	14. अर्य्याणी[f] (स्वयम्) अर्य्या[f] (स्यात्)
One of the *Kshatriya* tribe.	क्षत्रिया[f] क्षत्रियाण्य[2 f](ऽपि)
A female teacher.	उपाध्याया[f] (प्यु) पाध्यायी[3 f]
A spiritual instructress.	(स्याद्) आचार्य्या[f] (ऽपि च स्वतः)
The wife of a spiritual preceptor.	15. आचार्य्याणी[f] (तु पुंयोगे)
Wife of a *Vaisya*.	(स्याद्) अर्य्यी[f]
Wife of a *Kshatriya*.	क्षत्रियी[f] (तथा)
Wife of a tutor.	उपाध्याया[4 f]न्युपाध्यायी[5 f]
A masculine woman.[e]	पोटा[f] (स्त्रीपुंसलक्षणा

[1] शूद्रा. [2] —णी. [3] उ—. [4] —नी. [5] उ—.

[a] Or आली. [b] Or पलिता. [c] Whether belonging to the same or to a different tribe. [d] Milkman's wife; or a woman of his tribe. [e] Having breasts and a beard.

16. वीरपत्नी[f] वीरभार्य्या[f]	A hero's wife.
वीरमाता[1f] (च) वीरसूः[f]	A hero's mother.
जातापत्या[f] प्रजाता[f] (च) प्रसूता[f] (च) प्रसूतिका[f]	A woman who has borne a child. a
17. (स्त्री) नग्निका[f] कोटवी[fb] (स्याद्)	A naked woman.
दूती[fc] सञ्चारिके[2f] (समे)	A female messenger or go-betewen.
कात्यायन्य[3f](र्द्धवृद्धा या काषायवसनाधवा)	A middle-aged widow. d
18. सैरिंध्री[ff] (परवेश्मस्था स्ववशा शिल्पकारिका)	A female artisan in another's house. e
असिक्नी[fh] (स्यादवृद्धा या प्रेष्यांतःपुरचारिणी)	A female servant. g
19. वारस्त्री[f] गणिका[f] वेश्या[fi] रूपाजीवा[f]	A courtesan or harlot.
(ऽथ सा जनैः सत्कृता) वारमुख्या[f] (स्यात्)	The head of a set of harlots.
कुट्टनी[fj] शंभली[fk] (समे)	A bawd or procuress.
20. विप्रश्निका[f] (त्वी) क्षणिका[4f] दैवज्ञा[f]	A fortune-teller.
(ऽथ) रजस्वला	A woman in her courses.

---

[1] —सू. [2] —का. [3] —नी. [4] ई—.

[a] The two last of these synonyma are by some restricted to a woman recently delivered. [b] Likewise कोट्टवी. Some add कोटरी. [c] Also दूतिः. [d] Wearing a dress indicating the practice of austerity. [e] Being her own mistress, but living in another's house, and practising any art. [f] Also सैरंध्री. Some add सैरिंध्रिः. [g] Young and frequenting the apartments of the women. [h] And असिता. [i] Likewise वेषा. [j] Some add कुटनी. [k] Also सम्भली.

1f fa 2fb f 3f
स्त्रीधर्मिण्यविरात्रेयी मलिनी पुष्पवत्य (ऽपि)

4f 5f
21. ऋतुमत्य (पि) उदक्या (ऽपि)

6nc n 7n
The courses. (स्यात्) रजः पुष्पमार्त्तवं

f 8f
Longing, as in pregnancy. श्रद्धालुर्दोहदवती

fe f
Past child-bearing. d निष्कला विगतार्त्तवा

f 9f 10f f
Pregnant. 22. आपन्नसत्वा (स्यात्) गुर्विण्यन्तर्वत्नी (च) गर्भिणी

An assemblage of harlots. (गणिकादेस्तु) गाणिक्यं

n
—of pregnant women. गार्भिणं

nf
—of young women, यौवतं (गणे)

11f 12fh
A twice married woman. g 23. पुनर्भूर्दिधिषूरूढा (द्विः)

mi
Her second husband. (तस्या) दिधिषुः (पतिः)

m
One in whose family she presides. (स तु द्विजो) ऽग्रेदिधिषुः (सैव यस्य कुटुम्बिनी)

mj m
Son of an unmarried woman. 24. कानीनः कन्यकाजातः (सुतो)

m
Son of an auspicious mother. (ऽथ) सुभगासुतः

---

[1] —णी. [2] धा—. [3] —ती. [4] —ती. [5] उ—.
[6] —हु. [7] आ—. [8] दो—. [9] —णी. [10] अं—.
[11] —भू. [12] —षू.

[a] अविः and आवीः. [b] Some add आत्त्रेयी. [c] Also masc. रजः (—जस्) [d] Having ceased to menstruate. [e] Likewise निष्काशी and निष्कला or निष्कली. [f] Also यौवनं. [g] A virgin widow remarried. [h] Some add दिधिषुः. [i] Likewise दिधिषूः. [j] Fem. कानीनी. The daughter of such a woman.

सौभागिनेयः[m] (स्यात्)

पारस्त्रैणेय[m] (स्तु. परस्त्रियाः) — Son by another's wife.

25. पैतृष्वसेयः[m] (स्यात्) पैतृष्वस्रीय[m] (श्च पितृष्वसुः सुते।) — Paternal aunt's son.

(मातृष्वसुश्चैवं[a]) — Maternal aunt's son.

वैमात्रेयो[m] विमातृजः[m] — Step-mother's son.

26. (अथ) बान्धकिनेयः[m] (स्याद्) बन्धुल[m](श्चा) ऽसतीसुतः[m] — A bastard.[b]

कौलटेयः[m c] कौलटेरो[m d]।

(भिक्षुकी तु सती यदि — A son of a female beggar.

27. तदा) कौलटिनेयो[m](ऽस्याः)कौलटेयो[m](ऽपि चात्मजः)

आत्मजस्तनयः[m] [1 m] सूनुः[m] सुतः[m] पुत्रः[m e] — A son.

(स्त्रियान्त्वमी — A daughter.

28. आहुर्) दुहितरं[f f] (सर्वे[g])

---

[1]—त.

[a] Formed like the preceding terms, viz. मातृष्वसेयः and मातृष्वस्रीयः. Fem. मातृष्वसेयी and मातृष्वस्रीया. [b] Son of a disloyal wife. [c] Some add कौलटिनेयः. [d] Fem. कौलटेयी and कौलटेरा. [e] Also पुत्रकः. [f] Nom. दुहिता—(तृ). [g] All preceding terms for a son signify, in the feminine, a daughter, viz. आत्मजा, तनया, सूनुः, सुता, पुत्री, पुत्रिका or पुत्रका.

Offspring, male or female.	ऽपत्यं[n] तोकं[n] (तयोः समे)
A legitimate son. a	(स्वजाते त्वौ)[1m] रसोरस्यौ[m b]
Father.	तात[m] (स्तु) जनकः[m] पिता[2m]
Mother.	29. जनयित्री[f c] प्रसू[3f]र्माता[4f] जननी[f]
Sister.	भगिनी[f d] स्वसा[5f]
Husband's sister.	ननान्दा[6f e] (तु स्वसा पत्युः)
Grand-daughter. f	नप्त्री[f g] पौत्री[f h] सुतात्मजा[f]
Husband's brother's wife.	30. (भार्यास्तु भ्रातृवर्गस्य) यातरः[f i] (स्युः परस्परम्)
Brother's wife.	प्रजावती[f] भ्रातृजाया[f]
Maternal uncle's wife.	मातुलानी[f] (तु) मातुली[f]
Mother-in-law.	31. (पतिपत्न्योः प्रसूः) श्वश्रूः[f]
Father-in-law.	श्वशुर[m] (स्तु पिता तयोः)
Paternal uncle.	(पितुर्भ्राता) पितृव्यः[m] (स्यान्)
Maternal uncle.	(मातुर्भ्राता तु) मातुलः[m]
Wife's brothers.	32. श्यालाः[m j] (स्युर्भ्रातरः पत्न्याः)

---

[1] त्वौ—. [2] —तृ. [3] —सूः [4] मातृ. [5] —सृ. [6] —न्दृ.

[a] By a woman of the same tribe with her husband. [b] औरसः and उरस्यः. Some write औरस्यः. [c] Also जनित्री. [d] Likewise भग्नी. [e] Or ननन्दा (—न्दृ). Also नन्दिनी. [f] Either in the male or female line. [g] And नप्ता (—प्तृ), a grandson or grand-daughter. [h] Generally restricted to the son's daughter. Sing. याता (—तृ). [j] Sing. श्यालः. Also स्यालः.

m b m c

(स्वामिनो) देवृ देवरौ — Husband's brother. a

m m d

स्वस्रीयो भागिनेयः (स्यात्) — Sister's son.

m e m

जामाता दुहितुः पतिः — Daughter's husband.

m f 1 m

33. पितामहः पितृपिता — Father's father.

m g

(तत्पिता) प्रपितामहः — His father.

2 m h

(मातुर्) मातामहा (द्यैवं) — Maternal grandfather.

m i 3 m

सपिण्डा (स्तु) सनाभयः — Kinsmen

m m j m 4 m

34. समानोदर्य्य सोदर्य्य सगर्भ्य सहजाः (समाः) — A brother of the whole blood.

m m m m m 5 m

सगोत्र बांधव ज्ञाति बन्धु स्व स्वजनाः (समाः) — A distant kinsman.

n

35. ज्ञातेयं — Relationship.

f

बन्धुता (तेषां क्रमाद्भावसमूहयोः) — An aggregate of kinsmen

m m 6 m 7 m

धवः प्रियः पतिर्भर्त्ता — A husband.

8 m

जार (स्तु) पपतिः (समौ) — A paramour.

m

36. (अमृते जारजः) कुण्डो — An adulterine.

1—तृ. 2—ह. 3—ण्ड. 4—ज. 5—न.
6 पति. 7 भर्तृ. 8 उ—.

a Usually restricted to the younger brother. But some apply the first term to the elder brother; and the second to the younger. b Nom. देवा. Also देवः (—व). c Likewise देवरः. d Fem. स्वस्रीया and भागिनेयी; sister's daughter. e Also यामाता (—तृ). f Fem. पितामही, a grandmother. g Fem. प्रपितामही, a great-grandmother. h So प्रमातामहः, maternal great-grandfather. i Sing. सपिण्डः. j Also सोदरः and सहोदरः.

A widow's bastard.		*m* a (मृते भर्त्तरि) गोलकः
A brother's son.		*m* b 1 *m* भ्रात्रीयो भ्रातृजो
Brother and sister.		*m* du. *m* du. भ्रातृभगिन्यौ भ्रातराव् (उभौ)
Father and mother.	37.	*m* du. *m* du. *m* du. मातापितरौ पितरौ मातरपितरौ (च तौ)
Husband's or wife's father and mother		*m* du. *m* du. श्वश्रूश्वशुरौ श्वशुरौ
Son and daughter.		*m* du. पुत्रौ (पुत्रश्च दुहिता च)
Husband and wife	38.	*m* du. *m* du. *m* du. *m* du. दम्पती जम्पती जायापती भार्य्यापती (च तौ)
The womb. c		*m* *m* d *mn* *mn* गर्भाशयो जरायुः(स्याद्)उल्बं (च)कललो(ऽस्त्रियाम्)
The last month of gestation.	39.	*m* *m* सूतिमासो वैजननो
A fetus.		*m* *m* गर्भो भ्रूणो (इमौ समौ)
A eunuch.		*f* c *m* f *mn* *m* *n* तृतीया प्रकृतिः शण्ढः क्लीबं पण्डो नपुंसकम्
Childhood. g	40.	*n* *n* *n* शिशुत्वं शैशवं बाल्यं
Youth or manhood.		*n* *n* तारुण्यं यौवनं (समे)

1—ज.

[a] Or गोलः. [b] Likewise भ्रातृव्यः. [c] Some restrict the last, others the two last, to signify the embryo. [d] Also जरायुः, (—स्). [e] The compound term is properly तृतीयप्रकृतिः. [f] And षण्ढः or शण्डः. Some add सण्डः. [g] To the age of sixteen.

n n
(स्यात्) स्थाविरं (तु) वृद्धत्वं — Old age. a

m n b
वृद्धसंघे (ऽपि) वार्द्धकम् — An assemblage of old men.

n
41. पलितं (जरसा शौक्ल्यं केशादौ) — Greyness of hair. c

f f
विस्रसा जरा — Decrepitude.

f d f f f e
(स्याद्) उत्तानशया डिम्भा स्तनपा (च) स्तनन्धयी — An infant.

m g m
42. बाल (स्तु स्यान्) माणवको — A child. f

m 1 m 2 m
वयस्थस्तरुणो युवा — A young man. h

3 m m m m m 4 m
प्रवयाः स्थविरो वृद्धो जीनो जीर्णो जरन्न(ऽपि) — An old man.

5 m 6 m 7 m
43. वर्षीयान् दशमी ज्यायान् — One very aged.

m 8 m i m
पूर्वज (स्त्व्) अग्रियो ऽग्रजः — Elder brother; first born.

9 m m j m k m m
जघन्यजे (स्युः) कनिष्ठ यवीयो ऽवरजा ऽनुजाः — Younger brother.

m m m l
44. अमांसो दुर्बलश्छातो — Feeble; thin.

---

1 त—. 2—न्. 3—स्. 4 जरत्. 5—यस्. 6—न्. 7—यस्. 8 अ—. 9—ज.

[a] After seventy in men, or after fifty in women. [b] Also वार्धक्यं. The term likewise signifies old age. [c] Or पलितः, grey-haired. [d] Or, masc. उत्तानशयः, &c. For this and following (to v. 49) admit the three genders. [e] Some write स्तनन्धया. [f] Not exceedidg sixteen. [g] Fem. बाला. [h] Or one of the virile age, from sixteen to seventy. [i] Also अग्रिमः, अग्र्यः and अग्रीयः. [j] And कनीयान् (—यस्) or कन्यसः. [k] यवीयान् (—यस्). Likewise यविष्ठः. [l] छातः. Also शातः.

Strong; lusty.	बलवान्[1m] मांसलो[2m] ऽंसलः[3m]
Corpulent; pot-bellied.	तुन्दिल[m]स्तुन्दिक[m, a]स्तुन्दी[4m] बृहत्कुक्षिः[m] पिचण्डिलः[m, b]
Flat-nosed.	45. अवटीटो[m] ऽवनाट[m] (श्चा) ऽवभ्रटो[m] नतनासिके[5m]
Having much, or fine, hair.	केशवः[m] केशिकः[m] केशी[6m]
Flaccid.	वलिनो[m] वलिभः[m, c] (समौ)
Deformed. d	46. विकलाङ्ग[m] (स्तु) पोगण्डः[m, e]
A dwarf.	खर्वो[m] ह्रस्व[m] (श्च) वामनः[m, f]
Sharp-nosed	खरणाः[7m] (स्यात्) खरणसो[m]
Noseless.	विग्र[m] (स्तु) गतनासिकः[m]
Having a nose like a hoof.	47. खुरणाः[m] (स्यात्) खुरणसः[8m]
Bandy-legged. g.	प्रज्ञुः[m, h] प्रगतजानुकः[m]
Long shanked,	ऊर्द्ध्वज्ञु[m, j]रूर्द्ध्वजानुः[9m] (स्यात्)
Knock-kneed. k	संज्ञुः[m, l] संहतजानुकः[m]

---

[1]—त्. [2] मां—. [3] ऽंस—. [4]—न्. [5]—ष. [6]—न्. [7]—णस्. [8]—णस्. [9] ज्ञु—.

[a] तुन्दिकः or तुन्दिभः. [b] Also पिचण्डवान् (—त्). [c] Likewise वलिमान् (—त्). [d] Having a deficient, or a redundant, member; as a toe, or a finger, too many, or too few. [e] Also अपोगण्डः. [f] Fem. वामनी. [g] Or having the knees apart. [h] Also प्रज्ञः and प्रगतजानुः. [i] Or else thick-kneed. [j] And ऊर्द्ध्वज्ञः. [k] Or having the knees touching. [l] Likewise संज्ञः and संहतजानुः.

1 *m* *m* 48. (स्वाड्) एडे बधिरः	Deaf.
2 *m* *m* a कुब्जे गडुलः	Hump-backed.
m *m* c कुकरे कुणिः	Having a crooked arm. b
m d 3 *m* पृश्निरल्पतनौ	Small, short, or thin.
m *m* e श्रोणः पङ्गौ	A cripple.
m f *m* मुण्ड (स्तु.) मुण्डिते	Bald ; close-shaved.
m *m* 49. बलिरः केकरे	Squint-eyed.
m *m* खोडे खञ्ज	Lame.
g (त्रिषु जराऽवराः)	
m *m* 4 *m* जटुलः कालकः पिप्लुस्	A freckle or mark.
m 5 *m* तिलकस्तिलकालकः	A mole or spot. h

1—ड. 2 कुब्ज. 3 पृ—नु. 4 —प्लु. 5 ति—.

a And गण्डुलः. b Or a withered one. c Also कूणिः and कोणिः. d Likewise पृष्णिः. e पंगुः. Fem. पंगूः. f Fem. मुण्डा. g The preceding (from v. 41) vary the gender with that of the subject. h Or a person freckled or having moles.

SECTION II.

Health. 1. अनामयं (स्यात्) आरोग्यं

Physicking. चिकित्सा रुक्प्रतिक्रिया

Medicament. भेषजौषध भैषज्यान्यगदो जायु (रित्यपि)

A disease. 2. (स्त्री) रुग्रुजा (चोप) पताप रोग व्याधि गदामयाः

Pulmonary consumption. (पुमान्) यक्ष्मा क्षयः शोषः

Catarrh. प्रतिश्याय (स्तु.) पीनसः

Sneezing. 3. (स्त्री) क्षुत् क्षुतं क्षवः (पुंसि)

Cough. कास (स्तु.) क्षवथुः (पुमान्)

Intumescence. शोफ (स्तु.) श्वयथुः शोथः

Kibe.[e] पादस्फोटो विपादिका

Blotch. 4. किलासं सिध्म

Scab. कच्छ्वां (तु) पाम पामा विचर्चिका

---

[1] औ—. [2]—ज्य. [3]—द—. [4]रुज. [5]तु—. [6]आ—. [7]—न्. [8]—त्. [9]—न्. [10]—न.

[a] Likewise अयक्ष्मा (—न्) or अयक्ष्मः (—क्ष्म); and राजयक्ष्मा (—न्) or राजयक्ष्म (—न्). [b] Also प्रतिश्या and प्रतिश्यायः. [c] Likewise अपीनसः and पिनसः. [d] Also कासः. [e] A blister or sore on the foot. [f] Or सिध्मं. [g] कच्छूः. [h] पामा (—मन् and —मा) du. पामानौ and पामे.

f *f* *f* a

कण्डूः खर्जूः (च) कण्डूया — Itch.

m *mfn* b

विस्फोटः पिटक (स्त्रिषु) — Boil.

m f *n* c 1 *n*

5. व्रणो (ऽस्त्रियाम्) ईर्म्ममरुः — Sore or wound.

m

(क्लीबे) नाडीव्रणः (पुमान्) — Ulcer.

m *n*

कोठो मण्डलकं — Sort of leprosy. d

n *n* e

कुष्ठं श्वित्रे — Leprosy.

2 *n* 3 *n* f

दुर्नामकाऽर्शसी — Hemorrhoids.

m *m*

6. आनाह (स्तु) विबन्धः (स्याद्) — Epistasis. g

f h *f*

ग्रहणीरुक् प्रवाहिका — Diarrhœa.

f i *f* *f*

प्रच्छर्दिका वमि (च स्त्री पुमांस्तु) वमथुः (समाः) — Vomiting.

f k *m* l *m* m *m* n

7. (व्याधिभेदा) विद्रधिः (स्त्री) ज्वर मेह भगन्दराः — Various diseases. j

---

[1] अदस. [2] —का. [3] —स.

[a] Also कण्डूतिः. [b] Fem. पिटका:. Also पिटकः —का —कं. [c] Likewise, masc. ईर्मः. [d] White leprosy with round spots. [e] And श्वेतं or श्वेत्रं. [f] Likewise अर्शः (—र्स) Also masc. अर्शः (—र्श.) [g] Whether Ischury or Constipation. [h] Also ग्रहणी and ग्रहणिः. [i] Likewise, neut. छर्दिः (—स्); and fem. छर्दिः(—र्द) or छर्दी, &c. [j] Severally named in the text. [k] An abscess; an internal one. [l] Fever. [m] Also प्रमेहः, Gonorrhœa. Some interpret it simple gonorrhœa or seminal weakness; others, diabetes. [n] Fistula in ano.

f a n b

अश्मरी मूत्रकृच्छ्रं (स्यात्)

c

(पूर्वे शुक्रावधेस्त्रिषु)

m e 1 m 2 m f 3 m m

A Physician. d — 8. रोगहार्यगदंकारो भिषग्वैद्यौ चिकित्सके

m f n g m f n m f n m f n h

Recoverd from sickness. — वार्त्तो निरामयः कल्य उल्लाघो (निर्गतो गदात्)

m f n m f n i

Emaciated or weak. — 9. ग्लान ग्लास्नू

4 m f n m f n m f n m f n

Diseased. — आमयावी विकृतो व्याधितो ऽपटुः

m f n m f n m f n

आतुरो ऽभ्यमितो ऽभ्यांतः

m f n m f n

Scabby. — (समौ) पामन कच्छुरौ

m f n j 5 m f n

Afflicted with herpes. — 10. दद्रुणो दद्रुरोगी (स्याद्)

m f n m f n

—with hemorrhoids. — अर्शोरोगयुतो ऽर्शसः

---

[1] ग—. [2] द्यावे. [3] वैद्य. [4] —न. [5] —न.

[a] Stone or gravel. [b] Strangury. Some make the two last terms synonymous, as signifying dysury. [c] The following terms (inclusively to v. 12) admit the three genders. [d] Or, adjectively, 'practising medicine.' [e] रोगहारी (—न्.) [f] भिषक् (—ज्.) [g] Fem. वार्त्ता. [h] Some restrict the last term to convalescent or recently well from disease. [i] ग्लास्नुः [j] Also दद्रुघ्नः. Fem. दद्रूः, दद्रुः, दद्रूः or दद्रुः, herpes.

1 mfn 2 mfn
वातकी वातरोगी (स्यात्) — Afflicted with gout or rheumatism.

mfn mfn
सातिसारोऽतिसारकी — —with dysentery.

mfn mfn mfn mfn
11. (स्युः) क्लिन्नाक्षे चुल्लचिल्लपिल्लाः (क्लिन्नेऽक्ष्णि चाप्यमी)[a] — Blear-eyed

mfn 3 mfn
उन्मत्त उन्मादवति — Insane.

mfn mfn 4 mfn
श्लेष्मलः श्लेष्मणः कफी — Phlegmatic.

mfn
12. न्युब्जो (भुग्ने रुजा) — Gibbous, from disease. b

mfn c mfn
(वृद्धनाभौ) तुण्डिलतुण्डिभौ — Having an elevated navel.

5 mfn mfn
किलासी सिध्मलः — Having blotches.

mfn 6 mfn d
अन्धोऽदृक् — Blind.

mfn mfn mfn
मूर्च्छाले मूर्त्तमूर्च्छितौ — Fainting.

n e 7 n n f n n n g
13. शुक्रं तेजोरेतसी (च) बीजवीर्येन्द्रियाणि (च) — Seed.

m n
मायुः पित्तं — Bile.

m 8 m
कफः श्लेष्मा — Phlegm.

1—न्. 2—न्. 3—त्. 4—न्. 5—न्.
6—श्. 7—स्. 8—न्.

[a] These terms, in the neuter gender, signify the diseased eye. [b] The word also signifies a disease occasioning a gibbosity of the back. [c] Also तुन्दिलः. [d] अदृक् (—श्). [e] The preceding (from v. 8.) admit three genders, being used adjectively. [f] Sing. रेतः (—स्). [g] Sing. इन्द्रियं.

The skin. — (स्त्रियां तु) त्वगसृग्धरा [f a] [f b]

Flesh. — 14. पिशितं [n] तरसं [n] मांसं [n] पललं [n] क्रव्यम् [n] आमिषम् [n c]

Dry flesh. — उत्तप्तं [n] शुष्कमांसं [n] (स्याद्) वल्लूरं [m f n d] (त्रिलिङ्गकम्)

Blood. — 15. रुधिरे [n] ऽसृक् [n c] लोहिता [1 n] ऽस्र [n f] रक्त [n] क्षतज [n] शोणितम् [n]

The heart.[g] — बुक्का [m f n h] ऽग्रमांसं [n i] हृदयं [n] हृत् [2 n]

The serum of flesh.[j] — मेद [n k] (स्तु) वपा [f] वसा [f]

Muscles at the nape of the neck. — 16. (पश्चाद्ग्रीवा शिरा) मन्या [f]

A nerve, tendon or gut.[l] — नाडी [f m] (तु) धमनिः [f n] सिरा [f o]

The bladder. — तिलकं [3 n p] क्लोम

The brain.[q] — मस्तिष्कं [n] गोर्दं [n]

---

[1] लो—. [2] —त् or —द्. [3] —न्.

[a] त्वक् (—च्) and त्वचा or neut. त्वचं. [b] असृग्धरा or असृग्धारा. [c] आमिषं and अमिषं. [d] Fem. वल्लूरा. [e] असृक् (—ज्). [f] some add अस्रं. [g] Certain writers restrict the two first words to signify the heart; and the two last the thorax. [h] बुक्कः or बुक्का (—न्). Fem बक्का or बुक्की. Neut. बुक्कं or बुक्क (—न्). Also हक्कः, हक्का, हक्कं, and बृक्कः, बूक्का, बृक्कं, or हक्का, हक्क (—न्), and बृक्का, बृक्क (—न्). [i] Likewise बुक्काग्रमांसं. [j] Some interpret this the marrow of bones. [k] मेदः (—स्). Or masc. मेदः(—द). [l] Or any tubular vessel of the human body. [m] And नाडिः. [n] Or धमनी. [o] Also शिरा. [p] Also क्लोमं (—न). [q] Some make the preceding terms synonymous with these.

n mn
किट्टं मलो (ऽस्त्रियाम्) — An excretion.[a]

n 1mnb
17. अन्त्रं पुरीतत् — Entrails.

m 2mc
गुल्म (स्तु) प्लीहा (पुंस्य) — The spleen.

fd
(थ) वस्नसा — A tendon or muscle.

f
स्नायुः (स्त्रियां)

n 3n
कालखण्ड यकृती (तु समे इमे) — The liver.

fe f f
18. सृणिका स्यन्दिनी लाला — Saliva.

ff
दूषिका (नेत्रयोर्मलम्) — Rheum of the eyes.

n m
मूत्रं प्रस्राव — Urine.

m m m mg
उच्चारा ऽवस्करौ शमलं शकृत् — Fæces.

n n mn f fh
19. गूथं पुरीषं वर्चस्क (मस्त्री) विष्ठा विशौ (स्त्रियौ)

m mn
(स्यात्) कर्परः कपालो (ऽस्त्री) — The skull; cranium.

n n 4n
कीकसं कुल्यमस्थि (च) — Any bone.

m
20. (स्याच्छरीरास्थ्नि) कंकाल: — The skeleton.

1—त्. 2—न्. 3—त्. 4 थ—.

[a] Either excrement or excrescence; twelve are enumerated; (some count nine only:) as serum, seed, blood, marrow, urine, fæces, earwax, nails, phlegm, tears, rheum and sweat. See Menu. c.5.v.135. [b] Likewise परितत्. [c] Or प्लिहा (—न्). Also fem. प्लीहा. [d] Likewise स्नसा. [e] Or सृणीका. [f] And दूषी or दूषीका. [g] And शकन्. [h] Sing विट् (विश् or विष्). Also विषा.

The back-bone. — (पृष्ठास्थ्नि तु) कशेरुका [f a]

The skull; or bones of the head. — शिरोस्थ्नि (तु) करोटिः (स्त्री) [1 n, f b]

A rib. — पार्श्वास्थनि (तु) पर्शुका [2 n, f c]

A limb or member. — 21. अङ्गं प्रतीको ऽवयवो ऽपघनो [n m m m]

The body — (ऽथ) कलेवरम् [n]

गात्रं वपुः संहननं शरीरं वर्ष्म विग्रहः [n 3n n n 4n m]

22. कायो देहः (क्लीबपुंसोः स्त्रियां) मूर्त्तिस्तनु स्तनूः [m m n f f d 5f]

Point of the foot. — पादाग्रं प्रपदं [n n]

A foot. — पादः पद् ङ्घ्रिश्चरणो (ऽस्त्रियाम्) [m m e m f 6 m n]

The ancles. — 23. (तद्ग्रन्थी) घुटिके गुल्फौ [f g m n]

A heel. — (पुमान्) पार्ष्णि (र्द्वयोः) [n f]

A leg. — जङ्घा (तु) प्रसृता [f f]

A knee. — जानूरुपर्वा ऽष्ठीवद् (ऽस्त्रियाम्) [m n h 7 m n 8 m n]

A thigh. — 24. सक्थि (क्लीबे पुमान्) ऊरुस् [n 9 m]

1—नृ. 2—नृ. 3—स्. 4—नृ. 5—तनू. 6अ—. 7ज—नृ. 8—तृ. 9—रु.

[a] And कशेरुका. [b] Or करोटी. Also neuter करोटं. [c] Likewise पार्शुका and पर्शुः. [d] तनुः (—न and—नुस्). [e] पत् (—द्) ;and पदः (—द): also neut. पादं and पदं. [f] अंह्रिः and अंघ्रिः. Some make these neuter likewise. [g] Sing. घुटिका and घटिः or घुटी Also घुटः. [h] Masc. जानुः, ऊरुपर्वा, अष्ठीवान्. Neut. जानु, ऊरुपर्वं, अष्ठीवत्.

m (तत्संधिः पुंसि) वंक्षणः	The groin.
n 1 *n* *m* गुदं (तु) पानं पायु (र्ना)	The anus.
m f a वस्ति (र्नाभेरधो द्वयोः)	The abdomen.
m *n* c *f* d *f* e *f* 25. कटो (ना) श्रोणिफलकं कटिः श्रोणी ककुद्मती	The hip and loins. b
m (पश्चान्) नितम्बः (स्त्रीकट्याः)	A woman's buttocks.
(क्लीबे तु) जघनं (पुरः)	Mons veneris.
n f 26. (कूपकौ तु नितम्बस्थौ द्वयहीने) कुकुंदरे	Cavities of the loins.
2 *f* *m* g (स्त्रियां) स्फिचौ कटिप्रोथाव्	The buttocks.
उपस्थो (वक्ष्यमाणयोः)	Parts of generation. h
n *m f* i 27. भगं योनि (र्द्वयोः)	Vulva.
m *m* *n* j शिश्नो मेढ्रो मेहन शेफसी	Penis.
m *m* l *m* मुष्को ऽण्डकोषो वृषणः	The scrotum. k
n (पृष्ठवंशाधरे) त्रिकम्	The end of the spine. m

1 ष—. 2—थ्.

a Also fem. वस्ती. b Some distinguish the two first terms as signifying the hip. c Likewise श्रोणीफलं. d And कटी. e श्रोणिः or श्रोणी. f Also ककुन्दरं. g Sing. कटिप्रोथः. Likewise कटिः and प्रोथः. h Of either sex. i And fem. योनी. j शेफः (—स्) or शेपः (—स्). Also masc. शेफः (—फ), शेपः (—प) ; and शेवः. k Also the testicles. l And अण्डकोशः. m Consisting of three bones, Os sacrum, &c.

m a   m b   m n 1 n   n

The belly. 28. पिचण्ड कुक्षी जठरोदरं तुन्दं

m   m

The paps. c   स्तनौ कुचौ

m n d   n

A nipple.   चूचुकं (तु) कुचाग्रं (स्यान्)

f n f   n

The bosom. e   (न ना) क्रोडं भुजान्तरम्

2 n   n   n g

29. उरो वत्सं (च) वक्षश् (च)

n

The back.   पृष्ठं (तु चरमं तनोः)

m h   3 n   m n i

A shoulder; scapula.   स्कन्धो भुजशिरोऽंसो (ऽस्त्री)

n j

The collar bones.   (सन्धी तस्यैव) जत्रुणी

n   m k

The arm-pits. 30. बाहुमूले (उभे) कक्षौ

m n

A side.   पार्श्वं (मस्त्री तयोरधः)

m n   m n l   m n

The waist.   मध्यमं (चा) ऽवलग्नं (च) मध्यो (ऽस्त्री)

An arm.   (द्वौ परौ द्वयोः)

m f m   m f n   m   4 m o

31. भुज बाहू प्रवेष्टो दोः

m f p   m f q

An elbow.   (स्यात्) कफोणि (स्तु) कूर्परः

---

1 च—.   2—स्.   3—स्.   4—स्.

[a] Also पिचण्डः. [b] कुक्षिः and कुक्षः. [c] Sing. स्तनः, कुचः. [d] Also चुचुकं—कः. [e] Some separate the two first terms from the other three; distinguishing the breast between the shoulders (i. e. the first bone of the sternum) from the region of the Cartilago ensiformis. [f] Fem. क्रोडा. [g] वक्षः (—स्). [h] स्कंधः (—न्ध). Also neut. स्कंधः (—स्). [i] अंसः or अंसः. [j] Sing. जत्रु. [k] Sing. कक्षः. [l] Likewise विलग्नं. [m] Also fem. भुजा. [n] Masc. and fem. बाहुः. Also masc. बाहः. Fem. बाहा. [o] And fem. दोषा. [p] And कफणिः. Also fem. कफोणी and कफणी. [q] Fem. कूर्परा.

(अंसोपरि) प्रगण्डः[m] (स्यात्) — Humerus. [a]

प्रकोष्ठ[m] (स्तस्य चाप्यधः) — A fore arm.

32. (मणिबन्धादाकनिष्ठं करस्य) करभो[m] (बहिः) — Metacarpus. [b]

पञ्चशाखः[m] शयः[m c] पाणिस्[1 m] — A hand.

तर्जनी[f] (स्यात्) प्रदेशिनी[f d] — A fore finger.

33. अङ्गुल्यः[f e] करशाखाः[f] (स्युः) — Fingers.

(पुंस्य[2]) ङ्गुष्ठः[m] प्रदेशिनी[f] — The several fingers. [f]

मध्यमा[f]ऽनामिका[f g] (चापि) कनिष्ठा[f h] (चेति ताः क्रमात्)

34. पुनर्भवः[m i] कररुहो[m] नखो[m n]ऽ(स्त्री) नखरो[m n j]ऽ(स्त्रियाम्) — A nail.

प्रादेश[m k] ताल[m l] गोकर्णा[m m] (स्तर्जन्यादियुते तते) — A short span, of three kinds.

35. (अङ्गुष्ठे सकनिष्ठे स्याद्) वितस्ति[m f] (र्द्वादशाङ्गुलः) — A long span. [n]

1— षि. 2 षं—.

[a] From the shoulder to the elbow. [b] From the wrist to the little finger. [c] And शमः. [d] Or प्रदेशिनी. [e] Sing. अङ्गुलिः. Also अङ्गुली and अङ्गुरिः—री. Or अङ्गुलः and अङ्गुलं. [f] In their order; viz. the thumb, fore finger, middle finger, ring finger and little finger. [g] And अनामा. [h] Also कन्यसा, कनीनी, or कनीनिका. [i] Also पुनर्नवः. [j] Also fem. नखरा. [k] or प्रदेशः, from the tip of the thumb to that of the fore finger extended; Spithama. [l] To the tip of the middle finger. [m] गोकर्णः to the tip of the ring finger. [n] From the tip of the thumb to that of the little finger; a measure of twelve fingers.

The palm with extended fingers.
m a *m* b *m*
(पाणौ) चपेट प्रतल प्रहस्ता (विस्तृताङ्गुलौ)

Both such palms joined.
m c d
36. (द्वौ संहतौ) संहतलः (प्रतलौ वामदक्षिणौ)

The palm bent. e
m f
(पाणिर्निकुब्जः) प्रसृतस्

Both such palms joined.
m
(तौ युताव्) अञ्जलिः (पुमान्)

A cubit. g
m
37. (प्रकोष्ठे विस्तृतकरे) हस्तो

A short cubit. h
(मुष्ट्या तु बद्धया)
m f
रत्निः (स्याद्)

An intermediate one. i
m f
अरत्नि(स्तु निष्कनिष्ठेन मुष्टिना)

A fathom. j
m
38. व्यामो (बाह्वोः सकरयोस्ततयो स्तिर्यगन्तरम्)

The measure of a man's reach, k
m f n l
(ऊर्ध्वविस्तृतदोः पाणिपृमाने) पौरुषं (त्रिषु)
पौ

The throat.
m f n m *m*
39. कण्ठो गलो

The neck.
1 *f* *f* 2 *f* n
(ऽथ) ग्रीवायां शिरोधिः कन्धरे (त्यपि)

---

1 ग्रीवा. 2 —रा.

a Also चपेटः and चपटः. b Likewise तलं. c Or सिंहतलः. d By omitting the termination of the preceding term, this is made by some synonymous with it; in a less restricted sense. e As if to hold a liquid. f प्रसृतः. Also प्रसृतिः. g From the elbow to the tip of the middle finger; a measure of twenty-four fingers. h From the elbow to the extremity of the fist. i From the elbow to the tip of the little finger. j The space between the ends of the fingers, when the arms are extended; Orgya. k Equal to the height, to which he reaches, when elevating both arms with the fingers extended. l Fem. पौरुषी. m कण्ठः, कण्ठी or कण्ठा, कण्ठं. n Some add masc. कंधरः.

कम्बुग्रीवा [f] (त्रिरेखा सा)	One streaked with three lines. a
अवटुर्[mf] घाटा[1f] कृकाटिका[f]	Back of the neck. b
40. वक्त्रा[n]स्ये[2n] वदनं[n] तुण्ड[n]माननं[3n] लपनं[n] मुखम्[n]	The mouth. c
(क्लीबे) घ्राणं[n] गन्धवहा[f] घोणा[f] नासा[fd] (च) नासिका	The nose.
41. ओष्ठा[m]धरौ[me] (तु) रदनच्छदौ[m] दशनवाससी[4n]	The lips.
(अधः स्यात्) चिबुकं[nf]	The chin.
गण्डौ[m] कपोलौ[m]	The cheeks. g
(तत्परो) हनुः[mfh]	The jaw.
42. रदना[m] दशना[mn] दन्ता[mj] रदाः[5m]	Teeth. i
तालु[n] (तु) काकुदम्[n]	The palate.
रसज्ञा[f] रसना[fk] जिह्वा[fl]	The tongue.
(प्रान्तावोष्ठस्य) सृक्कणी[nm]	The corners of the mouth.
43. ललाट[n]मलिकं[mn] गोधिः[6m]	The forehead.

---

[1] घा—. [2] आस्य. [3] घा—. [4] —सू. [5] —द. [6] गोधि.

[a] Like a shell : it is reckoned a mark of great destiny. [b] Or, according to another interpretation, the raised or straight part of the neck. [c] Also the face. [d] And नसा or नस्या. [e] ओष्ठौ, अधरौ and ओष्ठाधरौ ; for properly the first (sing. ओष्ठः) is the upper lip ; and the second (sing. अधरः) signifies the lower lip. [f] Also चिबुः. [g] Sing. गण्डः, कपोलः, [h] Also fem. हनूः. [i] Sing. रदनः ; दशनः—न°, &c. [j] Sing. दंत. Some add दत्. [k] Or रसज्ञा. Also neut. रसनं°. [l] And masc. जिह्वः. [m] Sing. सृक्व (—क्), सृक्क (—क्), or सृक्वि (—क्) ; and सृक्वं (—क्कं), सृक्वं or सृक्वि ; also fem. सृक्वणी. [n] अलिकं. Likewise अलीकं.

U

The eye-brows. — (ऊर्द्ध्वं दृग्भ्यां) भ्रुवौ (स्त्रियाम्) [1 f a]

Space between the eye-brows. — कूर्च (मस्त्री) (भ्रुवोर्मध्यं) [m n]

Pupil of the eye. — तारका (ऽक्ष्णः) कनीनिका [f, f]

An eye. — 44. लोचनं नयनं नेत्रमीक्षणं चक्षुरक्षिणी [n, n, n, 2n, n b, n c]

दृग्दृष्टी (च) [3f, f]

A tear. — ऽश्रु नेत्राम्बु रोदनं (च) ऽस्रमश्रु (च) [n, n, n, n d, 4 n]

The outer corners of the eyes. — 45. अपांगौ (नेत्रयोरन्तौ) [m e]

A glance or side-look. — कटाक्षो (ऽपांगदर्शने) [m f]

An ear. — कर्णं शब्दग्रहौ श्रोत्रं श्रुतिः (स्त्री) श्रवणं श्रवः [m, 5 m, n g, f, m n, 6 n h]

The head. — 46. उत्तमांगं शिरः शीर्षं मूर्द्धा (ना) मस्तको (ऽस्त्रियाम्) [n, 7 n i, n, 8 m, m n j]

Hair. — चिकुरः कुंतलो बालः कचः केशः शिरोरुहः [m, m, m, m, m, m]

Head of hair. — 47. (तद्वृन्दे) कैशिकं कैश्यम् [n, n]

Curls. — अलकाश्चूर्णकुंतलाः [m n k, 9 m]

---

1 भ्रू. 2 ईं—. 3 दृश्. 4 चक्षु. 5 —ह्. 6 —स्. 7 —स्. 8 —न्. 9 चू—.

a Sing. भ्रूः. b चक्षुः (—स्). Some add चक्षु (—क्षु). c Sing. अक्षि. Some add अक्षं. d Or अस्रं. e Sing. अपांगः. f Also कटाक्षः. g Or श्रोत्रं. h Likewise masc. श्रवः (—व). i Also masc. शिरः (र). j Likewise मस्तः. k Sing. अलकः —कं.

(ते ललाटे) भ्रमरकाः [m]	The same on the forehead.
काकपक्षः [m] शिखण्डकः [m b]	Locks, left at the tonsure. a
48. कबरी [f d] केशवेशः [m]	A braid or tress. c
(ऽथ) धम्मिल्लः [m] (संयताः कचाः)	Braided hair. e
शिखा [f] चूडा [f] केशपाशी [f]	A lock left on the crown of the head.
(व्रतिनस्तु) जटा [f] सटा [f f]	An ascetic's clotted hair.
49. वेणिः [f] प्रवेणिः [f h]	Unornamented hair. g
शीर्षण्य [m] शिरस्यौ [1 m] (विशदे कचे)	Clean and unentangled hair.
पाशः [m] पक्ष [m] (श्च) हस्त [m] (श्च कलापार्थाः कचात्परे)	Much, or ornamented hair. i
50. तनूरुहं [m n j] रोम [2 n] लोम [3 n]	Hair of the body.
तद्वृद्धौ श्मश्रु [4 n] (पुंमुखे)	The beard.

[1]—स. [2]—न्. [3]—न्. [4]—श्रु or —श्रुन्.

[a] Interpretations differ: it is explained, three (some say, five) locks left at the solemn tonsure of children, or of the military class in particular; or else any lock left on the head. [b] Or शिखाण्डकः and शिखण्डः. [c] A mode of dressing the hair. [d] And masc. कबरः or neut.—रं. [e] Tied round the head; or with flowers intermixed, and covered with pearls, &c. [f] Some add छटा. [g] As worn by women in the absence of their husbands. [h] Also वेणी and प्रवेणी. [i] The terms are used in composition with one signifying hair; as केशपाशः, केशपक्षः, &c. [j] Likewise तनूरुहः,—हं.

SECTION III.

Dress or embellishment.

m m a n l n n

1. आकल्पवेषौ नेपथ्यं प्रतिकर्म प्रसाधनम्।

b

(दश ते त्रिषु)

Adorned.

2 m f n m f n m f n c

ऽलंकर्त्ता ऽलंकरिष्णु (श्च) मण्डितः

m f n m f n m f n m f n

2. प्रसाधितो ऽलंकृत (श्च) भूषित (श्च) परिष्कृतः

m f n d 3 m f n 4 m f n

Elegant.

विभ्राड्भ्राजिष्णु रोचिष्णु

f f e

Act of adorning.

भूषा (तु स्यात्) अलंक्रिया

Ornaments; jewels or trinkets.

m 5 n m n f

3. अलङ्कार (स्त्व्) आभरणं परिष्कारो विभूषणम्

मण्डनं (च)

n h m n

A crest. g

(अथ) मुकुटं किरीटं (पुन्नपुंसकम्)

1—मु. 2—र्त्तृ. 3 भ्रा—. 4—ष्णु. 5 वा—.

a Or वेषः. b The ten following nouns admit the three genders. c Some restrict the two first terms to signify a person disposed to decoration: others make the three first signify one who adorns. d Nom. विभ्राट् (—ज्). e Some omit the last three lines. f Also भूषणं. g An ornament of the head; worn upon a diadem or tiara. h Or मकुट.

4. चूडामणिः[m] शिरोरत्नं[n]	A gem on the crest.
तरलो[m] (हारमध्यगः)	The middle gem of a string.
बालपाश्या[f] पारितथ्या[f]	A trinket for the hair. a
पत्रपाश्या[f] ललाटिका[f]	—for the forehead. b
5. कर्णिका[f] तालपत्रं[n] (स्यात्)	—for the ear. c
कुण्डलं[n] कर्णवेष्टनम्[n]	An ear ring.
ग्रैवेयकं[n] कण्ठभूषा[f]	A collar. d
लम्बनं[n] (स्यात्) ललन्तिका[f]	A necklace. f
6. (स्वर्णैः) प्रालम्बिका[f]	A golden one.
(ऽथो) रःसूत्रिका[1 f] (मौक्तिकैः कृता)	One of Pearls.
हारो[m] मुक्तावली[f]	A garland of pearls, &c.
देवच्छन्दो[m] (ऽसौ) शतयष्टिकः[m]	One composed of 100 strings. g
7. (हारभेदा यष्टिभेदात्) गुच्छ[m i] गुच्छार्द्ध[m j] गोस्तनाः[m k]	Garlands of various sorts. h

¹ उ—.

ᵃ A plate, or a flat chain, of gold or silver, with or without jewels set in it; worn between the divided hair on the head. Some expound the first term a string of pearls binding the hair. ᵇ A jewel, or a golden or other trinket, worn on the forehead, below the partition of the hair; a star on the forehead. Some make these and the preceding terms synonymous. ᶜ A hollow cylinder thrust through the lobe of the ear. ᵈ Or short necklace. ᵉ Likewise ग्रैवेयं and ग्रैव°. ᶠ A loose one, reaching below the breast. ᵍ Some say 103. ʰ In their order: distinguished by the number of strings or rows. ⁱ Also गुच्छः. It consists of 32 rows. ʲ Or गुच्छार्धः. It contains 24 rows. ᵏ Composed either of 4 or of 34 strings.

m a m b

अर्द्धहारो माणवक

1 f

A single string. एकावल्ये(कयष्टिका)

f

One containing 27 pearls. 8. (सैव) नक्षत्रमाला (स्यात्सप्तविंशतिमौक्तिकः)

m m m n m n

A bracelet. c आवापकः पारिहार्य्यः कटको वलयो (ऽस्त्रियाम्)

m n 2 m n

Ornament of the arm. d 9. केयूरमङ्गदं (तुल्ये)

m n e 3 f

A finger-ring. अंगुलीयकमूर्मिका

4 f

A seal ring. (साक्षरा) शुक्तिमुद्रा (सा)

m n n

Ornament of the wrist. f कङ्कणं करभूषणम्

f f h f f i

A woman's girdle. g 10. (स्त्रीकट्यां) मेखला कांची सप्तकी रसना (तथा)

n

(क्लीवे) सारसनं (चा)

m f n j

A man's belt. (ऽथ पुंस्कट्यां) शृंखलं (त्रिषु)

n 5 m l 6 m n m n

Ornament of the feet. k 11. पादांगदं तुलाकोटिर्मञ्जीरो नूपुरो (ऽस्त्रियाम्)

1—डो. 2 अं—. 3 ज—. 4 अं—. 5—टि.

6 म—.

[a] Including 64 strings. [b] Comprising 20 rows. [c] Of gold, or of conch, &c. [d] Worn above the elbow. [e] Some add अंगुरीयकं. [f] A broad solid ring with or without pearls, &c. set on it. [g] The terms are here stated as synonymous; but they signify belts of various kinds, differing in the number of rows or strings. [h] Also कांचिः. [i] And रशना. [j] Fem. शृङ्खला. [k] Rings for the toes. Some distinguish the two last terms as signifying a distinct ornament. Or fem. तुलाकोटिः and तुलाकोटी.

हंसकः[m] पादकटकः[m]

किङ्किणी[f a] क्षुद्रघण्टिका[f] — Bells or tinkling ornaments.

12. (त्वक्फलकृमिरोमाणि) वस्त्रयोनिर्[1 f] — Materials of cloth. b

(दश त्रिषु)[c]

वाल्कं[m f n e] (क्षौमादि) — Made of bark. d

फालं[m f n] (तु) कार्पासं[m f n] बादरं[m f n] (च तत्) — Made of cotton.

13. कौशेयं[m f n f] कृमिकोशोत्थं[m f n] — Silken.

राङ्कवं[m f n g] मृगरोमजम्[m f n] — Woollen

अनाहतं[m f n] निष्प्रवाणि[m f n] तन्त्रकं[m f n] (च) नवाम्बरे[2 n h] — New and unbleached cloth.

14. (तत्स्याद्) उद्गमनीयं[n] (यद्धौतयोर्वस्त्रयोर्युगम्) — A pair of bleached cloths.

पत्रोर्णं[n] धौतकौशेयं[n] — Bleached silk. i

बहुमूल्यं[n] महाधनम्[n j] — Any thing precious.

1—नि. 2—र.

[a] Or किङ्कणी. [b] Of four kinds: 1st. bark of plants, as Rushy Crotalaria, Linum, hemp hibiscus, &c. 2d. fruit, viz. cotton; 3d. insects, viz. silk; 4th. hair and wool. [c] The ten following terms (Some say eleven; others say ten omitting two intermediate compound terms;) admit the three genders. [d] As linen, &c. Thus क्षौमं, linen. Fem. क्षौमी. [e] Fem. वाल्की. [f] Also कौषेयं. [g] Made of the hair of the *Rancu* (stated to be a sort of deer), or any other hair or wool. [h] Some include this among adjectives. [i] Or wild silk. [j] Some include this and the preceding terms among adjectives.

n a n

Wove silk. 15. क्षौमं दुकूलं (स्यात्)

m f n b m f n c

A veil or mantle. (द्वे तु) निवीतं प्रावृतं (त्रिषु)

m f pl. m f pl. d

Ends of a cloth. (स्त्रियां बहुत्वे वस्त्रस्य) दशाः (स्युर्) वस्तयो (र्द्वयोः)

n l m e m f

Length. 16. दैर्घ्यमायाम आरोहः

m f

Width. परिणाहो विशालता

n n

Old cloth. पटच्चरं जीर्णवस्त्रं

m h m

Dirty or tattered cloth. g (समौ) नक्तक कर्पटौ

n 2 n 3 n i 4 n j n 5 n

Cloth. 17. वस्त्रमाच्छादनं वासश्चेलं वसनमंशुकम्

m m n l

Fine cloth. k सुचेलकः पटो (ऽस्त्री स्यात्)

m n m f n o

Coarse cloth. m वराशिः स्थूलशाटकः

---

[1] आ—. [2] वा—. [3] —स्. [4] चे—. [5] अं—.

[a] Also क्षोमं. [b] Or निवृतं. [c] Fem. निवीता, प्रावृता. [d] Also sing. वस्तिः. [e] Likewise fem. आयतिः. [f] Some read आनाहः. [g] Interpretations differ much. Some make these terms synonymos with the following : others explain them, a handkerchief, a rag, a night-shift, &c. [h] Likewise नक्तकः. [i] Also masc. वासः. [j] And fem. चेली. [k] These terms are also said to be synonymous with the preceding. [l] Also fem. पटिः and पटी ; but this is a diminutive, and properly signifies a particular sort of cloth. [m] Some make these and the preceding terms synonymous. [n] Likewise वराशः. [o] Fem स्थूलशाटिका.

mfn b *m* 18. निचोलः प्रच्छदपटः	A cover or wrapper. a
m 1*m* (समौ) रल्लककम्बलौ	A blanket.
n 2*n* 3*n* 4*n* अन्तरीयोपसंव्यान परिधानान्यधोंऽशुके	Lower garment.
m 5*m* *f* 19. (द्वौ) प्रावारोत्तरासंगौ (समौ) बृहतिका (तथा)	Upper garment.
n 6*n* संव्यानमुत्तरीयं (च)	
mf d *mf* चोलः कूर्पासकः (स्त्रियाः)	A bodice. c
m 20. नीशारः (स्यात्प्रावरणे हिमानिलनिवारणे)	A warm cloak.
mn (अर्द्धोरुकं वरस्त्रीणां स्याच्) चण्डातकं (मंशुकं)	A petticoat.
7 *mfn* e 21. (स्यात्त्रिष्वा) प्रपदीनं (तत्प्राप्नोत्याप्रपदं हि यत्)	A dress reaching to the feet.
mn 8*m* (अस्त्री) वितानमुल्लोचः	An awning.
n f दूष्या (द्यं वस्त्रवेश्मनि)	A tent.
f *f* g *f* h 22. प्रतिसीरा जवनिका (स्यात्) तिरस्करणी (च सा)	A screen or wall of cloth.
9*n* j 10*m* परिकर्माङ्गसंस्कारः	Embellishment of person. i

1—ल. 2—उ. 3—न. 4अ—क. 5उ—ग.
6उ—. 7आ—. 8उ—. 9—र्म. 10अं—.

a Also a sheet; or else the cover of a litter, &c. Likewise a veil. b And निचुलः. Fem. निचोली. c Or a jacket. d Fem. चोली. e Fem. आप्रपदीना. f दूष्यं. Some read दुष्यं. g Also यवनिका or यमनिका. h And तिरस्कारिणी. i Dress for cleanliness; or else ornament by sandal wood and perfumes. j Also प्रतिकर्म.

V

Cleaning of it. [a] — (स्नान्) मार्ष्टिर्मार्जना मृजा

Cleaning with perfumes. — 23. उद्वर्त्तनोत्सादने (द्वे समे)

Bathing. — आप्लाव आप्लवः

स्नानं

Perfuming. [c] — चर्चा (तु) चार्चिक्यं स्थासकः

Reviving a fragrancy. — (ऽथ) प्रबोधनम्

24. अनुबोधः

Painting the person. [e] — पत्रलेखा पत्राङ्गुलि (रिमे समे)

A circle on the forehead. — तमालपत्र तिलक चित्रकाणि विशेषकम्

25. (द्वितीयं च तुरीयं च न स्त्रियाम्)

Saffron. — (अथ) कुंकुमं

काश्मीरजन्मा ऽग्निशिखं वरं वाह्लीक पीतने

26. रक्त संकोच पिशुनं धीर लोहितचन्दनं

---

1 त्रा—. 2 त्त—. 3—क. 4—न्. 5—न्.

[a] By wiping; or by bathing, rubbing with oil and sandal wood. [b] Also उत्सादनं. [c] By plastering the whole person with sandal wood, &c. [d] Erroneously by some written अनुरोधः. [e] Delineations with saffron or with musk, &c. on the breast, cheeks, &c. [f] Also पत्रावली and other synonyma. [g] Or काश्मीरजन्म (—न्.) [h] Or वरं. Also वार. [i] Likewise वाह्लिकं and बल्हीकः. [j] And other terms signifying red or blood. [k] Also रक्तचन्दनं, &c.

लाक्षा[f] राक्षा[f,a] जतु[n,b] (क्लीबे) यावो[m] ऽलक्तो[m] द्रुमामयः[m,c] — Lac.

27. लवङ्गं[n] देवकुसुमं[n] श्री[f] (संज्ञम्)[d] — Cloves.

(अथ) जायकम्[n,f] — A yellow fragrant wood.[e]

कालीयकं[n,g] (च) कालानुसार्यं[n] (च)

(ऽथ) समार्थकम्[t] — A gallochum.[h]

28. वंशिका[n,i] ऽगुरु[m,n] राजार्हं[n] लोहं[n] कृमिजं[n] जोङ्गकम्[n]

कालागुरु[1,n] अगुरुः[2,m,n] — A black kind.

(स्यात्तु) मङ्गल्या[f] (मल्लिगन्धि यत्) — A very fragrant sort.

29. यक्षधूपः[m] सर्जरसो[m] ऽराल[m,j] सर्वरसा[3,m] (वपि) — Resin.

बहुरूपो[m] (ऽप्य)

(ऽथ) वृकधूप[m,k] कृत्रिमधूपकौ[4,m] — Compounded perfume.

30. तुरुष्कः[m] पिण्डकः[m] सिह्लो[m,l] यावनो[m] (ऽप्य) — Incense.

(ऽथ) पायसः[m] — Terpentine.

1—व. 2 व—. 3—स. 4—क.

[a] Or रक्षा. [b] One author disjoins this from the preceding and following terms. [c] Some distinguish the four last terms ; others, the three last, from the preceding : the distinction seems to be the gum or or resin discriminated from the dye of the insect. [d] Or any other name of *Lacshmi*. [e] Perhaps yellow sandal wood. [f] And जापकं. [g] Or कालेयकं and कालियकं. [h] Perhaps Amyris Agallocha, R. [i] And वंशकं ; also fem. वंशिका. [j] Likewise रालः. [k] Or वृकधूप. [l] One reads सिल्ह.

m a m m 1 m

श्रीवासो वृकधूपो (ऽपि) श्रीवेष्ट सरलद्रवो

m b 2 m c f

Musk. 31. मृगनाभिर्मृगमदः कस्तूरी (चा

n

Bdellium. ऽथ) कोलकम्

n n

कक्कोलकं कोषफलम्

m n

Camphor. (अथ) कर्पूर (मस्त्रियाम्)

m 3 m d m e f

32. घनसार चंद्र (संज्ञः) सिताभ्रो हिमवालुका

m m n f 4 m n

Sandal wood. गंधसारो मलयजो भद्रश्रीचन्दनो (ऽस्त्रियाम्)

n n m n

Varieties of sandal wood. f 33. तैलपर्णिक गोशीर्षे हरिचंदन (मस्त्रियाम्)

f n h n n

Red sanders. g तिलपर्णी (तु) पत्राङ्गं रञ्जनं रक्तचंदनम्

n

34. कुचंदनं (चा

n i n j

Mace. ऽथ) जातीकोश जातिफले (समे)

1—व. 2कस्तू—. 3घं—. 4चं—.

[a] Also श्रीवासः (—सा) [b] Likewise मृगः and (fem.) नाभिः. [c] Also मदः. [d] Or any name of the moon. [e] Or सिताभ्रः. [f] Denominated from the countries in which they are produced : or, as some derive these terms, from other circumstances. The first sort is white ; the second, the colour of brass and very fragrant. The third is yellow and said to smell like a ripe mango. [g] Pterocarpus santolinus. Some interpret this, red lead (Minium). But medical writers disjoin these terms and make the *Patranga* to Sappan wood (Cæsalpinia sappan). [h] Also पतंगं and पत्तंगं. [i] And जातीकोषम्. [j] Likewise जातीफलं ; and जातिः or जाती and फलं.

(कर्पूरागुरुकस्तूरी कक्कोलैर्) यक्षकर्दमः [m]	Perfumed paste. a
35. गात्रानुलेपनी [f] वर्त्तिर्[f c 1] वर्णकं [m n] (स्याद्) विलेपनम् [n]	Perfume for the person. b
चूर्णानि [n e] वासयोगाः [m] (स्युर्)	Powder. d
भावितं [m f n] वासितं [m f n] (त्रिषु)	Perfumed.
36. (संस्कारो गंधमाल्याद्यैर्यः स्यात्तद्) अधिवासनम् [n]	Adjusting with perfumes. f
माल्यं [n] माला [f] स्रजौ [f g] (मूर्ध्नि) ²	A chaplet.
(केशमध्ये तु) गर्भकः [m]	One worn in the hair.
37. प्रभ्रष्टकं [n] (शिखालंबि)	Or suspended from the middle lock.
(पुरोन्यस्तं) ललामकम् [n]	Or falling over the forehead.
प्रालंबं [n] (मृजुलंबि स्यात्कण्ठाद्)	Or hung round the neck.
वैकक्षकं [n] (तु तत्)	Or worn as a scarf.
38. (यत्तिर्य्यक् क्षिप्तमुरसि)	
(शिखास्वा) पीड़ [2 m] शेखरौ [3 m]	Or tied on the crown.
रचना [f] (स्यात्) परिस्पन्द [m h]	Decoration of hair.
आभोगः [m] परिपूर्णता [f]	Completion or fullness.

[1] व—. [2] आ—. [3] —र.

[a] Consisting of camphor, agallochum, musk, bdellium, (or else the three first, with saffron and sandal wood,) in equal proportions. [b] Whether ground and pounded, or not; but some distinguish the two last as restricted to perfumes ground. [c] वर्त्तिः or वर्त्ती. [d] To be thrown on the clothes; red powder, &c. [e] Sing. चूर्ण. [f] With fragrant wreathes, resins &c. [g] Sing. स्रक् (—ज्). [h] Or परिस्यन्दः.

Meaning	Sanskrit	Marks above the words
A pillow.	39. उपधानं (तू) पबर्हः	1 m
A bed.	शय्यायां शयनीय (वत्)	2 f, n
	शयनं	m
A bedstead.	मंच पर्यंक पल्यङ्काः खट्वया (समाः)	m, m, m, 3 f
A ball to play with.	40. गेण्डुकः कन्दुको	m a, m
A lamp.	दीपः प्रदीपः	m, m
A chair or stool.	पीठमासनम्	n, 4 n
A casket.	समुद्गकः संपुटकः	m b, m
A spitting pot.	प्रतिग्राहः पतद्ग्रहः	m c, n
A comb.	41. प्रसाधनी कंकतिका	f, f d
Perfumed powder.	पिष्टातः पटवासकः	m, m
A mirror.	दर्पणे मुकुरादर्शौ	5 m n, m e, m f
A fan.	व्यजनं तालवृन्तकम्	n, n g

---

[1] उ—. [2] शय्या. [3] खट्वा. [4] आ—. [5] —ण.

[a] Also गेण्डूकः. [b] And समुद्गा. [c] Or प्रतिग्रहः. [d] Likewise कङ्कती and कङ्कतं. Also प्रसाधनं. [e] And मकुरः or मंकुरः. [f] अदर्शः and आदर्शः. [g] Or तालवृन्तं.

f 1n n 2n 3m m 1. संततिर्गोत्र जननकुलान्यभिजना ऽन्वयौ	Race or lineage.
m m m वंशो ऽन्ववायः सन्तानो	
m b वर्णाः (स्युर्ब्राह्मणादयः)	Tribes or classes. a
4m m 2. राजबीजी राजवंश्यो	Sprung from a royal house.
m m बीज्य (स्तु) कुलसंभवः	Sprung from any family.
m c m d 5m m m 6m महाकुलकुलीनार्य्य सभ्यसज्जनसाधवः	Of honourable parentage.
m m m m 3. ब्रह्मचारी गृही वानप्रस्थो भिक्षु (श्चतुष्टये)	The four orders. e
m n आश्रमो (ऽस्त्री)	An order, or religious state. f
m g 7m m h m द्विजात्यग्रजन्म भूदेव वाडवाः	A man of the sacerdotal tribe.
m m 4. विप्र (श्च) ब्राह्मणो	

---

[1]गो—. [2]—ल. [3]व—. [4]—श्. [5]आर्य्यं.
[6]—धु. [7]ज—न्.

[a] The sacerdotal, &c. [b] Sing. वर्णः. [c] Or महाकुलः. [d] कुलीनः. Also कुल्यः, कौलेयः and कौलेयकः. [e] In succession as enumerated : viz. 1st. The religious student, who has received investiture, and is unmarried. 2d. The householder or married man. 3d. The hermit or anchoret. 4th. The mendicant or ascetic. [f] Either of the four above enumerated. [g] द्विजातिः. Also द्विजः and द्विजन्मा (—न्). [h] Or भूमिदेवः.

One, practising the six-allowed acts. a

1 *m*

(ऽसौ) षट्कर्मा (यागादिभिर्युतः)

Wise or learned.

2 *m* 3 *m* 4 *m* 5 *m* *m* *m* *m*

विद्वान् विपश्चिद्दोषज्ञः सन्सुधीः कोविदो बुधः

m 6 *m* *m* *m* b 7 *m* *m* *m* e

5. धीरो मनीषी ज्ञः प्राज्ञः संख्यावान् पण्डितः कविः

8 *m* *m* d 9 *m* *m* 10 *m* *m*

धीमान् सूरिः कृती कृष्टिर्लब्धवर्णो विचक्षणः

11 *m* 12 *m* e

6. दूरदर्शी दीर्घदर्शी

A priest conversant with scripture.

m 13 *m*

श्रोत्रियच्छान्दसौ (समौ)

A teacher.

m *m*

उपाध्यायो ऽध्यापको

A spiritual parent. f

m

(ऽथ स्यान्निषेकादिकृद्) गुरुः

An instructor in holy writ.

m

7. (मंत्रव्याख्याकृद्) आचार्य्य

An employer of priests. g

14 *m*

(आदेष्टा त्वध्वरे) व्रती

The same for peculiar rites. h

15 *m* *n*

यष्टा (च) यजमान (श्च)

m

(स सोमवति) दीक्षितः

One, who frequently sacrifices.

m *m*

8. इज्याशीलो यायजूको

1—न्. 2—स्. 3—त्. 4 दो—. 5 सत्.
6—न्. 7—वत्. 8—मत्. 9—न्. 10 ल—. 11—न्.
12—न्. 13 श्रो—. 14—न्. 15 यष्टृ.

a Sacrifice, study, benefaction; assisting to sacrifice, teaching, accepting alms. b Fem. प्राज्ञी. Also masc. प्रज्ञः. c And fem. कवी. d Also सूरी (—न्). e Some disjoin the two last terms as signifying provident. f Either the natural father, or the spiritual preceptor. g One who employs them to perform a sacrifice. h For ceremonies which include the drinking of acid asclepias. Some make this term synonymous with two preceding words.

[1 m] यज्वा (तु विधिनेष्टवान्) — One who sacrifices in due form.

[m] (स गीष्पतीष्ट्या) स्थपतिः — -who does so in a certain form. a

[2 m] सोमपीती (तु) [m b] सोमपः — -who has drunk the juice of acid Asclepias.

9. [3 m] सर्ववेदाः (स येनेष्टो यागः सर्वस्वदक्षिणः) — -who has bestowed all his wealth. c

[m] अनूचानः (प्रवचने साङ्गेऽधीती) — -who is completely learned. d

(गुरोस्तु यः

10. लब्धानुज्ञः) [m] समावृत्तः — -who has taken leave of his preceptor. e

[4 m] सुत्वा (त्वभिषवे कृते) — -who has made ablutions. f

[5 m] छात्रान्तेवासिनौ [m g] शिष्ये [m] — A pupil.

[m i] शैक्षाः प्राथमकल्पिकाः [m] — Novices. h

11. (एकब्रह्मव्रताचारा मिथः) सब्रह्मचारिणः [m k] — Fellow students. j

[m m] सतीर्थ्या (स्त्वे) [6 m n] कगुरवः — Spiritual brethren. l

(श्चितवानग्निम्) अग्निचित् — A worshipper of fire. o

1—नृ. 2—नृ. 3—दस्. 4—नृ. 5—त्र. 6ए—रु.

[a] In that of the sacrifice named from VRIHASPATI. [b] Also सोमपाः (—पा.) [c] On the priests employed by him for a sacrifice called *Viśwajit*; at which the principal's whole property must be distributed in sacrificial fees. [d] In sacred knowledge; being conversant with the *védas* and six *védángas*. [e] To become a householder. [f] Preparatory to the performance of a sacrifice. [g] Sing. अन्तेवासी (नृ). [h] Students who have recently begun reading the *védas*. [i] Sing. शैक्षः [j] Pursuing together the same studies, with like austerities. [k] Sing. सब्रह्मचारी (—नृ.) [l] Pupils of the same preceptor. [m] Sing. सतीर्थ्यः and सतीर्थः. [n] Sing एकगुरुः. [o] One who has taken and placed or consecrated a sacrifical fire.

Traditional instruction. Untaught knowledge.

12. (पारंपर्योपदेशे स्यात्) ऐतिह्यमितिहा (ऽव्ययम्) [n, 1]

उपज्ञा (ज्ञानमाद्यं स्यात्) [f]

Deliberate commencement.

(ज्ञात्वारंभ) उपक्रमः [m]

A sacrifice.[a] The great sacraments.[b]

13. यज्ञः सवोऽध्वरो यागः सप्ततंतुर्मखः क्रतुः [m m m m m 2m m]

(पाठो होमश्चातिथीनां सपर्यातर्पणं बलिः

14. एते पंच) महायज्ञा (ब्रह्मयज्ञादिनामकाः) [m c]

An assembly or meeting.

समज्यापरिषद्गोष्ठी सभासमिति संसदः [f 3f 4f f f f d]

15. आस्थानी (क्लीबम्) आस्थानं (स्त्रीनपुंसकयोः) सदः [f n 5f n e]

A room in front of the offerings.[f] By-standers.[g]

प्राग्वंशः (प्राग्घविर्गेहात्) [m]

सदस्या विधिदर्शिनः [m h, 6m]

Members of the assembly. Reciters of the prayers.[j]

16. सभासदः सभास्ताराः सभ्याः सामाजिका(श्च ते) [m i, m, m, m]

अध्वर्यूद्गातृहोतारो (यजुः सामर्ग्विदः क्रमात्) [7m, 8 m k, m l]

---

[1] इ—ह. [2] स—. [3]—द. [4] गो—. [5]—स्. [6]—न्. [7]—र्. [8]उ—.

[a] Or ceremony in which oblations are presented. [b] Five acts of religion named the sacraments of the *Védas*, of the Gods, of guests, of the manes, of mundane beings : viz. 1. study of scripture ; 2. presenting of oblations to the gods ; 3. hospitable reception of geusts ; 4. libation of water to the manes of ancestors ; 5. casting of food on the ground, or in water, for the gods, or for mundane beings. [c] Sing. महायज्ञः. [d] Sing. संसद् (—द्). [e] Sing. fem. सदाः. Neut सदः. [f] In front of the apartment in which the intended oblations are stored ; it is allotted to the employer and his family and the by-standers. [g] Whose business it is to notice and correct mistakes. [h] Sing. सदस्यः विधिदर्शी. [i] Sing. सभासद् (—द्). [j] Being conversant with the several *Védas* respectively. [k] Sing. उद्गाता. Chanter of the *Sáma-véda*. [l] Sing. होता (—तृ).

m b *m* 17. (आग्नीध्राद्या धनैर्वार्या) ऋत्विजो याजकाश्च ते)	Officiating priest. a
m d वेदिः (परिष्कृता भूमिः)	The altar. c
n *n* (समे) स्थण्डिलचत्वरे	Sacrificial ground. e
m *m* 18. चषालो यूपकटकः	A ring on the post. f
f h कुम्बा (सुगहनावृतिः)	An enclosure. g
n 1*n* यूपाग्रं तर्म	Top of the post. i
2 *m f* k (निर्मन्थ्य दारुणि त्वरणि (द्वयोः)	Wood for lighting a fire. j
m 3 *m* *n* 19. दक्षिणाग्निर्गार्हपत्याहवनीयौ (त्रयो ऽग्नयः)	Three sorts of sacred fire. l

1—त्. 2 च—. 3 गा—.

a Hired to perform the sacrifice : and denominated according to their respective officers, अग्नीध्रः (or आग्नीध्रः), &c. Sixteen such are employed under different designations. b Sing. ऋत्विक् (—ज्). c Or spot prepared for binding the victim, or placing the vessels. d Also बेदी. e A spot levelled for the purpose. f A wooden ring on the top of the sacrificial post. Some say an iron ring at its base. g Round the place of sacrifice, to prevent prophane intrusion. h Some make this a synonymous term. Fem. सुगहना. i Of the sacrificial post (called यूपः) ; which is an octangular column of Bambus or of *C'hadira* wood (Mimosa Catechu) ; to which the victim is bound, to mark the conclusion of the sacrifice. j By the attrition of two pieces of wood. k अरणिः. Also fem. अरणी. l Severally stated : viz. दक्षिणाग्निः, a fire, taken from the consecrated one, or from a domestic fire, and placed towards the south. गार्हपत्यः, the fire perpetually maintained by a householder. आहवनीयः, fire thence taken and prepared for receiving oblations : a consecrated fire.

The three sacred fires. a Fire consecrated by prayers.

(अग्नित्रयमिदं) त्रेता [f]

प्रणीत: [m] (संस्कृतोऽनल:)

Sacrificial fire. b Sort of sacred fire. c

20. समूह्य: [m] परिचाय्योपचाय्याव् [m] (अग्नौ प्रयोगिण:) [l m]
(यो गार्हपत्यादानीय दक्षिणाग्नि: प्रणीयते

21. (तस्मिन्) आनाय्यो [m]

The wife of fire. d Prayer uttered to excite fire. e

(ऽथा) ऽग्नायी [f] स्वाहा [f] (च) हुतभुक्प्रिया [f]

(ऋक्) सामधेनी [f] धाय्या [f] (च या स्यादग्निसमिंधने

Metre. f

22. (गायत्री प्रमुखं) छंदो [2 n]

A prepared oblation for the gods. g

(हव्यपाके) चरु: [m] (पुमान्)

Curd of two milk whey.

आमिक्षा [f h] (सा शृतोष्णे या क्षीरे स्याद्दधियोगत:)

A leather fan. i

23. धुवित्रं [n j] (व्यजनं तद्रचितं मृगचर्मणा)

---

d हु—. 2 —सु.

a Collectively. b In general : or, as others interpret this, particular sacrificial fires. c The southern fire, taken from the householder's hearth, and consecrated. d A goddess presiding over the prayers with which burnt-offerings are made. e Used, when fuel is put on the fire. f Measure of verse in the *Védas* : of various sorts ; as गायत्री or गायत्त्री, 24 syllables (6×4). उष्णिक्(—ष्), 28 syllables (7×4). अनुष्टुप् (—भ्), 32 syllables (8×4). बृहती, 36 syllables (9×4). पंक्ति:, 40 syllables (10×4), &c. g Also for the manes. Some explain it, the vessel in which oblations are prepared. h Some write आमीक्षा. i Made of antelope's hide ; and used to fan the sacaificial fire. j Also धवित्रं.

दध्याज्यं (सदध्याज्ये)	Oblation of butter and curds.
परमान्नं (तु) पायसः	—of rice, milk, and sugar.
24. हव्य कव्ये (दैवपित्र्ये अन्ने)	Food of the gods and manes. a
पात्रं (स्रुवादिकम्)	A vase or vessel. b
ध्रुवोपभृज्जुहू(र्ना तु)स्रुवो (भेदाः)स्रुचः(स्त्रियः)	Various sorts. c
25. उपाकृतः (पशुरसौ योऽभिमन्त्र्य क्रतौ हतः)	A victim. i
परंपराकं शमनं प्रोक्षणं (च वधार्थकम्)	Immolation.
26. (वाच्यलिङ्गाः) प्रमीतोपसम्पन्नप्रोक्षिता (हते)	Slain or immolated.
सान्नाय्यं हविर्	An intended oblation. k
(अग्नौ तु हुतं त्रिषु) वषट्कृतम्	Burnt as a sacrifice. l

Superscript grammatical marks printed above words: दध्याज्यं n; परमान्नं n, पायसः m n; हव्य n, कव्ये n; पात्रं m n; ध्रुवा f d, उपभृत् 1 f e f f, जुहू f, स्रुवः m f g, स्रुचः 2 f h; उपाकृतः m; परंपराकं n, शमनं n j, प्रोक्षणं n; प्रमीत m f n, उपसम्पन्न 3 m f n, प्रोक्षित m f n; सान्नाय्यं n, हविर् 4 n; वषट्कृतम् m f n.

[1] स—स्. [2]—ष. [3] स—. [4]—स्.

[a] Respectively, viz. हव्यं, an oblation to the gods. कव्यं, an oblation to the manes. [b] Of any kind : including the undermentioned sorts ; besides others, as pestle and mortar, spoon, jar &c. [c] Severally named in the text. They are used in sacrifice and differ in shape : being respectively (as some describe them) round, square, semicircular, triangular, and lotus-shaped. [d] ध्रुवा, shaped like an Indian fig-leaf (Ficus Indica) and made of the wood of Flacourtia sapida. [e] उपभृत, a round vessel made of the wood of a holy fig tree (F. religiosa). [f] जुहूः or जुहुः, a semicicular vessel made of the wood of Butea (B. frondosa). [g] स्रुवः or fem. स्रुवा:, a ladle of *C'hadira* wood (Mimosa Catechu). [h] स्रुक् (—च्) same with the last, though some distinguish it. [i] Slain, or to be slain. [j] Also शसनं or संज्ञपनं. [k] The thing to be offered or sacrificed ; usually clarified butter. [l] Sacrificed in fire.

Supplemental sacrifice. [a] — 27. (दीक्षान्तो)[b] ऽवभृथो[n] (यज्ञे)

Suitable to a sacrifice. — (तत्कर्म्मार्हन्तु) यज्ञियम्[mfn c] (त्रिषु)

An act of sacrifice. d — (अथ क्रतुकर्म्म) इष्टं[1 n]

-of pious liberality. e — पूर्त्तं[n] (खातादिकर्म्मणि)

Remains of a sacrifice or oblation. f — 28. अमृतं[n] विघसो[m] (यज्ञशेषभोजनशेषयोः)

Gift or donation. — त्यागो[m] विहापितं[n] दानमुत्सर्ज्जन[n] विसर्ज्जने[2 n] [n]

29. विश्राणनं[n] वितरणं[n] स्पर्शनं[n] प्रतिपादनम्[n]

प्रादेशनं[n] निर्वपणमपवर्ज्जनम्[n 3 n] अंहतिः[4 f g]

Obsequies of a deceased person. — 30. (मृतार्थं तदहे दानं त्रिषु स्यात्) और्ध्वदेहिकम्[mfn h]

Gifts in honour of the deceased. — पितृदानं[n] निवापः[m i] (स्यात्)

Funeral repast. j — श्राद्धं[5 n] (तत्कर्म्मशास्त्रतः)

---

1 इष्ट. 2 उ—. 3 प्र—. 4 अं—. 5 श्राध.

[a] Performed to atone for any defect in the principal one. [b] Some make this a synonymous term. [c] Fem. यज्ञिया. [d] Oblation or other act of a sacrifice ; or the sacrifice itself. [e] Digging a pond or well ; erecting a temple or house ; planting an orchard, &c. [f] Respectively, viz. अमृतं, butter, &c. remaining of a sacrifice. विघसः, residue of food offered to the gods, to the manes, to a venerable guest, or to a spiritual parent, &c. [g] Or अंहती. Also अंहितिः. [h] Also और्ध्वदैहिकं, और्ध्वदेहिकं. Fem. और्ध्वदेहिकी. [i] And निवापः. [j] Feeding of priests and other prescribed ceremonies, in honour of ancesters.

31. अन्वाहार्य्यं [n b] मासिके. [1 n] — Monthly obsequies. [a]

(ऽंशो ऽष्टमो ऽह्नः) कुतपेा [m n] (ऽस्त्रियाम्) — Eighth hour of the day. [c]

पर्य्येषणा [f] परीष्टि [f] (श्चा) न्वेषणा [f] (च) गवेषणा [f] — Research or inquiry. [d]

32. सनि [f e] (स्त्व) ध्येषणा [2 f] — Request or solicitation.

याच्ञा [f] ऽभिशस्तिर्य्याचना [f] ऽर्थना [3 f] [f] — Asking or begging.

(षट् तु त्रिष्व) [f]

ऽर्घ्य [m f n h] (मर्घार्थे) — A respectful oblation. [g]

पाद्यं [m f n i] (पादाय वारिणि) — Water for ablution of the feet.

33. (क्रमाद्) आतिथ्या [m f n j] तिथेये [4 m f n k] (अतिथ्यर्थे ऽत्र साधुनि) — Proper for a guest.

(स्याद्) आवेशिक [m f n l] आगन्तुरतिथि [m f n m] [5 m n] (र्ना गृहागते) [o] — A guest.

1—क. 2 ध—. 3 या—. 4 आ—. 5 अ—.

[a] Funeral repast in honour of ancestors on the day of new moon. Some restrict this to the monthly ceremonies for one recently deceased. [b] Also अन्वाहार्य्यकं and अनुहार्य्यं. [c] Towards midday: for the day (or period of day light) comprises fifteen hours (*muhúrtas*). An offering to the manes at noon is reckoned best. [d] Especially the investigation of duty by reasoning, [e] Also सनी. [f] The following admit the three genders. [g] Water only; or else grass, flowers, &c. with water. [h] Fem. अर्घ्या. [i] Fem. पाद्या. [j] Fem. आतिथ्या. [k] Fem. आतिथेयी [l] Fem. आवेशिकी. [m] Likewise आगन्तुः. [n] Also fem. अतिथिः, or अतिथी. [o] Some include this among the synonyma.

Worship. a — 34. पूजा नमस्याऽपचितिः सपर्य्याऽर्चाऽर्हणाः (समाः)

Service. — वरिवस्या (तु) शुश्रूषा परिचर्य्या (प्यु) पासनम्

Roaming. b — 35. व्रज्याऽटाट्या पर्य्यटनं

Perseverance in austerities. — चर्य्या (त्वीर्य्यापथस्थितिः)

Sipping. f — उपस्पर्शं (स्त्वा) चमनम्

Silence. — (ऽथ) मौनमभाषणम्

Order, method. — 36. आनुपूर्वी (स्त्रियां) (वा) वृत् परिपाटी अनुक्रमः पर्य्याय (श्चा)

Neglect. i — ऽतिपात (स्तु स्यात्) पर्य्यय उपात्ययः

Meritorious act. j — 37. नियमो व्रत (मस्त्री तच्चोपवासादि) पुण्यकम्

A fast. — उपवस्तं (तू) पवासो

Discrimination. — विवेकः पृथगात्मता

Holiness. l — 38. (स्याद्) ब्रह्मवर्चसं वृत्ताध्ययनर्द्धिर्

1—उ. 2 आ—. 3 अ—. 4 आवृत. 5 उ—. 6 —र्द्धि.

[a] Whether adoration or respect. [b] Likewise परिसर्व्या. [c] Also fem. उपासना or उपास्तिः. [d] Wandering for alms: travelling for austerity. [e] Also अटा and अट्या. [f] Touching without swallowing. [g] Likewise, neut. आनुपूर्व्यं, आनुपूर्वं or आनुपूर्वकं. [h] And परिपाटिः. [i] Of what is enjoined or customary. [j] As fasting, &c. [k] Also उपोषितं, उपोषणं, औपवस्तं, &c. [l] Resulting from the study of scripture; and the observance of its injunctions.

(ऽथांजलिः	Joining both hands while reading the *Védas.* a
m पाठे) ब्रह्माञ्जलिः	
1 m (पाठे विप्रुषो) ब्रह्मबिन्दवः	Sanctified saliva. b
n 39. ध्यानयोगासने ब्रह्मासनं	A holy posture. c
m m m कल्पे विधिक्रमौ	A sacred precept. d
m मुख्यः (स्यात्प्रथमः कल्पो)	A chief injunction. e
m ऽनुकल्प (स्तु ततोऽधमः)	A secondary one. f
n h 40. (संस्कारपूर्वं ग्रहणं स्याद्) उपाकरणं (श्रुतेः)	Holy study. g
n j 2 n (समे तु) पादग्रहणमभिवादन (मित्युभे)	Obeisance. i
3 m m l 4 m 5 m m 6 m 41. भिक्षुः परिव्राट् कर्मन्दी पाराशर्य्य (पि) मस्करी	A mendicant. k

---

1—न्दु. 2 च—. 3—ज्. 4—न्. 5—न्. 6—न्.

[a] An act of humility, with a short prayer, at the beginning and end of a lesson : or else to mark, by the motion of the hands so joined, the accentuation, while reading the *Sáma-véda.* [b] Drops of spittle sputtered in reading the *Védas.* [c] Adapted to meditation and restraint of thought : sitting with the feet raised, or with fingers intertwined, &c. [d] Practice prescribed by the *Védas* for the effecting of certain consequences. [e] Regarding an act of religion : as 'sacrifice with rice ;' 'strew *Kus'a* grass.' [f] Or succedaneous : as 'for want of rice use *Nibári*' : 'for want of *Kus'a* employ *Cás'a* or *Durvá.*' [g] Reading of the *Védas* after initiation. [h] Also उपाकर्म (—न्) and उपग्रहणं. [i] A bow or prostration to a person addressed by name. [j] Likewise उपसंग्रहणं. [k] One who has entered the fourth order (or that of devotion), following the rules of CARMANDA or PA'RA'S'ARYA : a *Sannyási.* [l] And परिव्राजकः. [m] पाराशरी or पराशरी (—न्).

An ascetic. a — 1m तपस्वी m तापसः 2m पारिकांक्षी

A holy sage. b — m वाचंयमो mf मुनिः

Patient of austerity. — 42. m तपःक्लेशसहो m दांतो

Religious students. c — m वर्णिनो md ब्रह्मचारिणः

Saints. e — mf ऋषयः m सत्यवचसः

An initiated householder. g — m स्नातक (स्त्री) nh आप्लवव्रती

Sages with subdued senses. i — 43. (ये) निर्जितेन्द्रियग्रामा mj यतिनो m यतय mk (च, ते)

One, who sleeps on the bare ground. l — (यः स्थण्डिले व्रतवशाच्छे ते) 3m स्थण्डिलशाय्य (सौ)

1—नु. 2—नु. 3—यो. (—नु).

a Employed in devotion and seeking spiritual wisdom. Some make these terms synonymous with the preceding. b Practising rigid taciturnity; devoid of passions, and serene or unruffled by pain or pleasure. c Practising austerity during the study of the *Védas*. d Sing. वर्णी (—न्) and ब्रह्मचारी (—न्). e Infallible. Seven classes of them are distingnished, viz. *Maharshi*, *Dévarshi*, (as NA'RADA, &c.) *Brahmarshi*, (as CAS'YAPA, &c.), *Paramarshi*, *Can'darshi*, *S'rutarshi*, and *Rájarshi*. f Sing. ऋषिः or रिषिः. And fem. ऋषी, &c. g One, who has entered the second order, after passing through the first: having completed his noviciate, but without attaining a knowledge of the *Védas* (he is called *Vratasnátaca*): having attained that knowledge before the expiration of the prescribed period of study (he is termed *Vidyásnátaca*): having completed both his studies and probation (he is named *Ubhoyasnátaca*). h आप्लवव्रती (—न्.) and आप्लुतव्रती. i Whose organs are restrained from all that is blamable, as VAS'ISHT'HA and others. j Some exclude this from the synonyma. k Sing. यती (—न्) and यतिः. l By way of mortification.

44. स्थण्डिल[m] (शा) (ऽय) विरजस्तमस[1m]ः (स्युर्) द्वयातिगा[m]ः	Men perfectly virtuous. a
पवित्र[m]ः प्रयत[m]ः पूत[m]ः	A purified person. b
पाषण्डा[m d]ः सर्वलिङ्गि[2m]नः	Heretics and impostors. c
45. (पालाशो दण्ड) आषाढो[m f] (व्रते)	A student's staff. e
राम्भ[m] (स्तु, वैणवः)	One cut from a Bambu. g
(अस्त्री) कमण्डलु[m n]ः कुण्डी[f i]	His water-pot. h
(व्रतिनामासनं) वृषी[f k]	His cushion. j
46. अजिनं[n] चर्म[3n.] कृत्ति[f]ः (स्त्री)	A hide used by him. l
भैक्षं[n] (भिक्षाकदम्बकम्)	Aggregate of alms.
स्वाध्याय[m]ः (स्याज्) जप[m m]ः	Reading or muttering of prayers.

[1]—मस्. [2]—न्. [3]—न्.

[a] Devoid of every bad quality; having gained the knowledge of GOD, and attained beatitude in their life time: as VYA'SA and others. [b] Cleansed by a austerity and mortification. [c] Who assume the exteriors of the four tribes and orders; but whose practice is in contradiction to the *Védas*: for example (say the Commentators) the *Baud-d'has*, &c. [d] Sing. पाषण्डः or पाखण्डः. [e] Cut from a *Pălása* tree (Butea frondosa): and used by certain ascetics on the full moon of *A'shádd'ha*. [f] Also आषाढः. [g] Borne by students with a wisp of of *Kus'a* grass. Any other Bambu staff is named वैणवः. [h] A wooden or an earthen one. The student, as well as the ascetic in the third or fourth order, was anciently required to carry a water-pot. [i] Likewise कुण्डिका. [j] A seat made of *Kus'a* grass (Poa cynosuroides). [k] Or वृसी. [l] Commonly an antelope's skin. [m] Or जापः.

Religious bathing. a — सुत्या ऽभिषवः सवनं (च सा) [f m n]

An expiatory prayer. b — 47. (सर्वैनसामपध्वंसि जप्यं त्रिषु) अघमर्षणम् [1 m f n c]

Half-monthly sacrifice. d — दर्श (श्च) पौर्णमास (श्च, यागौ पक्षान्तयोः पृथक्) [m m]

A perpetual duty. e — 48. (शरीरसाधनापेक्षं नित्यं यत्कर्म तद्) यमः [m]

A voluntary one. f — नियम (स्तु. स यत्कर्मानित्यमागन्तुसाधनम्) [m]

The cord passed over the left shoulder. g — 49. उपवीतं (यज्ञसूत्रं प्रोद्धृते दक्षिणे करे) [n n h]

Over the right shoulder. i — प्राचीनावीत (मन्यस्मिन्) [n]

Suspended over the neck. — निवीतं (कण्ठलम्बितम्). [n]

Part of the hand sacred to the gods. j — 50. (अङ्गुल्यग्रे तीर्थं) दैवं [n]

---

1 अघ—.

a Preparatory to a sacrifice. Also, as some explain these terms, extracting the juice of acid asclepias, and drinking it. b Meditated while a drop of water is held to the nose. The name (which is also that of its author) signifies expiatory : it is supposed to atone even sins in thought. c Fem. अघमर्षणी. d At the change and full of the moon, respectively : performed by persons maintaining a perpetual fire. e As veracity, &c. See MANU, Ch. 10, v. 63. f As pilgrimage, fasting &c. g And under the right arm. MANU, 2. v. 63. It is the usual mode of wearing it. h This general term, for the sacerdotal string, is by some made synonymous with the preceding word. i And under the left arm. It is so worn during particular ceremonies. j Tips of the fingers (some exclude the thumb) : See MANU, 2. v. 59.

(स्वल्पांगुल्यो र्मूले) कायम् (n)	Part of the head sacred to the creator. a
(मध्येऽङ्गुष्ठाङ्गुल्योः) पैत्रं (n)	—to the manes. b
(मूले त्वङ्गुष्ठस्य) ब्राह्मम् (n)	—to the *Védas*. c
51. (स्याद्) ब्रह्मभूयं (n) ब्रह्मत्वं (n) ब्रह्मसायुज्य (n) (मित्यपि)	Deified state. d
देवभूया (n f) (दिकं तद्वत्)	Inferior deification. e
कृच्छ्रं (n) (सान्तपनादिकम्)	Penance. g
52. (संन्यासवत्यनशने पुमान्) प्रायो (m)	Fasting to die.
(ऽथ) वीरहा (1 m)	One who has left his sacred fire. h
नष्टाग्निः (m)	
कुहना (f) (लोभान्मिथ्येर्यापथकल्पना)	Hypocrisy. i
53. व्रात्यः (m) संस्कारहीनः (m) (स्याद्)	An uninitiated person. j
अस्वाध्यायो (m) निराकृतिः (m)	One who has not made his studies. k

1—न.

[a] To *Prajápati*. It is the root of the two smaller fingers. [b] Between the thumb and forefinger. [c] Under the root of the thumb. [d] Becoming united with *Brahme*. [e] Becoming identified with a god. [f] देवभूयं, देवत्वं or देवसायुज्यं. [g] That called *Sántapana* or any other: as the *Chándráyana* or *Prájápatya*, &c. See MANU, 11. v. 212, &c. [h] Having extinguished or neglected it; or having gone abroad, committing the charge of the perpetual fire to his family. [i] Practice of religious austerities through avarice, or from pride, &c. [j] For whom the prescribed ceremonies have not been performed: who has not received investiture. [k] Who has not duly read the *Védas*.

A hypocrite or impostor.[a] A violator of his vow.[b]

धर्मध्वजी लिंगवृत्तिर्
अवकीर्णी क्षतव्रतः

One who is asleep at sunset, or at sun rise.[c]

54\. (सुप्ते यस्मिन्नस्तमेति सुप्ते यस्मिन्नुदेति च
अंशुमान्) अभिनिर्मुक्ता ऽभ्युदितौ (तौ यथाक्रमम्)

One married before his elder brother.[d] The unmarried elder brother.

55\. परिवेत्ता (ऽनुजो ऽनूढे ज्येष्ठे दारपरिग्रहात्)
परिवित्ति (स्तु. तज्ज्यायान्)

Marriage.

विवाहोपयमौ (समौ)

56\. (तथा) परिणयोद्वाहोपयामाः पाणिपीडनम्

Copulation.

व्यवायो ग्राम्यधर्म्म (च) रतं निधुवनं (च सः)

Three human pursuits[i]

57\. त्रिवर्गो (धर्म्मकामार्थै श्च्)

Four objects.[k]

चतुर्वर्गः (समोक्षकैः)

The same equally potent.

(सबलैस्तै श्च्) चतुर्भद्रं

The bridegroom's friends.

जन्याः (स्निग्धावरस्य ये)

1—मृ. 2—चि. 3—नृ. 4 तृ—. 5 ह—. 6 ह—. 7 ह—.

[a] Who assumes the exteriors of religion for a livelihood. [b] Infringing, through incontinence, austerities begun by him. [c] Respectively. [d] This regards the first marriage. [e] Also परिवृक्तिः and परिवृत्तिः. [f] Also पाणिग्रहणं, &c. [g] Also रमणं, सुरतं, and रतिः. [h] Likewise मैथुनं. [i] Viz. duty, love, and wealth. [j] And त्रिगणः. [k] The three above mentioned; and final beatitude or release from transmigration. [l] Sing. जन्यः.

CHAPTER VIII.

SECTION I.

m m m m a 1m	
1. मूर्द्धाभिषिक्तो राजन्यो बाहुजः क्षत्रियो विराट्	A man of the military tribe.
mb 2m m 3mc md mc m	
राज्ञि राट् पार्थिव क्ष्माभृन्नृप भूप महीक्षितः	A king
m	
2. (राजा तु प्रणताशेषसामन्तः स्याद्) अधीश्वरः	An emperor. f
4m m	
चक्रवर्त्ती सार्वभौमो	A universal monarch. g
m	
(नृपो ऽन्यो) मण्डलेश्वरः	Any other prince.
3. येनेष्टं राजसूयेन मण्डलस्येश्वरश्च यः	A paramount. h
5m	
शास्ति यश्चाज्ञया राज्ञः स) सम्राड्	
n	
(अथ) राजकम्	An assemblage of princes.
n	
4. राजन्यकं (च नृपति.क्षत्रियाणां गणे क्रमात्)	— of soldiers.

---

1 राज्. 2—ज्. 3—त्. 4—न्. 5—ज्.

[a] Also क्षत्री (—न्) and क्षत्त्रः or क्षत्रः. [b] राजा (—न्.) [c] Likewise महीक्षित्, &c. [d] नृपः. So नृपतिः, नरपतिः, &c. [e] Also भूपालः, भूमिपाल, &c. [f] Paramount over all neighbouring princes. Some make this synonymous with the following. [g] Sovereign of the earth from sea to sea. [h] A sovereign prince who has performed a *Rájasúya* sacrifice, and exersises despotic sway over others. Or one, who has either of these qualifications.

1 m m m

A minister or counsellor. — मन्त्री धीसचिवोऽमात्यो

m a

Other ministers. — (ऽन्ये) कर्मसचिवा (स्ततः)

m m n b

The king's companions. — 5. महामात्राः प्रधानानि

2 m m

The priest or chaplain. — पुरोधा (स्तु) पुरोहितः

3 m 4 m

The judge. — (द्रष्टरि व्यवहाराणां) प्राड्विवाकाऽक्षदर्शकौ

m c m m d m m e

The warder or porter. — 6. प्रतीहारो द्वारपाल द्वास्थ द्वास्थित दर्शकाः

m 5 m

An armed guard. — रक्षिवर्ग (स्त्व) नीकस्थो

6 m 7 m

A superintendent. f — (ऽथा) ऽध्यक्षा ऽधिकृतौ (समौ)

m

An overseer of a village. — 7. स्थायुको (ऽधिकृतो ग्रामे)

m

An inspector of a district. — गोपो (ग्रामेषु भूरिषु)

m m

The treasurer. g — भौरिकः कनकाध्यक्षो

m m i

The master of the mint. h — रूप्याध्यक्ष (स्तु) नैष्किकः

m

The chamberlain. j — 8. (अन्तःपुरे त्वधिकृतः स्याद्) अन्तर्वंशिको (जनः)

1—न्. 2—धस्. 3—क. 4—क. 5 ऽथ—. 6—क्षं. 7—तृ.

[a] कर्मसचिवः. Also आमात्यः. [b] Sing. प्रधानं,—नः. [c] Also प्रतिहारः. [d] Or द्वाःस्थः. Likewise द्वारी (न्), द्वारिकः, दौवारिकः. [e] Also उपदर्शकः, and द्वास्थितदर्शकः. [f] Over any department some say, over that of receipt and disbursements. [g] Superintendent of the gold. [h] Superintendent of the silver coinage; or of the silver in general. [i] Also टङ्कपतिः. [j] Superintedent of the women's apartments.

सौविदल्ला: कंचुकिन: स्थापत्या: सौविदा (स् ते)	Attendants of the women. a
9. षंडो वर्षवर (सल्वौ)	A eunuch. c
सेवका ऽर्थ्यनुजीविन:	A servant.
(विषयानन्तरो राजा) शत्रुर्	A foe. h
मित्र (मृत: परम्)	A stranger or neutral. i
10. उदासीन: (परतर:)	A stranger. k
पार्ष्णिग्राह (स्तु पृष्ठत:)	An enemy in the rear.
रिपौ वैरि सपत्ना ऽरि द्विषद्द्वेषण दुर्हृद:	Any enemy.
11. द्विड् विपक्षा ऽहिता ऽमित्र दस्यु शात्रव शत्रव:	
अभिघातिपरा ऽरातिप्रत्यर्थिपरिपन्थिन:	
12. वयस्य: स्निग्ध: सवया	A friend and contemporary.

1—न्. 2—न्. 3—त्रु. 4—पु. 5—न्. 6 द्—. 7—द्. 8 त्रु. 9—न्. 10—न्. 11—स्.

[a] Guarding the apartments of the king's women. [b] Sing. कंचुकी (—न्.) [c] स्थापत्य: or स्थपति:. [d] सौविद: or सुविद:. [e] A castrated attendant. Some make the preceding synonymous with this. [f] One reads षंढ:, but erroneously; for the term is षंढ: and signifies impotent. [g] वर्षी (—न्). [h] A neighbouring prince; for enmity frequently arises between neighbours. [i] Being more distant. [j] Or मित्र॰. [k] Remote; showing neither friendship nor enmity. [l] वैरी (—न्). [m] Or सापत्न:. [n] द्विट् (—ष्). Also द्विष: (—ष्). [o] अभिघाती (न्) or अभिघाती (—न्) and अभिघाति: (—ति). [p] अराति: or आराति:.

n a l m b 2 m

A friend. — (स्य) मित्रं सखा सुहृत्

n n

Friendship. — सख्यं साप्तपदीनं (स्याद्)

m n

Complaisance. c — अनुरोधो ऽनुवर्त्तनम्

m m 3 m e 4 m m

A spy. d — 13. यथार्हवर्णः प्रणिधिरपसर्पश्चरः स्पशः

m 5 m

चार (श्च) गूढपुरुषश्

6 m f n m f n f

Trusted; confidential. — (चा) प्तः प्रत्ययित (त्रिषु)

m m g m m h

An astrologer. — 14. सांवत्सरो ज्यौतिषिको दैवज्ञ गणका (वपि)

m m 7 m m

(स्युर्)मौहूर्त्तिक मौहूर्त्त ज्ञानि कार्त्तांतिका(अपि)

m m

A man versed in any science. — 15. तांत्रिको ज्ञातसिद्धांतः

8 m j m

A generous householder. i — सत्री गृहपतिः (समौ)

m k m m l m

A scribe. — लिपिकारो ऽक्षरचणो ऽक्षरचुञ्चु (श्च) लेखके

1—मि. 2—हृ. 3 च—. 4 च—. 5—श. 6 चाप्त. 7—ज्ञ. 8—त्र.

b

a Or मित्र'. Invariably neuter : but some vary the gender ; masc. मित्रः fem. मित्रा. b Fem. सखी c The accomplishing of a desired object. Some explain this, service. d The two first, others say the three first, terms signify a secret agent under a disguise : and the rest an occasional emissary : or else a spy in general. e Or चरस्पश':. f Fem. आप्ता and प्रत्ययिता. g Or ज्योतिषिकः. h गणकः fem. गणकी. i Constantly giving alms and performing sacrifices. j Also सत्त्री. k Or लिपिकरः. and लिबिंकरः. l Also अक्षरचंचुः.

n a *n* b *f* 1*f* c 16. लिखिता ऽक्षरसंस्थाने लिपिर्लिबि (रुभे स्त्रियौ)	Scripture or writing.
m *m* d (स्यात्) संदेशहरो दूतो	A messenger or ambassador.
n e दूत्यं (तद्भावकर्मणि)	An embassy or message.
m f *m* *m* *m* g *m* 17. अध्वनीनो ऽध्वगो ऽध्वन्यः पान्थः पथिक (इत्यपि)	A traveller.
(स्वाम्यमात्यसुहृत्कोशराष्ट्रदुर्गबलानि च)	The requisites of regal administration. h
n *f* i 18. राज्याङ्गानि प्रकृतयः	
(पौराणां श्रेणयो ऽपि च)	Including citizens. j
m *m* *n* *n* *n* *m* (संधिर्ना विग्रहो यानमासनं द्वैधमाश्रयः)	Six expedients of defence. k
m l 19. (षड्) गुणाः	
f शक्तय (स्तिस्रः प्रभावोत्साहमंत्रजाः)	Power. m

[1] वि—.

[a] And लिखनं or लेखनं. [b] According to another reading (अक्षर विन्यासे), this and the preceding term are the interpretation of the two next words. [c] Likewise लिपी and लिबी. [d] Fem. दूती. [e] And दौत्यं. [f] Fem. अध्वनीना, अध्वगा, अध्वन्या. [g] Fem. पान्था, पथिकी. Some write पथिका erroneously as others observe. Also masc. पथकः. [h] Viz. 1st. the king or lord ; 2d. his counsellor or minister ; 3d. a friend or ally ; 4th. treasure ; 5th. territory ; 6th. a strong hold ; 7th. an army. [i] Sing. राज्याङ्ग and प्रकृतिः. [j] Some reckon eight requisites of regal administration including the companies of citizens : others nine with the spiritual adviser, &c. [k] Severally mentioned. Viz. Pacification. War. A progress or a march. A halt or the maintaining of a post. A double resource or a stratagem. Recourse to protection. [l] Sing. गुणः an expedient. [m] Of three sorts : as resulting from majesty, perseverance and counsel.

Threefold object. [a]		(क्षयः[m] स्थानं[n] च वृद्धि[f] श्च) त्रिवर्गो[m] (नीतिवेदिनाम्)
Majesty. [b]	20.	(स) प्रतापः[m] प्रभाव[m] (श्च यत्तेजः कोषदण्डजम्)
Four means of success. [c]		(भेदो दण्डः साम दानमित्यु) पाय[1 m] (चतुष्टयम्)
Punishment.	21.	साहसं[n] (तु) दमो[m] दण्डः[m]
Conciliation.		साम[2 n] सान्त्वम्[n d] (अथो समौ)
Disunion.		भेदो[m] पजापा[3 m] व्
Trial or test of honesty. [e]		उपधा[f] (धर्माद्यैर्यत्परीक्षणम्)
	22.	(पंच[f] त्रिष्व)
Secret. [g]		षडक्षीणो[m f n] (यस्तृतीयाद्यगोचरः)
Solitary, or private.		विविक्त[m f n h] विजन[m f n] च्छन्न[m f n i] निःशलाका[m f n] (स्तथा) रहः[4 n j]
	23.	रह[5] (श्चो) पांशु[6] (चालिंगे)
Occurring in private.		रहस्यं[m f n k] (तद्भवे त्रिषु)
Trust or confidence.		(समौ) विस्रम्भ[m l] विश्वासौ[m]

---

[1] उ—. [2] —न्. [3] उ—प. [4] —स्. [5] —स्. [6] उ—.

[a] Loss, evenness and gain : or disappointment, continuance of the same state, and success : or else expenditure, equality and profit. [b] The dignity arising from treasure and forces ; and from the power of punishment : the consequent high spirit and impatience of injury. [c] In reducing the foe : viz. Sowing of dissention, chastisement, conciliation and gifts. [d] Likewise शाम (—न्) and शान्त्व. [e] Trial of loyalty, of disinterestedness, of continence, and of intrepidity. [f] The five next terms admit the three genders. [g] Unknown to a third person. [h] Fem. विविक्ता. [i] छन्नः or छन्दः. [j] Likewise masc. रहः (स्) [k] Fem. रहस्या. [l] And विश्रंभः.

भ्रेषो (भ्रंशो यथोचितात्)	Deviation from right.
24. अभ्रेष न्याय कल्पा (स्तु) देशरूपं समञ्जसम्	Propriety or fitness.
युक्तमौपयिकं लभ्यं भजमानाऽभिनीत (वत्)	Right, fit or proper.
25. न्याय्यं (च त्रिषु षट्)	
संप्रधारणा (तु) समर्थनम्	Deliberation. [a]
अववाद (स्तु) निर्देशो निदेशः शासनं (च सः)	An order or command.
26. शिष्टि (श्चा) ज्ञा (च)	
संस्था (तु) मर्य्यादा धारणा स्थितिः	Continuance in the right way.
आगोऽपराधो मंतु (श्च)	Offence or transgression.
(समे तू) द्दानबन्धने	Binding.
27. द्विपाद्यो (द्विगुणो दण्डो)	Double penalty. [c]
भागधेयः करो बलिः	Royal revenue.
(घट्टादिदेयं) शुल्को (ऽस्त्री)	Toll. [e]
प्राभृतं (तु) प्रदेशनम्	A present. [f]

---

1 औ—. 2 आज्ञा. 3—सु. 4 उ—.

[a] On the propriety or impropriety of any thing : a determination thereon. [b] Also शास्तिः. [c] Twice the prescribed fine or punishment of the offence. [d] Also कारः. [e] Or duty of customs payable at ferries, and passes. [f] Some restrict the two first terms to signify an oblation of first fruits, &c. to the gods : or a present to a friend ; and the four last an humble offering to the king, &c. ; or else a bribe ; or generally any present. Others restrict all the terms to one or other of those various senses.

n 1 n 2 m 3 f

28. उपायनमुपग्राह्यमुपहार (स्तथो) पदा

A special gift. a

m b n

(यौतकादि तु यद्देयं) स दायो हरणं (च तत्)

Present time. c

m n d

29. तत्काल (स्तु) तदात्वं (स्याद्)

Future time.

f e

(उत्तरः काल) आयतिः

Immediate consequence.

n

सांदृष्टिकं (फलं सद्यः)

Future consequence.

m

उदर्कः (फलमुत्तरम्)

Casual and unseen danger. f

n

30. अदृष्टं (वह्नितोयादि)

Obvious danger. g

m

दृष्टं (स्वपरचक्रजम्)

Latent danger. h

n

(महीभुजाम्) अहिभयं (स्वपक्षप्रभवं भयम्)

Bearing of royal insignia.

f 4 m

31. प्रक्रिया (त्व) धिकारः (स्याच्)

A cow tail. i

n j n

चामरं (तु) प्रकीर्णकम्

A throne.

n n

नृपासनं (यत्तद्) भद्रासनं

One made of gold.

n

सिंहासनं (तु तत्)

---

1 उ—. 2 उ—. 3 उ—. 4 अ—.

[a] As a nuptial present (यौतकं), or alms to a student on his initiation, &c. [b] Likewise सुदायः. [c] The time when an act occurs. [d] Some say indec. [e] Also masc. आयतः. [f] As that of conflagration, inundation, &c. [g] As desolation and plunder of armies. [h] From one's own party: compared to a lurking serpent. [i] The tail of the Bos grunniens: used as a fan. [j] Likewise चमरं and fem. चामरा—री.

32. (छेत्रं)

n a 1 n छत्रं (त्रा) तपत्रं	A parasol.
2 n (राजस्तु) नृपलक्ष्म (तत्)	A royal one. b
m m भद्रकुम्भः पूर्णकुंभो	An auspicious jar. c
m f भृङ्गारः कनकालुका	A golden vase.

SECTION. II.

m n 1. निवेशः शिबिरं (षंढे)	A camp. d
n 3 n सज्जनं (तु) परक्षणम्	A sentry or guard.
n (हस्त्यश्वरथपादातं) सेनाङ्गं (स्याच्चतुष्टयम्)	Component part of an army. e

---

1 आ—. 2—वृ. 3 उ—.

a Or छत्र°. b With a golden staff. c A golden one, filled with water from a holy place, and used in consecrating a king. d Some say the royal residence. e Four such parts are distinguished : horse, foot, elephants and cars : besides boats, buffaloes, &c.

An elephant.

2. दंती दंतावलो हस्ती द्विरदो ऽनेकपो द्विपः

मतङ्गजो गजो नागः कुञ्जरो वारणः करी

3. इभः स्तम्बेरमः पद्मी

The leader of a wild herd. — यूथनाथ (स्तु) यूथपः

A rutting elephant. c — मदोत्कटो मदकलः

A young elephant. d — कलभः करिशावकः

A furious elephant. f — 4. प्रभिन्नो गर्जितो मत्तः

An elephant out of rut. g — (समाव्) उद्वान्त निर्मदौ

A herd of elephants. — हास्तिकं गजता (वृन्दे)

A female elephant. — करिणी धेनुका वशा

The temples. — 5. गण्डः कटो

The temporal juice. j — मदो दानं

Water emitted from the elephant's trunk. — वमथुः करशीकरः

His frontal globes. k — कुम्भौ (तु पिण्डौ शिरसः)

1—मृ. 2—म. 3—मृ. 4—मृ.

[a] Also मतङ्गः. [b] And पद्म. [c] From whose temples juice is beginning to flow. [d] Till twenty years : some restrict the term to a cub under five years. [e] Fem. कलभी. [f] From whose temples juice is flowing. [g] The juice having ceased to exude. [h] So हस्तिनी, पद्मिनी &c. Also करेणुः वासिता, &c. [i] Likewise करटः. [j] Which exudes when the elephant is in rut. [k] Lumps on his head ; which swell in the rutting season. [l] Sing. कुंभः,

(तयोर्मध्ये) विदुः[m][a] (पुमान्)	The hollow between them.
6. अवग्रहो[m][b] ललाटं[n] (स्यात्)	His forehead.
ईषिका[f][c] (त्वक्षिकूटकम्)	His eyeball.
(अपांगदेशो) निर्याणं[n]	Corner of his eye.
(कर्णमूलं तु) चूलिका[f]	Root of his ear.
7. (अधः कुंभस्य) वाहित्थं[n]	Part below the frontal globes. d
प्रतिमान[n] (मधो ऽस्य यत्)	Under that; between the tusks.
आसनं[n] स्कन्धदेशः[m] (स्यात्)	His withers. e
पद्मकं[n][g] बिन्दुजालकम्[n]	Marks on his face and trunk. f
8. पक्षभागः पार्श्वभागो[m]	His side or flank.
दन्तभाग[m] (स्तु योऽग्रतः)	His front.
(द्वौ पूर्वपश्चाज्जंघादिदेशौ) गात्रा[1][n] ऽवरे[2][n] (क्रमात्)	His shoulder and thigh. h
9. तोत्रं[n] वैणुकम्[n][j]	Pike to drive him. i
आलानं[n] बंधस्तंभे[m]	Post to which he is secured. k
(ऽथ) शृंखले[m f n][l]	Chain for his feet.

1—त्र. 2—र.

[a] Some add विदूः. [b] Also अवग्राहः. [c] And इषिका or ईषिका. Also इषीका, &c. [d] Or rather below the protuberances, beneath the forehead, which are named वातकुंभः. [e] Where his rider sits. [f] Red, white or yellow. [g] Or पद्मं. [h] The first part of his fore-leg and of his hind-leg, respectively. [i] A bamboo headed with iron. [j] Some read वेणुक. [k] Or the post and tie. [l] Fem. शृंखला.

Z

m a   m n

अंदुको निगडो (ऽस्त्री स्याद्)

m n   f b

Hook to guide him. — अंकुशो (ऽस्त्री) सृणिः (स्त्रियाम्)

f c   f d   f

Leathern girt. — 10. दूष्याकक्ष्या वरत्रा (स्यात्)

f   f

Dressing an elephant. e — कल्पना सज्जना (समे)

f g   1 n   m   m h   m f i

His trappings. f — प्रवेण्यास्तरणं वर्णः परिस्तोमः कुथो (द्वयोः)

n

Unfit for riding. j — 11. वीतं (त्वसारं हस्त्यश्वं)

f   f

An elephant-stable. — वारी (तु) गजबंधनी

m k   m l   m   m   m   m

A horse. — घोटके पीति तुरग तुरंगा ऽश्व तुरंगमाः

2 m   m 3 m   m   m m   m   4 m

12. वाजि वाहा ऽर्व गंधर्व हय सैन्धव सप्तयः

m n   m

Horses of a good breed. — आजानेयाः कुलीनाः (स्युर्)

m o   5 n

—trained for the manege. — विनीताः साधुवाहिनः

---

1 आ—.   2—न्.   3—न्.   4—नि.   5—न्.

a Also अंदूकः. b Or सृणीः. It is also masculine, say some: but others hold such instances of it to be erroneous. c Likewise दूषा and दुष्या or दूष्या. d Also कक्षा. e Ornamenting him with minium, &c. or caparisoning him for his owner's riding. f Coloured woolen cloth; thrown over his back. g प्रवेणिः or प्रवेणी. h Some write परिष्टोमः. i Fem. कुथा. Also neut. कुथं. j An elephant or horse unfit for war, &c. k And घोटः. l Or पीती (—न्). Also वीतिः. m Fem. हयी. n Sing. आजानेयः. Also अजानेयः. o Sing. विनीतः.

m b m c m m d	
13. वानायुजाः पारसीकाः काम्बोजा बाह्लिका(हयाः)	Horses of certain local breeds. a
1 m m	
ययुर् (श्वो) ऽश्वमेधीयो	A horse fit for sacrifice. e
m f m	
जवन (स्तु) जवाधिकः	A fleet horse; a courser.
m 2 m g	
14. पृष्ठ्यः स्थौरी	A pack horse.
m	
(सितः) कर्को	A white horse.
m	
रथ्यो (वोढा रथस्य यः)	A chariot-horse.
m m	
बालः किशोरो	A colt.
3 f 4 f f	
वाम्यश्वा वडवा	A mare.
n	
वाडवं (गणे)	A stud.
5 m f n h	
15. (त्रिष्वा) श्वीनं (यदश्वेन दिनेनैकेन गम्यते)	A day's journey for a horse.
n	
कक्ष्यं (तु मध्यमश्वानां)	A horse's flank.
f f i	
हेषा ह्रेषा (च निस्वनः)	Neighing.
m m	
16. निगाल (स्तु) गलोद्देशो	The throat.
n 6 n	
(वृन्दे त्व) श्वीयमाश्व (वत्)	A multitude of horses.

---

¹ययु. ²—री. ³—मी. ⁴ब—. ⁵आ—. ⁶आ—.

a Of the several countries indicated: but some make the two first terms synonymous; as also the two last. b So वनायुजः a horse from *Vanáyu*; and वानायुजः one from *Vánáyu*. c Sing. पारसीकः or पारशीकः a Persian horse. d बाह्लिकः or बाह्लीकः. e Fit to be immolated at an *As'wamédha.* f Some add जवनः also प्रजवी (—न्). g Likewise स्थूरी (—न्), and स्थोरी (—न्). Some explain this strong. h आश्वीनः.—ना.—नं. i Also ह्रेषा.

A horse's paces. a — आस्कंदितं धौरितकं रेचितं वल्गितं प्लुतम्

His paces generally. b — 17. (गतयो ऽमूः पंच) धारा

His nose. c — घोणा (तु) प्रोथ (मस्त्रियाम्)

The bit of the bridle. — कविका (तु) खलीनो (ऽस्त्री)

A horse's hoof. — शफं (क्लीबे) खुरः (पुमान्)

His tail. — 18. पुच्छो (ऽस्त्री) लूम लांगूले वालहस्त (श्च) वालधिः

A horse rolling himself. — (त्रिषू) पावृत्त लुठितौ (परावृत्ते मुहुर्भुवि)

A war chariot. — 19. (याने चक्रिणि युद्धार्थे) शतांगः स्यंदनो रथः

Any other car. i — (असौ) पुष्परथ (श्चक्रयानं न समराय यत्)

A covered car. k — 20. कर्णीरथः प्रवहणं डयनं (च समं त्रयम्)

A cart. — (क्लीबे) ऽनः शकटो (ऽस्त्री स्यात्)

A carriage drawn by oxen. — गंत्री (कंबलिवाह्यकम्)

A litter. — 21. शिबिका याप्ययानं (स्यात्)

---

1 वृ—. 2—स्.

[a] Viz. walk, trot, moving in the longe, (some say sidling,) gallop, and vaulting ; in order, as enumerated. [b] Sing. धारा a pace. [c] Or the extremity of his snout : or one term signifies the nostril ; and the other the snout. [d] And कविः or कवी. [e] Likewise खलिनः. [f] And क्षुरः. [g] Or लांगुलः. [h] Some restrict the two last terms to signify a hairy or bushy tail. [i] For travelling, &c. [j] Also पुष्परथः. [k] For the conveyance of women ; but some interpret this a small covered car for diversion ; or else a litter to be borne on men's shoulders. [l] And प्रवहणं. [m] Or ड्यनं. [n] Likewise गान्त्री.

f *f* दोला प्रेंखा (दिकाः स्त्रियाम्)	A hammock or swing. a
mfn *mfn* (उभौ तु) द्वैप वैयाघ्रौ (द्वीपिचर्मावृते रथे)	A car covered with tigerskin. c
22. (पांडुकम्बलसंवीतः स्यंदनः) पांडुकम्बली [1] *mfn*	—with white woollen cloth.
mfn *mfn*d (रथे) काम्बल वास्त्रा (दयः कम्बलादिभिरावृते)	—with blanket or cloth, &c.
23. (त्रिषु द्वैपादयो)[c]	
f *f* रथ्या रथकड्या (रथव्रजे)	A multitude of cars.
[2]*f*g *n* धूः (स्त्री क्लीवे) यानमुखं	Fore-part of a carriage. f
n [3]*m* (स्याद्) रथांगमुपस्करः	Any part of a carriage.
24. *n* *n* चक्रं रथांगं	A wheel.
*f*h *m* (तस्यांते) नेमिः (स्त्री स्यात्) प्रधिः (पुमान्)	Its periphery.
*f*j *f*k पिण्डिका नाभिर्	Its nave. i
m *mf*m अक्षाग्रकीलके (तु द्वयोर्) अणिः	The pin of the axle. l

[1]—नृ. [2]धुर्. [3]अ्—.

[a] Whether for travelling or for diversion. [b] Besides other terms, as खट्वा, &c. [c] The following terms are employed adjectively. Ex. द्वैपः रथः. [d] वास्त्रः, covered with cloth. चार्मः, covered with leather. क्षौमः, with linen. दौकूलः, with silk. [e] The foregoing are used adjectively. [f] Its pole ; or the part where the yoke is fixed. [g] Also धुरा. [h] And नेमी. [i] Or else the centre piece of the car itself. [j] Also पिण्डी or पिण्डिकः. [k] नाभिः and नाभी. [l] Or a pin at the extremity of the pole. [m] Likewise आणिः and fem. अणी.

f 1m

The fender of a carriage. a — 25. रथगुप्तिर्वरूथो (ना)

m m

The pole. b — कूबर (स्तु) युगंधरः

m c

Bottom of a carriage. — अनुकर्षो (दार्वधःस्थं)

m

A separate yoke. d — प्रासंगो (ना युगाद्युगः)

n f n n n g n

Any vehicle. e — 26. (सर्वं स्याद्) वाहनं यानं युग्यं पत्रं (च) धोरणम्

m n

A mediate one. h — (परम्परावाहनं यत्तद्) वैनीतकम् (ऽस्त्रियाम्)

m m m 2m

Elephant drivers. i — 27. आधोरणा हस्तिपका हस्त्यारोहा निषादिनः

3m 4m 5m m 6m m

A charioteer. — नियंता प्राजिता यंता सूतः क्षत्ता (च) सारथिः

m j m k

28. सव्येष्ट दक्षिणस्थौ (च संज्ञा रथकुटुम्बिनः)

m m

Warriors in chariots. — रथिनः स्यंदनारोहाः

n n

Horsemen. l — अश्वारोहा (स्तु) सादिनः

1थ—. 2—तृ. 3—तृ. 4—तृ. 5—तृ. 6—तृ.

a A piece of wood encompassing it, to secure it from collision. b Or wood to which the yoke is fixed. c Also अनुकर्षन् (न्). d For training young cattle and for similar purposes. e Horse, elephant, chariot, &c. f Also वाह्यं. g And पत्त्रं. h As a porter carrying a litter, or a horse dragging a carriage. i Some restrict the two first terms to the keeper, and the two last to the warrior riding an elephant. j सव्येष्टा (तृ) सव्येष्ठः (अ). k Some erroneously make the two last terms signify the carriage horses yoked right and left. l Sing. अश्वारोहः, सादी (न्).

29. भटा *m* योधा(श्च) *m* योद्धारः [1] *m*	Warriors generally.
सेनारक्षा(स्तु) *m* सैनिकाः *m*	Guards or sentinels.
(सेनायां समवेता ये) सैन्या(स्ते) *m* सैनिका(श्च ते) *m*	Arrayed troops.
30. (बलिनो ये सहस्रेण) साहस्रा(स्ते) *m* सहस्रिणः [2] *m*	A thousand strong.
परिधिस्थः *m* परिचरः *m*	A guard or attendant. [a]
सेनानीर्वाहिनीपतिः *m* [3] *m*	A general.
31. कंचुको *m* वारबाणो(ऽस्त्री) *m n* [b]	Armour; hawberk.
(यत्तु मध्ये सकंचुकाः) (बध्नंति तत्) सारसना [4] *n* ऽधिकांगे *n*	The girdle over the coat of mail.
(ऽथ) शीर्षकम् *m*	A helmet.
32. शीर्षण्यं *n* (च) शिरस्त्रे *n*	
(ऽथ) तनुत्रं *n* वर्म [5] *n* दंशनम् *n* [c]	Mail.
उरश्छदः *m* कंकटको *m* जागरः *m* [d] कवचो *m n* (ऽस्त्रियाम्)	
33. आमुक्तः *mfn* प्रतिमुक्त(श्च) *mfn* पिनद्ध(श्चा) *mfn* ऽपिनद्ध(वत्) *mfn*	Clothed, or accoutred.
सन्नद्धो *mfn* वर्मितः *mfn* सज्जो *mfn* दंशितो *mfn* व्यूढकंकटः *mfn* [e]	Armed or mailed.
34. (त्रिष्वामुक्तादयो) (वर्मभृतां) कावचिकं *n* (गणे)	Multitude of soldiers mailed.

---

[1]योद्धृ—. [2]—न्. [3]वा—. [4]—न्. [5]—न्.

[a] Bodyguard. [b] Also वारबाणः. [c] Or दंसनं. [d] And जगरः. [e] Or, according to a different reading, व्यूढकंकटः.

m m m m a 1 m

A foot-soldier. पदाति पत्तिपदग पादातिक पदातय:

m m

35. पद्ग (श्च) पदिक (श्चा)

n f

Infantry. (ऽथ) पादातं पत्तिसंहति:

m m c m m

A soldier by profession. d शस्त्राजीवे काण्डस्पृष्टा ऽयुधीया ऽयुधिका:(समा:)

m m m

Skilled in archery. 36. कृतहस्त: सुप्रयोगविशिख: कृतपुङ्ख (वत्)

m

Unskilled; missing the the butt. अपराद्धपृषत्को (ऽसौ लक्ष्याच्च्युतसायक:)

2 m 3 m m m d m e m

An archer or bowman 37. धन्वी धनुष्मान् धानुष्को निषङ्ग्यस्त्री धनुर्धर:

4 m m

One fighting only with arrows. (स्यात्) काण्डवां (स्तु) काण्डीर:

m m

A warrior armed with an iron-lance. शाक्तीक: शक्तिहेतिक:

m m

— with a club, or a battle-axe. f 38. याष्टीक पारश्वधिकौ (यष्टिपरश्वधहेतिकौ)

m m

— with a sword. नैस्त्रिंशिको ऽसिहेति: (स्यात्)

m m

— with a spear. (समौ) प्रासिक कौन्तिकौ

5 m m

— bearing a shield. 39. चर्मी फलकपाणि: (स्यात्)

6 m m

A standard bearer. पताकी वैजयन्तिक:

m m m m

A companion or follower. अनुप्लव: सहाय (श्चा) ऽनुचरो ऽभिसर: (समा:)

m m g m m m

A leader. 40. पुरोगा ऽग्रेसरप्रष्ठा ऽग्रत:सर पुर:सरा:

1—ति. 2—न्. 3—त्. 4—वत्. 5—न्. 6—न्.

[a] Also पादात:, पादातिक: and पादाविक:. [b] These and following to V. 45 inclusive, may be used adjectively. [c] Or काण्डपृष्ठ:. [d] निषंगी (—न्). [e] अस्त्री (—न्). [f] Respectively. [g] Or अग्रसर:.

m 1 *m*
पुरोगमः पुरोगामी

2 *m* *m*
मन्दगामी (तु) मन्थरः — Marching slow.

m a *m* b
41. जंघालो ऽतिजवः — Marching fast.

m *m*
(तुल्यौ) जंघाकरिक जांघिकौ — A runner or express.

3 *m* *m* 4 *m* 5 *m* *m* *m*
तरस्वी त्वरितो वेगी प्रजवी जवनो जवः

m
42. जय्यो (यः शक्यते जेतुं) — Able to conquer.

जेयो (जेतव्यमात्रके) — Fit for conquest.

m 6 *m*
जैत्र (स्तु) जेता — A conqueror. c

(यो गच्छत्यलं विद्विषतः प्रति)

m *m* *m*
43. (सो) ऽभ्यमित्रो ऽभ्यमित्रीयो (ऽप्य) ऽभ्यमित्रीण (इत्यपि) — One who ably faces the foe.

m 7 *m*
ऊर्जस्वलः (स्याद्) ऊर्जस्वी (य ऊर्जातिशयान्वितः) — Strong; powerful.

8 *m* 9 *m*
44. (स्याद्) उरस्वानुरसिलो — Broad-chested. d

m *m* f 10 *m*
रथिको रथिरो रथी — The owner of a car. e

m h 11 *m*
कामगाम्यनुकामीनो (स्य.) — One who goes as he lists. g

m
ऽत्यंतीन (स्तथा भृशम्) — One who moves much.

1—न्. 2—न्. 3—न्. 4—न्. 5—न्.
6—तृ. 7—न्. 8—त्. 9उ—. 10—न्. 11ख—.

[a] Or जंघिलः. [b] And अतिबलः. [c] Or according to another interpretation, one who effectually faces the foe. [d] Some interpret this strong. [e] Or a person riding in a car. [f] Some read रथिनः; but others condemn this variation. [g] Some interpret the second term, acting as he lists. [h] कामगामी (—न्). Also कामंगामी(—न्).

A hero. 45. शूरो वीर[a] (श्) विक्रान्तो

Victorious; used to conquer. जेता जिष्णु (श्) जित्वरः

Skilled in war. सांयुगीनो (रणे साधुः)

(शस्त्राजीवादयस्त्रिषु)[b]

An army; or forces. 46. ध्वजिनी वाहिनी[c] सेना पृतना[d]ऽनीकिनी चमूः

वरूथिनी बलं[e] सैन्यं चक्रं (च)ाऽनीक (मस्त्रियाम्)[f]

Array of troops. Different forms of array.[g] 47. व्यूह (स्तु) बलविन्यासो

(भेदा दण्डादयो युधि)

The rear. प्रत्यासारो[h] व्यूहपार्ष्णिः

Reserve.[i] (सैन्यपृष्ठे) प्रतिग्रहः[j]

A platoon.[k] 48. (एकेभैकरथा त्र्यश्वा) पत्तिः (पञ्चपदातिका)

Greater bodies.[l] (पत्त्यङ्गैस्त्रिगुणैः सर्वैः क्रमादाख्या यथोत्तरम्)

1—ह.

[a] Or वीरः. [b] The preceding from v. 35 admit the three genders. [c] Some write वाहिनी and add वाहना. [d] Also पूतना [e] Or बलम्. [f] Some distinguish the four last terms from the preceding seven, as signifying a part or member of an army: others as signifying either that, or an army in general. [g] Namely दण्डः in line, भोगः in column, मण्डलः in a circle, असंहतः in separate order (including a half moon, &c.). These admit various subordinate distinctions noticed in treatises on the art of war. [h] Or प्रत्यासरः. [i] A separate corps posted with the general, four hundred yards in the rear of the line. [j] And परिग्रहः or पतद्ग्रहः. [k] Comprising one elephant, one chariot, three horse, and five foot. [l] Increasing in geometrical progression. Three *pattis* are a *Sénámuc'ha*; and three of these are a *Gulma*.

n mn m f f f

49. सेनामुखं गुल्म गणौ वाहिनी पृतना चमूः

f a

अनीकिनी

1*f*

(दशानीकिन्यो) ऽक्षौहिणी — A complete army. b

f d

(ऽथ) सम्पदि — Success or prosperity. c

f f f

50. सम्पत्तिः श्री (श्च) लक्ष्मी (श्च)

f e 2*f* 3*f* f

विपत्त्यां विपदापदौ — Adversity.

n n n 4*n* g

आयुधं (तु) प्रहरणं शस्त्रमस्त्रम् — A weapon.

(अथा ऽस्त्रियौ) — A bow.

mn h 5*mn* 6*n* i *n n n*

51. धनुश्चापौ धन्व शरासन कोदण्ड कार्मुकम्

m

इष्वासो (ऽप्य)

n

(ऽथ कर्णस्य) कालपृष्ठं (शरासनम्) — The bow of KARNA.

mn mn

52. (कपिध्वजस्य) गाण्डीव गाण्डिवौ (पुंनपुंसकौ) — That of ARJUNA.

1—णी. 2 —द्. 3 आपद्. 4 अ—. 5 चाप. 6 —नु.

a Consisting of (3. 7) 2, 187 elephants, as many cars, thrice as many horse, and five times as many foot ; making in all 21, 870. b Ten times the last, or 109, 350 foot, 65, 610 horse, 21, 870 chariots, and 21, 870 elephants. c Increase of wealth, &c. d संपत् (—द्) and संपदा. e विपत्तिः. f Also विपदा and आपदा. g Some restrict the last term to a missile weapon ; and the preceding term to a weapon retained in the hand. h Masc. धनुः (—नुः), or धनुः (—नु), and धनूः (—नूः). Likewise fem. धनुः, &c. i धन्व (—न्व) or धन्वं (—न्वन्) ; also masc. धन्वा (—न्वन्).

Notched extremity of a bow. Leathern fence for the arm.

f a

(कोटिरस्या) ऽटनी

f *fn* b

गोधा तले (ज्याघातवारणे)

Middle of the bow.

m *n*

53. लस्तक (स्तु) धनुर्मध्यं

The bow-string.

f *f* *f* *m*

मौर्वी ज्या शिञ्जिनी गुणः

Two attitudes in shooting. c

n 1 *n*

(स्यात्) प्रत्यालीढमालीढ (मित्यादिस्थानपंचकम्)

A butt or mark.

n *n* *n* d

54. लक्ष्यं लक्षं शरव्यं (च)

Archery.

m *n*

शराभ्यास उपासनम्

An arrow.

m *m* 2 *m* *m* *m* 3 *m*

इषत्क बाण विशिखा अजिह्मग खगाशुगाः

m e *m* *m* f 4 *m* *m* *mf*

55. कलम्ब मार्गण शराः पत्री रोप इषु (र्द्वयोः)

Iron arrows.

m g *m*

प्रक्ष्वेडना (स्तु) नाराचाः

Feather of an arrow.

m *m*

पक्षो वाजः

h

(त्रिषूत्तरे)

Shot, as an arrow.

mfn

56. निरस्तः (प्रहिते बाणे)

Poisoned arrow.

mfn *mfn*

(विषाक्ते) दिग्ध लिप्तकौ

m i *m* j *m* *m* *mf*

तूणो पासंग तूणीर निषङ्गा इषुधि (र्द्वयोः)

1—या. 2—खु. 3 आ—. 4—षु.

a And अटनिः. b तला or तलं. c Out of five, viz. 1st. with left foot advanced, and right foot retired; 2d. With the knee advanced, but the left foot retired; 3d. समपदं with both feet even; 4th. विशाखः with feet a span apart; 5th. मण्डलं with both knees bent. d Likewise सरव्यं. e Also कादम्बः. f शरः or सरः. g Sing. प्रक्ष्वेडनः नाराचः. Also fem. प्रक्ष्वेडना and प्रक्ष्वेदना. h The following admit the three genders. i तूणः Also fem. तूणा. j उपासंगः. Likewise अपासंगः.

57· त्वरुयां[1 f]

खड्गे[m] (तु) निस्त्रिंश[m] चन्द्रहासा[m] ऽसिरिष्टय:[m][m a] — A scimitar.

कौक्षेयको[m] मण्डलाग्र:[m] करवाल:[m b] कृपाण[m] (वत्)

58. त्सरु:[m c] (खड्गादिमुष्टौ स्यात्) — A hilt or handle.

मेखला[f] (तन्निबन्धनम्) — A sword knot. d

फलको[m n] (ऽस्त्री) फलं[n e] चर्म[2 n f] — A shield.

संग्राहो[m] (मुष्टिरस्य य:) — The gripe of a shield.

59. द्रुघणो[m h] मुद्गर[m] घनौ[m] — A mallet. g

(स्यादी) ईली[f j] करपालिका[f k] — A cudgel. i

भिन्दिपाल:[m] सृग[m] (स्तुल्यौ) — A short arrow. l

परिघ:[m] परिघातन:[m] — A bludgeon. m

60· (द्वयो:) कुठार:[m f n] स्वधिति:[m f] परशु[m f o] (श्च) परश्वध:[m p] — An axe.

---

[1] त्सरुणी. [2] —र्म.

[a] रिष्टि: or ऋष्टि:. [b] Also करवाल:. [c] Some add सरु:. [d] A thong or chain passing from the hilt over the wrist, to secure the sword : some say the guard of the hilt. [e] Or फरं. [f] Also चर्म(—र्मं). [g] A weapon formed like a carpenter's hammer. [h] And द्रुघन:. [i] Some explain it a short sword ; others, a stick shaped like a sword. [j] Likewise इली and ईलि:. [k] Also करपालिका. [l] Thrown by the hand ; or, as others explain it, shot through a tube. [m] Or a staff mounted with iron ; shaped like a pestle. [n] Fem. कुठारी. [o] Also पर्शु:. [p] Likewise परस्वध: and पर्श्वध:.

A knife. — (स्याच्) छस्त्री[1 f] (चा) ऽसिपुत्री[f] (च) छुरिका[f] (चा) ऽसिधेनुका[f]

A javelin. — 61. (वा पुंसि) शल्यं[m n] शंकु[m] (र्ना)

An iron crow. — सर्वला[f a] तोमरो[m n] (ऽस्त्रियाम्)

A bearded dart. — प्रास[m b] (स्तु) कुन्तः[m]

Sharp edge of a sword. c — कौण[m] (स्तु स्त्रियः) पाल्य[f d]श्रि[f e] कोटयः[f f]

Assembling of a complete army. — 62. सर्वाभिसारः[m] सर्वौघः[m] सर्वसन्नहनं[2 m] (र्थकः)

Lustration of arms. g — लोहाभिहारो[m h] (ऽस्त्रभृतां राज्ञां नीराजनाविधिः)

March to repel an enemy. — 63. (यत् सेनयाभिगमनमरौ तद्) अभियानकम्[n]

March of an assailant. i — यात्रा[f] व्रज्या[f] ऽभिनिर्याणं[n] प्रस्थानं[n] गमनं[n] गमः[m]

Surrounding a foe. — 64. (स्याद्) आसारः[m] प्रसरणं[n j]

An army in motion. k — प्रचक्रं[n] चलिता[3 n] (र्थकम्)

A gallant attack. — (अहितान् प्रत्यभीतस्य रणे यानम्) अतिक्रमः[l]

1—शस्त्री. 2—नू. 3—त.

[a] Or शर्वला. [b] And प्रासः. [c] Some say its point. [d] पालिः, or पाली. [e] अश्रिः, or अश्री. [f] कोटिः or कोटी. [g] A religious ceremony on the 19th of *A's'wina*, preparatory to the opening of a campaign. [h] Some write लोहाभिसारः. [i] Or march generally. [j] Also fem. प्रसरणी, प्रसरणिः, and प्रसारणी. [k] Some explain it, foraging. [l] Or अभिक्रमः, for both readings occur.

65. वैतालिका[m] बोधकराश्[1 m] — Awakeners. a

चाक्रिका[m] घाण्टिका[m c] (र्थकाः) — Bards in throngs: b

(स्युर्) मागधा[m] (स्तु.) मगधा[m e] — Bards by birth. d

बन्दिनः[m g] स्तुतिपाठकाः[m] — Panegyrists. f

66. संशप्तका[m] (स्तु. समयात्संग्रामादनिवर्त्तिनः) — Chosen soldiers. h

रेणु[m f] (र्द्वयोः स्त्रियां) धूलिः[f i] पांशु[m j](र्ना न द्वयो) रजः[2 n k] — Dust.

67. चूर्णे[m n] क्षोदः[m] — Powder. l

समुत्पिञ्ज[m] पिञ्जलौ[m] (भृशमाकुले) — An army in great disorder.

पताका[f] वैजयन्ती[f] (स्यात्) केतनं[n] ध्वज[m n](मस्त्रियाम्) — A flag or banner. m

68. (सा) वीराशंसनं[n] (युद्धभूमिर्यातिभयप्रदा) — The post of danger.

(अहंपूर्वमहंपूर्वमित्य) हंपूर्विका[f] (स्त्रियाम्) — Emulative onset. n

69. आहोपुरुषिका[f] (दर्पाद्या स्यात्संभावनात्मनि) — Boasting.

1—र. 2—स्.

[a] Whose business it is to awaken the prince at dawn with music and song. [b] Who chant in chorus : or, as some explain this who ring bells before idols. [c] Sing. चाक्रिकः also घाण्टिकः. [d] Who recite the praises of kings in their presence. Some make this and the following synonymous. [e] Sing. मागधः or मगधः. Also मधुकः [f] Who attend on a march and chant deeds of valour. [g] Sing. बंदी (—न्). [h] Sworn not to recede ; and whose business is to recall fugitives. [i] Or धूली. Also masc. धूलिः [j] And पांशुः [k] Likewise masc. रजः (स). [l] Formed by pulverizing. Some make this and the preceding synonymous. [m] Some make the two last, others the four terms, signify the ensign-staff. [n] Act of running forward with emulation.

Conceit of superiority.

f

70. अहमहमिका (तु सा स्यात्परस्परं यो भवत्यहंकार:)

1 n n a n 2 n 3 n b

Strength or power. द्रविणंतर: सहो बल शौर्य्याणि स्थाम शुष्म (च)

f m m

71. शक्ति: पराक्रम प्राणौ

m f

Great power. c विक्रम (स्त्व) ऽतिशक्तिता

f c

Drink of warriors. d वीरपाणं (तु यत्पानं वृत्ते भाविनि वा रणे)

n 4 n n n n

War, battle, combat. 72. युद्धमायोधनं जन्यं प्रधनं प्रविदारणम्

n 5 n n n f n g

मृधमास्कंदनं संख्यं समीकं साम्परायिकम्

m m 6 n m m

73. (अस्त्रियां) समरा ऽनीक रणा: कलहविग्रहौ

m m m m h m

सम्प्रहारा ऽभिसम्पात कलि संस्फोट संयुगा:

m m m m 7 m

74. अभ्यामर्द समाघात संग्रामा ऽभ्यागमाहवा:

m 8 m f 9 f 10 f 11 f i

समुदाय: (स्त्रिय:) संयत्समित्याजि समिद्युध:

n n

Close fight; struggle. 75. नियुद्धं बाहुयुद्धे

m n j n

Mingled combat. (ऽथ) तुमुलं रणसंकुले

1—स. 2—र्य. 3—मृ. 4 आ—. 5 आ—. 6—ण.
7 आ—. 8—त्. 9—ति. 10 आ—. 11—त्.

[a] सह: (स्). Also masc. सह: (स). [b] शुष्मं (ष्म) and शुष्म (न्). [c] Or heroic valour. [d] Taken during battle for refreshment; or before it, to elavate courage. [e] Some admit वीरपानं. [f] Also अनीकं. [g] Or संपरायकं. [h] Likewise संस्फेट:. [i] Sing. युत् (ध्). [j] And तुमूलं. Also लड.रं.

f m
क्ष्वेडा (तु) सिंहनादः (स्यात्) — War-Whoop.

f f
(करिणां) घटना घटा। — Troop of elephants. a

m
76. क्रन्दनं योधसंरावो। — Mutual defiance of combatants. b

n n
बृंहितं करिगर्जितम्। — Roaring of elephants.

m c
विस्फारो (धनुषः स्वानः) — Twang of a bow.

m 1 m
पटहाडम्बरौ (समौ) — Drum used in battle.

n m m
77. प्रसभं (तु) बलात्कारो हठो। — Violence.

n n
(ऽथ) स्खलितं छलम्। — Fraud; stratagem; circumvention.

m n m n
अजन्यं (क्लीबम्) उत्पात उपसर्गः (समं त्रयम्) — A portent.d

f n e m
78. मूर्च्छा (तु) कश्मलं मोहो (ऽप्य) — Fainting.

m n
ऽवमर्द (स्तु.) पीडनम्। — Devastation.

n
अभ्यवस्कन्दनं (त्व्) ऽभ्यासादनं — Striking to disable the foe. f

m m
विजयो जयः — Victory.

f m n
79. वैरशुद्धिः प्रतीकारो वैरनिर्यातनं (च सा) — Revenge.g

m 2 m m 3 m m m
प्रद्रावो द्राव संद्राव संदावा विद्रवो द्रवः — Flight; retreat. h

n
80. अपक्रमो ऽपयानं (च)

m
(रणे भङ्गः) पराजयः — Defeat.

---

[1]स्वा—. [2]उ—. [3]—व.

[a] Assembled in battle. [b] Provoking each other to fight. [c] And विष्फारः. [d] As an earthquake, &c. [e] Or कश्मलं. [f] Some interpret this, facing the enemy. [g] Retaliating of an injury. [h] Some explain the first six terms, flight; andthe other two, retreat.

Defeated; vanquished.

m f n *m f n*
पराजित पराभूतौ (त्रिषु)

Missing; lost, having vanished.

m f n *m f n*
नष्टतिरोहितौ

Slaughter.

n a *n* b *n* *n* c
81. प्रमापणं निबर्हणं निकारणं निशारणम्
n *n* *n* *n*
प्रवासनं परासनं निषूदनं निहिंसनम्
n *n* *n* d 1 *n*
82. निर्वासनं संज्ञपनं निर्ग्रंथनमपासनम्
n *n* *n* *n*
निस्तर्हणं निहननं क्षणनं परिवर्जनम्
n *n* *n* *n*
83. निर्वापणं विशसनं मारणं प्रतिघातनम्
n *n* *n* 2 *n*
उद्वासन प्रमथन क्रथनोज्जासनानि (च)
m *m* *m* *m* 3 *m* *m*
84. आलंभ पिंज विशर घातोन्मन्थ वधा (अपि)

Death.

f e *m* *m* *m* *m*
(स्यात्) पंचता कालधर्मो दिष्टांत, प्रलयो ऽत्यय:
m *m* *m f* f 4 *n* *m n*
85. अंतो नाशो (द्वयोर्) मृत्युर्मरणं निधनो (ऽस्त्रियाम्)

Dead: having expired.

m f n *m f n* *m f n* *m f n* *m f n*
परासु प्राप्तपंचत्व परेत प्रेत संस्थिता:
m f n *m f n*
86. मृत प्रमीतौ (त्रिष्वेते)

A funeral pile. g

f *f* *f*
चिता चित्या चिति: (स्त्रियाम्)

---

1 क्ष—. 2 उ—म. 3 उ—. 4 म—.

a Some add प्रमापनं. b Or निर्बर्हणं. c And विशारणं. d Some read निर्गन्थनं. e Likewise पंचत्वं. f Also neut. मृत्यु. Likewise मृतं and fem. मृति:. g Or a place prepared for burning a body.

m n कबंधो (ऽस्त्री क्रियायुक्तमपमूर्द्धकलेवरम्)	A headless trunk.
n *m* b 87. श्मशानं (स्यात्) पितृवनं	A cemetery. a
m *m n* कुणपः शवम् (अस्त्रियाम्)	A dead body.
m 1 *m* *f* d प्रग्रहोपग्रहौ वंद्यां	A prisoner c
f *m* कारा (स्याद्) बंधनालये	A prison or jail.
2 *m* *m* 88. (पुंसि भूम्नि) ऽसवः प्राणा (श्चैवं)	Breath. e
m f *n* जीवो ऽसुधारणम्	Life.
n g *m* आयुर्जीवितकालो (ना)	Age ; duration of life.
m n 3 *n* जीवातुर्जीवनौषधम्	Drug to revive the dead.

1 ग्र—ह. 2 असु. 3 जी—.

a Or the place where bodies are burnt. b Also पितृकाननं, पितृवसतिः, &c. c Or any one (man or beast) confined. d Sing. वंदिः or वंदी. e Inspiration and respiration of five sorts (See book 1. ch. 1.) collectively pl. असवः. But, if one be meant, sing. असुः. f Also fem. जीवा and neut. जीवनं. g आयुः (—स्) or masc. आयुः (—यु).

CHAPTER IX.

m m m m 1m b m c

Men of the third tribe. a — 1. ऊरव्या ऊरुजा अर्य्या वैश्या भूमिस्पृशो विशः

m f f f 2n n

Livelihood; profession. — आजीवो जीविका वार्त्ता वृत्तिर्वर्त्तन जीवने

m n n c

Various professions. d — 2. (स्त्रियां)कृषिः पाशुपाल्यं वाणिज्यं (चेति वृत्तयः)

f 3f

Service. — सेवा श्ववृत्तिर्

n f f

Agriculture. — अनृतं कृषिर्

n g 4n

Gleaning. — उञ्छशिलं (त्वृ) तम्

n n

Alms solicited; or unsolicited. h — 3. (द्वे याचितायाचितयोर्यथासंख्यं) मृता मृते

n m

Traffic; commerce. — सत्यानृतं वणिग्भावः

n n

Debt. — (स्याद्) ऋणं पर्य्युदंचनम्

1—श्. 2व—. 3—त्ति. 4मृत.

[a] Of the class of merchants and husbandmen. [b] भूमिस्पृक् (—श्). [c] Sing. विट् (—श्). [d] Severally stated: viz. husbandry, pasture and merchandize. [e] And fem. वणिज्या. [f] Some read प्रमृतं. [g] Also उञ्छ-शिलं. Likewise उञ्छः or उञ्छ gathering of grains; and शिल gleaning ears of corn. [h] Severally stated, in their order.

4. उद्धारो (m)	
अर्थप्रयोग (m) (स्तु.) कुसीदं (n a) वृद्धिजीविका (f)	Profession of usury.
(याच्ञयाप्तं) याचितकं (n)	A thing borrowed for use. b
(निमयाद्) आपमित्यकम् (n)	Obtained by barter.
5. उत्तमर्णा (m) ऽधमर्णौ (m) (द्वौ प्रयोक्तृग्राहकौ क्रमात्)	Creditor and debtor. c
कुसीदिको (m) वार्धुषिको (m) वृद्ध्याजीव (m) (श्च) वार्धुषिः (m)	A usurer.
6. क्षेत्राजीवः (m) कर्षक (m d) (श्च) कृषिक (m) (श्च) कृषीवलः (m)	A husbandman.
(क्षेत्रं) व्रैहेय (m f n) शालेयं (m f n) (व्रीहिशाल्युद्भवोचितम्)	(Field) fit for corn and rice. e
7. यव्यं (m f n) यवक्यं (m f n) षष्टिक्यं (m f n) (यवादिभवनं हि यत्)	—producing barley, &c. f
तिल्यं (m f n) तैलीन (m f n) (वन्माषोमाणुभंगाद्वि. रूपता)	—producing sesamum, &c. g
8. मौद्गीनं (m f n) कौद्रवीणा (m f n). (दिशेषधान्योद्भवोचितम्)	—fit for other grain; as pulse, &c. h
बीजाकृतं (m f n) (उ) [1] प्तकृष्टं (m f n)	(Land) ploughed after sowing.

[1] उ—.

[a] And कुषीदं or कुषीदं. [b] Commodatum. [c] Severally mentioned. These and the following to v. 10. admit the three genders. [d] Or कार्षकः. [e] Severally. [f] Respectively for barley, forced rice, and quick-growing rice. [g] So माष्यं, माषीणं, producing black kidney beans (Phaseolus radiatus). उम्यं, औमीनं, growing linseed. अणव्यं, आणवीनं, bearing panic. भंग्यं, भांगीनं, yielding hemp. [h] Severally; fit for kidney beans (Phaseolus max and mungo), or for Paspalum (P. frumentaceum). So कौलत्थीनं fit for Dolichos biflorus. चाणकीनं fit for chich peas, &c.

Land any how ploughed or tilled.

m f n a *m f n* *m f n*
सीत्यं कृष्टं (च) हल्य (वत्)

Thrice ploughed.

m f n *m f n* *m f n* *m f n*
9. त्रिगुणाकृतं तृतीयाकृतं त्रिहल्यं त्रिसीत्य(मपि तत्क्षिन्)

Twice ploughed.

m f n b *m f n* c
द्विगुणाकृते (तु सर्व्वं पूर्व्वं) शम्बाकृत (मपोह)

Sown with certain measures of seed. d

m f n 1 *m f n*
10. (द्रोणाढकादिवापादौ) द्रौणिकाढकिका (दयः)

m f n
(खारीवापस्तु) खारीक

e
(उत्तमर्णादयस्त्रिषु)

A field. A multitude of fields.

m n *m* *n*
11. (पुंनपुंसकयोर्) वप्रः केदारः क्षेत्रम्
(अस्य तु)

n *n* *n* *n* f
कैदारकं (स्यात्) कैदार्य्यं क्षैत्रं कैदारिकं (गणे)

Clods of earth. g

m n *m*
12. लोष्टानि लेष्टवः (पुंसि)

A harrow.

m h *m* i
कोटिशो लोष्टभेदनः

A goad.

n j *n* *n* k
प्राजनं तोदनं तोत्रं

A spade or hoe.

n 2 *n*
खनित्रमवदारणम्

---

1 खा—. 2 च—.

[a] Or सीत्यं. [b] So द्वितीयाकृतं, द्विहल्यं, द्विसीत्यं. [c] Also शंबाकृतं. [d] Or capable of containing so much. Thus द्रौणिकः, (fem. द्रौणा and द्रौणिकी) ; holding one *Dróna*. आढकिकः, आढकीनः, (fem. आढकी, आढकीना), holding one *A'd'h'aca*. So प्रास्थिकः, holding one *Prost'ha* and कौडविकः, holding one *Cudava*. But खारीकः, holding one *C'ha'rí*. [e] The foregoing from v. 5. admit the three genders. [f] Also केदारं. [g] Sing लोष्टं and लेष्टुः. [h] Or कोटीशः. [i] Likewise लोष्टघ्नः and लेष्टघ्नः. [j] And प्रवयणं. [k] Or तोत्त्रं.

13. दात्रं[n] लवित्रम्[n]	A sickle.
आबन्धो[m] योत्रं[n] योक्त्रम्[n]	The tie of the yoke. a
(अथो) फलं[n c]	The body of the plough. b
निरीशं[n d] कुटकं[n]	
फालः[m n] कृषिको[m f]	The plough-share. e
लाङ्गलं[n] हलम्[n g]	A plough.
14. गोदारणं[n] (च) सीरो[m h]	
(ऽथ) शम्या[f] (स्त्री) युगकीलकः[m]	The pin of the yoke.
ईषा[f i] लाङ्गलदण्डः[m] (स्यात्)	The pole or shaft of the plough.
सीता[f j] लाङ्गलपद्धतिः[f]	A furrow.
15. (पुंसि) मेधिः[m] (खले दारु न्यस्तं यत्पशुबन्धने)	Post of the threshing floor. k
आशु[m n] व्रीहिः[m l] पाटलः[m m] (स्यात्)	Rice ripening in the rains.
सितशूक[m n] यवौ[m] (समौ)	Barley.
16. तोक्म[m] (स्तु, तत्र हरिते)	Green or unripe barley.

[a] With which the ox is yoked to the plough : or with which the yoke is fastened to the plough. [b] The wood, exclusive of the pole and share. [c] Some read फलं, and make it explanatory. [d] Or निरीषं. [e] Some make the preceding terms synonymous with these. [f] Or कृषकः. Also fem. कृषिका. [g] And masc. हलः. [h] Or शीरः. [i] Likewise ईशा. [j] And शीता. [k] Round which cattle turn to tread out the grain. [l] Some unite the terms, आशुव्रीहिः. [m] Also पाटलिः. [n] And शितशूकः.

Peas.[a] — कलाय[m] (स्तु) सतीनकः[m b]

हरेणु[m] खण्डिकौ[m] (चास्मिन्)

Sort of grain.[c] — कोरदूष[m] (स्तु) कोद्रवः[m d]

Lentil.[e] — 17. मङ्गल्यको[m] मसूरो[m f]

Sort of kidney bean.[g] — (ऽथ) मयुष्टक[m h] मपष्ठकौ[m i]

वनमुद्ग[m]

Mustard seed.[j] — सर्षपे[m k] (तु द्वौ) तन्तुभ[m l] कदम्बकौ[m m]

The white sort.[n] — 18. सिद्धार्थ[m] (स्त्वेषु धवलो)

Wheat. — गोधूमः[m] सुमनः[m o] (समौ)

Half ripe barley.[p] — (स्याद्) यावक[m] (स्तु) कुल्माषश्[1 m q]

Chich pea.[r] — चणको[m] हरिमन्थकः[m s]

1—श्.

[a] Some writers distinguish the three first terms as names of three kinds of pulse. [b] Or सतीलः. Also सोतीनकः or सतीनकः and सातीनकः. [c] Paspalum frumentaceum, Koen. or P. Kora, Willd. [d] And कुद्रवः. [e] Ervum lens or Cicer lens. [f] Or मसुरः. Also fem. मसूरा, मसुरा. [g] Phaseolus lobatus. [h] And मकुष्टकः or मकूष्टकः. Also मकुष्टका. [i] And मयष्टकः or मपष्टकः. Likewise मयुष्टकः. [j] Sinapis dichotoma, Roxb. [k] Or सरिषपः. [l] And तंतुकः. [m] Also कटुस्नेहः. [n] Sinapis glauca, Roxb. [o] Also सुमनाः (—नस्.) [p] Interpretations differ greatly : some make this awnless barley ; others forced rice (*Bo'r*) ; others again, different species of Phaseolus, (*Ra'jama'sha*), or of Dolichos (*Culatt'ha*). [q] Or कुल्मासः. [r] Cicer arietinum. Some erroneously make these synonymous with the preceding ; others, with *Chi'naca*, Panicum Pilosum, Roxb. [s] And हरिमंथजः.

19. (द्वौ तिले) तिलपेज[m] (श्च) तिलपिञ्ज[m] (श्च निष्फले)	Barren sesamum.[a]
क्षवः[m] क्षुधाभिजननो[m c] राजिका[f] कृष्णिका[f] ऽसुरी[f d]	Black mustard.[b]
20. (स्त्रियौ) कङ्गु[f] प्रियङ्गू[f f] (द्वे)	Panick seed.[e]
अतसी[f] (स्याद्) उमा[f] क्षुमा[f]	Lin; and linseed.[g]
मातुलानी[f] (तु) भङ्गायां[1 f]	Hemp.[h]
व्रीहिभेद[m] (स्त्व्) ऽणुः[m] (पुमान्)	*China'*.[i]
21. किंशारुः[m] शस्यशूकं[m] (स्यात्)	Beard of corn.
कणिशं[m n j] शस्यमञ्जरी[f]	Ear or spike.
धान्यं[n] व्रीहिः[m] स्तम्बकरिः[m]	Corn or rice.
स्तम्बो[m] गुच्छ[m k] (स्तृणादिनः)	Clump of grass, &c.
22. नाडी[f] नालं[n l] (च) काण्डो[m] (ऽस्य)	Stalk or culm.
पलालो[m n] (ऽस्त्री स निष्फलः)	Straw.
कडङ्गरो[m] बुसं[n m] (क्लीबे)	Chaff.
(धान्यत्वचि पुमां) स्तुषः[2 m n]	Husk of rice or corn.

[1] भंगा. [2] तूष.

[a] Bearing no blossom; or its seed containing no oil. [b] Sinapis Ramosa, Roxb. [c] Or क्षुताभिजनः. [d] आसुरी or असुरी. [e] Panicum Italicum. [f] कंगुः or कंगूः and प्रियंगुः. [g] Linum usitatissimum. Some confound this with *San'a* (Crotalaria Juncea). [h] Cannabis Sativa. But other interpretations are stated; and some confound it with linseed, and others with Crotalaria. [i] Panicum pilosum, Roxb. But other interpretations are also given. [j] And कणिषं. [k] Or गुत्सः. [l] Also नालो, and नाडं. [m] Or बुषं. [n] Or तुस.

An awn. — 23. शूको (ऽस्त्री श्लक्ष्ण तीक्ष्णाग्रे)
m n

A legume or pod. — शमी शिम्बा
f *f* [a]

(त्रिषूत्तरे)
[b]

Stored, as grain. c — ऋद्धमावसितं (धान्यं)
m f n [1] *m f n* [d]

Threshed out and winnowed. — पूतं (तु) बहुलीकृतम्
m f n *m f n*

Grain in pods. e — 24. (माषादयः) शमीधान्ये
n

Bearded corn. f — शूकधान्य (यवादयः)
n

Rice. g — शालयः (कलमाद्या श्च षष्ठिकाद्या श्च पुंस्यमी)
[2] *m* [h]

Wild grains. i — 25. तृणधान्यानि नीवाराः
m *n*

Coix. j — (स्त्री) गवेडुर्गवेधुका
f [k] [3] *f*

A pestle for cleaning rice. — अयोग्रं मुसलो (ऽस्त्री स्याद्)
m n *m n* [l]

A mortar. — उदूखलमुलूखलम्
[4] *n*

1—चा. 2 शालि. 3 ग—. 4 उ—.

[a] Also शिंबा and शिंबिः. [b] The following admit the three genders. [c] After cleaning it ; some say, before. [d] Also अवसितं. [e] As peas and other pulse. [f] As barley, wheat, &c. [g] Of two classes : white rice, &c. growing in deep water ; or red rice, &c. requiring only a moist soil. [h] The above-mentioned names of species of corn and pulse are masculeine. [i] Growing with little or with no culture : viz. नीवारः, wild rice. Besides other kinds ; as श्यामाकः Panicum frumentaceum, Roxb. [j] Coix barbata, Roxb. [k] And गवेधुः or गवेडुका. [l] Likewise मुषलः.

n m n a

26. प्रस्फोटनं शूर्पम् (अस्त्री) — A winnowing basket.

f b m

चालनी तितउः (पुमान्) — A sieve or cribble.

m c m

स्यूत प्रसेवौ — A sack.

m m c

कण्डोल पिटौ — A granary. d

m m

कट किलिञ्जकौ — A mat. f

27. (समानौ)

1 f n m n

रसवत्यां तु पाकस्थान महानसे — A kitchen.

m g

पौरोगव (स्तदध्यक्षः) — Overseer of the kitchen.

m m h

सूपकारा (स्तु) बल्लवाः — Cooks.

m m m m m

28. आरालिका आन्धसिकाः सूदा औदनिका गुणाः

m m m i j

आपूपिकः कान्दविको भक्ष्यकार (इमे त्रिषु) — A baker.

n k n l 2 f f m 3 f n

29. अश्मन्तमुद्धानमधिश्रयणी चुल्लिरन्तिका — A furnace or fire-place.

f 4 f 5 f

अङ्गारधानिकाऽङ्गारशकट्य् (पि) हसन्त्य् (पि) — A portable furnace.

1—स्त्री. 2 अ—. 3 अ॰—. 4—टी. 5—न्ती.

[a] Or शूर्पं. [b] Also neut. चालनं. [c] Likewise स्योतः and स्यूनः or स्योनः. [d] Constructed of bamboos : some say, a basket to hold grain. [e] Also पिटकः or पेटकः. [f] Or else a screen made of grass; or a twist of straw. [g] This and the following admit the variation of gender. [h] Some resrict these two first terms to mean one who prepares sauces, &c. [i] Or भक्ष्यकारः. [j] The preceding are used adjectively. [k] And अश्मन्तं. [l] उद्धानं and उद्धायं or उद्धारं. [m] Also चुल्ली. [n] अन्तिका or अन्दिका.

1f

30. इसन्य (प्य)

A fire brand. a — mn n n (ऽथ न स्त्री स्याद्) अङ्गारो ऽलातमुल्मुकम्

A frying pan. — n b m (क्लीवे) ऽम्बरीषं भ्राष्ट्रो (ना)

An iron plate or pan. c — mfn f कन्दु (र्वा) स्वेदनी (स्त्रियाम्)

A jar. — m d n 31. अलिञ्जर: (स्यान्) मणिकं

A pitcher. — 2f fc 3f कर्कर्यालुर्गलन्तिका

A pot. — mf fg fh ni पिठर: स्थाल्युखा कुण्डं

A waterpot. — mfn j कलश (स्तु, त्रिषु द्वयो:)

mn mn 4mn
32. घट: कुट निपाव्

A lid. — mnk mn (अस्त्री) सरावो वर्द्धमानक:

A seether or boiler. — nl n ऋजीषं पिष्टपचनं

A goblet. m — mnn mn कंसो (ऽस्त्री) पानभाजनम्

1—नी. 2—री. 3ग—. 4 निप.

a Whether burning or extinguished; but some interpret the first term, charcoal; and the two last, half burnt wood. b And अम्बरीषं. c Some make this and the preceding synonymous. d Or अलंजर:. e माल: and अत्रु: or मात्र:. f Also fem. पिठरी. g स्थाली and neut. स्थालं. h उखा or—ऊखा. i Or fem. कुण्डी. j Or कलस:. Fem कलशि:,—शी,—सि:, or—सी. Neut. कलसं—शं. k And सराव:. l Also ऋचीषं. m A metallic vessel to drink in. n Or कंस:. Also कांस्यं.

f
33. कुतूः (कृत्तेः स्नेहपात्रं) — A leather bottle for oil.

m
(सैवाल्पा) कुतुपः (पुमान्) — A small one.

n a *n* *m n* *n* *n*
(सर्वम्) आवपनं भाण्डं पात्राऽमत्रे (च) भाजनम् — Any vessel.

f *f b* *f c*
34. दर्विः कम्बिः खजाका (च स्यात्) — A ladle or spoon.

m f *1 m*
तर्दूर्दारुहस्तकः — A wooden ladle.

n *n* *2 m d*
(अस्त्री) शाकं हरितकं शिग्रुर् — A potherb.

(अस्य तु नाडिका) — Its stalk.

m *m*
35. कडम्ब (श्च) कलम्ब (श्च)

m e *m*
वेसवार उपस्करः — A condiment.

n *m n* *n*
तिन्तिडीक (ञ्च) चुक्र (ञ्च) वृक्षाम्लम् — Acid seasoning.

n
(अथ) वेल्लजम् — Pepper.

n f *n* *n* *n g* *n*
36. मरीचं कोलकं कृष्णमूषणं धर्मपत्तनम्

m *m* *f* *f*
जीरको जरणोऽजाजी कणाः — Cumin.

(कृष्णे तु जीरके) — *Calo'njī.* [h]

f i *f* *f* *3 f* *4 f*
37. सुषवी कारवी पृथ्वी पृथुः कालोपकुञ्चिका

n *m*
आर्द्रकं शृङ्गवेरं (स्याद्) — Ginger.

f *m*
(अथ) छत्रा वितुन्नकम् — Coriander.

---

[1] दा—. [2] —पु. [3] काला. [4] उ—.

[a] Some include this in the interpretation. [b] Also दर्वी and कम्बी. [c] Likewise masc. खजः. [d] Or शिग्रुः. [e] Also वेषवारः or वेशवारः. [f] Or मरिचं. [g] ऊषणं and उषणं. [h] Nigella Indica, Roxb. [i] सुषवी and सुसवी.

n a n b

38. कुस्तुम्बुरु (च) धन्याकम्

f c n d

Dry ginger (अथ) शुण्ठी महौषधम्

f n e n f n

(स्त्रीनपुंसकयोर्) विश्वं नागरं विश्वभेषजम्

n n 1 n f 2 n

Sour gruel. 39. आरनालक सौवीर कुल्माषा ऽभिषुतानि (च)

n n 3 n n g

अवन्तिसोम धान्याम्ल कुंजलानि (च) काञ्जिके

n n n h m n n i

Assa fœtida. 40. सहस्रवेधि जतुकं बाह्लिकं हिङ्गु रामठम्

f j f f f k f l f

Hingupatri. तत्पत्री कारवी पृथ्वी बाष्पिका कबरी पृथुः

f m f f f f

Turmerick. 41. निशाख्या काञ्चनी पीता हरिद्रा वरवर्णिनी

n n n n n o

Sea salt. सामुद्रं (यत्तु) लवणमक्षीवं वशिरं (च तत्)

m n n p n q n

Rock salt. 42. सैन्धवो (ऽस्त्री) शितशिवं माणिमन्थ (च) सिंधुजे

1—च. 2—ग. 3—ल.

[a] Likewise तुम्बरु, and fem. कुस्तुम्बुरी and तुम्बुरी. [b] Also धान्यकं. धनिकं, धनीयकं, धनेयकं, धान्यं and fem. धन्या. [c] Or शुण्ठिः. [d] Also fem. महौषधी. [e] Fem. विश्वा. [f] Or कुल्माषः, कुल्माषः and कुल्माषाभिषुतं. [g] Also कांचिकं or कांजीकं and fem, कांजिका. [h] Or बाह्लिकं. [i] And रमठं. [j] That is हिङ्गुपत्री. But some read त्वक्पत्री. [k] Or बाष्पीका. [l] Also करंरी. [m] And निशा or other terms signifying night. [n] अक्षीवं or अक्षिवं. [o] Also वषिरं [p] And शितशिवं शीतशिवं or शीतशिवं and शितशिवं. [q] Also माणिमन्थं.

n b n रौमकं वसुकं	Another sort. a
n n n पाक्यं विड (च) क्षतके (द्वयम्)	Factitious salt. c
n n n 43. सौवर्चले ऽक्षरुचके	*Sóchal* salt: white.
n तिलकं (तत्र मेचके)	The same: black. d
f n f मत्स्यण्डी फाणितं (खण्डविकारौ)	Raw sugar. e
f f शर्करा सिता	Refined sugar. g
f h f 44. कूर्चिका क्षीरविकृतिः (स्याद्)	Inspissated milk.
f रसाला (तु) मार्जिता	Curds with sugar and spices.
n n (स्यात्) तेमनं (तु) निष्ठानं	Sauce or condiment.
i (त्रिलिङ्गा वाच्यितावधेः)	
m f n m f n 1 m f n 45. शूलाकृतं भटित्रं (स्याच्) छूल्यं	Roasted on a spit.
f n m f n उख्यं (तु) पैठरम्	Boiled in a caldron.

[1] शूल्य.

[a] The same with *Sa'mbhar* salt, denominated *Raumaca*, as some say, from a mountain of salt called *Ruma'*; or, as others affirm, from a river or lake of the same name. [b] Also रोम. [c] Obtained by boiling clay found on the sea shore; or other earth impregnated with salt. Some remark, that the two first terms are names of different kinds of salt which are equally factitious. [d] This appears to be the same with black salt or *Vit'alavana*: a factitious salt containing sulphur. [e] The first term signifies granulated sugar; and the second inspissated juice of sugarcane. [f] Some, making this one of the exhibited terms, state three synonyma of syrup. [g] Clayed: others say, candied. [h] And कुर्चिका. [i] The following to v. 46 admit the three genders.

Dressed. — *m f n* 1 *m f n* — प्रणीतमुपसंपन्नं

Seasoned. — *m f n* *m f n* — प्रयस्तं (स्यात्) सुसंस्कृतम्

Sauce mixed with rice-gruel. a — *m f n* *m f n* b — 46. (स्यात्) पिच्छिलं (तु) विजिलं

Strained. — *m f n* *m f n* — संमृष्टं शोधितं (समे)

Bland, soft. — *m f n* *m f n* *m f n* — चिक्कणं मसृणं स्निग्धं

Scented. — *m f n* *m f n* c — (तुल्ये) भावित वासिते

Food half dressed. d — *n* *m* 2 *m* e — 47. आपक्वः पौलिरभ्यूषो.

Fried grain. — *m* pl. f *n* g — लाजाः (पुंभूम्नि च) ऽक्षतम्

Rice, &c. flattened. — *m* *m* h — पृथुकः (स्याच्) चिपिटको.

Fried barley or rice. — *f* pl. — धाना (भ्रष्टयवे स्त्रियाम्)

Cake. — *m* *m* *m* — 48. पूपोऽपूपः पिष्टकः (स्यात्)

—mixed with curds. — *m* i 3 *m* pl. — करंभो दधिसक्तवः

---

¹उ—. ²भ्य—. ³—क्तु.

a Or else any sauce, or condiment, with gravy ; otherwise explained moist split pulse. b Also विचिलं and विज्जलं or विजयिलं. c The foregoing are used adjectively. d To be eaten from the hand ; some say bread ; others, green barley fried. e Also अभ्युषः and अभ्योषः. f Or fem. लाजा. g Or, as some read, masc. pl. अक्षताः. This is explained by others, whole rice. h And चिपिटः or चिपुटः. Likewise चिपिटः, &c. i Also करंब.

f[a] n n[b] n 1mn m

भिस्सा (स्त्री)भक्तमन्धो ऽन्नमोदनो(ऽस्त्री स)दीदिविः Boiled rice.

fc f

49. भिस्सटा दग्धिका — The same scorched.

mn

(सर्वरसाग्रे) मण्ड (मस्त्रियाम्) — Scum.

m 2m m[d]

मासराचाम निस्रावा (मण्डे भक्तसमुद्भवे) — Scum of boiled rice.

f 3f f f f

50. यवागूरुष्णिका श्राणा विलेपी तरला (च सा) — Rice gruel.

mfn

गव्यं (त्रिषु गवां सर्वं) — Belonging to a cow.

4fn 5mn

गोविड्गोमय (मस्त्रियाम्) — Cowdung.

mn

51. (तत्तु शुष्कं) करीषो (ऽस्त्री) — Dry cowdung.

n n 6n

दुग्धं क्षीरं पयः (समम्) — Milk.

n

पयस्य (माज्यदध्यादि) — Prepared from milk.[e]

n[f]

द्रप्सं (दधि घनेतरत्) — Thin or diluted curds.

n 7n 8f 9f

52. घृतमाज्यं हविः सर्पिर् — Clarified butter.

n n

नवनीतं नवोद्धृतम् — Fresh butter.

---

1 ओ—. 2 आ—. 3 उ—. 4 —ट्. 5 गो—.
6 —स्. 7 आ—. 8 —स्. 9 —स्.

[a] One writes भिक्षा. [b] अन्धः (स्). [c] And भिस्सिटा or भिस्मिटा, भिस्सिटा, भिस्सिका. [d] Likewise निस्रावः. [e] Butter, curds, &c. [f] Also द्रप्स' and द्रप्य'. Some read सरं, and interpret it floating curds.

Butter of yesterday's milk.[a]	(तत्तु) हैयंगवीनं[n] (यत् ह्योगोदोहोद्भवं घृतम्)
Butter-milk.	53. दण्डाहतं[n] कालशेय[n b] मरिष्ट[1 n] (मपि) गोरसः[m]
—with proportions of water.	तक्रं[n c] (ह्यु) दश्विन्मथितं[2 n d, n e] (पादाम्ब्वर्धाम्बुनिर्जलम्)
Whey of curds.	54. (मण्डं दधिभवं) मस्तु[n]
Milk of a cow which lately calved.[f]	पीयूषो[m g] (ऽभिनवं पयः)
Hunger.	अशनाया[f] बुभुक्षा[f] क्षुद्[3 f h]
A mouthful.	ग्रास[m] (स्तु.) कवलः[4 m] (पुमान्)
Drinking together.	55. सपीतिः[f] (स्त्री) तुल्यपानं[n]
Eating together.	सग्धिः[f] (स्त्री) सहभोजनम्[n]
Thirst.	उदन्या[f] (तु) पिपासा[f] तृट्[5 f i] तर्षो[m]
Food.	जग्धि[f] (स्तु.) भोजनम्[n]
	56. जेमनं[n j] लेह[m] आहारो[m] निघसो[m k] न्याद[m] (इत्यपि)

1 ध्य—. 2 श्च—द्. 3 —ध्. 4 —स. 5 —ड्.

[a] Some explain it butter from new milk. [b] Or कालसेयं. [c] With a fourth part of water. [d] With an equal part of water. [e] Without water. [f] Within the first seven days. [g] Also पेयूषः—षं and पीयूषं. Some make the last signify milk after the seventh day from the cow's calving. [h] क्षुद् (—ध्). Also क्षुधा. [i] Or तृषा. Also तृष्णा. Or जमनं. [k] Likewise निघसः.

n n f
सौहित्यं तर्पणं तृप्तिः — Satiety.

f b *n*
फेला भुक्तसमुज्झितम् — Outs, leavings. a

i i i 1 *i* 2 *i* *i*
57. कामं प्रकामं पर्य्याप्तं निकामेष्टं यथेप्सितम् — Voluntarily.

m m m m c 3 *m* d *m*
गोपे गोपाल गोसंख्य गोधुगाभीर बल्लवाः — Herdsman.

n e
58. (गोमहिष्यादिकं) पादबन्धनं — Stock of cattle.

m
(द्वौ) गवीश्वरे — Owner of kine.

4 *m* 5 *m*
गोमान् गोमी

n n f *m*
गोकुलं (तु) गोधनं (स्याद्) गवां व्रजः — A herd.

6 *m f n* g
59. (त्रिष्वा) शितंगवीनं (तद्गावो यत्राशिताः पुरा) — Formerly grazed by cattle.

m m h *m m m*
उक्षा भद्रो बलीवर्द ऋषभो वृषभो वृषः — A bull or ox.

7 *m* i *m* 8 *m*
60. अनड्वान् सौरभेयो गौर्

n
(उक्ष्णां संहतिर्) औक्षकम् — A herd of oxen.

f f
गव्या गोत्रा (गवां) — A herd of kine.

n n
(वत्सधेन्वोर्) वात्सक धैनुके — —of calves, and milch-cows. j

1—र्य. 2 ष्ट'. 3 पा—. 4—न्. 5—न्.
6 आ—. 7—डुह्. 8 गो.

a Left at the meal; or, otherwise interpreted, dropped from the mouth. b And फेलिः. Also masc. फेलक. c गोधुक (ह्). Also गोदुहः. d Or आभीरः. e Or, according to a different reading, यादवं. f Some add धनं, as a synonymous term. g आशितंगवीनः, ना, नं; or अशितंगवीनः, ना, नं. Also उषितंगवीनः, ना, नं, where cattle have dwelt. h And बरीवर्दः or बलीवर्द्दः. i Fem. अनडुाही and अनडुही. j Respectively.

A large bull or ox. — 61. (उक्षा महान्) महोक्षः[m] (स्याद्)

An old bull. — वृद्धोक्ष[m] (स्तु.) जरद्गवः[m a]

A bullock. — (उत्पन्न उक्षा) जातोक्षः[m]

A new-born calf. — (सद्योजातस्तु) तर्णकः[m]

A calf. — 62. शकृत्करि[m b] (स्तु.) वत्सः[m] (स्याद्)

A steer. — दम्य[m] वत्सतरौ[m] (समौ)

One fit to be set free. — आर्षभ्यः[m] (षण्डतायोग्यः)

A bull at liberty. — षण्डो[m c] गोपति[1 m] रिट्चरः[2 m d]

A bull's shoulder. — 63. (स्कन्धदेशस्तु.) वहः[m]

His dewlap. — सास्ना[f] (तु) गलकम्बलः[m]

An ox, with a rein through his nose. — (स्यान्) नस्तित[m] (स्तु.) नस्योतः[m]

Young cattle in training. — प्रष्ठवाड्[m e] युगपार्श्वगः[m f]

Cattle yoked, &c. g — 64. (युगादीनान्तु वोढारो) युग्य[m] प्रासङ्ग्य[m] शाकटाः[3 m]

Ploughman; plough-cattle, &c. h — (खनति तेन तद्वोढास्येदं) हालिक[m] सैरिकौ[m]

Cattle for burden. — 65. धूर्वहे[m i] धुर्य[m] धौरेय[m] धुरीणाः[m] (स) धुरंधरः[m]

1—ति. 2 ष—. 3—ट.

[a] Fem. जरद्गवी. [b] Or शकृत्करिः. [c] And षण्ढः or षण्डः. [d] Also इट्चरः. [e] प्रष्ठवाट् (ह). [f] Or युगपार्श्वकः. [g] Respectively; one yoked, or one in training with a frame on his neck, or one trained to draught. [h] The third acceptation of both terms is 'of or belonging to a plough.' [i] Or धूर्धरः.

m *1m* *2m* (उभाव्) एकधुरीणै कधुरावे कधुरावहे	Cattle for special burden.
m *m* 66. (सतु) सर्व्वधुरीणः (स्यादोवै) सर्वधुरावहः	—for any carriage.
f *f* *f* *3f* *f* *f* माहेयी सौरभेयी गौरुस्रा माता (च) शृङ्गिणी	A cow.
4f *5f* *f* 67. अर्जुन्यघ्न्या रोहिणी (स्यादु)	
f[a] (उत्तमा गोषु) नैचिकी	An excellent one.
f[b] 68. (वर्णादिभेदात्संज्ञाः स्युः) शबली धवला (दयः)	Cows brindle, white, &c.
f *f* द्विहायनी द्विवर्षा (गौर्)	A heifer two years old.
f *6f* एकाब्दा (त्वे) कहायनी	—one year old.
f *f* 69. चतुरब्दा चतुर्हायणी	—four years old.
f *f* (एवं) त्र्यब्दा त्रिहायणी	—three years old.
f *f* वशा वंध्या	A barren cow.
f[c] *f* ऽवतोका (तु) स्रवद्गर्भा	A cow miscarrying by accident.
f (ऽथ) सन्धिनी	One which has gone to the bull.[d]
70. (आक्रांता वृषभेणा)	
7f *8f* (ऽथ) वेहद्गर्भोपघातिनी	Miscarrying from going unseasonably.

---

1 ए—र. 2 ए—. 3 उस्रा. 4 —र्नी. 5 घ्न—. 6 ए—. 7 —द्. 8 ग—.

[a] Also नैचिकी or नैचिका and निचिकी. [b] Likewise शबला and शबली. Also कृष्णा, black. कपिला, tawny. Or distinguished by other circumstances, as ह्रस्वा and वामनी, short; लम्बकर्णी, with long ears; वक्रशृङ्गी, with crooked horns, &c. [c] And वतोका. [d] Some interpret it, a cow with calf.

Fit for the bull.	काल्या[f] पसर्या[1f] (प्रजने)
A pregnant heifer. a	प्रष्ठौही[f] बालगर्भिणी[f]
A tractable cow.	71. (स्याद्) अचण्डी[f] (तु) सुकरा[f]
A cow bearing many calves.	बहुसूतिः[f] परेष्टुका[f]
	चिरसूता[f] बष्कयणी[f b]
One, which has lately calved.	धेनुः[f] (स्यात्) नवसूतिका[f]
Easily milked.	72. सुव्रता[f] सुखसन्दोह्या[f c]
with a large udder.	पीनोघ्नी[f] पीवरस्तनी[f]
Yielding a *dróna* of milk.	द्रोणक्षीरा[f] द्रोणदुग्धा[f]
Standing at the diary. d	धेनुष्या[f] (बन्धके स्थिता)
Calving every year.	73. समांसमीना[f] (सा यैव प्रतिवर्षं प्रसूयते)
An udder	ऊधः[2 n e] (तु. क्लीबम्) आपीनं[n]
A pillar. f	(समौ) शिवक[m] कीलकौ[m]
A rope or cord. g	74. (नपुंसि) दाम[3 f n h] संदानं[n]
A string or tie. i	पशुरज्जु[f] (स्तु.) दामनी[f j]

1 प—. 2—स्. 3—स्.

[a] Or a cow with calf for the first time. [b] Likewise बष्कयनी, and बष्कयिणी, or बष्कयवणी. Also बष्कयवी, &c. [c] सुखसंदुह्या. [d] Some interpret this a cow pledged. [e] Also ऊधः and आपीनः. [f] For cows to rub themselves upon; or, otherwise interpreted, for tying cows or calves. [g] To which cows are tied; or a string to bind a cow's hind-legs when milked. [h] Fem. दामा (नन्) or दामा (आ). [i] For binding the legs of cattle, or for tying the cattle themselves. [j] Likewise दावनी and बंधनी.

वैशाख[m] मन्थ[m a] मन्थान[m] मन्थानो[m] मन्थदण्डके[m] — A churning-stick.

75. कुठरो[m c] दण्डविष्कम्भे[m] — A post, round which its string winds. b

मन्थनी[f] गर्गरी[f] (समे) — A churn.

उष्ट्रे[m] क्रमेलक[m] मय[m] महाङ्गाः[m] — A camel.

करभः[m] शिशुः[m] — A young one. d.

76. (करभाः स्युः) शृङ्खलका[1 m] (दारवैः पादबन्धनैः) — Young camels clogged. e

अजा[f] छागी[f] — A she-goat.

स्तुभः[m f] छाग[m g] बस्त[m] छगलका[m h] अजे[m] — A he-goat.

77. मेढ्रो[m i] ऽरभ्रो[2 m] ऽरणो[3 m] र्णायु[4 m] मेष[m] वृष्णय[5 m] एडकाः[m j] — A ram.

(उष्ट्रोरभ्राजवृन्दे स्यात्) औष्ट्रकौ[n][6 n] ऽरभ्रकाजकम्[7 n] — Herd of camels ; flock of sheep and goats. k

78. चक्रीवन्त[8 m] (स्तु) वालेया[m] रासभा[m m] गर्दभाः[m] खराः[m] — Asses. l

वैदेहकः[m n] सार्थवाहो[m] नैगमो[m] वाणिजो[m o] वणिक्[9 m] — A trader.

79. पण्याजीवो[m] (ह्या) पणिकः[10 m] क्रयविक्रयिक[m] (श्च सः)

1—लाः. 2 उ—. 3 उ—. 4 ऊ—. 5—ष्णि. 6 औ—. 7 आ—. 8—त्. 9—ज्. 10 आ—.

[a] मन्था (—न्). [b] Or else the lid of the churn, contrived to support the stick. [c] Also कुठरः. [d] Or any young animal. [e] With wooden rings on their feet. [f] Also स्तभः and स्तम्भः or शुभः. [g] छागः or छगः. [h] छगल and छागलः. [i] Or मेढ्रः. [j] Masc. एडकः. Fem. एडकाः. [k] Respectively. [l] Sing. चक्रीवान्, वालेयः, &c. [m] Also रासभः. [n] Or वैदेहः. [o] And वणिजः or वाणिजिकः. Also वाणिजः.

A vender. — विक्रेता[1 m] (स्याद्) विक्रयिकः[m]

A buyer. — क्रायक[m] क्रयिकौ[m] (समौ)

Traffic. — 80. वाणिज्यं[n a] (तु) वणिज्या[f] (स्यान्)

Price. — मूल्यं[n] वस्नो[m] (ऽप्य्) अवक्रयः[2 m]

Capital; principal. — नीवी[f b] परिपणं[m n] मूलधनं[n]

Gain, profit. — लाभो[m] (ऽधिकं) फलम्[m]

Barter. — 81. परिदानं[n c] परीवर्त्तो[m d] नैमेय[m] निमया[m e] (वपि)

A deposit. — (पुमान्) उपनिधि[m] न्यासः[3 m]

The return of it. — प्रतिदानं[n f] (तदर्पणम्)

Exposed for sale. — 82. (क्रये प्रसारितं) क्रय्यं[m f n]

Purchasable. — क्रेयं[m f n] क्रेतव्य[m f n] (मात्रके)

Vendible. — विक्रेयं[m f n] पणितव्यं[m f n] (च) पण्य[m f n] (क्रय्यादयस्त्रिषु)[g]

Ratification of a bargain. — 83. (क्लीबे) सत्यापनं[m h] सत्यंकारः[m] सत्याकृतिः[f] (स्त्रियाम्)

1—तृ. 2 वा—. 3 न्या—.

a Or वणिज्य. b And नीविः. c Some read प्रतिदान. d And परिवर्त्तः. e Likewise नैमेयः, निमयः and विनिमयः. f Some read परिदानं. g The foregoing admit the three genders. h Also fem. सत्यापना.

m m
विपणो विक्रयः — Contract of sale.

a
(संख्याः संख्येये ह्यादश त्रिषु — Numerals.

b
84. विंशत्याद्याः सदैकत्वे सर्वाः संख्येयसंख्ययोः

c
संख्यार्थे द्विबहुत्वे स्तः तासु चानवतेः स्त्रियः

d
85. पंक्तेः शतसहस्रादिक्रमाद्दशगुणोत्तरम्)

n e n n 1 n
यौतवं द्रुवयं पाय्य (मिति) माना (र्थकं त्रयम्) — Measure.

f f m
86. (मानं) तुला ऽङ्गुलिप्रस्थैर् — Of three sorts. f

2 m h
(गुञ्जाः पञ्चा) द्यमाषकः — A *Ma'sha.* g

m m n
(ते षोडशा) ऽक्ष कर्षो (ऽस्त्री) — Sixteen times as much.

n
पलं (कर्षचतुष्टयम्) — Four times the last.

m n m n
87. सुवर्ण बिस्तौ (हेम्नो ऽक्षे) — A *karsha* of gold.

कुरुविस्त (स्तु तत्पले) — A *pala* of gold.

1—ब. 2 चा—.

[a] Numerals, from 1 to 18, agree in gender with the subject numbered. [b] Other numerals, (19) 20, &c. are singular; but may be dual or plural, if used distributively, Ex. विंशती, two scores. [c] The numerals, 20 to 90, are invariably feminine. [d] Numeration proceeds in decuple proportion. [e] Also पौतवं. [f] By weight, measure of length, and measure of capacity. [g] Equal to five rettis or seeds of the abrus precatorius. [h] Also माष; or माषः.

100 *Palas.* — तुला [f] (स्त्रियां पलशतं)

Twenty times as much. — भारः [m a] (स्याद्विंशतिस्तुलाः)

Ten times the last. — 88. आचितं [m n] (दशभाराः स्युः)

A cartload. — (शाकटो भार) आचितः [m n]

A *karsha* of silver. b — कार्षापणः [m c] कार्षिकः [m] (स्यात्)

A *pana* of copper. d — (कार्षिके ताम्रिके) पणः [m]

Various measures of capacity. e — 89. (अस्त्रियाम्) आढक [m n f] द्रोणौ [m n] खारी [f g] वाहो [m] निकुञ्चकः [m]
कुडवः [m h] प्रस्थ [m] (इत्याद्याः परिमाणार्थकाः पृथक्)

A quarter. — 90. पाद [m] (स्तुरीयो भागः स्यात्)

A part, share, or portion. — अंश [m i] भागौ [m] (तु) वण्टकः [m]

Substance, thing or wealth. — द्रव्यं [n] वित्तं [n] स्वापतेयं [n] रिक्थ [n] मृक्थं [1 n] धनं [n] वसु [n]

Wrought and unwrought gold, &c. k — 91. हिरण्यं [n] द्रविणं [n] द्युम्न [n] मर्थ [2 m] रै [m j] विभवा [m] (अपि)
(स्यात्) कोश [m l] (श्च) हिरण्यं (च हेमरूप्ये कृताकृते)

1 ऋ—. 2 च—.

[a] Likewise भरः. [b] Same with पुराणः, equivalent to 16 *Panas* of cowries. [c] Some add कार्षापणकः. [d] Equivalent to 80 cowries. [e] Severally, viz. 4 *A'd'hacas* = 1 *Dróna*; and = 16 D. = 1 *C'hári.* Also 20 D. = 1 *Kumbha*; and 10 C. = 1 *Váha.* Some state $\frac{Ch.}{4}$ = 1 *Máni.* $\frac{M.}{4}$ = 1 *Dróna.* $\frac{D.}{4}$ = 1 *A'd'haca.* $\frac{A.}{4}$ = 1 *Prast'ha.* $\frac{P.}{4}$ = 1 *Kudava.* $\frac{C.}{4}$ = 1 *Nicunchaca.* [f] Also fem. आढकी and आढकिका. [g] Likewise खारिः and masc. खारः. [h] And कुडपः or कुटपः. [i] Or अंशः. [j] Masc. nom. राः (रै). [k] Some disjoin the terms; कोश, wrought gold; हिरण्यं, unwrought silver. [l] And कोषः or कोषं.

92. (ताभ्यां यदन्यत्तत्) कुप्यं [n a]	Base metals.
रूप्यं [n] (तद्द्वयमाहतम्)	Bullion.
गारुत्मतं [n] मरकतम् [n] अश्मगर्भं [1 n] हरिन्मणिः [m]	An emerald.
93. शोणरत्नं [n] लोहितकः [m] पद्मरागो [m]	A ruby.
(ऽथ) मौक्तिकम् [n]	A pearl.
मुक्ता [f]	
(ऽथ) विद्रुमः [m] (पुंसि) प्रवालं [m n] (पुंनपुंसकम्)	Coral.
94. रत्नं [n] मणि [m f b] (र्द्वयोरश्मजातौ मुक्तादिकेऽपि च)	Any gem.
स्वर्णं [n] सुवर्णं [n] कनकं [n] हिरण्यं [n] हेम [2] हाटकम् [n]	Gold.
95. तपनीयं [n] शातकुम्भं [n c] गाङ्गेयं [n] भर्म [3 n d] कर्बुरम् [n e]	
चामीकरं [n] जातरूपं [n] महारजत [n] काञ्चने [n]	
96. रुक्मं [f n] कार्तस्वरं [n] जाम्बूनदम् [n] अष्टापदो [4 n m] (ऽस्त्रियाम्)	
(अलंकार सुवर्णं यच्) शृङ्गीकनक [5 m n g] (मित्यदः)	Gold for ornaments.
97. दुर्वर्णं [n] रजतं [n] रूप्यं [n] खर्जूरं [n h] श्वेत [n] (मित्यपि)	Silver.

---

1 अ—. 2—न्. 3—न्. 4 अ—. 5 शृ—.

[a] Or अकुप्यं. [b] Also fem. मणी. [c] Or शातकौम्भं. [d] Also भर्मं. [e] And कर्बूरं. Likewise कर्चुरं. [f] Or रुग्मं. [g] Some divide the terms: शृङ्गी or शृङ्गिः (also neut. शृङ्गि) and कनकं. [h] Or खर्ज्जूरं.

Brass. — रीतिः[f a] (स्त्रियाम्) आरकूटो[m n b] (न स्त्रियाम्)

Copper. — (अथ) ताम्रकम्[m]

98\. शुल्बं[n c] म्लेच्छमुखं[n] द्व्यष्टं[n d] वरिष्ठो[n]दुम्बराणि[n e] (च)

Iron. — लोहो[m n f](ऽस्त्री)शस्त्रकं[n] तीक्ष्णं[n] पिण्डं[n] कालायसा[1 n g] ऽयसी[n h]

99\. अश्मसारो[m n]

Rust of iron. — (ऽथ) मण्डूरं[m n] सिंहान[n i] (मपि तन्मले)

Any thing metallic. — (सर्वं च तैजसं) लौहं[m j]

Wrought iron; bar iron. — (विकारस्त्वयसः) कुशी[f]

Glass. — 100. क्षारः[m] काचो[m]

Quicksilver. — (ऽथ) चपलो[m] रसः[m] सूत[m n] (श्च) पारदे[m n k]

Buffalo's horn. — गवलं[n] (माहिषं शृङ्गम्)

Talc. — अभ्रकं[n] गिरिजा[2 n] ऽमले[n]

Antimony. — 101. स्रोतोञ्जन[n] (न्तु) सौवीरं[n] कापोताञ्जन[n l]यामुने[n]

Blue vitriol. — तुत्थाञ्जनं[n m] शिखिग्रीवं[n] वितुन्नक[n] मयूरके[n]

1—स. 2 ज.

[a] Also रीती. And neut. रैत्यं. [b] Likewise आरः. [c] Or शुल्वं. [d] And द्विष्टं. [e] उदुम्बरं, उडुम्बरं or औडुम्बरं. [f] And लोहं or लोहः. [g] Likewise कृष्णायसं. [h] अयं (स्). Also आयसं. [i] And सिंघाण, or सिंहाणं, सिंघाणं. [j] And लोहं. [k] Also पारतः, or पारः. [l] And कपोताञ्जनं. [m] Also तुत्थं.

102. कर्परी[f b] दार्विका[f] (क्वाथोद्भवं) तुत्थं — Collyrium.[a]

रसाञ्जनम्[n] — Another sort.[c]

रसगर्भं[n] तार्क्ष्यशैलं[n]

गंधाश्मनि[1 n] (तु) गन्धकः[m d] — Sulphur.

103. सौगंधिक[m e] (स्तु)

चक्षुष्य[f] कुलाल्यौ[2 f] (तु) कुलत्थिका[f g] — A blue stone used as a collyrium.[f]

रीतिपुष्पं[n] पुष्पकेतु[n] पौष्पकं[n h] कुसुमाञ्जनम्[n i] — Calx of brass.

104. पिञ्जरं[n] पीतकं[n] तालमालं[n][n j] (च) हरितालके[n] — Yellow orpiment.

गैरेयमर्थ्यं[n][3 n] गिरिजमश्मजं[n][4 n] (च) शिलाजतु[n] — Red chalk.[k]

105. बोल[m] गंधरस[m l] प्राण[m] पिण्ड[m] गोप[m m] रसाः[m n] (समाः) — Myrrh.

1—नृ. 2—ही. 3 च—. 4 च—.

[a] Extracted from Amomum Zanthorhizon, Roxb. [b] Some grammarians include this in the synonyma of blue vitriol. Medical authors write it खर्परी or खर्परं, and make it a distinct sort of collyrium. [c] Some join this article with the preceding, omitting कर्परी from the synonyma: this agrees with the medical books. [d] And गन्धिकः. [e] Or सुगंधिकः. [f] Some make these three terms synonymous with the following. [g] And कुलत्था. Likewise कुलं. [h] And पुष्पकं. [i] Also पुष्पांजनं. [j] चार्व्वं or चार्वं. Also गार्वं. [k] According to a different explanation, bitumen. [l] Or रसगंधः. [m] And गोलः. Also पिण्डगोलः. [n] Or प्राणः. Also गोलप्राणः.

Cuttle fish bone. — डिण्डीरो[m a] ऽब्धिकफः[m b] फेनः[m]

Minium, or red lead. — सिन्दूरं[n] नागसंभवम्[n]

Lead. — 106. नाग[n] सीसक[n] योगेष्ट[n] वप्राणि[1 n c]

Tin. — त्रपु[n] पिच्चटम्[n d]

रंग[n] वंगे[n]

Cotton. — (ऽथ) पिचु[m] स्तूलो[2 m e]

Safflower; carthamus. — (ऽथ) कमलोत्तरम्[n]

107. (स्यात्) कुसुंभं[n] वह्निशिखं[n] महारजन[n] (मित्यपि)

A woollen blanket. — मेषकम्बल[m] ऊर्णायुः[m]

Hare's or rabbit's hair. — शशोर्णं[n] शशलोमनि[3 n]

Honey. — 108. मधु[n] क्षौद्रं[n] माक्षिका[4 n] (दि)

Wax. — मधूच्छिष्टं[n] (तु) सिक्थकम्[n]

Red arsenic. — मनःशिला[f f] मनोगुप्ता[f] मनोह्वा[f g] नागजिह्विका[f]

Nitre; saltpetre. — 109. नेपाली[f] कुनटी[f h] गोला[f i]

यवक्षारो[m] यवाग्रजः[m]

1—प्र. 2 तूल. 3—सू. 4—क.

[a] दिण्डीरः or पिण्डीरः. Also डिण्डिहरः. [b] Or समुद्रफेनः. [c] Some read वर्ध्रं. Also वप्र°. [d] Some include the two first terms with the preceding, as names of lead. [e] And पिचव्यः. Also पिचुतूलः or तूलपिचुः. [f] Likewise मनःशिला. Also masc. मनःशिलः. [g] And मनोह्वा. [h] Some read कुलटी or कनटी. [i] Some make the last term the name of a different species; and the two preceding terms, its explanation.

पाक्यो[m]

(स्य) सर्जिकाक्षारः[m a] कापोतः[m] सुखवर्चकः[m] — Natron; alkali.

110. सौवर्चलं[n] (स्यादु) रुचकं[n b]

त्वक्क्षीरा[f] वंशरोचना[f c] — Manna of bamboos.

शिग्रुजं[n] श्वेतमरिचं[n] — Seed of morunga. d

मोरटं[n] (मूलमैक्षवम्) — Root of sugarcane.

111. ग्रन्थिकं[n] पिप्पलीमूलं[n] चटिकाशिर[1 n e] (इत्यपि) — Root of long pepper.

गोलोमी[f] भूतकेशो[m] (ना) — Root of sweet flag.

पत्राङ्गं[n] रक्तचन्दनम्[n] — Red-wood.

112. त्रिकटु[n] त्र्यूषणं[n g] व्योषं[n] — Three spices. f

त्रिफला[f h] (तु) फलत्रिकम्[n] — Three myrobalans.

1—स.

[a] Or सर्जिकाक्षारः. Also सर्जिका and क्षारः. [b] Some disjoin the two last terms, and make them names of Borax. [c] Or वंशलोचना. [d] Of Hyperanthera or Guilandina morunga. [e] And चटकाशिरः (स). Or masc. चटिकाशिरः (र). Also चटका and शिरः. [f] Black pepper, dry ginger and long pepper. [g] Or त्र्यूषणं. [h] And त्रिफली or त्र्यफला.

CHAPTER X.

Men of the fourth tribe. — 1. शूद्रा[m][a] (श्चा) ऽवरवर्णा[m] (श्च) वृषला[m] (श्च) जघन्यजाः[m]

Men of mixed orgin. b — (आचण्डालात्तु) संकीर्णा[m] (अम्बष्ठ करणादयः)

A scride. c — 2. (शूद्राविशो स्तु) करणो[m]

A physician. d — ऽम्बष्ठो[m] (वैश्याद्विजन्मनोः)

An *Ugra*. e — (शूद्रा क्षत्रिययोर्) उग्रो[m]

A bard. f — मागधः[m] (क्षत्रियाविशोः)

A *Ma'hishya*. g — 3. माहिष्यो[m] (ऽर्याक्षत्रिययोः)

A *Kshattri*. h — क्षत्ता[1m] (ऽर्याशूद्रयोः सुतः)

A charioteer. i — (ब्राह्मण्यां क्षत्रियात्) सूतः[m]

A trader. j — (तस्यां वैदेहको[m] (विशः)

1—शू.

[a] Sing. शूद्रः, &c. [b] From the intermarriages of the other tribes. [c] Or man of a class which sprung from the 3d and 4th tribes. [d] Sprung from the 1st and 3rd tribes. [e] From the 2d and 4th. [f] From the 3d and 2d. [g] From the 2d and 3d classes. [h] From the 4th and 3d. [i] From the 2d and 1st. [j] From the 3d and 1st.

4. रथकार[m] (स्तु माहिष्यात् करण्यां यस्य संभवः)	A car-maker.
(स्याच्च)चाण्डाल[m][b](स्तु जनितो ब्राह्मण्यां वृषलेन यः)	A *Chanda'la.*[a]
5. कारुः[m][c] शिल्पी[1][m]	An artisan.
(संहतैस्तैर्द्वयोः) श्रेणिः[m][f][d] (सजातिभिः)	A company of artists.
कुलकः[m][e] (स्यात्) कुलश्रेष्ठी[2][m][f]	One eminent by birth.
मालाकार[m] (स्तु) मालिकः[m]	A florist.
6. कुंभकारः[m] कुलालः[m] (स्यात्)	A potter.
पलगण्ड[m] (स्तु) लेपकः[m]	A bricklayer or plaisterer.
तन्तुवायः[m][g] कुविन्दः[m][h] (स्यात्)	A weaver.
तुन्नवाय[m] (स्तु) सौचिकः[m]	A taylor.
7. रङ्गाजीव[m] चित्रकरः[3][m]	A painter.
शस्त्रमार्जो[m] ऽसिधावकः[m]	An armourer.
पादूकृ[4][m][i]च्चर्मकारः[5][m][j] (स्याद्)	A shoemaker.
व्योकारो[m] लोहकारकः[m]	An iron-smith.[k]
8. नाडीन्धमः[m] स्वर्णकारः[m] कलादो[m][l] रुक्मकारके[m]	A gold-smith.

1—न्. 2—नृ. 3 चि—. 4—कृ. 5 च—.

[a] Sprung from the 4th aud 1st tribes. [b] Also चण्डालः. [c] Likewise fem. कारुः. [d] Also fem. श्रेणी. [e] Or कुलिकः. [f] Likewise कुलः and श्रेष्ठी. [g] And तन्त्रवायः or तन्तूवायः. Also तन्त्रवापः. [h] Or कुपिन्दः. [i] Or पादुकृत्. [j] Also चर्मारः. [k] Some separate the terms as severally signifying a founder and a smith. [l] Or कषादः.

A shell-cutter. (स्याच्) छांखिकः[1 m] काम्बविकः[m]

A copper-smith. शौल्विक[m a] स्ताम्रकुट्टकः[2 n]

A carpenter. 9. तक्षा[3 m] (तु) वर्द्धकि[m]स्त्वष्टा[4 m] रथकार[m] (श्च) काष्ठतट्[5 m]

One working for the village. (ग्रामाधीनो) ग्रामतक्षः[m]

One independent. कौटतक्षो[m] (ऽनधीनकः)

A barber. 10. क्षुरि[6 m] मुण्डि[7 m] दिवाकीर्त्ति[m] नापिता[m] ऽन्तावसायिनः[8 m]

A washerman. निर्णेजकः[m] (स्याद्) रजकः[m b]

A distiller. शौण्डिको[m] मण्डहारकः[m]

A goatherd. 11. जाबालः[m] (स्याद्) अजाजीवो[m]

An attendant on an idol. देवाजीवी[9 m c] (तु) देवलः[m]

A female juggler. (स्यान्) माया[f] शाम्बरी[f d]

A juggler. मायाकार[m e] (स्तु) प्रातिहारिकः[m f]

Dancers and tumblers. 12. शैलालिन[10 m] (स्तु) शैलूषा[m] जायाजीवाः[m] कृशाश्विनः[11 m]

भरता[m g] (इत्यपि) नटाश्[m h]

Dancers and mimics. चारणा[m] (स्तु) कुशीलवाः[m]

---

1 शां—. 2 ता—. 3—न्. 4 त्वष्टृ. 5—ष्. 6—न्. 7—न्. 8—न्. 9—न्. 10—न्. 11—न्.

[a] And शौल्विकः. [b] Fem. रजकी. [c] Or देवाजीवः. [d] And शाम्बरी or शांवरी. &c. [e] And मायावी (न्) or मायी (न्). [f] And प्रतिहारः, प्रातिहारः or प्रातिहारकः. [g] And भारतः. [h] Sing. नटः.

13. मार्दङ्गिका[m] मौरजिका[m]:	Players on drums.
पाणिवादा[m] (स्तु) पाणिघा[m]	Striking with their hands only.
वेणुध्माः[m] (स्युर्) वैणविका[m]	Players on the flute.
वीणावादा[m] (स्तु) वैणिका[m]:	—on the lute.
14. जीवान्तकः[m a] शाकुनिको[m]	A fowler or bird-catcher.
(द्वौ) वागुरिक[m] जालिकौ[m]	A hunter using nets.
वैतंसिकः[m] कौटिक[m] (श्च) मांसिक[m] (श्च समं त्रयम्)	A vender of flesh-meat. [b]
15. भृतको[m] भृतिभुक्[1][m] कर्मकरो[2][m] वैतनिको[m] (ऽपि सः)	A hireling; a servant or labourer.
वार्त्तावहो[m] वैवधिको[m c]	A chandler.
भारवाह[m] (स्तु) भारिकः[m d]	A porter.
16. विवर्णः[m] पामरो[m] नीचः[m] प्राकृत[m] (श्च) पृथग्जनः[m]	A low man. [e]
निहीनो[m] ऽपसदो[m f] जाल्मः[m] क्षुल्लक[m g] (श्चे) तर[3][m] (श्च सः)	
17. भृत्ये[m] दासेर[m] दासेय[m] दास[m h] गोप्यक[m i] चेटकाः[m j]	A servant or slave.
नियोज्य[m] किंकर[m k] प्रैष्य[m l] भुजिष्य[m] परिचारकाः[m]	

[1]—भ्. [2] क—. [3] ह्—.

[a] Or जीवन्तिकः. [b] Selling the flesh of beasts or birds. [c] And विवधिकः. [d] Likewise भारी (न्). [e] Following a degrading profession. [f] Or अपशदः. [g] Likewise क्षुद्रकः. [h] Or दाशः. Fem. दासी—शी. [i] And गोप्यः. [j] Or चेटः. Also चेडः, चेलकः. Fem. चेटिका, चेटी, चेडी. [k] Fem. किङ्करा or किङ्करी. [l] Also प्रैषः and प्रेष्यः.

One nourished by a stranger. a

m m b m c m
18. पराचित परिस्कन्द परजात परैधिताः

A lazy man.

m 1 m d m m m m
19. मन्दस्तुन्दपरिमृज आलस्यः शीतकोऽलसोऽनुष्णः

A dextrous person.

m m m c 2 m m m
दक्षे (तु) चतुर पेशल पटवः सूत्थान उष्ण (श्च)

A *Chanda'la*.

m m m m m f
20. चण्डाल प्लव मातङ्ग दिवाकीर्ति जनङ्गमा

m g m h 3 m m m i
निषाद श्वपचावन्तेवासि चाण्डाल पुक्कसाः

Barbarians. j

m
21. (भेदाः किरातशबरपुलिन्दा) म्लेच्छ (जातयः)

A hunter, or deer-killer.

m m m 4 m
व्याधो मृगवधाजीवो मृगयुर्लुब्धको (ऽपि सः)

A dog.

m m m k m
22. कौलेयकः सारमेयः कुक्कुरो मृगदंशकः

m l m 5 m m
शुनको भषकः श्वा (स्यात्)

A mad dog.

m n
अलर्क (स्तु. स योगितः)

A dog trained for the chase.

m
23. (श्वा) विश्वकद्रु (र्मृगयाकुशलः)

A bitch.

f f
सरमा शुनी

---

1 तु—. 2 पटु. 3 अ—सिन्. 4 लु—. 5 भन्.

a Some include this line in the synonyma of slave. b Likewise परिस्कन्दः, परिष्कन्दः, परिस्कन्नः, पारस्कन्दः. c And परजितः. d Or तुन्दपरिमार्जः. e And पेशलः or पेषलः. f Also जनङ्गमः. g And निषादः. h Sing. श्वपचः. Likewise श्वपच् (च्). i Also पुक्कशः, पुक्कसः. j Of various tribes, mountaineers, savages, &c As किरातः, living in forests and armed with a bow. शबरः or मल्लशबरः, wearing feathers (a peacock's tail, &c). पुलिन्दः or पुंलिन्दः, speaking no intelligible language. k And कुकुरः l Or शुन and शुनिः. m Also श्वानः. n Likewise अलकः.

m m m a

विट्चरः शूकरो ग्राम्ये। — A village hog.

m c

वर्कर (तरुणः पशुः) — Any young animal. b

n n m f

24. आच्छोदनं मृगव्यं (स्यात्) आखेटो मृगया (स्त्रियाम्) — Chase; hunting.

1 m

(दक्षिणावर्त्त प्रयोगात्) दक्षिणेर्म्मा (कुरङ्गकः) — A deer wounded on its right side.

2 m d 3 m e m f m m m

25. चौरैकागारिक स्तेन दस्यु तस्कर मोषकाः — A thief or robber.

4 m g 5 m m h m

प्रतिरोधि परास्कन्दि पाटच्चर मलिम्लुचाः

f i n n n

26. चौरिका स्तैन्य चौर्य्ये (च) स्तेयं — Theft, robbery.

n j

लोप्त्रं (तु तद्धनम्) — Booty.

m l

वीतंस (स्तूपकरणं बन्धने मृगपक्षिणाम्) — A net, chain, or cage. k

m n

27. उन्माथः कूटयन्त्रं (स्यात्) — A snare or trap. m

f f

वागुरा मृगबन्धिनी — A net. n

n o m p f m f n m q

शुल्बं वराटकः (स्त्री तु) रज्जु (स्त्रि.पु) वटी गुणः — A cord, rope, or string.

1—मृ. 2—र. 3 ऐ—. 4—मृ. 5—मृ.

[a] Some make the first, others the second, term, explanatory. [b] Or a lamb in particular. [c] Fem. बर्करी. [d] Also चोरः. Fem. चोरः. [e] Fem. ऐकागारिकी. [f] Or स्तेनः. Also स्तैन्यः. [g] And प्रतिरोधकः. [h] Likewise पटच्चरः. [i] Also चोरिका. [j] And लोत्रं or लोतं. [k] Any instrument for confining birds or beasts. [l] Also वितंसः. [m] Some make the preceding term synonymous with these. [n] For confining deer. [o] Adn शुल्वं or शुल्बं. Also masc. शुल्बः and fem. शुल्बा or शुल्वी. Likewise शुल्वं according to a different reading. [p] Or वराटः. But some read वटाकरः. [q] Likewise वटीगुणः.

Rope and bucket of a well. a — 28. उद्घाटनं[n] घटीयन्त्रं[n] (सलिलोद्वाहनं प्रहेः)

A loom. — (पुंसि) वेमा[1,m,n,b] वायदण्डः[m,c]

Threads. — सूत्राणि[n,d] (नरि) तन्तवः[m,e]

Weaving. — 29. वाणि[f,f] र्व्यूतिः[2,f,g] (स्त्रियौ तुल्ये)

Plaistering. h — पुस्तं[n] (लेप्याऽदिकर्मणि)

A doll or puppet. i — पाञ्चालिका[f,j] पुत्रिका[f] (स्याद्वस्त्रदन्तादिभिः कृता)

A basket. k — 30. पिटकः[m] पेटकः[m] पेटा[f,l] मञ्जूषा[f,m]

A pole for carrying burdens. — (ऽथ) विहङ्गिका[f,n]

भारयष्टिस्[3,f]

Its string. — (तदालम्बि) शिक्यं[n,o] काचो[m]

A shoe. — (ऽथ) पादुका[f]

31. पादू[f]रुपानत्[4,f] (स्त्री)

A boot. — (सैवा) ऽनुपदीना[f] (पदायता)

A thong. — नद्ध्री[f] वर्ध्री[f,p] वरत्रा[f] (स्याद्)

A whip. — (अश्वादेस्ताडनी) कशा[f,q]

1—नू. 2 व्यू—. 3—ष्टि. 4 उ—ष.

[a] A rope and jar to drow water from a well ; or any machine for raising water. [b] Likewise वेमः. [c] Or वायदण्डः. [d] Sing. सूत्रं. [e] Sing. तन्तुः. Also सूत्रतन्तुः. [f] And वेणिः. [g] Or व्युतिः. [h] Or painting images, &c. [i] Or figure made of cloth, ivory, &c. [j] And पञ्चालिका. [k] The two last of these four terms are by some separated, and made to signify a large basket. [l] And पेडा or पेटा. [m] Some add मञ्जूषा; erroneously. [n] Or विहङ्गमा. [o] Likewise शिक्य (क्य). [p] And वार्ध्री or वाध्री [q] Also कषा or कशा.

32. चाण्डालिका *f* [a] (तु) कण्डोलवीणा *f* [b] चण्डालवल्लकी *f*	A vulgar lute.
नाराची *f* (स्यात्) एषणिका *f*	Goldsmith's scales.
शाण *m* (स्तु) निकषः *m* कषः *m* [c]	A touch-stone.
33. व्रश्चनः *n* पत्रपरशुः [1] *m*	An iron chisel. [d]
ईषिका *f* [f] तूलिका *f* [g] (समे)	A pencil or brush. [e]
तैजसावर्त्तनी *f* मूषा *f* [h]	A crucible.
भस्त्रा *f* चर्मप्रसेविका *f* [i]	Bellows.
34. आस्फोटनी *f* [j] वेधनिका *f*	An gimlet or auger.
कृपाणी *f* कर्त्तरी *f* (समे)	Scissors or shears. [k]
वृक्षादनी *m* वृक्षभेदी [2] *m*	A carpenter's chisel.
टङ्कः *m* [m] पाषाणदारणः *m*	A hatchet. [l]
·35. क्रकचो *m n* [n] (ऽस्त्री) करपत्रं *n*	A saw.
(स्यात्) आरा *f* चर्मप्रभेदिका *f*	Shoemaker's knife.

1—षु. 2—नु.

[a] And चण्डालिका. [b] Likewise कटोलवीणा. [c] Some read शानः निकसः and कसः. [d] Or else a small saw. [e] Some explain this a fibrous stick; others a mould for ingots; or else what is thrown into a crucible to try whether the metal be melted. [f] Also इषीका and ईषीका or ईषिका. [g] Likewise तुलिः, तूली. [h] Also मुषा and मूषी or मूषिका. [i] Or masc. चर्मप्रसेवकः. [j] And आस्फोडनी. [k] Also a dagger. [l] Likewise a stone-cutter's chisel. [m] Or तङ्कः. [n] And क्रकरः.

An image of iron. a	*f* b *f* *f* सूर्मी स्थूणा लोहप्रतिमा
An art.	*n* शिल्पं (कर्म कलादिकम्)
An image; statue or picture.	*n* *n* *f* *f* *f* 36. प्रतिमानं प्रतिबिम्बं प्रतिमा प्रतियातना प्रतिच्छाया *f* 1*f* 2*m* प्रतिकृतिरर्चा (पुंसि) प्रतिनिधिर्
Resemblance. c	*f* 3*n* उपमोपमानं (स्यात्)
Like, similar.	*mfn* *mfn* *mfn* *mfn* 4*mfn* 37. (वाच्यलिङ्गाः) समस्तुल्यः सदृक्षः सदृशः सदृक् *mfn* d *mfn* साधारणः समान (श्च)
(In composition) Like.	e (स्युरुत्तरपदे त्वमी) *mfn* *mfn* *mfn* f *mfn* g 5*mfn* h 38. निभ सङ्काश नीकाश प्रतीकाशोपमा (दयः)
Wages or hire.	*f* *f* *f* 6*f* 7*n* *n* कर्मण्या (तु) विधा भृत्या भृतयो भर्म वेतनम् *n* i *n* *n* *m* *m* 39. भरण्यं भरणं मूल्यं निर्वेशः पण (इत्यपि)
Spirituous liquor.	*f* *f* *f* 8*f* 9*f* सुरा हलिप्रिया हाला परिस्रुद्वरुणात्मजा

---

1 कृ—. 2—धि. 3 उ—. 4—क्. 5 उपमा. 6—ति. 7—न्. 8—त्. 9 सु—.

[a] So most commentaries explain this : but one says an anvil. [b] Or सूर्मिः. Also स्थूर्मी or स्थूर्मिः. And सूर्मी, सूर्मिः or सूर्मः. [c] Some include this with the preceding. [d] Fem. साधारणी. or साधारणा. [e] The following are used only in composition. Ex. पितृनिभः, like his father. [f] Also निकाशः. [g] And प्रतिकाशः, प्रतिकाशः, or प्रतीकाशः. [h] Besides other terms similarly employed in composition : as भूतः रूपः कल्पः. [i] Also fem. भरण्या.

f f 1 f a 2 f f

40. गन्धोत्तमा प्रसन्नेरा कादम्बर्य्यः परिस्रुता

f n n

मदिरा कश्य मद्ये (चाप्य्)

m

ऽवदंश (स्तु भक्षणम्) — Eating what excites thirst.

f n

41. शुण्डापानं मदस्थानं — A tavern.

m m b

मधुवारा मधुक्रमाः — Tippling.

m m d m n e

मध्वासवो माधवको मधु माध्वीक (मद्वयोः) — Spirit, distilled from Bassia. c

n 3 m 4 m n g

42. मैरेयमासवः सीधुर् — Rum. f

m m

मेदको जगलः (समौ) — Vinous liquor for distilling.

n m

सन्धानं (स्याद्) अभिषवः — Distillation.

m i m j

किण्वं (पुंसि तु) नग्नहूः — Ferment. h

m k m

43. कारोत्तरः सुरामण्ड — Yeast, barm, froth.

n f

आपानं पानगोष्ठिका — Place where people drink together.

m n n m n 5 n m

चषको (ऽस्त्री) पानपात्रं सरको (ऽप्य) नुतर्षणम् — A drinking vessel. l

---

1 इरा. 2 —री. 3 —सव—. 4 —धु. 5 —ष—.

a Also प्रसन्नेरा. b Sing. मधुवारः, मधुक्रमः. c From the blossoms of the Bassia latifolia. Some divide the synonyma, making the two last terms signify wine obtained from grapes. d And माध्वकं, or माद्वीकं. e Also मधुमाध्वीकं. f The three terms signify different kinds; the first distilled from blossoms of Lythrum fruticosum, with sugar, &c. the second from the raw juice of suger-cane, the third from molasses. g Some connect the last term with the following article. h A drug used for that purpose. i Or कण्वं. j Also neut. नग्नहु. k And कारोत्तमः. l Some separate the two last terms of this line, and interpret them the distribution of liquor. m Also masc. अनुतर्षः.

A gamester. — 44. धूर्त्तो (m) ऽक्षदेवी (m, 1) कितवो (m) ऽक्षधूर्त्तो (m) द्यूतकृत् (m) (समाः)

Sureties. — (स्युर्) लग्नकाः (m) प्रतिभुवः (m)[a]

Keepers of gaming houses. — सभिका (m)[b] द्यूतकारकाः (m)

Gaming. — 45. द्यूतो (m, n) (ऽस्त्रियाम्) अक्षवती (f) कैतवं (n) पण (m) (इत्यपि)

पणो (m) (ऽक्षेषु) ग्लहो (m)

Dice. — ऽक्षा (m) (स्तु) देवनाः (m) पाशका (m) (श्च ते)

Moving a piece at play. — 46. परिणाय (m)[c] (स्तु शारीणां समन्तान्नयने) (ऽस्त्रियौ)

A checkered board or cloth. — अष्टापदं (m, n) शारिफलं (m, n)

A match of cocks, &c. — प्राणिद्यूतं (n) समाह्वयः (m)

47. (उक्ता भूरिप्रयोगत्वादेकस्मिन् ये ऽत्र यौगिकाः

ताद्धर्म्यादन्यतो वृत्तावूह्या लिङ्गान्तरे ऽपि ते)

1—भू.

[a] Sing. लग्नकः, and प्रतिभूः. Some reckon these synonymous with the following. [b] Sing. सभिकः and द्यूतकारकः. [c] Also परीणायः.

BOOK III.

CHAPTER I.

1. विशेष्यनिघ्नैः संकीर्णैर्नानार्थैरव्ययैरपि
लिङ्गादिसंग्रहैर्वर्गाः सामान्ये वर्गसंश्रयाः

2. स्त्रीदाराद्यैर्यद्विशेष्यं यादृशैः प्रस्तुतं पदैः
गुणद्रव्यक्रियाशब्दास्तथा स्युस्तस्य भेदकाः ।

1 *m f n* 2 *m f n* *m f n*
3. सुकृती पुण्यवान् धन्यो — Fortunate, well-fated. a

m f n *m f n*
महेच्छ (स्तु) महाशयः — Magnanimous.

m f n *m f n* b
हृदयालुः सुहृदयो — Good-hearted.

m f n *m f n*
महोत्साहो महोद्यमः — Persevérant, diligent.

m f n *m f n* *m f n* *m f n* *m f n* *m f n*
4. प्रवीणे निपुणाऽभिज्ञ विज्ञनिष्णात शिक्षिताः — Skilful, conversant.
m f n c *m f n* 3 *m f n* *m f n* d
वैज्ञानिकः कृतमुखः कृती कुशल (इत्यपि)

m f n *m f n*
5. पूज्यः प्रतीक्ष्यः — Venerable.

m f n *m f n*
सांशयिकः संशयापन्नमानसः — Dubious. e

1—न्. 2—वत्. 3—न्.

a Fem. सुकृतिनी, पुण्यवती, धन्या. b Or सहृदयः. Also हृदयी(—न्) हृदयिकः, हृदयवान् (—वत्). c Or विज्ञानिकः. d Likewise कुशलः. e Uncertain or questionable. Some refer this to the person; irresolute, unsettled in opinion.

Meriting a fee or reward.
m f n   m f n   m f n a
दक्षिणीयो दक्षिणार्ह (स्तत्र) दाक्षिण्य (इत्यपि)

Munificent.
m f n b   m f n c   m f n   m f n
6. (स्युर्) वदान्य स्थूललक्ष्य दानशौण्डा बहुप्रदे

Long-lived.
m f n d   1 m f n
जैवातृकः (स्याद्) आयुष्मान्

Skilled in sacred sciences.
m f n   2 m f n
अन्तर्वाणि (स्तु) शास्त्रवित्

Acutely investigating.
m f n   m f n
7. परीक्षकः कारणिको

Granting a prayer. e
m f n   m f n
वरद (स्तु) समर्धकः

Joyful, cheerful.
m f n   m f n 3 m f n f   m f n
हर्षमाणो विकुर्वाणः प्रमना हृष्टमानसः

Sad, perplexed.
4 m f n   4 m f n   4 m f n
8. दुर्मना विमना अन्तर्मनाः (स्याद्)

Regretting.
m f n   5 m f n
उत्क उन्मनाः

Sincere, candid.
m f n   m f n 6 m f n
दक्षिणे सरलो दारौ

Liberal in giving and using.
m f n
सुकलो (दातृभोक्तरि)

Diligent, attentive. g
m f n   7 m f n
9. (तत्परे) प्रसितासक्ताव्

Zealously active. h
m f n i   m f n
इष्टार्थोद्युक्त उत्सुकः

1—त्.   2—द्.   3—नस्.   4—स्.   5—स्.
6 उ—.   7 आसक्त.

[a] And दक्षिण्यः. [b] Or वदन्यः. [c] And स्थूललक्षः. [d] Fem. जैवातृका:. [e] As a deity, at the instance of a votary. [f] Also प्रमनाः (—स्). [g] Some include the two next terms in these synonyma; others, varying the reading, add आविष्टः, to this article. [h] Making exertions for a gratifying purpose. [i] According to another reading, उद्युक्ताः.

m f n   m f n   m f n   m f n   m f n   m f n

प्रतीते प्रथित ख्यात वित्त विज्ञात विश्रुताः — Known, celebrated, famous.

m f n   1 m f n a

10. (गुणैः प्रतीते तु) कृतलक्षणा हतलक्षणौ — Noted for good qualities.

m   m b * 2 m*

इभ्य आढ्यो धनी — Opulent, wealthy.

m   4 m c * 5 m   6 m*

स्वामी (त्वी) श्वरः पतिरीशिता — An owner or master.

m   7 m   8 m   m   m   m

11. अधिभूर्नायको नेता प्रभुः परिवृढोऽधिपः

m f n   m f n

अधिकर्द्धिः समृद्धः (स्यात्) — Every way happy.

m

कुटुम्बव्यापृत (स्तु.यः) — Attentive to support his family.

m n   m d

12.(स्याद्)अभ्यागारिक(स्तस्मिन्)उपाधि(श्च पुमानयम्)

m

(वराङ्गरूपोपेतो यः) सिंहसंहननो (हि सः) — Handsome and well-shaped.

m f n e

13. निर्वार्य्यः (कार्य्यकर्त्ता यः सम्पन्नः सत्वसम्पदा) — Acting fearlessly.

m f n f * m f n*

अवाचि मूको — Dumb.

m f n g * m f n*

(ऽथ) मनोजवः (स) पितृसन्निभः — Fatherly.

m i

14. (सत्कृत्यालंकृतां कन्यां यो ददाति स)कूकुदः — Giving a girl in marriage.[h]

---

1 आ—.   2 —न्.   3 —न्.   4 ई—.   5 —ति.
6 ईशित्.   7 ना—.   8 —ढ.

[a] Some read आहितलक्षणः. [b] Fem. इभ्या, आढ्या, धनिनी. [c] Fem. ईश्वरा or ईश्वरी. [d] Invariably masc.: even with a feminine or neuter substantive. [e] Some read निर्वार्यः. [f] अवाक् (च्). [g] Some erroneously read मनोजवसः [h] In due form; decorating her with ornamets. [i] Or कुकुदः.

Prosperous, happy. — *1mfn mfn mfna 2mfn* — लक्ष्मीवान् लक्ष्मणः श्लीलः श्रीमान्

Affectionate. — *mfn mfn* — स्निग्ध (स्तु) वत्सलः

Compassionate. — *mfn mfn mfn mfnb* — 15. (स्याद्) दयालुः कारुणिकः कृपालुः सूरतः (समाः)

Unrestrained. — *mfn mfn 3mfnc mfn mfnd* — स्वतन्त्रो ऽपावृतः स्वैरी स्वच्छन्दो निरवग्रहः

Dependent. — *mfn mfn 4mfn 5mfn* — 16. परतन्त्रः पराधीनः परवान्नाथवान् (अपि)

Docile. e — *mfn mfn mfn mfn mfn* — अधीनो निघ्न आयत्तो ऽस्वच्छन्दो गृह्यको (ऽप्यमी)

A sweeper. — *mfn mfnf* — 17. खलपूः (स्याद्) बहुकरो

Dilatory, slow. — *mfn 6mfn* — दीर्घसूत्रश्चिरक्रियः

Acting inconsiderately. — *mfn 7mfn* — जाल्मो ऽसमीक्ष्यकारी (स्यात्)

Indolent. — *mfn* — कुण्ठो (मन्दः क्रियासु यः)

Competent to an act. — *mfn mfn* — 18. कर्मक्षमो ऽलंकर्मीणः

Engaged in a business. — *8mfn mfn* — क्रियावान् कर्मसूद्यतः

Laborious. — *mfng mfn* — (स) कार्मः कर्मशीलो (यः)

Finishing carefully. — *mfn mfn* — कर्मशूर (स्तु) कर्मठः

1—त्. 2—त्. 3—न्. 4—त्. 5 मा—त्.
6 श्चि—. 7—न्. 8—त्.

[a] And श्रीलः. [b] Also सुरतः. [c] And स्वैरः. [d] Also निर्यन्त्रणः and निरंकुशः. [e] Some make the terms in this and the preceding line synonymous. [f] Fem. बहुकरी and बहुकरा. [g] Fem. कार्मी.

1 *m f n* a 2 *m f n*
19. अरण्यभुक्कर्मकरः — Working for hire.

m f n *m f n*
कर्मकार (स्तु.) तत्क्रियः — Working without wages.

m f n *m f n*
अपस्नातो मृतस्नात — Bathing after mourning. b

3 *m f n* *m f n* c
आमिषाशी (तु) शौष्कलः — Eating fish and flesh.

m f n *m f n* 4 *m f n* 5 *m f n*
20. बुभुक्षितः (स्यात्) क्षुधितो जिघत्सुरशनायितः — Hungry.

m f n *m f n*
परान्नः परपिण्डादो — Feeding at another's cost.

m f n *m f n* *m f n*
भक्षको घस्मरो ऽद्मरः — Gluttonous.

m f n *m f n*
21. आद्यूनः (स्याद्) औदरिको (विजिगीषाविवर्ज्जिते) — Shamelessly voracious.

m f n *m f n*
(उभाव) आत्मम्भरिः कुक्षिम्भरिः (स्वोदरपूरके) — Selfishly voracious. d

m f n 6 *m f n*
22. सर्वान्नीन (स्तु.) सर्वान्नभोजी — Eating every thing. e

m f n *m f n*
गृध्नु (स्तु.) गर्द्धनः — Covetous, greedy.

m f n *m f n* 7 *m f n* f
लुब्धो ऽभिलाषुक स्तृष्णक्

m f n *m f n*
(समौ) लोलुप लोलुभौ — Very covetous. g

1—ण्. 2 क—. 3—न्. 4—सु. 5 घ—.
6—न्. 7 तृष्णज्.

a Or कर्मण्यभुक् (—ज्). b Some interpret this, dying after ablutions before the ceremony is complete. c And शाष्कलः or शुष्कलः. d With disregard to those, whom he is bound to support. e Eating all manner of food, or—food proper to various tribes. f Also तृष्णकः and तृषितः or तर्षितः. g Some make these synonymous with the preceding.

Mad; insane.	*m f n* a *1 m f n* 23. उन्मद (स्तू) न्मादिष्णुः (स्यात्)
Misbehaving.	*m f n m f n* अविनीतः समुद्धतः
Drunk.	*m f n m f n 2 m f n m f n* मत्ते शौण्डोत्कट क्षीबाः
Lustful.	*m f n 3 m f n m f n* कामुके कमिताऽनुकः
	m f n 4 m f n m f n m f n m f n m f n 24. कम्रः कामयिताऽभीकः कमनः कामनोऽभिकः
Compliant.	*m f n 5 m f n* b *m f n m f n* विधेयो विनयग्राही वचनेस्थित आश्रवः
Governable. c	*m f n m f n* 25. वश्यः प्रणेयो
Modest. d	*m f n m f n m f n* e निभृत विनीत प्रश्रिताः (समाः)
Impudent, shameless.	*m f n m f n* f *6 m f n* धृष्टे धृष्णग्वियात (श्च)
Bold, present.	*m f n m f n* प्रगल्भः प्रतिभान्वितः
Ashamed.	*m f n m f n* 26. (स्याद्) अधृष्टे (तु) शालीनो
Astonished.	*m f n m f n* विलक्षो विस्मयान्विते
Confused.	*m f n m f n* g अधीरे कातरस्
Timid.	*7 m f n m f n* h *m f n m f n* त्रस्ते भीरु भीरुक भीलुकाः

1 उ—. 2 उ—. 3—क. 4—क. 5—व.
6 वि—. 7—रू.

a Or उन्मादः. Some read शोन्मादः or उन्मादः and उन्मदः. b Or वचनग्राही (ग्रृ). c Some make these synonymous with the preceding. d Having passions restrained: or else humble, nor arrogant. e Or प्रश्रतः. f धृष्णज् (—क्). Also धृष्णुः. g कातरः—रा —रं. h Also त्रस्तः, भीतः, &c.,

1 *m f n* 2 *m f n* 27. आशंसुराशंसितरि	Wishing blessings.
3 *m f n* *m f n* a गृहयालुर्ग्रहीतरि	Disposed to take.
m f n श्रद्धालुः (श्रद्धया युक्ते)	Faithful; believing.
m f n *m f n* पतयालु (स्तु) पातुकः	Habitually falling.
4 *m f n* 28. (लज्जाशीले) ऽपत्रपिष्णुर्	Bashful.
5 *m f n* 6 *m f n* वन्दारुरभिवादके	Civil; polite.
m f n 7 *m f n* *m f n* शरारुर्घातुको हिंस्रः	Mischievous.
m f n *m f n* (स्याद्) वर्द्धिष्णु (स्तु) वर्द्धनः	Thriving; growing.
m f n 8 *m f n* 29. उत्पतिष्णु (स्तू) त्पतिता	Jumping up.
m f n *m f n* ऽलङ्करिष्णु (स्तु) मण्डनः	Inclined to ornament.
m f n 9 *m f n* 10 *m f n* भूष्णुर्भविष्णुर्भविता	Faring well.
m f n 11 *m f n* वर्त्तिष्णुर्वर्त्तनः (समौ)	Stationary.
m f n *m f n* b 30. निराकरिष्णुः क्षिप्नुः (स्यात्)	Obstructive.
m f n *m f n* सान्द्रस्निग्ध (स्तु) मेदुरः	Very smooth.
12 *m f n* *m f n* 13 *m f n* ज्ञाता (तु) विदुरो विन्दुर्	Knowing; intelligent.
14 *m f n* c *m f n* विकासी (तु) विकस्वरः	Expanding.

1—सु. 2 आ—तृ. 3—लु. 4—ष्णु. 5—रु. 6 अ—.
7 श—. 8 उ—तृ. 9 भ—. 10 भ—तृ. 11 व—. 12—तृ.
13—रु. 14—न्दु.

[a] ग्रहीता (—तृ) or गृहीता (—तृ). [b] Or क्षिप्णुः. [c] Also विकाशी (न्) and विकश्वरः or विकासी (न्) and विकस्वरः.

Flowing or creeping.	mfn mfn 1mfn 2mfn 31. विसृत्वरो विसृमरः प्रसारी (च) विसारिणि
Patient, content. a	mfn mfn 3mfn mfn 4mfn 5mfn सहिष्णुः सहनः क्षन्ता तितिक्षुः क्षमिता क्षमी
Passionate; wrathful.	mfn mfn 6mfnb 32. क्रोधनोऽमर्षणः कोपी
Very passionate.	mfn 7mfn चण्ड (स्त्व) त्यन्तकोपनः
Wakeful.	mfn 8mfn जागरूको जागरिता
Rolling, as in sleep.	mfn mfn घूर्णितः प्रचलायितः
Sleepy, sluggish.	9mfn mfn 10mfn 33. स्वप्नक् शयालुर्निद्रालुर्
Asleep.	mfnc mfn निद्राणशयितौ (समौ)
Averting the face.	mfn mfn पराङ्मुखः पराचीनः
Down-looked. d	11mfne mfnf (स्याद्) अवाङ् (प्य) धोमुखः
Adoring deities. g	12mfnh 34. (देवानञ्चति) देवद्र्यङ्
Going everywhere.	13mfni विश्वद्र्यङ् (विष्वगञ्चति)
Accompanying.	14mfnj (यः सहाञ्चति) सध्र्यङ् (स)
Moving tortuously.	15mfnk (स) तिर्यङ् (यस्तिरोऽञ्चति)

1—नु. 2—रिनु. 3 घंत्र. 4—क्षु. 5—तृ. 6—नृ. 7ष्ठ—. 8—ऊक. 9—क्. 10 नि—लु. 11—च्. 12—च्. 13—च्. 14—च्. 15—च्.

[a] Some distinguish the three first terms as signifying patient; and the other three, contented. [b] Also कोपनः. [c] Likewise निद्रितः. [d] Also headlong. [e] Fem. अवाची. [f] Fem. अधोमुखी. [g] The same term signifies approaching idols. [h] Fem. देवद्रीची. Neut. देवद्र्यक्. [i] Fem. विष्वद्रीची. Neut. विष्वद्र्यक्. Also विश्वद्र्यङ् (—च्),—द्रीची,—द्र्यक्. [j] Fem. सध्रीची. Neut. सध्र्यक्. Also सम्यङ् (—च्). [k] Fem. तिरश्ची.

35. वदो वदावदो वक्ता (*m f n*, *m f n*, 1 *m f n*)	Speaking sensibly. a
वागीशो वाक्पतिः (समौ) (*m f n*, *m f n*)	Eloquent.
वचोयुक्तिपटुर्वाग्मी वावदूक (श्च) वक्तरि: (*m f n* c, 2 *m f n* d, *m f n*, 3 *m f n*)	Speaking much. b
36. (स्यात्)जल्पाक(स्तु)वाचालो वाचाटो बहुगर्ह्यवाक् (*m f n* f, *m f n* g, *m f n*, 4 *m f n*)	Talking nonsense. e
दुर्मुखे मुखरा ऽबद्धमुखौ (*m f n*, *m f n*, *m f n*)	Foul-mouthed, scurrilous.
शक्लुः प्रियम्वदे (*m f n* h, *m f n*)	Speaking civilly.
37. लोहलः (स्याद्) अस्फुटवाग् (*m f n*, 5 *m f n*)	Lisping.
गर्ह्यवादी (तु) कद्वदः (6 *m f n*, *m f n*)	Speaking ill.
(समौ) कुवाद कुचरौ (*m f n*, *m f n*)	Censorious, detracting.
(स्याद्) असौम्यस्वरो ऽस्वरः (*m f n*, *m f n*)	Having a bad voice.
38. रवणः शब्दने (*m f n*, *m f n*)	Sonorous.
नान्दीवादी नान्दीकरः (समौ) (7 *m f n*, *m f n* j)	Speaker of a prologue. i

1—क्तृ. 2—न्. 3—क्तृ. 4—च्. 5—च्.
6—न्. 7—न्.

a Or knowing how to speak. Some interpret this simply, speaking or speaker. b Some separate the two first terms as signifying one who speaks as is fit; and the other two, as signifying loquacious. c Or वाचोयुक्तिः, and पटुः. d वाग्ग्मी (न्) or वाग्मी (न्). e Or simply, talkative: or else, saying much that is blamable. f Fem. जल्पाकी. g This term also occurs in a good sense. h Also शक्तः, शक्रः, and शक्त. i Some say player of the overture. The prologue of an Indian drama is a benediction joined with compliments to the audience. j Or नान्दिकरः.

Idiot, stupid.	*m f n* a *m f n* जडो ऽज्ञ.
Deaf and dumb.	*m f n* b एडमूक (स्तु. वक्तुं श्रोतुमशिक्षिते)
Silent.	*m f n* *m f n* 39. तूष्णींशील (स्तु.) तूष्णीको।
Naked.	*m f n* 1 *m f n* *m f n* नग्नो। ऽवासा। दिगम्बरे
Expelled.	*m f n* c *m f n* निःकासितो। ऽवकृष्टः (स्याद्)
Cursed.	*m f n* *m f n* अपध्वस्त (स्तु.) धिक्कृतः
Humbled: subdued. d	*m f n* *m f n* e 40. आत्तगर्वो। ऽभिभूतः (स्याद्)
Condemned; or adjudged. f	*m f n* g *m f n* दापितः साधितः (समौ)
Removed; set aside.	*m f n* *m f n* *m f n* *m f n* प्रत्यादिष्टो। निरस्तः (स्यात्) प्रत्याख्यातो। निराकृतः
	m f n *m f n* 41. निकृतः (स्याद्) विप्रकृतो।
Deceived, tricked.	*m f n* *m f n* विप्रलब्ध (स्तु.) वञ्चितः
Disappointed.	*m f n* *m f n* *m f n* *m f n* मनोहतः प्रतिहतः प्रतिबद्धो हत (श्च सः)
Turned away. h	*m f n* *m f n* 42. अधिक्षिप्तः प्रतिक्षिप्तो।
Confined. i	*m f n* *m f n* *m f n* बद्धे कीलित संयतौ

1—नञ्.

a Fem. जडा. b Also अनेडमूकः. c One reads निष्कासितः. d Some make the preceding synonymous with this. e Also पराभूतः. f Either the person cast; or the thing awarded; some interpret this, amerced; others, the person, by whom, or to whom, payment is made. g Likewise दायितः. h Some explain it sent or despatched. i Bound; some say fettered or confined in stocks, &c. others say imprisoned.

m f n *m f n* आपन्न आपत्प्राप्तः (स्यात्)	Distressed.[a]
m f n *m f n* कांदिशीको भयद्रुतः	Put to flight.
m f n *m f n* *m f n* 43. आक्षारितः क्षारितोऽभिशस्ते	Calumniated.[b]
m f n *m f n* संसुकोऽस्थिरे	Unsteady.[c]
m f n 1 *m f n* व्यसनार्तोपरक्तौ (द्वौ)	Afflicted.[d]
m f n *m f n* विक्लवः व्याकुलौ (समौ)	Confounded, perplexed.
m f n *m f n* 44. विक्लवो विह्वलः	Overcome by fear, &c.[e]
m f n *m f n* (स्यात्तु) विवशोऽरिष्टदुष्टधीः	Apprehensive of death.
m f n *m f n* कश्यः कशार्हे	Deserving a whipping.
m f n 2 *m f n* *m f n*[g] सन्नद्धे (त्वा) ततायी वधोद्यते	Murderous; a felon.[f]
m f n *m f n* 45. द्वेष्ये (त्व) ऽक्षिगतो	Hateful, detestable.
m f n *m f n* वध्यः शीर्षच्छेद्य (इमौ समौ)	Meriting beheading.
m f n विष्यो (विषेणयो वध्यो)	Meriting death by poison.
m f n[h] मुसल्यो (मुसलेन यः)	—by knocks of a pestle.

---

1 उ—ऋ. 2 आ—तृ.

[a] Overtaken by calamity. [b] Especially by a false accusation of adultery: some explain it, accused of adultery; others say, guilty of a crime. [c] Some interpret this uncertain. [d] Suffering pain from a cause human or divine. [e] Unable to contain himself. [f] Including assassins, incendiaries, robbers, &c. [g] Most commentators exclude the last, others the first and last, of these terms, from the synonyma. [h] Or मुषल्यः.

m f n 1 *m f n* a
Innocent. — 46. विभिन्नदानो ऽक्षाणकर्मा

m f n 2 *m f n*
Inconsiderately guilty. b — चपल श्चिकुरः (समौ)

3 *m f n* 4 *m f n*
Malevolent and censorious. c — दोषैकदृक् पुरोभागी

m f n *m f n* *m f n*
Wicked; perverse. — निकृत (स्त्व) ऽनृजुः शठः

m f n *m f n* *m f n* d
Informer. — 47. कर्णेजपः सूचकः (स्यात्) पिशुनो

m f n *m f n*
Mischief-maker. — दुर्जनः खलः

m f n *m f n* *m f n* *m f n*
Destructive, mischievous. — नृशंसो घातुकः क्रूरः पापो

m f n *m f n*
Fraudulent; crafty. — धूर्त (स्तु) वञ्चकः

m f n *m f n* e *m f n* *m f n* *m f n* f *m f n*
Idiot. — 48. अज्ञ मूढ यथाजात मूर्ख वैधेय बालिशाः

m f n *m f n* *m f n* *m f n* *m f n* g
Miser; avaricious. — कदर्ये कृपण क्षुद्र किम्पचान मितम्पचाः

m f n *m f n* *m f n* *m f n* *m f n* h
Poor; indigent. — 49. निःस्व(स्तु)दुर्विधो दीनो दरिद्रो दुर्गतो(ऽपि सः)

m f n i *m f n* *m f n* *m f n* 5 *m f n*
Beggar; mendicant, — वनीयको याचनको मार्गणो याचका ऽर्थिनौ

1—नु. 2 चि—. 3—घ. 4—नु. 5—नु.

[a] Many commentators read अक्षणकर्मा (नु); and expound that with the preceding term, sinful or criminal. [b] Committing a crime without considering the guilt. [c] Remarking only ill qualities. [d] Some include this in the next article; others make the five words synonymous. [e] Also ज्ञः. [f] Fem. वैधेयी. [g] Some read किम्पचः and मितम्पचः. [h] Likewise दुस्थः. [i] Or वनीपकः.

1 *m f n* a 2 *m f n*

50. अहङ्कारवानहंयुः (स्यात्) — Proud.

m f n *m f n* b

शुभंयु (स्तु.) शुभान्वितः — Happy.

m f n

दिव्योपपादुका (देवाः) — Of divine origin. c

m f n

(नृगवाद्या) जरायुजाः — Viviparous. d

m f n

51. स्वेदजाः (कृमिदंशाद्याः) — Engendered by damp. e

m f n

(पक्षिसर्पादयो) ऽण्डजाः — Oviparous. f

1—यत्. 2 थ—.

[a] Some make this to be only explanatory of the other term. [b] This also is by some made only explanatory. [c] Divine beings, produced without any apparent cause. [d] Produced from a viviparous being; as man, horses, bulls, &c. [e] As worms and insects. [f] Produced from an egg: birds, serpents, &c.

CHAPTER II.

m

Vegetables.[a] 1. उद्भिद (तरुगुल्माद्या)

1 m f n m f n b 2 m f n

Sprouting; germinating. उद्भिदुद्भिज्ज मुद्भिदम्

m f n c m f n m f n m f n m f n m f n

Beautiful or pleasing. सुन्दरं रुचिरं चारु सुषमं साधु शोभनम्

m f n m f n d m f n m f n m f n m f n e

2. कान्तं मनोरमं रुच्यं मनोज्ञं मञ्जु मञ्जुलम्

m f n f

Charming. (तद्) ऽसेचनकं (तृप्ते र्नास्त्यन्तो यस्य दर्शनात्)

m f n m f n m f n m f n m f n m f n

Beloved, desired. 3. अभीष्टे ऽभीप्सितं हृद्यं दयितं वल्लभं प्रियम्

m f n m f n 3 m f n m f n g m f n m f n h m f n

Inferior; low. निकृष्ट प्रतिकृष्टा र्व रेफ याप्या ऽवमा ऽधमाः

m f n m f n m f n m f n m f n m f n i

4. कुपूय कुत्सिता ऽवद्य खेट गर्ह्या ऽणकाः (समाः)

m f n m f n j m f n m f n k

Foul, dirty. मलीमसं (तु) मलिनं कच्चरं मलदूषितम्

1—हृ. 2 उ—. 3—नृ.

[a] As trees, shrubs, &c. [b] उद्भिज्जं or उद्भिन्नं. [c] Fem. सुन्दरी and सुन्दरा. [d] Also मनोहरं, and मनोहारि (न्). [e] Some add सौम्यं, मधुरं, रमणीयं, and रामणीयकं. [f] असेचनकं or आसेचनकं. [g] Or रेपः. Also रेफः (स्) and रेपः (स्). [h] Some read अरमः. [i] अणकः or आणकः, also अनकः. [j] Likewise म्लानं. [k] Some discriminate the two first terms as signifying simply dirty; and the other two spoiled by dirt.

m f n m f n m f n

5. पूतं पवित्रं मेध्यं (च) — Purified.

m f n m f n

वीध्रं (तु) विमला (र्थकम्) — Clean.

m f n m f n m f n m f n 1 m f n

निर्णिक्तं शोधितं मृष्टं निःशोध्यमनवस्करम् — Cleansed.

m f n m f n

6. असारं फल्गु — Pithless.

m f n a *m f n m f n m f n*

शून्य (न्तु.) वशिकं तुच्छ रिक्तके — Void, empty.

n c *m f n m f n m f n 2 m f n*

(क्लीबे) प्रधानं प्रमुख प्रवेका ऽनुत्तमोत्तमाः — Chief; principal. b

m f n d *m f n m f n m f n m f n*

7. मुख्य वर्य वरेण्या (श्च) प्रबर्हो ऽनवरार्ध्य (वत्)

m f n m f n m f n m f n m f n m f n e *3 m f n*

परार्ध्याग्र ऽग्र प्राग्रहर प्राग्र्या ऽग्र्या ऽग्रीयमग्रियम्

4 m f n m f n m f n m f n m f n

8. श्रेयान् श्रेष्ठः पुष्कलः (स्यात्) सत्तम (श्चा) ऽतिशोभने — Excellent. f

m m 5 m m

(स्युरुत्तरपदे) व्याघ्र पुङ्गवर्षभ कुञ्जराः — Pre-eminent g (in comp.)

m m m h

9. सिंह शार्दूल नागा (द्याः पुंसि श्रेष्ठार्थगोचराः)

---

1 श्च—. 2 ष्ठ—. 3 श्च—. 4 —श्रेष्ठ. 5—ह.

a Or शून्यं. b Some restrict the synonyma to the first line; others to the first eight terms: while others extend them to three lines, or even to four. c Invariably neuter. Instances of this word used in the masculine and in the feminine gender, are poetical licenses. d Also मुखः. e Also प्राग्र्यो:—ग्री—ग्रि. f Some join this with the preceding article; others take in the two last lines; or the last line and a half including fourteen terms. g Ex. पुरुषव्याघ्रः, an eminent man. मुनिपुंगवः, a pre-eminent sage. h Besides other terms as हंसः, चन्द्रः, &c.

m f n n 1 n

Secondary, subordinate. अप्राग्र्यं (द्वयहीने द्वे) अप्रधानोपसर्जने

m f n a m f n 2 m f n 3 m f n m f n 4 m f n

Great. 10. विशङ्कटं पृथु बृहद्विशालं पृथुलं महत्

m f n b 5 m f n m f n

वड्रोरु विपुलं

m f n 6 m f n c m f n m f n

Fat; large. पीन पीव्नी (तु) स्थूल पीवरे

m f n m f n m f n m f n m f n m f n m f n m f n

Little, small. d 11. स्तोकाऽल्प क्षुल्लकाः सूक्ष्मं श्लक्ष्णं दभ्रं कृशं तनु

f e f f m g m m h 7 m

(स्त्रियां) मात्रा त्रुटी(पुंसि)लव लेश कणाऽणवः

m f n m f n 8 m f n 9 m f n j 10 m f n

Very small. i 12. अत्यल्पेऽल्पिष्ठमल्पीयः कनीयोऽणीय(इत्यपि)

m f n m f n m f n 11 m f n m f n m f n

Much, many. प्रभूतं प्रचुरं प्राज्यमदभ्रं बहुलं बहु

m f n k m f n m f n m f n 12 m f n l m f n

13. पुरुहं पुरु भूयिष्ठं स्फारं भूय (श्) भूरि (च)

m f n

Countless. m परःशता (द्यास्ते येषां परा संख्या शतादिकात्)

---

1 अ—. 2—थु. 3 वि— 4—लं. 5 व—. 6—नू.
7—णु. 8 अ—ठ. 9—णु. 10—णु. 11 प—. 12—हू.

[a] Fem. विशङ्कटा, or—टी. [b] Also वड्रं. [c] Fem. पीवरी. [d] One author divides this article into four, making the three first terms signify small; the five next minute; the two terms following very minute; and the four last atom-like. [e] This and the following are invariably feminine. [f] Or त्रुटिः. [g] This and the following are invariably masculine. But some make them vary the gender. Others restrict the three first of them to the abstract sense. [h] Also fem. कणी or कणीका. [i] Some omit this line. [j] Also कनीयः (स). [k] Likewise पुरुहू. [l] Also भूम (न्). [m] In this compound term, the first word is indeclinable. Ex. परःशताः, —ता,—तं. But others make it vary with the gender. Ex. Neut. परंशतं, more than a hundred. So परःसहस्राः (परंसहस्र), above a thousand; परोलक्षाः, above a hundred thousand.

m f n *m f n*

14. गणनीये (तु) गणेयं — Numerable.

m f n *m f n*

संख्याते गणितम् — Numbered, counted.

m f n *m f n*

(अथ) समं सर्वम् — All; entire.

m f n 1 *m f n* *m f n* *m f n* *m f n* 2 *m f n* *m f n*

विश्वमशेषं कृत्स्नं समस्तनिखिलाऽखिलानि निःशेषम्

m f n *m f n* *m f n* a 3 *m f n* *m f n* b

15. समग्रं सकलं पूर्णमखण्डं (स्याद्) अनूनके

m f n *m f n* *m f n*

घनं निरन्तरं सान्द्रं — Coarse grass. c

m f n *m f n* *m f n*

पेलवं विरलं तनु — Delicate, fine. d

m f n *m f n* 4 *m f n* *m f n* *m f n*

16. समीपे निकटाऽऽसन्न सन्निकृष्ट सनीड (वत्) — Near, proximate.

m f n *m f n* e *m f n* *m f n* *m f n* f

सदेशाऽभ्याश सविधः समर्याद सवेश (वत्)

m f n *m f n* *m f n* *m f n* i

17. उपकण्ठाऽन्तिकाऽभ्यर्णाऽभ्यग्रा (अपि) ऽभितो

(ऽव्ययम्)

m f n *m f n* 5 *m f n* g

संसक्ते (त्व) ऽव्यवहितमपदान्तर (मित्यपि) — Adjoining, contiguous.

m f n *m f n* h

18. नेदिष्ठमन्तिकतमं — Very near.

m f n *m f n* i

(स्याद्) दूरं विप्रकृष्टकम् — Distant.

---

1 कृ—. 2 स—स्त. 3 अ—. 4 आ—. 5 अ—.

a Likewise पूर्ण°. b Or अनूनं. c Without interstices. d With interstices. e Or अभ्यासः. f Also सवेशः. g Likewise अपदान्तरं. h Also अन्तिकं. i And विप्रकृष्ट°.

Very remote. 1 mfn mfn mfn
दवीय (श्च) दविष्ठं (च) सुदूरं

Long. mfn 2mfn
दीर्घमायतम्

Round. a mfn mfn mfn
19. वर्तुलं निस्तलं वृत्तं

Uneven, wavy. b mfn c 3mfn
बन्धुरं (तू) न्नतानतम्

High, tall. d mfn mfn 4mfn 5mfn 6mfn 7mfn e
उच्च प्रांशून्नतोदग्रोच्छ्रितास्तुङ्गे

Short. mfn
(ऽथ) वामने

mfnf 8mfn mfng mfn
20. न्यङ्नीच खर्व ह्रस्वाः (स्युर्)

Bending, stooping. mfn mfn 9mfn h
अवाग्रे ऽवनतानतम्

Crooked. i mfn mfn mfn 10mfn mfn mfn
अरालं वृजिनं जिह्ममूर्मिमत्कुञ्चितं नतम्

mfn mfn mfn mfn mfn
21. आविद्धं कुटिलं भुग्नं वेल्लितं वक्र (मित्यपि)

Strait. 11 mfn 12 mfn mfn
ऋजावजिह्म प्रगुणौ

Confounded. mfn 13 mfn 14 mfn
व्यस्ते (त्व) प्रगुणाकुलौ

Eternal. mfn mfn mfn mfn mfn
22. शाश्वत (स्तु) ध्रुवो नित्य सदातन सनातनाः

1—सु. 2 आ—. 3 उ—. 4 उ—. 5 उ—. 6 उ—.
7 तु—. 8 नीच. 9 आ—. 10 ऊ—तृ. 11—जु. 12 अ—.
13 अ—. 14 आ—.

a Either circular or globular. b Some interpret this, naturally even, but factitiously depressed in some place. c Or बन्धूर. d Some make the preceding terms synonymous with these. e Also उन्नतानतः. f न्यञ्च, fem. नीची, nent. न्यक्. g Or खर्वः. h Also नतं. i Some make the preceding article synonymous with this.

m f n *m f n* 1 *m f n*
स्थास्नुः स्थिरतरः स्थेयान् — Permanent, firm. a

(एकरूपतया तु यः)

m f n
23. (कालव्यापी स) कूटस्थः — Uniform; perpetually the same. b

m f n
स्थावरो (जङ्गमेतरः) — Immovable.

m f n 2 *m f n* *m f n* *m f n* 3 *m f n* *m f n*
चरिष्णुर्जङ्गम चर त्रस मिङ्ग चराचरम् — Movable.

m f n d *m f n* *m f n* *m f n* *m f n* *m f n*
24. चलनं कम्पनं कम्प्रं चलं लोलं चलाचलम् — Shaking, moving. c

m f n *m f n* *m f n* *m f n*
चञ्चलं तरलं (चैव) पारिप्लव परिप्लवे

m f n *m f n*
25. अतिरिक्तः समधिको — Exceeding.

m f n *m f n*
दृढसन्धि (स्तु) संहतः — Strong knit. e

m f n f *m f n* *m f n* *m f n* g *m f n* *m f n*
कक्खटं कठिणं क्रूरं कठोरं निष्ठुरं दृढम् — Hard, solid.

m f n h
26. जठरं

4 *m f n* 5 *m f n*
मूर्त्तिमन्मूर्त्तं — Material, corporeal. i

m f n *m f n* 6 *m f n*
प्रवृद्धं प्रौढमेधितम् — Full-grown.

m f n j *m f n* *m f n* *m f n* *m f n*
पुराणे प्रतनं प्रत्न पुरातन चिरन्तनाः — Old, ancient.

1—स्नु. 2 ञ—. 3 इं—. 4—त्. 5 मू—. 6 ए—.

[a] Some make these synonymous with the preceding. [b] As the soul, the etherial expanse, &c. [c] Some interpret the three first terms, tremulous; and the seven last trembling: others, the three first moving, and the seven last quaking. [d] Also चपलं and चटुलं. [e] Some apply this to a man whose limbs are strongly knit; others to any thing, which has no interstices. [f] Also खक्खटं. [g] Or कठोलं. [h] Fem. जठरा. Also जरठः,—ठा,—ठं. [i] Some join these with the preceding synonyma. [j] Fem. पुराणा,—णी.

m f n m f n m f n m f n m f n m f n

New. 27 प्रत्यग्रो ऽभिनवो नव्यो नवीनो नूतनो नवः

m f n

नूत्न (श्च)

m f n m f n m f n m f n

Soft. सुकुमारं (तु) कोमलं मृदुलं मृदु

1 m f n a 2 m f n 3 m f n i

Following. 28. अन्वगन्वक्षमनुगे ऽनुपदं क्लीबमव्ययम्)

m f n c m f n

Perceptible. b प्रत्यक्षं (स्याद्) ऐन्द्रियकम्

m f n e 4 m f n

Imperceptible. d अप्रत्यक्षमतीन्द्रियम्

m f n m f n 5 m f n 6 m f n

Closely attentive. f 29. एकतानो ऽनन्यवृत्तिरे.काग्रैकायना (वपि)

7 m f n m f n 8 m f n

(अप्ये) कसर्ग एकाग्र्यो (ऽप्ये) कायनगतो (ऽपि च)

9 m g m f n m f n m f n 10 m f n h

Prior; first; initial. 30. पुंस्यादिः पूर्वं पौरस्त्य प्रथमाद्या

(अथास्त्रियाम्)

m n i m f n m f n 11 m f n m f n j m f n k

Last, ultimate. अन्तो जघन्यं चरममन्त्य पाश्चात्त्य पश्चिमाः

m f n m f n

Vain, useless. 31. मोघं निरर्थकं

m f n m f n m f n 12 m f n

Apparent, evident. स्पष्टं स्फुटं प्रव्यक्तमुल्बणम्

1—क्ष. 2 क्ष—. 3 क्ष—. 4 क्ष—. 5 ए—. 6 ए—त्ति.
7 ए—. 8 ए—. 9 आदि. 10 आद्य. 11 अ—. 12 उ—.

[a] अन्वक्, अन्वीकी, अन्वक्ष. [b] Or perceived : present. [c] Likewise अध्यक्ष. [d] Or unperceived : absent. [e] Also असमक्ष. Likewise परोक्ष. [f] With the mind fixed attentively on one object. [g] Invariably masculine. [h] Also आदिमः and अग्रिमः. [i] Even with a feminine noun, it remains masculine or neuter. [j] Some write पाश्चात्यः. [k] Also अन्तिमः.

m f n a n
साधारणं (तु) सामान्यम् — Common.

1 m f n 2 m f n m f n
एकाकी (त्वे) क एककः — Alone, solitary.

m f n m f n b m f n m f n c m f n m f n
32. भिन्ना(र्थका) अन्यतर एकस्त्वो ऽन्येतरा (वपि) — Other different.

m f n 4 m f n
उच्चावचं नैकभेदम् — Various.

m f n 5 m f n d
उच्चण्डम् अविलम्बितम् — Quick, expeditious.

m f n 6 m f n
33. अरुन्तुद (स्तु) मर्मस्पृक् — Sharp, corrosive.

f m f n m f n
अबाधं (तु) निरर्गलम् — Unobstructed.

m f n m f n m f n 7 m f n
प्रसव्यं प्रतिकूलं (स्याद्) अपसव्यम् अपष्ठु (च) — Contrary.

m f n m f n
34. वामं (शरीरं) सव्यं (स्याद्) — Left.

m f n e m f n
अपसव्यं (तु) दक्षिणम् — Right.

m f n m f
सङ्कटं (ना तु) सम्बाधः — Narrow.

m f n m f n
कलिलं गहनं (समे) — Impervious.

m f n h m f n m f n
35. सङ्कीर्णे संकुलाकीर्णे — Crowded, confused. g

m f n m f n
मुण्डितं परिवापितम् — Shaved.

1—मु. 2 एक. 3 इ—र. 4 च—. 5—म. 6 च—. 7 वा—.

a Fem. साधारणी—णा. b Some read एकतरः. c त्यः (resulting from two radical pronouns, त्य and त्यद्, which differ in accent). d Or अविलम्बनं. e Or अपसव्यं. Some make one term explanatory of the other. f Invariably masculine. g Some make this and the preceding article synonymous. h Also सङ्कीर्णं.

Strung; tied.	*mfn*[a] *mfn*[b] *mfn* ग्रन्थितं सन्दितं दृब्धं
Spread; diffuse.	*mfn mfn mfn* विसृतं विस्तृतं ततम्
Forgotten.	*mfn mfn* 36. अन्तर्गतं विस्मृतं (स्यात्)
Placed.[e]	*mfn*[d] *mfn* प्राप्तप्रणिहिते (समे)
Shaken.	*mfn mfn* 1 *mfn mfn* 2 *mfn mfn* वेल्लितं प्रेङ्खिताधूत चलिताकम्पिताधुते
Thrown, cast, sent.	*mfn mfn mfn mfn* 3 *mfn mfn* 4 *mfn* 37. नुत्त नुन्ना ऽस्तनिष्ठ्यूताविद्धक्षिप्तेरिता: (समा:)
Intrenched.	*mfn mfn* परिक्षिप्तं (तु) निवृतं
Stolen.	*mfn* 5 *mfn* मूषितं मुषिता (र्थकम्)
Expanded; dispersed.	*mfn mfn* 38. प्रवृद्ध प्रसृते
Deposited.	*mfn mfn* न्यस्त निसृष्टे
Multiplied.	*mfn* 6 *mfn* गुणिताहते
Plaistered.	*mfn* 7 *mfn* निदिग्धोपचिते
Hidden.	*mfn mfn* गूढ गुप्ते
Pounded.	*mfn*[e] *mfn* गुण्ठित रूषिते
Melted.	*mfn mfn* 39. द्रुता ऽवदीर्णे
Raised, held up.	*mfn* 8 *mfn* उद्गूर्णोद्यते
Suspended n a swing.	*mfn mfn* काचित शिक्यिते

1 आ—. 2 आ—. 3 आ—. 4 ई—. 5—त

6 आ—. 7 उ—. 8 उ—.

[a] Or ग्रथितं. Also गुम्फितं and गुफितं. [b] Or सदितं. Likewise सितं. [c] Also, obtained. [d] And आप्तं. [e] Or गुण्ठितं.

m f n m f n
घ्राणघ्राते — Smelled.

m f n m f n
दिग्धलिप्ते — Smeared, anointed.

m f n 1 *m f n*
समुदक्तोद्धृते (समे) — Drawn: raised from a deep place.

m f n *m f n* *m f n* *m f n* 2 *m f n*
40. वेष्टितं (स्यात्) वलयितं संवीतं रुद्धमावृतम् — Surrounded. a

m f n m f n
रुग्णभुग्ने — Bent, crooked.

m f n *m f n* 3 *m f n* b *m f n*
(ऽथ) निशितक्ष्णुतशातानि तेजिते — Sharpened, whetted.

m f n m f n
41. (स्याद्) विनाशोन्मुखं पक्वं — Mature.

m f n *m f n* *m f n*
ह्रीणह्रीतौ (तु) लज्जिते — Ashamed.

m f n *m f n* *m f n* c
वृते (तु) वृत्तवावृतौ — Chosen; appointed.

m f n d *m f n*
संयोजित उपाहितः — Joined; annexed.

m f n m f n *m f n*
42. प्राप्यं गम्यं समासाद्यं — Attainable.

m f n m f n m f n m f n
स्यन्नं रीणं स्रुतं स्नुतम् — Flowing, dropping.

m f n *m f n*
संगूढः (स्यात्) सङ्कलिते — Arranged; or heaped. e

m f n *m f n*
ऽवगीतः ख्यातगर्हणः — Detested.

---

1 उ—. 2 आ—. 3 शात.

a Some restrict the two first terms to signify encompassed; and the other three, secured from access. b Also निशातं. c Some, disallowing the root of this word, read व्यावृत्तः. Also वावृत्तः. d Or संयोगितः. e Or, as otherwise interpreted, brought in contact.

Various, multiform.	*m f n* *m f n* *m f n* *m f n* 43. विविधः (स्याद्) बहुविधो नानारूपः पृथग्विधः
Censured, blamed.	*m f n* *m f n* अवरीणो धिक्कृत (श्चाप्य.)
Coarsely pounded.	*m f n* a *m f n* ऽवध्वस्तो ऽवचूर्णितः
Diluted decoction. b	*m f n* *m f n* 44. अनायासकृतं फाण्टं
Sounded; making a noise.	*m f n* *m f n* स्वनितं ध्वनितं (समे)
Bound.	*m f n* *m f n* *m f n*c 1*m f n*d *m f n* *m f n* बद्धे सन्दानितं मूतमुद्दितं सन्दितं सितम्
Decocted.	*m f n* *m f n* 45. निष्पक्वे क्वथितं
Boiled. e	*m f n* (पाके क्षीराज्यपयसां) शृतम्
Departed. f	*m f n* निर्वाणो (मुनिवह्न्यादौ)
Become calm. g	*m f n* निर्वात (स्तु, गते ऽनिले)
Mature, ripe.	*m f n* *m f n* 46. पक्वं परिणते
Passed (as ordure).	*m f n* *m f n* गूनं हन्ने
Passed (as urine).	*m f n* *m f n* मीढं (न्तु) मूत्रिते
Nourished.	*m f n* *m f n* पुष्टे (तु) पुषितं
Borne. h	*m f n* *m f n* सोढे क्षान्तम्
Vomited.	*m f n* i 2 *m f n* उद्वान्तमुद्गते

1 उ—. 2 उ—.

a Also अवध्वस्तः. b Made by an extemporary and simple preparation. c And मूर्तं. d उद्दितं. e Water, milk, or liquid butter. f As a saint who has attained beatitude, a fire which is extinguished, a beast which is infirm, &c. g Wind no longer blowing. h Also patient. i Likewise उद्वानं and उद्यानं or उद्यान्तं.

m f n *m f n*
47. दान्त (स्तु.) दमिते — Tamed, subdued or trained.

m f n *m f n*
शान्तः शमिते — Pacified, appeased.

m f n *m f n*
प्रार्थिते ऽर्दितः — Asked, requested.

m f n *m f n*
ज्ञप्त (स्तु.) ज्ञपिते — Made known.

m f n 1 *m f n*
छन्नश्छादिते — Covered.

m f n *m f n* a
पूजिते ऽञ्चितः — Worshipped revered.

m f n *m f n*
48. पूर्ण (स्तु.) पूरिते — Filled : full.

m f n *m f n*
क्लिष्टः क्लिशिते — Tired, fatigued.

m f n *m f n*
ऽवसिते सितः — Finished.

m f n *m f n* 2 *m f n* *m f n*
प्रुष्ट प्लुष्टोषिता दग्धे — Burnt.

m f n *m f n* *m f n*
तष्ट त्वष्टौ तनूकृते — Pared ; made thin.

m f n 3 *m f n* *m f n*
49. वेधितच्छिद्रितौ विद्धे — Pierced.

m f n *m f n* *m f n*
विन्न वित्तौ विचारिते — Judged, discussed.

m f n *m f n* *m f n*
निःप्रभे विगता ऽरोकौ — Gloomy, obscured.

m f n *m f n* *m f n*
विलीने विद्रुत द्रुतौ — Liquid.

m f n *m f n* *m f n*
50. सिद्धे निर्वृत्त निष्पन्नौ — Accomplished.

m f n *m f n* *m f n*
दारिते भिन्न भेदितौ — Split.

m f n *m f n* 4 *m f n*
ऊतं स्यूतमुतं (चेति त्रितयं तन्तुसन्तते) — Woven

---

1 छा—. 2 प्लु—. 3 छि—. 4 स्यू—.

a And अर्चितः

m f n m f n m f n 1 *m f n*

Saluted, honoured. 51. (स्यादू) अर्हिते नमस्यितं नमसितमपचायिता

m f n m f n

ऽर्चिता ऽपचितम्

m f n m f n 2 *m f n* 3 *m f n*

Served, adored. वरिवसिते वरिवस्यितमुपासित (ञ्चो) पचरितं (च)

m f n m f n m f n m f n m f n

Suffering pain. 52. सन्तापित सन्तप्तौ धूपित धूपायितौ (च) दून (श्च)

m f n m f n 4 *m f n m f n m f n m f n*

Pleased, glad, content. हृष्टे मत्तस्तृप्तः प्रह्लन्नः प्रमुदितः प्रीतः

m f n m f n m f n m f n m f n m f n m f n m f n

Cut. 53. छिन्नं छातं लूनं कृत्तं दातं दितं छितं वृक्णम्

m f n m f n m f n m f n m f n m f n m f n

Fallen. स्रस्तं ध्वस्तं भ्रष्टं स्कन्नं पन्नं च्युतं गलितम्

m f n m f n m f n m f n 5 *m f n m f n*

Obtained. 54. लब्धं प्राप्तं विन्नं भावितमासादितं (च) भूतं (च)

m f n m f n 6 *m f n m f n m f n*

Sought. अन्वेषितं गवेषितमन्विष्टं मार्गितं मृगितम्

m f n m f n m f n m f n m f n m f n 7 *m f n*

Wet; moistened. 55. आर्द्रं सार्द्रं क्लिन्नं तिमितं स्तिमितं समुन्नमुत्तं (च)

m f n m f n m f n 8 *m f n m f n m f n*

Preserved, saved, guarded. त्रातं त्राणं रक्षितमवितं गोपायितं (च) गुप्त (म्)

m f n 9 *m f n m f n m f n m f n*

Disregarded, despised. 56. अवगणितमवमता ऽवज्ञाते ऽवमानितं(च)परिभूते

m f n m f n m f n m f n m f n 10 *m f n*

Abandoned, left. त्यक्तं हीनं विधुतं समुज्झितं धूतमुत्सृष्टम्

m f n m f n 11 *m f n m f n* 12 *m f n* 13 *m f n m f n*

Spoken, said. 57. उक्तं भाषितमुदितं जल्पितमाख्यातमभिहितं लपितम्

---

1 अ—. 2 उ—. 3 उ—. 4 ह्ल—. 5 आ—. 6 अ—. 7 उ—. 8 अ—. 9 अ—. 10 उ—. 11 उ—. 12 आ—. 13 अ—.

m f n *m f n* *m f n* *m f n* *m f n* 1*m f n* *m f n*

बुद्धं बुधितं मनितं विदितं प्रतिपन्नमवसिताऽवगते Known, understood.

m f n a 2*m f n* 3*m f n* 4*m f n* *m f n*

58. ऊरीकृतमुररीकृतमङ्गीकृतमाश्रुतं प्रतिज्ञातम् Promised.

m f n *m f n* *m f n* b *m f n* 5*m f n* 6*m f n*

सङ्गीर्णं सम्विदितं संश्रुतं समाहितोपश्रुतोपगतम्

m f n *m f n* *m f n* *m f n* *m f n* *m f n* 7*m f n*

59. ईडितशस्तपणायितपनायितप्रणुतपणितपनितानि Praised.

m f n c *m f n* *m f n* 8*m f n* 9*m f n*

अपिगीर्णं वर्णिताऽभिष्टुतेडितानि स्तुता(ऽर्थानि)

m f n *m f n* *m f n* d *m f n* *m f n* e *m f n* *m f n*

60. भक्षितचर्वितलिप्तप्रत्यवसितगिलितखादितप्सातम् Eaten.

m f n *m f n* *m f n* f *m f n* *m f n* *m f n* *m f n*

अभ्यवहृताऽन्नजग्धग्रस्तग्लस्ताऽशितं भुक्तं

m f n g *m f n* h *m f n* i *m f n* j *m f n* k *m f n* l

61. क्षेपिष्ठक्षोदिष्ठप्रेष्ठवरिष्ठस्थविष्ठबंहिष्ठाः Certain irregular superlatives.

(क्षिप्रक्षुद्राभीप्सितपृथुपीवबहुलप्रकर्षार्थाः)

m f n m *m f n* n *m f n* o *m f n* p *m f n* q *m f n* r

62. साधिष्ठद्राघिष्ठस्फेष्ठगरिष्ठह्रसिष्ठवृन्दिष्ठाः

(बाढव्यायतबहुगुरुवामनवृन्दारकातिशये)

---

1 अ—. 2 ऊ—. 3 आ—. 4 आ—. 5 उ—.
6 उ—. 7 —त. 8 ईडित. 9 स्तुत.

[a] And उरीकृतं. [b] Also प्रतिश्रुतं. [c] And गीर्णं. [d] Likewise चोढ. [e] And गिरितं. [f] Also अन्नं. [g] Most quick. [h] Most small. [i] Most dear. [j] Most large. [k] Most corpulent. [l] Most numerous. [m] Most hard. [n] Most long. [o] Most firm. [p] Most heavy. [q] Most short. [r] Most abundant.

CHAPTER III.

1. (प्रकृतिप्रत्ययाद्यर्थैः सङ्कीर्णे लिङ्गमुन्नयेत्)

Action. — कर्म[1 n a] क्रिया[f]

Continual.[b] — (तत्सातत्ये गम्ये स्युर्) अपरस्पराः[m f n c]

Totality. — 2. (साकल्यासङ्गवचने) पारायण[n d]

Adherence, attachment. — परायणे[m f n e]

Wilfulness, independence. — यदृच्छा[f] स्वैरिता[f f]

Vain and causeless state. — (हेतु शून्या त्वास्था) विलक्षणम्

Quiet.[g] — 3. शमथ[m] (स्तु) शमः[m] शान्तिर्[2 f]

Self-command.[h] — दान्ति[f](स्तु) दमथो[m] दमः[m]

Approved occupation.[i] — अवदानं[n j] (कर्मवृत्तं)

A desirable gift. — काम्यदानं[n] प्रवारणम्[n k]

1—नृ. 2—न्ति.

[a] One authority makes this term masc. and neut. in both its acceptations, of action and of act. Others add, in both genders, कर्मः, and कर्मं. [b] In respect of action. [c] Adjectively अपरस्परः, रा:, रं. Adverbially,—रं. [d] Invariably neuter even with nouns of other genders. [e] Some read तुरायणं or त्वरायणं. [f] Also स्वैरता. [g] Absence of passion. [h] Endurance of the pain of austerities. [i] Some interpret this an act accomplished. [j] Also अपदानं. [k] Likewise प्रवारणं.

4. वशक्रिया *f* संवदनं *n* [b]	Subduing by charms.[a]
मूलकर्म *1n* (तु) कार्म्मणम् *n*	Magic.
विधूननं *n* विधुवनं *n* [c]	Tremour.
तर्पणं *n* प्रीणना *n* ऽवनम् *n*	Satisfaction.[d]
5. पर्य्याप्तिः *f* (स्यात्) परित्राणं *n* हस्तवारण *n* [e] (मित्यपि)	Warding of a blow.
सेवनं *n* सीवनं *n* स्यूतिर् *2f*	Sewing.
विदरः *m* स्फुटनं *n* [f] भिदा *f*	Tearing, rending.
6. आक्रोशनम् *n* अभीषङ्गः *3m* [g]	Curse, imprecation.
संवेदो *m* वेदना *fn* (न ना)	Sensation, perception.
सम्मूर्च्छनम् *n* अभिव्याप्तिर् *4f*	Co-extending, pervading.
याच्ञा *f* भिक्षा *f* ऽर्थना *fn* ऽर्दना *fn*	Begging.
7. वर्द्धनं *n* छेदने *n*	Cutting.
(ऽथ द्वे) आनन्दन *n* [i] सभाजने *n* [j]	Courtesy; welcome or adieu.[h]
आप्रच्छन्नम् *n*	
(अथा) म्नायः *5m* सम्प्रदायः *m*	Received doctrine.[k]
क्षये *m* क्षिया *f*	Loss.

1—मू. 2—ति. 3 ष—. 4—च्छि. 5 आ—.

[a] Bringing into one's power by drugs, charms or incantations; or the drugs and charms by which that is effected. [b] Or संवदना. Also संवननं. [c] And विधुननं. [d] Whether the act of pleasing or the state of being pleased. [e] Or हस्तधारणं. [f] And स्फोटनं. [g] Likwise अभिषङ्गः. [h] Civility in receiving a friend, or in taking leave of him: embracing, friendly inquiry, adieu. [i] And आमन्त्रणं. [j] Also सभाजनं. [k] Traditional and right.

Taking.[a]	8. ग्रहे ग्राहो	m m
Wish, desire.	वशः कान्तौ	m 1f
Protection, defence.	रक्ष्णस्त्राणे	m b 2n
Sound, noise.	रणः क्वणे	m c m
Perforation, piercing.	व्यधो वेधे	m m
Maturity.	पचा पाके	f m
Calling; challenging.	हवो हूतौ	m 3f
Engaging; appointing.[d]	वरो वृतौ	m 4f
Combustion, burning.	9. ओषः प्लोषे	m m e
Guiding, directing.	नयो नाये	m m
Wearing, growing old.	ज्यानिर्जीर्णौ	f 5f
Whirling, going round.	भ्रमो भ्रमौ	m 6f
Increase, growth.	स्फातिर्वृद्धौ	f 7f
Fame, notoriety.	प्रथा ख्यातौ	f 8f
Touch, contact.	स्पृष्टिः पृक्तौ	f 9f
Oozing, dripping.	स्नवः स्रवे	m f f

1—न्ति. 2 त्रा—. 3—ति. 4—ति. 5 जीर्णिः.
6—न्ति. 7 वृद्धि. 8—ति. 9—क्ति.

[a] Whether by seizure or acceptance. [b] Some read रक्षा. [c] Also क्वाणः. [d] Prevailing on a person to undertake a business. Both terms also signify requesting, and encompassing. [e] Also प्लोषः. [f] And स्फायः. Also स्रवः

f a 1*f*
10. एधा समृद्धौ — Thriving.

n b *n* c
स्फुरणं स्फुरणे — Throbbing.

2*f* *f*
प्रमितौ प्रमा — True knowledge.

f *m*
प्रसूतिः प्रसवे — Bringing forth (as young).

m d *m*
श्च्योते प्राघारः — Pouring forth; aspersion.

m *m*
क्लमथः क्लमे — Fatigue.

m *m*
11. उत्कर्षोऽतिशये — Excellence.

f *m*
सन्धिः श्लेषे — Union, junction.

m *m* e
विषय आश्रये — Refuge; asylum.

3*f* *n*
क्षिपायां क्षेपणं — Sending; directing. f

f 4*f* g
गीर्णिर्गिरौ — Swallowing.

n h 5*m*
गुरणमुद्यमे — Effort, exertion.

m *m*
12. उन्नाय उन्नये — Raising.

m *n*
श्रायः श्रयणे — Reliance; taking refuge.

n *m* i
जयने जयः — Conquest, victory.

1—ऋध. 2—मि. 3—पा. 4 गिरि. 5 उ—.

a Some read विधा. b And स्फुरणं or स्फोरणं. Also स्फुरः and स्फुरणा. c Likewise स्फारणं. d And श्चोतः. e Or आश्रयः. f Also interpreted passing away time. g Also गिलिः and गिलनं. h Likewise गूरणं and गोरणं. i According to another reading, जपनं, जपः, inaudible repetition.

Discourse, speech. — निगादो[m] निगदे[m]

Pride.[a] — मादो[m] मद[m]

Regret. — उद्वेग[m] उद्भ्रमे[m]

Trituration of perfumes. — 13. विमर्दनं[m] परिमले[m]

Conferring of a benefit.[b] — ऽभ्युपपत्ति[1 m]रनुग्रहः[2 m]

Disfavour. — निग्रह[m c] स्तद्विरुद्धः स्याद्)

Attack, onset.[d] — अभियोग[m] (स्त्व)भिग्रहः[3 m]

Clinching of the fist. — 14. मुष्टिबन्ध[m] (स्तु.) संग्राहो[m]

Affray, assault.[e] — डिम्बे[m] डमर[m f] विप्लवौ[m]

Ligament, fetters. — बन्धनं[n] प्रसितिश्[f]चारः[4 m g]

Morbid heat.[h] — स्पर्शः[m i] स्प्रष्टो[5 m j]पतप्तरि[6 m]

Injury.[k] — 15. निकारो[m] विप्रकारः[m] (स्याद्)

Hint, sign, token.[l] — आकार[m]स्त्विङ्ग[7 m] इङ्गितः[m]

---

[1] —ति. [2] अ—. [3] अ—. [4] चार. [5] —ष्टृ.
[6] उ—प्तृ. [7] इ—.

[a] Also joy. [b] By doing good, or by preventing ill. [c] Or विग्रहः. Also, according to a varied reading, निरोधः and विरोधः; but here a different acceptation is intended: viz. restraint or confinement. [d] Some explain this, a challenge to fight. [e] A conflict without weapons. Also terrifying the enemy by shouts or gestures. Likewise devastation and predatory or irregular war. [f] And डामरः. [g] Some read चारः, and connect it with the next article. [h] The line is by some divided into three articles, instead of two: viz. ligament; business of a scout or spy (चारः स्पशः); morbid heat. [i] Also स्पर्शः. [j] Or स्प्रष्टा (ष्टृ). [k] Also wickedness. [l] Indication of sentiment.

m m f 1f परिणामो विकारो (द्वे समे) विकृति विक्रिये	Change of form. a
m 2m 16. अपहार (स्तु) पचयः	Loss.
m m समाहारः समुच्चयः	Assemblage. b
m n प्रत्याहार उपादानं	Abstraction. c
m m विहार (स्तु.) परिक्रमः	Walking for pleasure.
m e n 17. अभिहारोऽभिग्रहणं	Robbery. d
m n निर्हारोऽभ्यवकर्षणम्	Extraction.
m m अनुहारोऽनुकारः (स्यात्)	Imitation.
m (अर्थस्यापगमे) व्ययः	Expenditure.
m f 18. प्रवाह (स्तु.) प्रवृत्तिः (स्यात्)	Stream. f
m प्रवहो (गमनं बहिः)	Going forth, issuing.
m m m m m m वियामो वियमो यामो यमः संयाम संयमौ	Forbearance. g
3n m 19. हिंसाकर्माऽभिचारः (स्यात्)	Incantation to destroy.
f h m f जागर्या जागरा (द्वयोः)	Waking, watching.

1—या. 2 अ—. 3—र्म.

[a] Some distinguish the terms, making the two first signify a total change, and the other two a partial or temporary alteration. [b] Gathering together in fact, or in thought. [c] Restraining the organs of sense. Also abridgment. [d] Or seizure in one's presence. [e] Likewise अभ्याहारः. [f] Or continual flow. Likewise commencement of action. [g] This line is by some divided into three articles: the two first terms signifying various distress; the two next decease; and the two last, forbearance. [h] Also जागरिया and जागर्त्तिः. Likewise जागरणं.

Obstacle, impediment. — विघ्नो[m] ऽन्तरायः[m] प्रत्यूहः[m]

Contiguous support.[a] — (स्याद्) उपघ्नो[m] ऽन्तिकाश्रये[m]

Enjoyment. — 20. निर्वेश[m] उपभोगः[m] (स्यात्)

Encompassing; surrounding. — परिसर्पः[m] परिक्रिया[m]

Separation. — विधुर[n] (न्तु) प्रविश्लेषो[m]

Meaning, intention. — ऽभिप्रायश्[m] छन्द[1][m][b] आशयः[m]

Abridgment. — 21. संक्षेपणं[n] समसनं[n]

Contradiction. — पर्यवस्था[f][c] विरोधनम्[n]

Perambulation.[d] — परिसर्या[f][e] परीसारः[m]

Stay. — (स्याद्) आस्या[f] (त्वा) सना[2][f] स्थितिः

Diffusion. — 22. विस्तारो[m][f] विग्रहो[m] व्यासः[m]

Prolixity. — स च (शब्दस्य) विस्तरः[m]

Rubbing of the person. — (स्यान्) मर्दनं[n] सम्बाहनं[n]

Disappearance. — विनाशः[m] (स्याद्) अदर्शनम्[n]

Acquaintance. — 23. संस्तवः[m] (स्यात्) परिचयः[m]

Spreading. — प्रसर[m] (स्तु) विसर्पणम्[m]

Scarcity. — नीवाक[m] (स्तु) प्रयामः[m] (स्यात्)

Proximity. — सन्निधिः[m][g] सन्निकर्षणम्[n]

1 स—. 2 आ—.

[a] As a tree, of a creeper. [b] Also neut. छन्दः (स्). [c] And प्रत्यवस्था. [d] Moving about, on the ground: some interpret it near approach. [e] Or परीसर्या. [f] And विस्तरः. [g] Also सन्निधं.

m m n
24. लवो ऽभिलावो लवने — Reaping.

m n m
निष्पावः पवने पवः — Winnowing, cleaning.

m m
प्रस्तावः (स्याद्) अवसरः — Occasion, opportunity.

m b n
त्रसरः सूत्रवेष्टनम् — A shuttle. a

m m
25. प्रजनः (स्याद्) उपसरः — First pregnancy of cows. c

m d m
प्रश्रय प्रणयौ (समौ) — Affectionate solicitation.

f 1 m
धीशक्तिर्निष्क्रमो — Intellectual faculty. e

m n g m h
(ऽस्त्री तु) संक्रामो दुर्गसञ्चरः — Difficult progress. f

m i m j
26. प्रत्युत्क्रमः प्रयोगार्थः — Act tending to a main object.

m m
प्रक्रमः (स्याद्) उपक्रमः — Beginning. k

n 2 m l m
(स्याद्) अभ्यादानमुद्घात आरम्भः

m 3 f m
संभ्रमस्त्वरा — Haste, hurry.

---

1 नि—. 2 उ—. 3 त्व—.

a Also act of weaving. b Or तसरः. c Some interpret it, the season of impregnation. Others explain it, the first going of a cow to a bull; or the first impregnation; or simply her impregnation by the bull, or her pregnancy. d Also प्रसरः. e Power of the understanding: as attention, comprehension, reasoning, &c. f Towards a place scarcely accessible. g And संक्रमः. h Likewise दुस्सञ्चारः. i Or प्रत्युत्क्रान्तिः. j Some read प्रयुक्तार्थः; and explain this article, beginning of battle: others interpret it, war or combat. k Some divide this article; making the two first terms signify a first beginning, and the three last a commencement in general: others explain the two first, a beginning; and the three last, a thing begun. l Also उपोद्घातः m And त्वरिः.

Impediment.[i] — 27. प्रतिबन्धः[m] प्रतिष्टम्भो[m a]

Causing to descend. — ऽवनाय[m b] (स्तु.) निपातनम्[n c]

Apprehension.[d] — उपलम्भ[m] (स्त्व्) ऽनुभवः[m]

Smearing.[e] — समालम्भो[m] विलेपनम्[m]

Separation of lovers.[f] — 28. विप्रलम्भो[m] विप्रयोगो[m]

Liberality.[g] — विलम्भ[m] (स्त्व्) अतिसर्जनम्[1 n]

Celebrity. — विश्राव[m] (स्तु) प्रविख्यातिर्[2 f h]

Attention. — अवेक्षा[f] प्रतिजागरः[m]

Reading; lecture. — 29. निपाठ[m] निपठौ[m] पाठे[m]

Wetness.[i] — तेमस्तेमौ[m m] समुन्दने[n]

Distress, from disease, &c. — आदीनवा[m]स्रवौ[3 m j] क्लेशे[m]

Meeting; union. — मेलके[m] सङ्ग[m] सङ्गमौ[m k]

Research. — 30. सम्वीक्षणं[n l] विचयनं[n] मार्गणं[n] मृगणा[n] मृगः[m m]

Embrace. — परिरम्भः[m n] परिष्वङ्गः[m] संश्लेष[n] उपगूहनम्[n]

Sight; seeing; looking. — 13. निर्वर्णनं[u] (तु) निध्यानं[n] दर्शना[4 n o]लोकने[5 n]क्षणम्[6 n]

---

1 स—. 2—ति. 3 स्रा—. 4—न. 5 स्रा—. 6 ई—.

[a] Likewise विष्टम्भः. [b] And अवनयः. [c] Or निपातनं. [d] Conception otherwise than from memory. [e] With saffron, sandalwood, &c. [f] Also solitude, and disagreement. [g] Some explain it, appointing, engaging. [h] Also प्रतिख्यातिः. [i] One explains this, wet. [j] Or आस्रवः. [k] Also सङ्गमं and साङ्गमः. [l] Likewise समीक्षणं and समेक्षणं, or गवेषणं. [m] Some read मृगया. [n] Or परीरम्भः. [o] According to another reading, आलोकः and ईक्षणं.

n n m f

प्रत्याख्यानं निरसनं प्रत्यादेशो निराकृतिः — Rejection; disallowance.

m m

32. उपशायो विशाय (श्च पर्य्यायशयनार्थकौ) — Watching alternately.

n f b f c f

अर्त्तनं (च) ऋतीया(च)हृणीया(च) घृणा (र्थके) — Censure, reproach. a

m m m m c

33. (स्याद्) व्यत्यासो विपर्य्यासो व्यत्यय(श्च) विपर्य्यये — Contrariety; opposition. d

m g m m m

पर्य्ययो ऽतिक्रम (स्तस्मिन्न) ऽतिपात उपात्ययः — Transgression. f

n

34. (प्रेषणं यत्समाहूय तत्र स्यात्) प्रतिशासनम् — Mission after calling. h

m

(स) संस्तावः (क्रतुषु या स्तुतिभूमिर्द्विजन्मनाम्) — Place where the priests stand. i

m

35. (निधाय तक्ष्यते यत्र काष्ठे काष्ठं स) उद्घनः — A carpenter's work-bench.

m m k

स्तम्बघ्न(स्तु) स्तम्बघनः (स्तम्बो येन निहन्यते) — Tool for cutting corn and grass. j

m

36. आविधो (विध्यते येन तत्र) — An auger. l

m

(विष्वक्समे) निघः — Round, circular.

m m

उत्कार (श्च) निकार(श्च द्वौ धान्योत्क्षेपणार्थकौ) — Winnowing of corn. m

---

[a] One commentator remarks, that two of these terms, ऋतीया and हृणीया, which properly signify shame, are here inserted by mistake. [b] Also रोच्या. [c] Likewise हृणिया and ह्रिणीया or हृणीया. [d] One interprets this, misapprehension. [e] And विपर्यासः. [f] Some make the four terms, others the two first of them, synonymous with the preceding. [g] And पर्यायः. [h] Sending of a servant on an errand after calling him. [i] At a solemn act of religion; reciting hymns and prayers. [j] For eradicating clusters of gramineous plants: some say for cutting the stalks: others explain the term a basket to receive heads of Indian corn, &c. [k] Also स्तंबघनन',—नी. [l] Turned by a string. [m] Or piling it up.

m 1m m 2m

Swallowing, &c. a — 37. निगारोद्गारः विक्षावोद्ग्राहा (स्तु. गरणादिषु)

3f 4f 5f mb

Stopping, ceasing. — आरत्यवरति विरतय उपरामे

mfc

Spitting. — (वा स्त्रियां तु)निष्ठेवः

f 6n n

38. निष्ठ्यूति निष्ठेवनं निष्ठीवन (मित्यभिन्नानि)

n fd

Speed. — जवने जूतिः

f n

Conclusion. e — सातिस्तु) ऽवसाने (स्यादथ)

m f

Fever. — (अथ) ज्वरे जूर्तिः

m n

Driving of cattle. — 39. उदज (स्तु.) पशुप्रेरणम्

m f

Curse. — अकरणि (रित्यादयः शापे)

7n

Aggregate patronymic. g — (गोत्रान्तेभ्यस्तस्य वृन्दमित्यौ) पगवका (दिकम्)

m m

Multitude of loaves and pies. h — 40. आपूपिकं शाष्कुलिक (मेवमाद्यमचेतसाम्)

---

1 उ—. 2 उ—. 3—ति. 4 ग्र— 5—ति.
6 नि—. 7 औ—क.

a The four terms, here exhibited, differ in signification. निगारः, swallowing. उद्गारः, vomiting. विक्षावः, cough; some say, sound. उद्ग्राहः, taking up: also, replying in argument. b Or उपरमः. c Fem. निष्ठेवा. Some say, also neuter निष्ठेवं. d Likewise जुतिः. Some add जतिः and जवनं. e End of action. f So similar terms of imprecation. As अजननिः, अजीवनिः, अपग्राहः, निग्राहः, &c. Ex. तस्याजीवनिरेवास्तु, May he not live! g Instanced in the text; औपगवकं, a multitude of descendants of Upagu So गार्गकं, a multitude of descendants of Garga. दाक्षकं,—of Daksha. h Respectively: stated as instances of nouns of multitude of inanimate things.

n a
(माणवानान्तु) माणव्यं — Multitude of boys.

f
(सहायानां) सहायता — —of coadjutors.

f
41. हल्या (हलानां) — —of ploughs.

n n
ब्राह्मण्य वाडव्ये (तु द्विजन्मनाम्) — —of priests.

n n
(द्वे पर्शुकानां पृष्ठानां) पार्श्वं पृष्ठ्य (मनुक्रमात्) — —of ribs and back-bones. b

f f
42. (खलानां) खलिनी खल्या (ऽप्य) — —of threshing floors.

n
(ऽथ) मानुष्यकं (नृणाम्) — —of men.

f f f f f
ग्रामता जनता धूम्या पाश्या गल्या(पृथक् पृथक्) — —of villages, &c. c

n n n 1n
43. (अपि) साहस्र कारीष वार्मणाथर्वणा (दिकम्) — —of thousands, &c. d

---

[1] णा—ष.

[a] Some read माणवकं. [b] Respectively. [c] In order : multitude of people ; accumulation of smoke ; abundance of fetters ; great quantity of reeds, (or multitude of ropes or of throats : for गल has all these senses.) [d] In order : multitude of pieces of dry cow-dung ; abundance of hides (or of shields) ; collection of prayers and incantations delivered by the sage AT'HARVAN : besides other similar terms : as वार्मणं, assemblage of coats of mail ; वार्मिणं, multitude of men in armour ; चार्मिणं,—of men holding shields ; आङ्गारं,—burning or burnt coals ; क्षैत्रं,—of fields.

CHAPTER IV.

SECTION I.

1. (नानार्थाः केऽपि कान्तादिवर्गेष्वेवात्र कीर्त्तिताः
भूरि प्रयोगा ये येषु पर्य्यायेष्वपि तेषु ते)

1 Sky, ether. 2 Heaven. — 2. (आकाशे त्रिदिवे) नाको[m]

1 World. 2 People. — लोकः[m] (तु भुवने जने)

1 Verse. 2 Glory. — (पद्ये यशसि च) श्लोकः[m]

1 Arrow. 2 Sword. — (शरे खड्गे च) सायकः[m a]

1 Shakal. 2 God of water. — 3. जम्बुकौ[m] (क्रोष्टु वरुणौ)

1 Fried rice flattened. 2 Infant. — पृथुकौ[m] (चिपिटार्भकौ)

1 Sight, look. 2 Light. — आलोकौ[m] (दर्शनोद्योतौ)

1 A double drum. 2 A large drum.[b] — (भेरी पटहम्) आनकौ[m]

1 Mark. 2 Flank.[c] — 4. (उत्सङ्ग चिह्नयोर्) अङ्कः[m]

1 Spot. 2 Defamation. — कलङ्को[m] (ऽङ्कापवादयोः)

---

[a] Or शायकः. Some read घातकः. [b] Some reverse the interpretations: one of these instruments is a large drum beaten at both extremities; the other, at one end only. [c] The side above the hip, where women place young children in carrying them. Also 3 A cypher or figure. 4 An act of a drama. 5 Variegated or spotted.

तक्षका (नागवर्द्धक्योर्)	1 A carpenter. 2 The chief of snakes. a
अर्कः (स्फटिकसूर्य्ययोः)	1 Crystal. 2 The sun. b
5. (मारुते वेधसि ब्रध्ने पुंसि) कः	1 Wind. 2 *Brahma.* 3 Sun. 4 Soul.
कं (शिरोऽम्बुनोः)	5 Head. 6 Water. c
(स्यात्) पुलाक (स्तुच्छधान्ये संक्षेपे भक्तसिक्थके)	1 Shrivelled grain. 2 Brevity. d
6. (उलूके करिणः पुच्छमूलोपान्ते च) पेचकः	1 An owl. 2 Root of a tail. e
(कमण्डलौ च) करकः	Water-pot. f
(सुगते च) विनायकः	A *Buddha* or saint. g
7. किष्कु (हस्ते वितस्तौ च)	1 Cubit. h 2 A span.
(मृककीटे च) वृश्चिकः	Scorpion. i
(प्रतिकूले) प्रतीक (स्त्रि.षु.कदेशे च पुंस्ययम्)	An integrant part. j

(Gender marks printed above the words: m over तक्षका, अर्कः, कः, कं, पुलाक, पेचकः, विनायकः, किष्कु, वृश्चिकः, प्रतीक; m n over करकः.)

---

[a] Or of demi-gods shaped like snakes, abiding in the infernal regions. Also 3 Speaker of the prologue to a drama. [b] Also 3 Asclepias gigantea. 4 Copper. 5 A title of *Indra.* [c] Also 7 Joy. [d] Others say, 2 Celerity. 3 Lump of boiled rice. [e] That is of an elephant's tail. [f] Especially a hollow Cocoanut, or gourd . Also m. f. 2 Hail. m. 3 Pomegranate. 4 A bird (Curlew.) m. n. 5 A box to hold betle-leaf. [g] Also 2 Title of GANE´SA. 3 Title of YAMA. 4 Name of VISHNU's eagle. 5 A spiritual teacher. 6 Obstacle ; difficulty. [h] Whether the measure, or the forearm. [i] The insect ; as well as the sign of the zodiac. Also, 2 The month during which the sun is in Scorpio. Likewise, 3 A crab. 4 A hairy caterpillar. 5 Name of a tree (Vangueria Spinosa). [j] And m. f. n. 2 Contrary : not consonant. 3 Inverse.

1 Gentian. a 2 A fragrant grass. b — 8. (स्त्री) भूनिम्ब (न्) भूनिम्बे कत्तृणे भूस्तृणे ऽपि च)

Sorts of Cucurbitaceous plants. c — (ज्योत्स्निकायां च घोषे च) कोशातकी

(ऽथ कट्फले

A white sort of Mimosa. e — 9. सिते च खदिरे) सोमवल्कः (स्त्री)

(ऽथ सिह्लके

1 Incense. 2 Meal of seame. f — तिलकल्के च) पिण्याकेा

Asafœtida. g — बाह्लीकं (रामठे ऽपि च)

1 INDRA. 2 Bdellium. 3 Owl. i — 10. (महेन्द्रगुग्गुलूलूकव्यालग्राहिषु) कौशिकः

1 Diseas. e 2 Pain. 3 Fear. k — (रुक्तापशङ्कास्व.ा) तङ्कः

Small. l — (स्वल्पे ऽपि) क्षुद्रक (त्रि.षु)

1—की. 2 का—.

[a] Gentiana Chirayta, Roxb. [b] Andropogon Schoenanthus: and another kind. Some, varying the interpretation, make this a name of the *Káyaphal*. [c] Vizt. 1 Trichosanthes diœca. 2 Luffa Pentandra and Acutangla, R. Likewise 3 Achyranthes aspera. Also 4 Night. [d] And कोशातकी. [e] Also 2 the *Káyaphal*. [f] Likewise 3 Oilcake of sesame. 4 Asafœtida. 5 Saffron. [g] Also 2 Saffron. And m. 3 Name of a country. 4 Horse bred in that country. 5 Man of a low tribe. [h] And बाह्लिकं, वाह्लिकं, or बह्लीकं. [i] Also 4 Snakecatcher. Likewise 5 Ichneumon (viverra mungo). 6 Title of VISWA'MITRA. 7 Skilled in dictionaries. And f. कौशिकी. 8 Title of GAURI'. 9 Name of a river in Bengal. Or कौशिकः—की. [k] Also 4 Sound of a drum. [l] Also 2 Hard. 3 Low, vile. 4 poor, indigent. 5 Youngest. [m] Fem. क्षुद्रका. Also क्षुद्रकः—का.

11. जैवातृकः[m] (शशाङ्केऽपि) — The moon. [a]

(खुरेऽप्यश्वस्य) वर्तकः[m] — A horse's hoof. [b]

(व्याघ्रेऽपि) पुण्डरीको[m] (ना) — A leopard. [c]

(यवान्यामपि) दीपकः[m][e] — An aromatic seed. [d]

12. शालावृकाः[1 m] (कपि क्रोष्टु श्वानः) — 1 Ape. 2 Dog. 3 Shakal.

(स्वर्णेऽपि) गैरिकम्[n] — Gold. [f]

(पीडार्थेऽपि) व्यलीकं[m] (स्यात्) — Pain. [g]

अलीकं[n] (त्वप्रिये ऽनृते) — 1 Falsehood. 2 Any thing displeasing. [h]

13. (शीलान्वयाव्) ऽनूके[n] (द्वे) — 1 Disposition. 2 Race, family. [i]

शल्के[n] (शकलवल्कले) — 1 part. 2 Scale of a fish. 3 Bark.

३—क.

[a] Also m. f. n. 2 Long-lived 3 Thin. [b] And m. f. 2 A quail. [c] Also 2 The elephant posted in the S. E. to uphold the world. 3 A proper name (the author of a dictionary). 4 A variety of the suger-cane. Likewise n. 5 A white lotos. 6 A white umbrella. 7 A medicinal drug. [d] Ligusticum Ajowan, Roxb. Or else Apium involucratum, R. Also 2 Cumin (Cuminum Cyminum). 3 Celosia Cristata. 4 A lamp. 5 In rhetoric, a certian elegance of construction. [e] Or दीप्यकः m. n. 1 Ligusticum Ajowan R. 2 Apium involucratum, R. 3 Celosia cristata. [f] Also 2 Red orpiment. 3 Red chalk. [g] Likewise 2 Any thing displeasing. 3 Unfit to be done. 4 Strange. 5 Reverse. Also m. 6 Addicted to an unnatural crime. [h] Also : 3 The forehead. [i] Likewise m. 3 A former state of existence.

1 A weight. a 2 Gold. 3 Ornament on the breast.

(साष्टे शते सुवर्णानां हेम्न्युरोभूषणे पले

m n

14. दीनारे ऽपि च) निष्को (ऽस्त्री)

m n

1 Sin. 2 Fraud. b

कल्को (ऽस्त्री शमलैनसोः

दम्भे ऽप्य)

m n

1 SIVA'S bow. 2 Trident. c

(ऽथ) पिनाको (ऽस्त्री शूलशङ्करधन्वनोः)

f

A female elephant. d

15. धेनुका (तु करेण्वां च)

f

Cloudiness. e

(मेघजाले च) कालिका

f

1 Agony. 2 Explanatory verse. f

कारिका (यातनावृत्त्योः)

f

An earring. g

कर्णिका (कर्णभूषणे

---

[a] One of 108 *suvarnas*. Also one of 4 *suvarnas*. Likewise one of 2 *karshas*. [b] Also 3 Dirt. 4 Ordure. 5 Sediment. 6 Levigated powder. 7 The belleric myrobalan. And m. f. 8 Sinful; wicked. [c] *Siva's*; some say, any trident. Also 3 A shower of dust. [d] Also 2 A milch cow; especially one which has recently calved. 3 Dagger. Likewise m. 4 Proper name; a demon slain by KRISHNA. n. 5 A herd of kine. 6 Gesture of a woman. [e] A multitude or succession of clouds. Also: 2 A dark cloud threatening rain. 3 A fog or mist. 4 Blackness. 5 Black. 6 The Goddess GAURI'. 7 Name of a terrific goddess. 8 A female crow. 9 A black scorpion. 10 Spikenard. 11 A sort of potherb. 12 A branch of a Cucumber plant. 13 A line of hair reaching to the navel. 14 Price of a commodity on credit. 15 Interest at a monthly rate. 16 Spirituous liquor. 17 A stain or defect in gold, &c. [f] Or, as otherwise read, 3 Interest at any stipulated rate. 4 Action in general. Also 5 An art or profession. 6 A female rope-dancer and tumbler. [g] Also 2 The pericarp of a lotos. 3 The tip of an elephant's trunk. 4 The middle finger.

16. करिहस्ताङ्गुलौ पद्मबीजकोश्यां।

(त्रिषूत्तरे)[a]

m f n वृन्दारकौ (रूपिमुख्याव्) — 1 Handsome. 2 Chief, Principal. b

m f n एके (मुख्यान्यकेवलाः) — 1 Chief. 2 Other. 3 Alone. 4 One.

17. (स्याद्दाम्भिकः) *m f n* कौक्कुटिको (यश्चादूरेरितेक्षणः) — Hypocritical. c

m f n लालाटिकः (प्रभोर्भालदर्शी कार्याक्षमश्च यः) — 1 Attentive. 2 Indolent. d

18. (भूभृन्नितम्बवलये चक्रे च) *m n* कटको (ऽस्त्रियाम्) — 1 Side of a hill. 2 Bracelet. 3 Circle. e

(सूच्यग्रे क्षुद्रशत्रौ च रोमहर्षे च) *m* कण्टकः — 1 A thorn. 2 A paltry foe. 3 Hair on end. f

---

[a] The following admit the three genders. [b] Also m. 3 A god. 4 A general or leader of an army. [c] Also, 2 One who never looks far before him; but steps with caution for fear of treading on insects. [d] Watchful of his master's looks. 2 Careless or incapable of work. 3 Mode of embrace. [e] Also 4 A ring on an elephant's tooth. 5 An army. 6 A metropolis. 7 Sea salt. [f] Also 4 A fishbone. 5 Finding fault. This and the preceding line are omitted by most commentaries.

SECTION II.

1 Bright-ness. 2 Ray of light. 3 Flame. a — 19. मयूख (स्त्विट्कर ज्वालासु)

1 A bee. 2 An arrow. — (ऽलिबाणौ) शिलीमुखौ

An auriferous gem. b — शंखो (निधौ ललाटास्थ्नि कम्बौ न स्त्री)

Organ of sense. c — (इन्द्रिये ऽपि) खम्

1 Ray of light. 2 Flame. d — 20. (घृणिज्वाले अपि) शिखे

SECTION III.

1 A mountain. 2 A tree. e — (शैलवृक्षौ) नगावगौ

1 Wind. 2 An arrow. f — आशुगौ (वायुविशिखौ)

1 An arrow. 2 The sun. 3 A bird. g — (शरार्कविहगाः) खगाः

1 A bird. 2 The sun. h — 21. पतङ्गौ (पक्षिसूर्यौ च)

1 Areca. i 2 Multitude. — पूगः (क्रमुकवृन्दयोः)

1—खा. 2 अग. 3 धग.

[a] Also 4 Beauty. [b] And 2 The bones of the forehead. m. n. 3 A shell, a conch. 4 In numeration, the twelfth place of figures. [c] Also 2 Vacuity. 3 A cypher. 4 Heaven. 5 The sky. 6 Auspiciousness. [d] Likewise 3 A branch. 4 A radicant branch. 5 Crest of a peacock. 6 Lock of hair on the head. 7 Chief, principal. [e] Also 3 A serpent 4 The sun. [f] Likewse m. f. n. 3 Fleet, moving with speed. [g] Also 4 A planet. 5 A grasshopper. 6 A god. 7 Sound. [h] Also 3 A grasshopper. 4 Brasil-wood. [i] Masc. The palm (Areca faufel). Neut. Its nut.

(पशावपि) मृगाः ^{m}	Cattle. a
वेगः ^{m} (प्रवाहजवयोरपि)	1 Stream. 2 Speed. b
22. परागः ^{m} (कौसुमे रेणौ स्नानीयादौ रजस्यपि)	1 Pollen of flowers. 2 Dust. c
(गजेऽपि) नागमातङ्गौ $^{m\ m}$	An elephant. d
अपाङ्गः ^{m} (तिलकेऽपि च)	A circlet on the forehead. e
23. सर्गः ^{m} (स्वभावनिर्मोक्षनिश्चयाध्यायसृष्टिषु)	1 Nature. 2 Relinquishment. f
योगः ^{m} (संनहनोपायध्यानसङ्गतियुक्तिषु)	1 Armour. 2 Means. g
24. भोगः ^{m} (सुखे स्त्र्यादिभृतावहेश्च, फणकाययोः)	1 Enjoyment. 2 Hire. h
(चातके हरिणे पुंसि) सारङ्गः $^{m\ j}$ (शबले त्रिषु)	1 Sort of bird. 2 A deer. i

[a] Likewise 2 Deer. 3 An elephant with white marks on his forehead. 4 A constellation (the head of Orion). 5 Search. [b] Also 3 Rapid transition, as of mind or wind. 4 Call of nature. [c] And 3 Fragrant powder. Also 4 Eclipse. 5 Coral. [d] Also नागः. 2 A snake (Coluber naja: and a sort of demigod shaped as a serpent). 3 A cruel person. 4 Name of a country. 5 In comp. Pre-eminent. 6 Mesua ferrea. 7 Rottlera tinctoria, R. 8 Cyperus pertenuis, R. Likewise मातङ्गः. 2 A race of mountaineers. 3 The sacred fig-tree (Ficus religiosa). [e] Also 2 Corner of the eye. 3 A lame or maimed person. [f] Likewise 3 Certainty. 4 A chapter or section. 5 Creation. Also 6 Perseverance. [g] And 3 Meditation. 4 Union. 5 Junction. Also 6 Keeping a fixed posture. 7 Lucky conjuncture. 8 In astrology. A mode of reckoning the moon's longitude. [h] And 3 Expanded head of a serpent. 4 Body of a serpent. Also 5 Eating. 6 Nurture. [i] And m. f. n. 3 Variegated. Also m. 4 An elephant. 5 A bee. 6 A peacock. [j] Or सारङ्गः.

An ape. a — 25. (कपौ च) प्लवगः *m*

1 Curse.
2 Defeat. b — (शापे तु.) ऽभिषङ्गः *m* (पराभवे)

1 A yoke.
2 A pair.
3 An age. c. — (यानाद्यङ्गे) युगः *m* (पुंसि)

युगं *n* (युग्मे कृतादिषु)

1 Heaven.
2 An arrow
3 A bull.
4 Speech. d — 26. (स्वर्गेषुपशुवाग्वज्रदिङ्नेत्रघृणिभूजले
लक्ष्यदृष्ट्या स्त्रियां पुंसि) गौर् *m f* e

1 A mark.
2 Privy part. f — लिङ्गं *n* (चिह्नशेफसोः)

1 Preferableness.
2 Summit. g — 27. शृङ्गं *n* (प्राधान्यसान्वोश्च)

1 The head.
2 Privy part. h — वराङ्गं *n* (मूर्धगुह्ययोः)

1 Prosperity. i — भगं *n* (श्रीकाममाहात्म्यवीर्ययत्नार्ककीर्तिषु)

---

[a] Also 2 A frog. 3 Sort of bird (a diver). 4 The dawn: the charioteer of the sun. [b] Also 3 Oath. 4 Groundless imputation. 5 Embrace. [c] The *Kṛita, Trétá, Dwápara,* and *Kali.* Also 4 A measure of four cubits. [d] And 5 The thunderbolt. 6 A region or quarter. 7 An eye. 8 A ray of light. 9 The earth. 10 Water. Likewise 11 The sun. [e] Masc. in some senses; and fem. or even neut. in others. [f] Membrum virile. Also 3 A sign or token. 4 The Symbol of SIVA. [g] Of a mountain. Likewise 3 A home. Also fem. 4 A sort of fish (Silurus pungentissimus). 5 A poisonous plant. [h] Pudendum muliebre. [i] Or 2 Beauty. And 3 Love, desire. 4 Pudendum muliebre. 5 Excellence (virtue, knowledge, &c.) 6 Strength, Vigour. 7 Care. 8 Glory, fame. And m. n. 9 One of the twelve suns. Also 10 The Moon.

SECTION IV.

28. *m* परिघः (परिघाते ऽस्त्रे ऽप्य)	1 Destruction. 2 An iron club. a
m ओघो (वृन्दे ऽम्भसां रये)	1 Multitude. 2 A current. b
मूल्ये पूजाविधाव) *m* ऽर्घो	1 Price. 2 Mode of adoration. c
(ऽंहो दुःखव्यसनेष्व) *n* ऽघम्	1 Sin. 2 Pain. 3 Passion.
29. (त्रिष्विष्टे ऽपि) *m f n* लघुः	Pleasing. d.

SECTION V.

m काचाः (शिक्यमृद्भेददृग्रुजः)	1 A swing. e 2 Glass. f
m विपर्यासे विस्तरे च) प्रपञ्चः	1 Reverse. 2 Copiousness. g
(पावके) *m* शुचिः	1 Fire. 2 A tried minister. 3 A month. h
30. (मास्यमात्ये चात्युपधे पुंसि मेध्ये सिते त्रिषु)	
(अभिष्वङ्गे स्पृहायाञ्च गभस्तौ च) *f* रुचिः (स्त्रियाम्)	1 Passion. 2 Desire. i

---

[a] Or 3 A club armed with iron. 4 In astrology, One of the *Yógas.* [b] Of water. Also 3 Succession. [c] Or of showing respect. [d] Also 2 Small. 3 Light. And n. 4 Quick. [e] For suspending a load. [f] And 3 A disease of the eye. [g] And 3 Error or illusion. 4 Prolixity. 5 Abundance. Also 6 Delusion. [h] That of *A'shád'ha* or of *Jyaisht'ha.* Or 4 The Hot season. 5 The sentiment of love. And m. f. n. 6 Pure. 7 White. [i] And 3 A ray of light. Or 4 Intentness. 5 Splendour. 6 Beauty.

SECTION VI. a

1 Clear. 2 A bear. b	31. (प्रसन्ने भल्लुकेऽप्य) ऽच्छो *m*
1 A cluster. 2 Sort of necklace. c	गुच्छः *m f n* (स्तबकहारयोः)
1 Hem of a garment. d	(परिधानाञ्चले) कच्छो *m* (जलप्रान्ते त्रिलिङ्गकः)

SECTION VII.

1 A peacock. 2 VISHNU's bird.	32. (केकितार्क्ष्याव) ऽहिभुजौ *m*
1 A tooth. 2 A regenerate man. e	(दन्तविप्राण्डजा) द्विजाः *m*
1 VISHNU. 2 SIVA. 3 A goat. f	अजा *m* (विष्णुहरच्छागा)
1 A cowpen. 2 A road. g	(गोष्ठाध्वनिवहा) व्रजाः *m*
1 A deified saint. 2 YAMA. h	33. धर्म्मराजौ *m* (जिनयमौ)
An elephant's tooth. i	कुञ्जो *m n* (दन्ते ऽपि न स्त्रियाम्)

---

[a] The stanza, constituting this section, is omitted by most commentators. [b] Also 3 Crystal. [c] Likewise 3 A clump. 4 A multitude or assemblage. [d] And m. f. n. (some say m.) 2 Bank or shore. Also m. 3 Sort of tree (Hibiscus Populneoides). [e] Of the three first tribes. And 3 An oviparous animal: a bird, &c. [f] Also 4 *Brahmá*. 5 Cupid. 6 A sheep. 7 Proper name; Son of RAGHU. [g] And 3 A multitude. [h] Also 3 Title of YUD'HIST'HIRA. [i] Likewise 2 An arbour.

n
वलजे (क्षेत्रपूर्द्वारे) — 1 A field. 2 A city gate. a 3 A pretty woman.

f
वलजा (वल्गुदर्शना)

1 f
34. (समे क्ष्मांशे रणे ऽप्या) जिः — 1 Even ground. 2 War.

f
प्रजा (स्यात्सन्ततौ जने:) — 1 Progeny. 2 People.

m
अब्जौ (शङ्खशशाङ्कौ च) — 1 A conch. 2 The moon. b

m f n
(स्वके नित्ये) निजं (त्रिषु) — 1 Own. 2 Perpetual.

SECTION VIII.

m
35. (पुंस्यात्मनि प्रवीणे च) क्षेत्रज्ञः (वाच्यलिङ्गकः) — 1 Soul. c

f
संज्ञा (स्याच्चेतनानामहस्ताद्यैश्चार्थसूचना) — 1 Thought. 2 Name. 3 Hint. d

m
36. दोषज्ञौ (वैद्यविद्वांसौ) — 1 A physician. 2 A wise man.

m
ज्ञः (विद्वान्सोमजो ऽपि च) — 1 A wise man. 2 BUD'HA. e

---

1 आजि.

a Also 3 War. b Also 3 *Dhanwantari*. 4 A tree (Eugenia acutangula). And n. 5 A Lotos. c And m. f. n. 2 Skilful. d Also 4 Proper name: the wife of the sun. e First of the lunar race.

SECTION IX.

A crow. a — (काकेभगण्डौ) करटौ [m]

An elephant's cheek. 2 The hip. b — (गजगण्डकटी) कटौ [m c]

1 Bald. 2 Without prepuce. d — 37. शिपिविष्ट (स्तु खलतौ दुश्चर्मणि महेश्वरे) [m e]

1 divine artist. f — (देवशिल्पिन्यपि) त्वष्टा [1 m g]

Destiny. h — दिष्टं (दैवे ऽपि न द्वयोः) [n]

Pungency. — 38. (रसे) कटुः [m]

Improper act. i — कटु (कार्य्ये त्रिषु मत्सरतीक्ष्णयोः) [2 n]

1 Happiness. 2 Ill luck. j — रिष्टं (क्षेमाशुभाभावेषु) [n]

Happiness. 2 Misery. k — ऽरिष्टे (तु शुभाशुभे) [n]

1 Illusion. 2 Fraud. — 39. (मायानिश्चलयन्त्रेषु कैतवानृतराशिषु

1—ष्टृ. 2 कटु.

[a] And 2 An elephant's cheek. Also 3 A person speaking nonsense. 4 One following a blamable profession. [b] Also 3 A mat. 4 A dead body. And f. (करटी). 5 Long pepper. [c] Nom. कटः. But some, by a slight variation of the reading and interpretation, make कटिः the term in both acceptations; or else कटिः and कटः. [d] Naturally so. Or 3 A leper. 4 Title of Siva. 5 Krîshn'a. [e] And शिपिविष्टः or शिविपिष्टः. [f] Vis'wakarma'. Also 2 A carpenter. 3 In mythology, One of the twelve suns. [g] Or त्वष्टा (ष्टृ). [h] Also m. 2 Time. [i] And m. f. n. 3 Envious. 4 Fierce. 5 Displeasing. Also f. 6 Mustard. 7 A medicinal plant. vulg. *Catuci*. [j] And 3 The reverse of ill luck. Also 4 Destruction. 5 Sin. [k] Also 3 Sign of death. 4 Spirituous liquor. Likewise m. Garlic. 6 Melia azadderckht. 7 A crow.

m n
अयोघने शैलशृङ्गे सीराङ्गे) कूट (म्स्त्रियाम्) — 2 Lic. 4 Assemblage. 5 Summit. a

f
40. (सूक्ष्मैलायां) त्रुटिः (स्त्री स्यात्काले ऽल्पे संशये ऽपि सा) — 1 Small cardamum. 2 An instant. b

1 f
(अत्युत्कर्षाश्रयः) कोट्यः — 1 End of a bow. 2 Eminence. c

f
(मूले लग्नकचे) जटा — 1 A root. 2 Clotted hair. d

f
41. व्युष्टिः (फले समृद्धौ च) — 1 Consequence. 2 Opulence. e

f
दृष्टि (ज्ञानेऽक्ष्णि दर्शने) — 1 Knowledge 2 An eye. 3 Sight.

f
इष्टि (यागेच्छयोः) — 1 A sacrifice. 2 Desire. f

f h
सृष्ट (निश्चिते बहुले त्रिषु) — 1 Certain. g

m f n
42. कष्टे (तु कृच्छ्रगहने) — 1 Painful. 2 Difficult. i

(दक्षामन्दागदेषु तु)

m f n
पटु (द्वौ वाच्यलिङ्गौ च) — 1 Diligent. 2 Skilful. j

1—टि.

[a] Of a mountain. And 6 Ploughshare. 7 Body of a plough. 8 Uniform substance (as the etherial element, &c.). 9 A trap for deer. 10 A hammer. Likewise 11 A jar. 12 Name of a plant. [b] And 3 An atom. 4 Doubt. [c] And 3 Edge of a weapon. 4 A corner or angle. 5 In numeration, Ten millions. [d] Also 3 Spikenard. [e] Also 3 Praise. [f] Likewise 3 A memorial verse. [g] The subject of ascertainment. And m. f. n. 3 Much. Also f. 4 Creation. [h] Or सृष्ट°. Likewise Created, fabricated. [i] Not easily attainable. [j] And 3 Fierce. 4 Cruel. 5 Hale. Also m. 6 A plant (Trichosanthes dioica) n. 7 Salt.

SECTION X.

SIVA. [a] — *m* नीलकण्ठः (शिवे ऽपि च)

1 The stomach. 2 A granary. [b] — 43. (पुंसि) *m* कोष्ठो (ऽन्तर्जठरं कुसूलो ऽन्तर्गृहं तथा)

1 Confirmation. [c] — *f* निष्ठा (निष्पत्तिनाशान्ताः)

1 Excellence. 2 Limit. 3 Region. [d] — 1 *f* काष्ठो(त्कर्षे स्थितौ दिशि)

Pre-eminent. [e] — 44. (त्रिषु) *m f n* ज्येष्ठो (ऽतिशस्ते ऽपि)

1 Very young. 2 Small. [f] — *m f n* कनिष्ठो (ऽतियुवाल्पयोः)

A staff. [g] — *m n* दण्डो (ऽस्त्री लगुडे ऽपि स्यात्)

1 A globe or ball. 2 Raw suger. [h] — *m* गुडो (गोलेक्षुपाकयोः)

1 A serpent. 2 A carnivorous beast. [i] — 45. (सर्पमांसात्पशू *m* (व्याडौ

---

1 काष्ठा.

[a] Also 2 A peacock. 3 A blue jay (Coracias Indica, &c.) 4 A gallinule. [b] And 3 An apartment. Also 4 Own. [c] And 2 Disappearance. 3 Destruction. Or 4 Stop. 5 Steady practice. [d] Or quarter. Also 4 A measure of time ; 18 twinklings of an eye. 5 A place. 6 A plant (Amomum Anthorhiza). Likewise n. 7 Wood. [e] Also 2 Eldest. 3 Very old. Likewise m. 4 The month so called. And f. 5 The constellation. [f] Also 3 Youngest. And f. 4 The little finger. [g] Likewise 2 A measure of four cubits. 3 A churning stick. 4 A measure of time : 24 minutes. 5 Punishment. 6 YAMA ; the Judge of the next world. 7 A companion of the sun. 8 A column of troops. 9 A stem or trunk. [h] Also f. 3 Euphorbia Tirucalli, &c. [i] As a tiger, &c. Also 3 A wicked man.

1f f b गोभूवाचस्त्वि) डा इला:	1 A cow. 2 The earth. 3 Speech. a
f क्ष्वेडा (वंशशलाकापि)	A bambu rod. c
f नाडी (काले ऽपि षट्क्षणे)	An Indian hour. d
m n 46. काण्डो (ऽस्त्री दण्डबाणार्ववर्गावसरवारिषु)	1 A stem. 2 An arrow. e
n (स्याद्) भाण्ड (मश्वाभरणे ऽमत्रे मूलवणिग्धने)	Trappings of a horse. f

SECTION XI.

n 47. (भृशप्रतिज्ञयोर्) बाढं	1 Much. 2 Promise. g
n प्रगाढं (भृशकृच्छ्रयो:)	1 Much. 2 Difficult. h
m f n (शक्तस्थूलौ त्रिषु) दृढौ	1 Able. 2 Bulky. i
m f n व्यूढौ (ऽविन्यस्तसंहतौ)	1 Arranged. 2 Compact. j

---

1 इला.

[a] And 4 Wife of BUDHA and daughter of IKSHWÁKU. [b] The word is written both ways. [c] Likewise 2 A war whoop. And m. 3 Venom. [d] Equivalent to 24 minutes. Also 2 A pipe or tube. 3 A vein or artery. 4 The guts. 5 A fistulous sore. 6 The hollow stalk of a lotos, &c. [e] And 2 Bad. 3 A chapter. Or 4 A horse. 5 Multitude. Likewise 6 Opportunity. 7 Water. Also 3 A Cluster ; or a shrub. 9 A branch of a tree. [f] Some say, his saddle. And 2 A vessel. 3 Stock or capital. Also 4 An ornament. [g] Some make the term indeclinable. [h] Or 3 Pain. 4 Firm [i] Also 3 Strong. 4 Firm. 5 Confirmed. 6 Much. [j] Likewise 3 Large.

1 Child. 2 Human fœtus.

48. भ्रूणो[m] ऽर्भके स्त्रैणगर्भे)

1 Son of BALI. 2 An arrow. a

बाणो[m] (बलिसुते शरे)

1 A particle. 2 Eye of corn. b

कणो[m] (ऽतिसूक्ष्मे धान्यांशे)

1 Multitude. c

(संघाते प्रमथे) गणः[m]

1 A stake at play. 2 Wages. d

49. पणो[m] (द्यूतादिषूत्सृष्टे भृतौ मूल्ये धनेऽपि च)

1 A bow string. 2 Quality. e

(मौर्व्यां द्रव्याश्रिते सत्वशुक्लसन्ध्यादिके) गुणः[m]

1 State of being unemployed. f

50. (निर्व्यापारस्थितौ कालविशेषोत्सवयोः) क्षणः[m]

1 Tribe. 2 Colour. g

वर्णो[m] द्विजादौ शुक्लादौ स्तुतौ)

वर्णं[m n] (तु वाक्षरे)

1 The Sun. h

51. अरुणो[m] (भास्करेऽपि स्याद्वर्णभेदेऽपि च त्रिषु)

1 SIVA. i

स्थाणुः[m] (शर्वे ऽप्य)

1 A raven. j

(ऽथ) द्रोणः[m] (काकेऽपि च)

1 Sound. k

(रवे) रणः[m l]

---

[a] Also 3 Sound. And m. f. 4 A plant (blue Barleria). 5 Wages of weaving. [b] Also 3 A spark of any gem. And f. 4 Long pepper. 5 Cuminum cyminum. [c] And 2 S'IVA's attendants. [d] And 3 Price. 4 Wealth. 5 A commodity. 6 Business. 7 A weight; two *tólas*. 8 In tale, twenty *gandás* of cowries. [e] And 3 Epithet. 4 A rope. 5 A cook. [f] And 2 A minute of time (the 6th part of a *ghat'í*; some say the 12th part of a *muhurta*). 3 A moment. 4 A festival. 5 Dance and song. [g] Also 3 Praise. 4 Narration. m. n. 5 A letter of the Alphabet. [h] And m. f. n. 2 Dark red. Also m. 3 The Charioteer of the sun. 4 The dawn. And f. 5 Madder. [i] And m. n. 2 A pollard, or trunk of a lopped tree. 3 A spear. 4 A nest of termites. [j] And 2 A measure of capacity. 3 Proper name: the military preceptor of the *Pán'davas*. [k] And m. n. 2 War, battle. [l] This stanza is omitted by many commentators.

52. ग्रामणी *m* (नापिते पुंसि श्रेष्ठे ग्रामाधिपे त्रिषु)	1 A barber. a
ऊर्णा *f* c (मेषादिलोम्नि स्त्रावर्त्ते चान्तरा भ्रुवोः)	1 Wool, felt, &c. b
53. हरिणी *f* (स्यान्मृगी हेमप्रतिमा हरिता च या)	1 A doe. 2 A golden image. d
(त्रिषु पाण्डौ च) हरिणः *m f n*	Yellowish white. e
स्थूणा *f* (स्तम्भेऽपि वेश्मनः)	A house post. f
54. तृष्णे *f* (स्पृहापिपासे द्वे)	1 Desire. 2 Thirst.
(जुगुप्साकरुणे) घृणे *f*	1 Blame. 2 Pity
(वणिक्पथेऽपि) विपणिः *f*	1 A market. g
(सुराप्रत्यक् च) वारुणी *f*	1 Spirituous liquor. 2 The west.
55. करेणु *f* i (रिभ्यां स्त्रीनेभे)	A female elephant. h
द्रविणं *m n* (तु बलं धनम्)	1 Strength. 2 Wealth. j
शरणं *n* (गृहरक्षित्रोः)	1 A house. 2 Preserver. k
श्रीपर्णं *n* (कमलेऽपि च)	A lotos. l

[a] And m. n. 2 Excellent. 3 A superintendent of a village. [b] And 2 A circle of hair between the eye-brows; esteemed a token of greatness. [c] Or ऊर्णा. [d] And 3 Green. Also 4 Sort of metre. 5 A description of women. [e] Also m. 2 A deer. [f] Likewise 2 An iron image. [g] Also 2 A stall or shop. See Book II. ch. 2. 2. 3 A commodity for sale. [h] And m. A male elephant. [i] Or fem. करेणू. [j] Also 3 Gold. [k] Likewise 3 Preservation. 4 Killing. [l] Nelumbium speciosum. Also 2 Premna spinosa and longifolia.

1 Poison. 2 War. a

56. (विषाभिमरलोहेषु) तीक्ष्णं [n] (क्लीबे खरे त्रिषु)

1 Proof. 2 Limit. b

प्रमाणं [n] (हेतुमर्यादाशास्त्रेयत्ताप्रमातृषु)

1 Instrument. 2 Field. c

57. करणं [n] (साधकतमं क्षेत्रगात्रेन्द्रियेष्वपि)

1 Birth. 2 Unresisted march of troops. d

(प्राण्युत्पादे) संसरणं [n] (मसंबाधचमूगतौ

58. घण्टापथे)

1 Food vomited. 2 Raising. e

(ऽथ वान्ताने) समुद्गिरणं [n f] (मुन्नये)

(अतस्त्रिषु) [g]

1 A horn. 2 Elephant's tooth.

विषाणं [m f n] (स्यात्पशुशृङ्गेभदन्तयोः)

1 Declivity. 2 Humble. h

59. प्रवणः [m f n] (क्रमनिम्नोर्व्यां प्रह्वे ना तु चतुष्पथे)

1 Miscellaneous. 2 Impure. i

संकीर्णो [m f n] (निचिताशुद्धाव्)

1 Desert. 2 Salt and barren soil.

इरिणं [m f n j] (शून्यमूषरम्)

---

[a] Or 3 Death. 4 Iron. 5 A weapon. 6 Any thing metallic. 7 Haste. 8 Sea salt. And m. f. n. 9 Sharp. 10 Hasty. Also m. 11 Nitre. [b] And 3 Sacred ordinance. 4 Quantity. 5 Authority. [c] And 3 Body. 4 Organ of sense. Also 5 Cause. m. 6 A tribe sprung from the third and fourth classes. [d] Or 3 Beginning of war. And 4 A highway. Or 5 A resting place. [e] As of water from a well. Or 3 Eradicating of a tree, &c. [f] And उद्गरण°. [g] The following admit the three genders. [h] And m. 3 A place where four roads meet. Also m. f. n. 4 Generous. 5 Principal. [i] Or 3 Mixed. 4 Of an impure or mixed tribe. [j] And ईरण°.

SECTION XII.

60. (देवसूर्यौ) विवस्वन्तौ [1 m]	1 A god. 2 The sun.
सरस्वन्तौ [2 m] (नदार्णवौ)	1 A river. 2 The sea. a
(पक्षितार्क्ष्यौ) गरुत्मन्तौ [3 m]	1 A bird. 2 VISHNU's bird.
शकुन्तौ [4 m] (भासपक्षिणौ)	1 The Indian vulture. 2 A bird. b
61. (अग्न्युत्पातौ) धूमकेतू [5 m]	1 Fire. 2 A comet. c
जीमूतौ [m] (मेघपर्वतौ)	1 A cloud. 2 A mountain. d
हस्तौ [m] (तु पाणिनक्षत्रे)	1 A hand. 2 The asterism. e
मरुतौ [6 m g] (पवनामरौ)	1 Wind. 2 A deity. f
62. यन्ता [7 m] (हस्तिपके सूते)	1 An elephant driver. 2 A charioteer. h
भर्ता [8 m f n] (धातरि पोष्टरि)	1 A holder. 2 A nourisher. i
(यानपात्रे शिशौ) पोतः [m]	1 A boat. 2 A young animal. j
प्रेतः [m] (प्राण्यन्तरे मृते)	1 A departed soul. k

1—त्. 2—त्. 3—त्. 4—न्त. 5—तु.
6—त or —त्. 7—न्तृ. 8—र्तृ.

[a] Also m. f. n. 3 Juicy. f. 4 Goddess of speech. 5 A river. [b] Likewise 3 An insect. [c] Also 3 A falling star. [d] Likewise 3 The plant called *Deōtār*. [e] Corvus. Also 3 An elephant's trunk. 4 A cubit. 5 (In composition with कोष) multitude; pre-eminence. [f] Of a particular order. Also n. 4 Medicago esculenta. [g] मरुत् or मरुतः. [h] Likewise m. f. n. 3 Any person who restrains. [i] And m. 3 A husband. [j] Also 3 Site of a house. [k] And m. f. n. 2 Dead.

1 The moon's descending node. a — 63. (ग्रहभेदे ध्वजे) केतुः [m]

1 A king. 2 A son. b — (पार्थिवे तनये) सुतः [m]

1 An architect. c — स्थपतिः [m] (कारुभेदे ऽपि)

1 A mountain. 2 A king. — भूभृद् [1 m] (भूमिधरे नृपे)

1 A king. d — 64. मूर्द्धाभिषिक्तो [m] (भूपे ऽपि)

A woman's courses. e — ऋतुः [m] (स्त्रीकुसुमे ऽपि च)

Vishnu. f — (विष्णावप्य) ऽजिता [m] ऽव्यक्तौ [2 m]

1 A Cartwright. 2 A charioteer. g — सूत [m] (स्त्वष्टरि सारथौ)

Wise, learned. h — 65. व्यक्तः [m f n] (प्राज्ञे ऽपि)

1 A science. 2 An example. i — दृष्टान्ताव् [3 m] (उभे शास्त्रनिदर्शने)

1 Charioteer. 2 A porter. j — क्षत्ता [4 m] (स्यात्सारथौ द्वाःस्थे क्षत्रियायां च शूद्रजे)

1 Topic. 2 Mode. k — 66. वृत्तान्तः [m] (स्यात्प्रकरणे प्रकारे कार्त्स्न्यवार्त्तयोः)

1—वृ. 2—क्ष. 3—न्त. 4—सू.

[a] Reckoned as the ninth planet. 2 A flag or standard. 3 A mark or symbol. 4 A comet. 5 An enemy. [b] Or 3 A king's son. And 4 fem. सुता, a daughter. [c] Or 2 A head carpenter. Also 3 A person performing a sacrifice to the planet Jupiter. And m. f. n. 4 Chief. [d] Or 2 A man of the military tribe. 3 A mixed class sprung from the 1st and 2d. 4 A chief minister. [e] And 2 A season; spring, summer, &c. [f] Also अजितः. 2 One of the *Jinas*. m. f. n. 3 Unconquered. And अव्यक्तः. 2 *Siva*. n. 3 The Supreme soul. 4 Any invisible principle. m. f. n. 5 Indistinct. [g] Likewise 3 A mixed class sprung from the 2d and 1st. 4 Quicksilver. m. f. n. 5 Generated. [h] Also 2 Evident. 3 Ascertained. [i] Likewise 3 Death. [j] And 3 A mixed class sprung from the 4th and 2d. 4 One sprung from the 4th and 3d. Likewise 5 Son by a female slave. [k] And 3 Whole. 4 Rumour. Story.

आनर्त्तः (समरे नृत्यस्थाननीवृद्विशेषयोः) *m*	1 War. 2 A stage. a
67. कृतान्तो (यमसिद्धान्तदैवाकुशलकर्मसु) *m*	1 YAMA. 2 Right conclusion. b
(श्लेष्मादि रसरक्तादि महाभूतानि तद्गुणाः	
68. इन्द्रियाण्यश्मविकृतिः शब्दयोनिश्च[1]) धातवः *m*	1 Principle of the body. c
(कक्षान्तरेऽपि) शुद्धान्तो (नृपस्यासर्वगोचरे) *m*	The seraglio. d
69. (कासूसामर्थ्ययोः) शक्तिर् *f* [f]	1 An iron spear. 2 Power. e
मूर्त्तिः(काठिन्यकाययोः) *f*	1 Matter. 2 Body. g
(विस्तारवल्ल्योर्) व्रततिर् *f* [h]	1 Expansion. 2 A creeping plant.
(वसती[2]) रात्रिवेश्मनोः) *f*	1 Night. 2 A house. i
70. (क्षयार्चयोर्) अपचितिः *f*	1 Loss. 2 Worship. j
साति (दानावसानयोः) *f* [k]	1 Gift. 2 Destruction.

1—श्च. 2—ति or —ती.

[a] Or 3 A theatre. 4 Name of a Country on the N. W. coast of India. 5 Inhabitant of that country. [b] Demonstrated doctrine. And 3 Destiny. 4 Sinful act. [c] Viz. phlegm, wind and bile. 2 Constituent part: as blood, flesh, marrow, &c. 3 The primary elements; earth, water, fire, air, and ether. 4 Their qualities, odour, flavour, colour, touch, and sound. 5 The organs of sense, nose, tongne, eye, skin and ear. 6 Fossil. 7 Metal. 8 Root of words; crude verb. [d] The king's private palace, or apartments of his women. Also 2 The king's wife, or concubine. [e] Likewise 3 Energy of a divinity: as GAURI´ of SIVA. [f] शक्तिः or शक्ती. [g] Or a definite form. [h] व्रततिः or व्रततिः. [i] Also 3 Stay, abode. [j] Likewise 3 Expense. 4 Exclusion. [k] Some add सतिः and सन्तिः.

1 Pain. 2 End of a bow. — *f* [a] अर्त्तिः (पीडा धनुष्कोट्योः)

1 Kind or sort. 2 Birth. b — *f* जातिः (सामान्यजन्मनोः)

1 Usage. 2 Oozing. c — 71. (प्रचारस्यन्दयो) [1] *f* रीतिर्

1 Calamity of season. d — *f* ईतिर् (डिम्बप्रवासयोः)

1 Gain. 2 Obtaining. e — (उदये ऽधिगमे) *f* प्राप्तिः

1 Three sacrificial fires. f — *f* त्रेता (त्व ऽग्नित्रये युगे)

A harp. g — 72. (वीणाभेदे ऽपि) *f* महती

1 Ashes. 2 Success. h — *f* भूति (र्भस्मनि सम्पदि)

1 River of snakes. 2 City of serpents. i — (नदीनगर्य्यौर्नागानां [2] *f* भोगवत्य्

(ऽथ सङ्गरे

1 Combat. 2 Company. 3 Assembly. — 73. संगे सभायां) *f* समितिः

1 Wane, loss. 2 Adode. j — (क्षयवासावपि) *f* क्षितिः

1 Sun-beam. 2 Weapon. 3 Flame. — (रवेरर्चिश्च शस्त्रं च वह्निज्वाला च) [3] *f* हेतयः

1 The world. 2 Sort of metre. k — 74. *f* जगती (जगति छन्दोविशेषे ऽपि क्षितावपि)

1—ति. 2—ती. 3—ति.

[a] Or आर्त्तिः. [b] Also 3 Sort of metre. 4 Jasmin. 5 Nutmeg. 6 Lineage. [c] Likewise 3 Brass. 4 Scoria of metals. [d] And 2 Travelling abroad. [e] Or 3 Rise. 4 Improvement, success. [f] And 2 Second age of the world. [g] NA'RADA's lute with 100 (some say seven) strings. 2 Solanum melongena. [h] Also 3 Super-human power, as rendering oneself invisible, &c. 4 Production. [i] Both situated in the infernal regions. Also m. भोगवान् (—वत्). A serpent. [j] Also 3 The earth. 4 Period of general destruction. [k] And 3 The earth.

f पंक्ति (च्छन्दो ऽपि दशमं)	1 A metre. 2 Ten. a
1 *f* (स्यात्प्रभावे ऽपि चा)यतिः	Majesty or dignity. b
75. *f* पत्ति (र्गतौ च)	Motion. c
f (मूले तु) पक्षतिः (पक्षभेदयोः)	1 Root of a wing. d
f प्रकृति (र्योनिलिङ्गे च)	1 Origin. 2 Sex. e
2 *f* (कैशिक्याद्याश्च) वृत्तयः	Style of composition. f
76. *f pl.* h सिकताः (स्युर्वालुकापि)	Sand. g
f (वेदे श्रवसि च) श्रुतिः	1 Holy scripture. 2 An ear. i
f वनिता (जनितात्यर्थानुरागायां च योषिति)	Beloved woman. j
77. *f* गुप्तिः (क्षितिव्युदासे ऽपि)	A cavern. k
f धृति (र्धारणधैर्य्ययोः)	1 Holding. 2 Steadiness. l
f बृहती (क्षुद्रवार्त्ताकी च्छन्दोभेदे महत्यपि)	1 An egg-plant. 2 A metre. m

1 चा—. 2—कि.

[a] Also 3 A row. [b] Likewise 2 Breadth. 3 Future time. 4 Restraint of mind. [c] Also 2 A platoon. And m. 3 A foot soldier. [d] And 2 First day of a lunar month. [e] Or 3 Pudendum muliebre. And 4 Natural disposition. 5 Material nature. 6 Original matter. 7 Root of a word. [f] And 2 Livelihood or profession. 3 Exposition or gloss. [g] Also 2 Sandy ground. 3 Stony nodules. [h] Some admit the singular number. [i] Likewise 3 Listening. 4 A rumour. 5 A quarter of a musical tone. [j] Or 2 A woman in general. 3 m. f. n. Solicited, begged. [k] Or 2 A hole in the ground. 3 A sink. Also 4 A prison. 5 Concealment. [l] Likewise 3 Satisfaction. 4 One of the astrological *Yógas*. And m. 5 A religious ceremony. [m] And 3 A large lute. 4 A mantle.

1 A woman. 2 A female elephant. a — 78. वासिता [f] [b] (स्त्रीकरिण्योश्च)

1 Livelihood. 2 Rumour. c — वार्त्ता [f] (वृत्तौ जनश्रुतौ)

1 Chaff. 2 Health. d — वार्त्तं [n] (फल्गुन्यरोगे च त्रिषु)

Water. e — (ऽप्सु च) घृता [n] ऽमृते [n]

1 Silver. 2 Gold. — 79. कलधौतं [n] (रूप्यहेम्नोर्)

1 Cause. 2 Token. — निमित्तं [m] (हेतुलक्ष्मणोः)

1 Science. f — श्रुतं [n] (शास्त्रावधृतयोर्)

1 The golden age. 2 Enough. g — (युगपर्य्याप्तयोः) कृतम् [n]

1 Great dread. 2 Valiant act. — 80. अत्याहितं [n] (महाभीतिः कर्म्मजीवानपेक्षि च)

An element. h — (युक्ते क्ष्मादावृते) भूतं [n] (प्राण्यतीते समे त्रिषु)

1 Verse. 2 Conduct. i — 81. वृत्तं [n] (पद्ये चरिते त्रिष्वतीते दृढनिस्तले)

Realm. j — महद् [n] (राज्यं च)

1 Calumny. k — ऽवगीतं [n] (जन्ये स्याद्गर्हिते त्रिषु)

---

[a] Also n. 3 The cry of birds. m. f. n. 4 Perfumed. [b] Or वाशिता. [c] Or 3 A profession. 4 News. [d] And m. f. n. 3 Healthy. [e] And 2 Liquid butter. Also अमृतं. 3 Nectar. 4 Residue of a sacrifice. 5 Unsolicited alms. 6 Exemption from transmigration. [f] And m. f. n. 2 Heard. 3 Understood. [g] Also m. f. n. 3 Done. 4 Hurt. [h] And m. f. n. 2 Right. 3 True. 4 Past. 5 (in conposition) Like. 6 Been. Also n. 7 A living being. m. n. 8 A demon. And m. 9 A class of demi-gods. [i] And m. f. n. 3 Past. 4 Firm. 5 Round. 6 Studied. 7 Covered. Also n. 8 Profession. [j] Also m. 2 The intellectual principle. 3 m. f. n. Great. f. 4 A harp or large lute. [k] And m. f. n. 2 Blamed, censured. 3 Wicked.

82. श्वेतं[n] (रूप्ये ऽपि) — Silver. a

रजतं[n] (हारे रूप्ये सिते त्रिषु) — 1 A necklace. 2 Silver. b

त्रिषिते।[c]

जगद्[1 m f n] (इङ्गे ऽपि) — Movable, locomotive. d

रक्तं[m f n] (नील्यादिरागि च) — Died, tinged. e

83. अवदातः[m f n] (सिते पीते शुद्धे) — 1 White. 2 Yellow. 3 Clean.

(बद्धार्जुनौ) सितौ[m f n] — 1 Bound. 2 White. f

(युक्ते ऽतिसंस्कृते मर्षिण्य.) ऽभिनीतः[m f n] — 1 Fit. 2 Excellent. g

(ऽथ) संस्कृतम्[m f n] — 1 Wrought, finished. h

84. (कृत्रिमे लक्षणोपेते ऽपि)

ऽनन्तो[m f n]! (ऽनवधावपि) — Infinite, endless. i

(ख्याते हृष्टे) प्रतीतः[m f n] — 1 Famous, 2 Glad. j

ऽभिजात[m f n] (कुलजे बुधे) — 1 Noble. 2. Learned. k

---

h—त्.

[a] And m. f. n. 2 White. m. 3 Name of an island. 4 Name of a mountain. f. 5 A cowry. [b] Or, according to a different reading, 3 Gold (Ex. जातरूपं). And m. f. n. 4 White. [c] The following admit the three genders. [d] Also n. 2 The world. m. 3 Air. [e] Also 2 Red. 3 Fond. And n. 4 Blood. 5 Copper. 6 Saffron. [f] Also 3 Destroyed. And f. 4 Clayed sugar. [g] Or 3 Much ornamented. And 4 Patient. Or 5 Impatient. [h] Or 2 Adorned. 3 Excellent. 4 Prepared. And n. 5 Language grammatically correct. [i] Likewise m. 2 Vishnu. 3 The king of serpents (*Sésha*). f. 4 The earth. 5 The goddess Pa'rvati. 6 A grass (Agrostis linearis). 7 A myrobalan. n. 8 The sky or atmosphere. [j] Also 3 Known. 4 Respectful. [k] Likewise 3 Fit.

1 Pure. 2 Desert. a — *m f n* 85. विविक्तौ (पूतविजनौ)

1 Foolish. 2 High, tall. b — *m f n* मूर्छितौ (मूढसोच्छ्रया)

1 Sour; Vinegar. 2 Harsh. — *m f n* (द्वौ चाम्लपरुषौ) शुक्तौ

1 White. 2 Black. — *m f n* c शितौ (धवलमेचकौ)

1 True. 2 Right. d — 1*m f n* 86. (सत्ये साधौ विद्यमाने प्रशस्तेऽभ्यर्हिते च) सन्

1 Revered. 2 Distrest by foes. e — *m f n* पुरस्कृतः (पूजितेऽरात्यभियुक्तेऽग्रतः कृते)

1 Secure. f — *m f n* 87. निवातावाश्रयावातौ शस्त्राभेद्यं च वर्म यत्)

1 Produced. 2 High. g — *m f n* (जातोन्नद्धप्रवृद्धाः स्युर्) उच्छ्रिता

m f n उत्थिता (स्त्वमी

1 Increased. h — 88. वृद्धिमत्प्रोद्यतोत्पन्ना)

1 Respectful. 2 Respected. — *m f n* आदृतौ (सादरार्चितौ)

---

1 सत्.

a Or Lonely. Also 3 Discriminated. b And 3 Insensible. c शितिः—ती.—ति. Also शितिः. d And 3 Being, existing. 4 Excellent. 5 Respected, venerable. Fem. (सती). 6 A faithful wife. 7 The goddess PA´RVATI´. e Or 3 Facing the enemy and endeavouring to overcome him. 4 Placed in front. f As an abode. 2 Calm, free from wind. 3 Safe, as strong armour. g And 3 Grown large. h And 2 Endeavouring. 3 Born or produced.

SECTION XIII.

m अर्थो (ऽभिधेयो रैवस्तुप्रयोजननिवृत्तिषु)	1 Meaning. 2 Wealth. a
89. (निपानागमयोस्) तीर्थम् (ऋषिजुष्टजले गुरौ) n on तीर्थम्	1 Piece of water. b
m f n समर्थं (स्त्रि.षु शक्तिष्ठे सम्बन्धार्थे हिते ऽपि च)	1 Powerful. c
m 90. दशमीस्थौ (क्षीणरागवृद्धौ)	1 Impotent. 2 Very old.
f वीथी (पदव्यपि)	A road. d
f (आस्थानीयत्नयोर्) आस्था	1 Assembly. 2 Care. e
m n प्रस्थो (ऽस्त्री सानुमानयोः)	1 Side of a hill. f

SECTION XIV.

1 m 91. (अभिप्रायवशौ) छन्दाव्	1 Meaning, opinion. 2 Subjection.
m g अब्दौ (जीमूतवत्सरौ)	1 A cloud. 2 A year.

1—छन्दः.

[a] And 3 Thing. 4 Purpose. 5 Prohibition. 6 Object. 7 Cause. 8 Request. [b] And 2 Sacred science. 3 Holy spot visited by pilgrims; especially sacred water. 4 Holy instructor. 5 Sacrifice. [c] And 2 Connected in sense. 3 Benevolent. [d] Also 2 A line. 3 Terrace in front of a house. 4 A shop. 5 Sort of drama. [e] Likewise 3 Consideration, regard. 4 State. [f] And 2 A measure of quantity. [g] Some write अब्द; in both acceptations; others in the last.

1 Defamation. 2 Command.	अपवादौ[m][a] (तु निन्दाज्ञे)
1 Son. 2 Kinsman.	दायादौ[m] (सुतबान्धवौ)
1 A ray of light. 2 A foot. b	92. पादा[m] (रश्म्यङ्घ्रितुर्य्यांशाः)
1 The moon. 2 Fire. 3 The sun.	(चन्द्राग्न्यर्कास् तमोनुदः)[1][m]
Ill report. c	निर्वादो[m] (जनवादे ऽपि)
1 Mud. 2 Young grass.	शादो[m] (जम्बालशष्पयोः)
1 Cry. d	93. (आरावे रुदिते त्रातर्य्या) क्रन्दो[2][m] (दारुणे रणे)
Favour. e	(स्यात्) प्रसादो[m] (ऽनुरागे ऽपि)
Sauce or condiment. f	सूदः[m] (स्याद्व्यञ्जने ऽपि च)
A cowherd. g	94. (गोष्ठाध्यक्षे ऽपि) गोविन्दो[m]
Joy. h	(हर्षे ऽप्या) मोद[3][m] (वन्) मदः[m]
1 Chief. 2 Royal insignia. i	(प्राधान्ये राजलिङ्गे च वृषाङ्गे) ककुदो[m][n][j] (ऽस्त्रियाम्)

1—दृ, or —द. ² आ—. ³ आ—.

[a] Or अपवादः. [b] And 3 A fourth part. Also 4 A root. 5 A measure of a verse, or one verse of a stanza. [c] Likewise 2 Disregard. 3 A controversy decided. 4 Absence of contest. [d] Exclamation in pain, or simply a cry. And 2 Lamentation, with or without noise. 3 A defender in general, or 4 An abetter of an enemy who attacks in the rear of the army. 5 Terrific war. [e] Also 2 Brightness. 3 Cleanness. [f] Likewise 2 Split pease. 3 A cook. [g] Also 2 KRISHN´A. [h] Likewise आमोदः. 2 Fragrancy; delightful odour. And मदः. 2 Intoxication. 3 Inebriating liquor. 4 Insanity. 5 Pride. 6 The juice exuding from the temples of a rutting elephant. [i] And 3 Hump of a bull. 4 Summit of a hill. [j] Or fem. ककुद् (—द्).

95. (स्त्री)संविज् [1 f] (ज्ञानसंभाषाक्रियाकाराजिनामसु) — 1 Knowledge. 2 Cry. a

(धर्मे रहस्यु) पनिषत् [2 f] — 1 Religious and moral merit. b

(स्यादृतौ वत्सरे) शरत् [3 f] — 1 The sultry season. 2 A year.

96. पदं [n] (व्यवसितित्राणस्थानलक्ष्माङ्घ्रिवस्तुषु) — 1 Industry. 2 Defence. c

गोष्पदं [n] (सेविते माने) — 1 Spot frequented by kine. d

(प्रतिष्ठाकृत्ययोः) आस्पदम् [n] — 1 Dignity. 2 Business. e

97. (त्रिष्विष्टमधुरौ) स्वादु [4 m f n] — 1 Desired. 2 Sweet.

मृदू [5 m f n] (चातीक्ष्णकोमलौ) — 1 Blunt. 2 Soft. f

(मूढाल्पापटुनिर्भाग्याः) मन्दाः [6 m f n] (स्युः) — 1 Foolish, dull. 2 Little. g

(द्वौ तु) शारदौ [m f n] — 1 New. 2 Diffident. h

98. (प्रत्यग्राप्रतिभौ)

(विद्वत्सुप्रगल्भौ) विशारदौ [m f n] — 1 Learned. 2 Confident.

1—द्. 2 ष—द्. 3—द्. 4—दु. 5—दु. 6—न्द.

[a] As in battle. And 3 Agreement, contract. 4 War, combat. 5 Name. [b] And 2 Privacy. Also 3 The theological portion of scripture. 4 Principle. [c] And 3 Place. 4 Mark. 5 Token. 6 Foot. 7 Footstep. 8 Thing. 9 Word. 10 Sound. [d] And 2 A mesaure of quantity; as much as a cow's footstep will hold. [e] And 3 A place. [f] And 3 Gentle. [g] And 3 Slow. 4 Unlucky. 5 Low (a tone). Also m. 6 The planet Saturn. [h] Also 3 Produced in the sultry season. And m. 4 A year. f. 5 A title of DURGA.

SECTION XV.

1 A fathom. a 2 The Indian fig tree. — (व्यामो वटश्च) न्यग्रोधाव्

1 Body. 2 Height. — उत्सेधः (काय उन्नतिः)

1 A yoke for burdens. 2 A highway. b — 99. (पर्य्याहारश्च मार्गश्च) विवधौ वीवधौ (च तौ)

1 A branch of a tree at a sacrifice. d — परिधि (र्यज्ञियतरोः शाखायामुपसूर्य्यके)

1 A pledge. 2 A calamity. c — 100. (बन्धकं व्यसनं चेतः पीडाधिष्ठानम्) आधयः

1 A reconciling of differences. f — (स्युः समर्थननीवाकनियमाश्च) समाधयः

1 Offence or guilt. g — 101. (दोषोत्पादे) ऽनुबन्धः (स्यात्प्रकृत्यादिविनश्वरे
मुख्यानुयायिनि शिशौ प्रकृतस्यानुवर्त्तने)

1 VISHNU. 2 The moon. h — 102. विधु (र्विष्णौ चन्द्रमसि)

1 Limit. 2 A hole. i — (परिच्छेदे बिले) ऽवधिः

1—ष. 2—धि. 3—धि.

[a] Measured by the extended arms. [b] Or 3 Storing of corn, &c. 4 A load. [c] Spelt both ways. [d] Stuck in the ground, to tie the victim to it. And 2 The sun's image. [e] And 3 Mental agony. 4 Site or place. 5 Expectation. [f] And 2 Silence. 3 Promise or vow. 4 Collecting grain on account of a dearth. 5 Deep meditation. 6 Perseverance in a difficult undertaking. [g] And 2 An element of language; root, affix, augment or permutation. 3 In grammar, an indicatory letter not sounded. 4 A person following an example. 5 A child. Or 6 A child following example. 7 Continuation. [h] And 3 Camphor. [i] Also 3 Period. 4 Situation, place.

m विधि (विधाने दैवे च) — 1 Rule, form. 2 Fate. a

m प्रणिधिः (प्रार्थने चरे) — 1 Request. 2 A spy. b

103. *m m* बुधवृद्धौ (पण्डिते ऽपि) — Learned. c

m स्कन्धः (समुदये ऽपि च) — Multitude. d

(देशे नदविशेषे ऽब्धौ) *m* सिन्धु (र्ना सरिति स्त्रियाम्) — 1 Name of a country. 2 — of a river. e

104. *f g* विधा (विधौ प्रकारे च) — 1 Form or rule. 2 Manner, sort. f

1 *mfn* स्वादु (रम्ये ऽपि च त्रिषु) — Handsome, pleasing. h

f वधू (भार्या स्नुषा स्त्री च) — 1 A wife. 2 Daughter-in-law. i

f सुधा (लेपे ऽमृतं स्नुही) — 1 Plaister. 2 Nectar. j

105. *f* सन्धा (प्रतिज्ञा मर्य्यादा) — 1 Promise. 2 State.

f श्रद्धा (सम्प्रत्ययः स्पृहा) — 1 Belief, confidence. 2 Fondness.

1—धु.

[a] Likewise 3 BRAHMA', or providence. 4 Command, injunction. [b] Also 3 Situation, place. [c] Likewise बुधः. 2 The regent of the planet Mercury. Or बुधः. 2 A deified saint. 3 Known or understood. वृद्धः. 2 Old. 3 Grown or increased. [d] Also 2 A shoulder. 3 The fork of a tree; or its principal branch. 4 Part of an army. [e] And 3 The sea. 4 The juice exuding from the temples of a rutting elephant. f. 5 A river. [f] Also 3 Fodder. 4 Prosperity, thriving. 5 Piercing. [g] Some state विधः as a separate term with the same acceptations. [h] Likewise 2 Right, fit. 3 Good, virtuous. m. 4 An usurer. [i] And 3 Any woman. 4 A sister-in-law. 5 A bride. [j] And 3 Euphorbia Tirucalli, &c.

1 Ardent spirit. 2 Nectar of flowers. a — *n* मधु (मद्ये पुष्परसे क्षौद्रे ऽप्य)

Darkness. b — *n* ऽन्धं (तमस्यपि)

c

106. (अतस्त्रिषु)

1 Conceited of learning. d — *m* समुन्नद्धौ (पण्डितंमन्यगर्वितौ)

A reproachful appellative. e — *m f n* f ब्रह्मबन्धु (रधिक्षेपे निर्देशे).

1 Relied on. 2 Near. g — (ऽथावलम्बितः

m f n

107. अविदूरोऽप्य) ऽवष्टब्धः

1 Notorious. 2 Adorned. — *m f n* प्रसिद्धौ (ख्यातभूषितौ)

SECTION XVI.

1 The Sun. 2 Fire. — 1 *m* (सूर्यवह्नी) चित्रभानू

1 Ray of light. 2 The sun. — 2 *m* भानू (रश्मिदिवाकरौ)

1—नु. 2—नु.

[a] And 3 Honey. 4 Water. 5 Milk. Also m. 6 Bassia latifolia. 7 The season of spring. 8 The month of *Chaitra*. 9 Name of a demon slain by Vishnu. f. 10 Liquorice. [b] And m. f. n. 2 Blind. [c] The following admit the three genders. [d] And 2 Proud. 3 Elevated. [e] Indicating that the man neglects his duty, and is only a *Bráhmana*. So क्षत्रबंधुः in speaking of a *Kshatriya*. 2 An indefinite appellation to avoid the use of a name. [f] Fem. ब्रह्मबन्धूः or न्धुः. [g] Also 3 Wrapt up. 4 Bound. 5 Surrounded ; assailed on all sides.

108. भूतात्मानौ[1 m] (धातृदेहौ)	1 BRAHMA. 2 Body. a
(मूर्खनीचौ) पृथग्जनौ[m]	1 An ignorant man. 2 One of a low tribe.
ग्रावाणौ[2 m] (शैलपाषाणौ)	1 A mountain. 2 A rock or stone.
पत्रिणौ[3 m] (शरपक्षिणौ)	1 An arrow. 2 A bird. b
109. (तरुशैलौ) शिखरिणौ[4 m]	1 A tree. 2 A mountain. c
शिखिनौ[5 m] (वह्निबर्हिणौ)	1 Fire. 2 A peacock. d
प्रतियत्नाव्[6 m] (उभौ लिप्सोपग्रहाव्)	1 Desire. 2 Making prisoner. e
(अथ) सादिनौ[7 m]	1 Charioteer. 2 Horseman. f
110. (द्वौ सारथिहयारोहौ)	
वाजिनो[8 m] (ऽश्वेषु पक्षिणः)	1 A horse. 2 An arrow. 3 A bird.
(कुले ऽप्य्) ऽभिजनो[m] (जन्मभूम्यामप्य्)	1 Family 2 Native spot. g
(ऽथ) हायनाः[m]	1 A year. 2 Ray of light. h

1—त्मन्. 2—वन्. 3—न्. 4—न्. 5—न्.
6—त्न. 7—न्. 8—न्.

[a] Or, according to another reading. 3 Component part of an animated body, as blood, flesh, &c. [b] Also 3 A falcon. 4 A carriage. [c] Likewise 3 Clitoria ternatea. f. 4 शिखरिणी, sort of metre. [d] Also 3 A gallinaceous fowl. 4 A tree. 5 An arrow. m. f. n. 6 Crested. [e] Also 3 Comprehension. [f] Or 3 A person riding on an elephant. [g] Or 3 Head of a family. 4 Place where the family is. [h] And m. 3 Red rice. 4 Wild rice.

111. (वर्णार्चिर्व्रीहिभेदाः स्युः)

1 The moon. 2 Fire. 3 The sun. a — (चन्द्राग्न्यर्का) विरोचनाः [m]

Hair. b — (केशे ऽपि) वृजिनो [m]

1 The sun. 2 The artist of the gods. c — विश्वकर्मा[1 m] (ऽर्कसुरशिल्पिनोः)

1 Care. 2 Firmness. d — 112. आत्मा[2 m] (यत्नो धृतिर्बुद्धिः स्वभावो ब्रह्म वर्ष्म च)

1 INDRA. 2 A vicious elephant. e — (शक्रो घातुकमत्तेभो वर्षुकाब्दो) घनाघनः [m]

1 Pride of wealth, &c. 2 Knowledge. f — 113. अभिमानो [m] (ऽर्थादिदर्पे ज्ञाने प्रणयहिंसयोः)

1 A cloud. 2 Solidity. g — घनो [m] (मेघे मूर्तिगुणे त्रिषु मूर्ते निरन्तरे)

1 The sun. 2 A master. h — 114. इनः [m] (सूर्ये प्रभौ)

1 The moon. 2 A soldier by tribe. i — राजा[3 m] (मृगाङ्के क्षत्रिये नृपे)

1—र्मन्. 2—त्मन्. 3—जन्.

[a] Also 4 A proper name : the son of PRAHLA´DA and father of BALI. [b] Likewise n. 2 Sin. m. f. n. 3 Crooked, bent. [c] Also 3 Name of a sage. [d] And 3 Intellect. 4 Natural disposition. 5 The supreme BRAHMA. 6 Body. 7 Vivifying soul. 8 Sentient soul. 9 Mind. [e] Or 3 Mischievous. 4 A rutting elephant. 5 A rainy cloud. 6 Collision. [f] And 3 Affection. 4 Request. 5 Killing. [g] And m. f. n. 3 Solid, material. 4 Uniformly extended. 5 Smooth. Also m. 6 Extension. 7 Assemblage. 8 An anvil. 9 Cyperus rotundus. n. 10 Cymbal, bell, &c. 11 Mode of dancing. [h] Or 3 A king. 4 A husband. [i] And 3 A king. 4 A master. 5 INDRA. 6 A *Yaksha* or attendant of KUVE´RA.

1 *f* b वाहिन्यौ (नर्त्तकीमत्ते)	1 A dancing girl. a
f (स्रवन्त्यामपि) वाहिनी	A river. c
2 *f* 115. ह्रादिन्यौ (वज्रतडितौ)	1 The thunderbolt. 2 Lightning.
f (वन्द्यायामपि) कामिनी	A climbing plant. d
f (त्वग्देहयोरपि) तनुः	1 The skin. 2 Body. e
f सूना (ऽधोजिह्विकापि च)	The uvula. f
m n 116. (क्रतुविस्तारयोरस्त्री) वितानं (त्रिषु तुच्छके मन्दे)	1 A sacrifice. 2 Expansion. g
n (ऽथ) केतनं (कृत्ये केतावुपनिमन्त्रणे)	1 Indispensable act. h
3 *n* 117. (वेदस्तत्त्वं तपो) ब्रह्म	1 Holy writ. 2 True knowledge. i
4 *m* ब्रह्मा (विप्रः प्रजापतिः)	1 A priest by birth. 2 The creator. j

1—नी. 2—नी. 3—न्. 4—न्.

[a] And 2 A woman intoxicated. 3 A woman fond of gratification. [b] Or वाहिनी. [c] Also 2 An army. [d] Likewise 2 A loving woman. And m. कामी—न्. 3 An amorous man. 4 A dove. 5 A ruddy goose (Anas Casarca). [e] And m. f. n. 3 Thin. 4 Small. 5 Separate. [f] Also 2 Place of execution. 3 Place of slaughter (as the kitchen hearth, &c. of a householder. Manu 3. 69.) 4 Daughter. And n. 5 Bringing forth young. 6 A flower. m. f. n. 7 Blossoming. [g] And m. f. n. 3 Empty, vacant. 4 Bad. Or 5 Dull, stupid. Also n. 6 A sort of metre. m. n. 7 A canopy. [h] Or 2 Business. 3 A standard, or a symbol. 4 An invitation. 5 An abode. [i] Or 3 The supreme being. 4 Devotion. [j] Likewise 3 A superintending priest at religious rites. 4 One of the astrological *yôgas*.

1 Perseverance. 2 Destruction. a		(उत्साहने च हिंसायां सूचने चापि) गन्धनम्[n]
1 Calcining. b	118.	आतञ्चनं[n] (प्रतीवापजवनाप्यायनार्थकम्)
1 A mark or token. 2 A beard. c		व्यञ्जनं[n] (लाञ्छनं श्मश्रु निष्ठानावयवेष्वपि)
1 Detraction. d	119.	(स्यात्) कौलीनं[n] (लोकवादे युद्धे पश्वहिपक्षिणाम्)
1 Going forth, exit. e		(स्याद्) उद्यानं[n] (निःसरणे वनभेदे प्रयोजने)
1 Leisure. 2 Place. f	120.	(अवकाशे स्थितौ) स्थानं[n]
1 Sport, play. g		(क्रीडादावपि) देवनम्[n]
1 Manly exertion. 2 An army. h		उत्थानं[n] (पौरुषे तन्त्रे सन्निविष्टोद्गमेऽपि च)
1 Turning away. 2 Opposition. i	121.	व्युत्थानं[n] (प्रतिरोधे च विरोधाचरणेऽपि च)

[a] And 3 Intimation. Or 4 Hint to kill. 5 Manifestation. [b] By casting a powder into melted gold, &c. Or 2 A powder adapted to that purpose. 3 Casting any thing, for example buttermilk, into fresh milk to turn it. 4 Danger, calamity; as a pestilence or epidemic. 5 Speed. 6 Gratifying. [c] And 3 Sauce or condiment. 4 Private part of male or female. Also 5 A consonant. 6 A day. [d] Or 2 Rumour, report. 3 Combat of animals, whether quadrupeds, birds, serpents, &c. 4 Cockfight or other match of animals for a bet. 5 High birth. [e] And 2 A garden. 3 Purpose, motive. [f] Also 3 Stay, or continuance without increase or diminution. [g] And 2 Emulation, desire to surpass. 3 Splendour. 4 Praise. 5 Motion. 6 Affair, business. 7 Grief. Also m. 8 A die. [h] Or 3 Business of a family or of a realm, as the care of dependants and subjects. [i] Also 3 Independence.

(मारणे मृतसंस्कारे गतौ द्रव्ये ऽर्थदापने — 1 Killing. 2 Obsequies. 3 Motion. a

n

122. निर्वर्त्तनोपकरणानुव्रज्यासु च) साधनम्

n

नियीतनं (वैरशुद्धौ दाने न्यासार्पणे ऽपि च) — 1 Revenge. 2 Gift. b

n

123. व्यसनं (विपदि भ्रंशे दोषे कामजकोपजे) — 1 Calamity. 2 Fall. 3 Fault. c

1 n

पक्ष्म(ऽक्षिलोम्नि किञ्जल्के तन्त्वाद्यंशे ऽप्यणीयसि) — 1 Eyelash. 2 Filament of a flower. d

2 n

124. (तिथिभेदे क्षणे) पर्व — 1 Certain days of the lunar month. e

3 n

वर्त्म (नेत्रच्छदे ऽध्वनि) — 1 Eyelid. 2 A road.

n

(अकार्य्ये गुह्ये) कौपीनं — 1 Wrong or unfit act. f

n

मैथुनं (सङ्गतौ रतौ) — 1 Union. 2 Copulation. g

n

125. प्रधानं (परमात्मा धीः) — 1 The supreme soul. 2 Intellect. h

n

प्रज्ञानं (बुद्धिचिह्नयोः) — 1 Knowledge. 2 A mark, token.

---

1 पक्ष्मन्. 2—न्. 3—न्.

[a] And 4 Substance. 5 Enforcement of delivery of any thing. 6 Accomplishing. 7 Materials ; or instrument. 8 Following. Also 9 An army. 10 Means. 11 Cause. 12 Generative organ of a male. [b] And 3 Delivery of a deposit. 4 Payment of a debt. [c] Arising from desire (as hunting, gaming, drinking, wenching), or from aversion (as calumny, battery, or pecuniary injury). Also 4 Sin. 5 Ill destiny. 6 Fated consequence. 7 Vain effort. [d] And 3 A short thread. 4 Any thing small. 5 A wing. [e] Viz. the full and change of the moon, and the 6th, 8th and 10th of each half month. 2 A festival. 3 The day of the equinox, solstice, &c. 4 A book or chapter. 5 A knot or joint. [f] And 2 Privy part. 3 Covering of it. [g] Or 3 Marriage. [h] Also 3 Nature. 4 An elephant-driver. And (invariably sing.) 5 Chief.

1 A blossom. 2 A fruit. — प्रसूनं *n* (पुष्पफलयोर्)

1 A family. 2 Disappearance. a — निधनं *n* (कुलनाशयोः)

1 Weeping. 2 Lamenting. — 126. क्रन्दने *n* (रोदनाह्वाने)

1 Body. 2 Measure. b — वर्ष्म [1] *n* (देहप्रमाणयोः)

1 A house. 2 Body. 2 Light. c — (गृहदेहत्विट्प्रभावा) धामन् [2] *n*

1 Meeting of four roads. d — (ऽथ चतुष्पथे

127. सन्निवेशे च) संस्थानं *n*

1 A mark, token. 2 Chief. — लक्ष्म [3] *n* (चिह्नप्रधानयोः)

1 Covering, clothing. e — आच्छादने *n* (सन्निधानमपवारणमित्युभे)

1 Accomplishment. f — 128. आराधनं *n* (साधने स्यादवाप्तौ तोषणे ऽपि च)

1 A wheel. 2 A town. g — अधिष्ठानं *n* (चक्रपुरप्रभावाध्यासनेष्वपि)

Excellent of its kind. h — 129. रत्नं *n* (स्वजातिश्रेष्ठे ऽपि)

1 Water. 2 A forest. i — वनं *n* (सलिलकानने)

1—न्. 2—धामन्. 3—न्.

[a] Or 3 Head of a family. 4 Death. [b] Also 3 A handsome form. 4 Weight, elevation. [c] And 4 Dignity or majesty. [d] And 2 Fabrication or construction. 3 Form. 4 Death. [e] And 2 Concealment. 3 Deception. [f] And 2 Attainment, acquisition. 3 Gratifying. [g] And 3 Dignity or majesty. 4 Approach. 5 Fixing. 6 Adjustment. [h] Also 2 A gem. [i] Likewise 3 Abode. 4 A house or dwelling.

m f n

तलिनं (विरले स्तोके) — 1 Separate. 2 Small. a

b

(वाच्यलिङ्गास्त्रयोऽत्तरे)

m f n

130. समानाः (सत्समैके स्युः) — 1 Virtuous. 2 Similar. 3 Same. c

m f n

पिशुनौ (खलसूचकौ) — 1 Wicked. 2 A whisper. d

m f n 1mfn

हीनन्यूनाव् (ऊनगर्ह्यौ) — 1 Deficient. 2 Blamable.

2 m f n

(वेगिशूरौ) तरस्विनौ — 1 Swift. 2 Valiant.

m f n

131. अभिपन्नो (ऽपराद्धो ऽभिग्रस्तव्यापद्गतावपि) — 1 Guilty. 2 Subdued. e

SECTION XVII.

m

कलापो (भूषणे बर्हे तूणीरे संहते ऽपि च) — 1 An ornament. 2 A string of bells. f

m

132. (परिच्छदे) परीवापः (पर्युप्तौ सलिलस्थितौ) — 1 Furniture. 2 Sowing around. g

m

(गोधुग्गोष्ठपती) गोपौ — 1 A herdsman. 2 The head of a cowpen. h

3 m

(हरविष्णू) वृषाकपी — 1 SIVA. 2 VISHNU. i

m

133. बाष्पाव् (ऊष्माश्रु) — 1 Vapour. 2 A tear

4 m n

कशिपु (त्वन्नमाच्छादनं द्वयम्) — 1 Food. 2 Clothing. j

1—नृ. 2—नृ. 3—पि. 4—पु.

[a] Also 3 Clear, transparent. 4 Inferior, situated beneath. [b] The following are adjectives agreeing in gender with the subject. [c] Likewise m. One of the five breaths. [d] Also 3 A crow. [e] And 3 Involved in calamity. 4 Fugitive. 5 Seeking refuge. [f] Worn by women round their waist. 3 The eye in a peacock's tail. 4 A quiver. 5 Multitude; assemblage. [g] And 3 Standing water. 4 A piece of water. [h] Also 3 A superintendent of a district. 4 A king. [i] Likewise 3 Fire. [j] Also du. 3 Food and apparel.

1 A bed. 2 An upper story. a — *m n* तल्पं (शय्याट्टदारेषु)

1 A clump or cluster. b — (स्तम्बेऽपि) *m n* विटपो (ऽस्त्रियाम्)

1 Learned. 2 Pleasing. — 134. *mfn* आप्तरूप *mfn* स्वरूपो *mfn* ऽभिरूपो (बुधमनोज्ञयोः
भेद्यलिङ्गा अमी)

1 A female turtle. 2 A sort of lute. c — (कूर्मी वीणाभेदश्च) *f* कच्छपी

SECTION XVIII.

1 The letter R. d — 135. (रवर्णे पुंसि) *m* रेफः (स्यात्कुत्सिते वाच्यलिङ्गकः)

SECTION XIX.

1 Spirit after death. e — (अन्तराभवसत्त्वे ऽश्वे) *m* गन्धर्वो (दिव्यगायने)

1 A ring. 2 A conch or shell. — 136. *m* कम्बु (र्ना वलये शंखे)

1 A serpent. 2 A whisperer or informer. — *m* द्विजिह्वौ (सर्पसूचकौ)

---

[a] Likewise 3 A wife. [b] Also 2 A branch above the principal one. 3 Expansion. [c] SARASWATI's lute. Likewise 3 A disorder of the spleen. [d] And m. f. n. 2 Vile, bad. [e] And previous to its being born again. Also 2 A horse. 3 A celestial quirister. 4 Spirits frequenting the sky. 5 A black cuckoo. 6 Sort of deer.

m f n [b] पूर्वः (ऽन्यलिङ्गः प्रागाह पुम्बहुत्वे ऽपि पूर्वजान्)	1 Eastern. 2 Prior. [a]
137. *m f n* कुम्भौ (घटेभमूर्द्धांशौ)	1 A jar. [c]
m डिम्भौ (तु शिशुबालिशौ)	1 A child. 2 An ignorant man.
m स्तम्भौ (स्थूणाजडीभावौ)	1 Post or pillar. 2 Insensibility.
1 m शंभू (ब्रह्मत्रिलोचनौ)	1 BRAHMA. 2 SIVA. [d]
138. (कुक्षिभ्रूणार्भका) *m* गर्भाः	1 The belly. 2 A fetus. A child.
m विस्रम्भः (प्रणये ऽपि च)	3 Acquaintance. [e]
(स्याद्भेर्यां) *m* दुन्दुभिः (पुंसि स्यादक्षे) *f* दुन्दुभिः (स्त्रियाम्)	1 A large drum. [f]
139. (स्यान्महारजनं क्लीबे) *n* कुसुम्भं (करके पुमान्)	1 Safflower. [g]
(क्षत्रिये ऽपि च) *m* नाभि (र्ना)	A *Kshatriya* [h]
m सुरभि (र्गवि च स्त्रियाम्)	A cow. [i]

ɪ—ऋ.

[a] And m. pl. 3 Forefather. [b] पूर्वः or पूर्वेः. [c] And 2 Frontal globe of an elephant's head. Also 3 The sign aquarius. 4 Proper name, the nephew of RA'VANA. 5 The paramour of a prostitute. n. 6 Bdellium. f. 7 Bignonia chelonoides. [d] Also 3 A deified saint or JINA. 4 VISHNU. [e] Or 2 Amorous solicitation. 3 Playful dispute. 4 Trust, confidence. [f] Also 2 VARUN'A. 3 Name of a demon. And f. 4 A die. 5 A stake at play. [g] And 2 Gold. m. 3 A water-pot. 4 A pomegranate. [h] Also 2 An emperor. 3 The nave of a wheel. m. f. 4 The navel. f. 5 Musk. [i] Or 2 The cow which, being milked, yields every wish. m. 3 Spring. 4 Nutmeg. 5 Michelia champac. m. f. n. 6 Fragrant. 7 Pleasing.

1 An assembly. 2 One of a company. a — 140. सभा (संसदि सभ्ये च)

A superintendent. b — (त्रिष्वध्यक्षे ऽपि) वल्लभः m/n

1 A ray of light. 2 A rein. — (किरणप्रग्रहौ) रश्मी 1 m

1 An ape. 2 A frog. — (कपिभेकौ) प्लवङ्गमौ m

1 Desire. 2 Love, Cupid. c — 141. (इच्छामनोभवौ) कामौ m

1 Power. 2 Exertion. d — (शक्त्युद्योगौ) पराक्रमौ m

1 Moral and religious merit. e — धर्माः m (पुण्ययमन्यायस्वभावाचारसोमपाः)

1 Deliberate undertaking. f — 142. (उपायपूर्व आरंभ उपधा चाप्यु) पक्रमः 2 m

1 A market. 2 A town 3 Holy writ. g — (वणिक्पथः पुरं वेदो) निगमो m

1 A citizen, a towns-man. 2 A trader. h — (नागरो वणिक्)

1—त्रिषु. 2 उ—.

[a] Likewise 3 A house. 4 Gaming. [b] Or 2 A chief herdsman. Also 3 Beloved. 4 A horse with good marks. [c] Likewise n. 3 Independent. 4 Semen genitale. 5 Desirable [d] To subdue the foe. 3 Valour. [e] And 2 YAMA. 3 Fitness, propriety. 4 Nature, character. 5 Usage, practice. 6 One who drinks the juice of acid asclepias at a sacrifice. 7 Any sacrifice. 8 Resemblance. 9 Innoxiousness. 10 A bow. 11 A theological treatise from the *Véda*. 12 Virtue personified; the father of YUD'HISHT'HIRA. [In some of its acceptations the word admits the neuter gender.] [f] With knowledge of means. 2 A stratagem. 3 Valour. [g] Also 4 Trade. [h] Likewise 3 A theological portion of the *Véda*.

143. नैगमौ[m] (द्वौ)

(बले) रामो[m] (नीलचारुसिते त्रिषु) — 1 BALA'RA'MA. a

(शब्दादि पूर्वो वृन्दे ऽपि) ग्रामः[m] — In comp. A multitude. b

(क्रान्तौ च) विक्रमः[m] — Walking. c

144. गुल्मा[m] (रुक्स्तम्बसेनासु) — 1 A disease of the spleen. d

जामिः[f][e] (स्वसृकुलस्त्रियोः) — 1 A sister. 2 A chaste woman.

(क्षितिक्षान्त्योः) क्षमा[f] (युक्ते) क्षमं[n] (शक्ते हिते त्रिषु) — 1 The earth. 2 Patience. f

145. (त्रिषु) श्यामौ[m f n] (हरित्कृष्णौ) श्यामा[f] (स्याच्छारिवा निशा) — 1 Green. 2 Black. g

ललामं[n][i] (पुच्छपुण्ड्राश्वभूषाप्राधान्यकेतुषु) — 1 A tail. h

146. सूक्ष्म[n] (अध्यात्ममप्यु) — The supreme soul. j

(आदौ प्रधाने) प्रथम[m f n] (त्रिषु) — 1 First. 2 Chief.

---

[a] Also 2 PARAS'URA'MA. 3 RA'MACHANDRA. 4 Sort of deer. m. f. n. 5 Black. 6 Pleasing. 7 White. [b] Likewise 2 A village or township. 3 An octave in music. [c] Also 2 Power. 3 Valour. [d] And 2 A clump of grass, &c. 3 Body of troops consisting of 9 platoons. [e] Or यामिः. [f] And n. 3 Right, propriety. m. f. n. 4 Able. 5 Benevolent. 6 Patient. [g] Also m. 3 A black cuckoo. 4 A cloud. 5 A sacred fig-tree at *Prayága*. 6 A sort of pot-herb: Convolvulus argenteus. n. 7 Black peppor. f. 8 A plant; vulgarly *Syámlatá*. 9 Night. 10 Indigo. 11 A description of women. [h] Also 2 A mark on the forehead of a horse, bull, &c. 3 A horse. 4 An ornament. Or 5 Ornament of a horse. 6 Chief. 7 A flag or symbol. 8 A horn. 9 Mane. [i] Or ललाम (—म्). [j] Also m. 2 An atom. m. f. n. 3 Little.

1 Pleasing. 2 Reverse, contrary. a — *m f n* वामौ (वल्गुप्रतीपौ द्वाव्)

1 Low. 2 Vile. — *m f n* अधमौ (न्यूनकुत्सितौ)

1 Old. 2 Used. — 147. (जीर्णं च परिभुक्तं च) *m f n* यातयाम (मिदं द्वयम्)

SECTION XX.

1 A horse. 2 VISHNU'S bird. b — (तुरङ्ग गरुडौ) *m* तार्क्ष्यौ

1 A house. 2 Less. c — (निलयापचयौ) *m* क्षयौ

1 Husband's brother. 2 Wife's brother. — 148. *m* श्वशुर्यौ (देवरश्यालौ)

1 A brother's son. 2 An enemy. — *m* भ्रातृव्यौ (भ्रातृजद्विषौ)

1 A thunder-cloud. 2 INDRA. d — *m* पर्जन्यौ (रसदब्देन्द्रौ)

1 A master. 2 A man of the 3d tribe. e — (स्याद्) *m* अर्य्यः (स्वामि वैश्ययोः)

1 The 8th asterism. 2 The 4th age. f — 149. *m* तिष्यः (पुष्ये कलियुगे)

1 Opportunity. 2 Succession. g — *m* पर्य्यायः (ऽवसरे क्रमे)

1 Subjected. 2 Oath, ordeal. h — *m* प्रत्ययः (ऽधीनशपथज्ञान विश्वासहेतुषु

---

[a] Likewise 3 Left, not right. m. 4 An udder. 5 Cupid. 6 SIVA. n. 7 Wealthy f.—वा. 8 A woman—स्त्री. 9 A mare. 10 A she-ass. 11 A female shakal. 12 A young female elephant. [b] Also 3 The dawn. n. 4 A collyrium. [c] Likewise 3 A phthisis or consumption. 4 General destruction. [d] Also 3 Any cloud. 4 Thunder. [e] Likewise m. f. n. 3 Excellent. [f] Also f. 3 The Emblic myrobalan. [g] Likewise 3 Mode, manner, form. [h] And 3 Knowledge, apprehension. 4 Trust, confidence. 5 Cause. 6 A hole. 7 An affix. Also 8 Celebrity. 9 Practice, usage.

150. रंध्रे शब्दे)	
(ऽथा) ऽनुशयो[m] (दीर्घद्वेषानुतापयोः)	1 An old enmity. 2 Repentance.
स्थूलोच्चय[m] (स्त्वसाकल्ये गजानां मध्यमे गते)	1 Incompleteness. a
151. समयाः[m] (शपथाचारकालसिद्धान्तसंविदः)	1 An oath. 2 Usage. 3 Time. b
(व्यसनान्यशुभं दैवं विपदित्य) ऽनया[m] (स्त्रयः)	1 Vice. 2 Ill fortune. 3 Calamity.
152. अत्ययो[m] (ऽतिक्रमे कृच्छ्रे दोषे दण्डे ऽप्यु)	1 Transgression. 2 Distress. c
(ऽथापदि युद्धायत्योः) सम्परायः[m]	1 Calamity. 2 War. 3 Futurity.
पूज्य[m] (स्तु श्वशुरे ऽपि च)	A father-in-law. d.
153. (पश्चादवस्थायिबलं समवायश्च) सन्नयौ[m]	1 Rear guard. 2 Multitude.
(संघाते सन्निवेशे च) संस्त्यायः[m]	1 Assemblage. 2 Vicinity e
प्रणया[m] (स्त्वमी	1 Acquaintance. 2 Solicitation. f
154. विस्रम्भ याच्ञा प्रेमाणो)	
(विरोधे ऽपि) समुच्छ्रयः[m]	Enmity. g
विषयो[m] (यस्य यो ज्ञातस्तत्र शब्दादिकेष्वपि)	1 Frequented and known. h

[a] And 2 An elephant's middle pace, neither quick nor slow. 3 A hill at the foot of a mountain. [b] And 4 Demonstrated conclusion. 5 Agreement, bargain. 6 Hint. 7 Leisure. [c] And 3 Fault, guilt. 4 Punishment by fine, &c. [d] Also 2 A teacher. m. f. n. 3 Worthy of respect. [e] Likewise 3 A house. [f] And 3 Affection. [g] Also 2 Elevation, height. [h] And 2 Object of sense, as sound, &c. 3 Country, province.

Infusion, extract. a — 155. (निर्यासे ऽपि) कषायो (ऽस्त्री) [m n]

Assembly. b — (सभायां च) प्रतिश्रयः [m]

1 Abundance, frequency. c — प्रायो (भूम्न्यन्तगमने) [m]

1 Distress. 2 A sacrifice. 3 Anger. d — मन्यु (र्दैन्ये क्रतौ क्रुधि) [m]

1 A secret. 2 Privy part. e — 156. (रहस्योपस्थयोर्) गुह्यं [n]

1 An oath. 2 Truth. f — सत्यं (शपथतथ्ययोः) [n]

1 Animal strength. 2 Dignity. g — वीर्य्यं (बले प्रभावे च) [n h]

1 Right, fit. 2 Substance. i — द्रव्यं (भव्ये गुणाश्रये) [n]

1 A place. 2 A house. j — 157. धिष्ण्यं (स्थाने गृहे भेऽग्नौ) [n k]

1 Destiny. 2 Goodluck. 3 Ill fate. — भाग्यं (कर्म्मशुभाशुभम्) [n]

1 A pignut. 2 Gold. l — (कशेरुहेम्नोर्) गाङ्गेयं [n]

A plant. m — विशल्या (दन्तिकापि च) [f]

---

[a] Or 2 Exudation of a tree. 3 Astringent taste. 4 Perfume rubbed on the body. [b] Also 2 Refuge. 3 House. [c] And 2 Starving oneself to death. 3 (In composition) Similar, like. [d] Also 4 Grief, sorrow. [e] Likewise m. 3 A tortoise. 4 Pride. [f] Also 3 The first age of the world. m. f. n. 4 True. [g] Likewise 3 Semen virile. 4 Splendour. 5 Valour. [h] Or वीर्यं. [i] The substratum of qualities. Likewise 3 Wealth. 4 Drug. 5 Brass. [j] And 3 An asterism. 4 Strength. m. n. 5 Fire. [k] Or धिष्ण्यः and धिष्ण्य. [l] Also m. 3 BHISHMA son of *Gangá*. [m] Named *Dantí*. Also certain other plants, as Menispermum glabrum, &c.

158. वृषाकपायी (श्रीगौर्योर्)[f] — 1 The goddess LAKSHMI′. 2 GAURI′. a

अभिख्या (नामशोभयोः)[f] — 1 A name. 2 Beauty. b

(आरम्भो निष्कृतिः शिक्षा पूजनं सम्प्रधारणम् — 1 Beginning, undertaking. 2 Atonement. c

159. उपायः कर्म चेष्टा च चिकित्सा च नव) क्रियाः[f]

छाया (सूर्यप्रिया कान्तिः प्रतिबिम्बमनातपः)[f] — 1 Wife of the sun. 2 Beauty. d

160. कक्ष्या (प्रकोष्ठे हर्म्यादेः काञ्च्यां मध्येभबन्धने)[f] — 1 Enclosure of an edifice. e

कृत्या (क्रियादेवतयोस्त्रिषु भेद्ये धनादिभिः)[f] — 1 An act. 2 A certain deity. f

161. जन्यः (स्याज्जनवादेऽपि)[m f n] — A rumour. g

जघन्यो (ऽन्त्येऽधमेऽपि च)[m f n] — 1 Last, ultimate. 2 Low, vile.

(गर्ह्याधीनौ च) वक्तव्यौ[m f n] — 1 Reprehensible. 2 Subject, dependent. h

कल्यौ (सज्जनिरामयौ)[m f n] — 1 Ready, prepared. 2 Healthy. i

---

[a] Likewise 3 *Swáhá,* wife of the regent fire. 4 SACHI′, wife of INDRA. [b] Also 3 Glory. [c] And 3 Study. 4 Worship. 5 Disquisition. 6 Means, expedient. 7 Act. 8 Bodily action. 9 Remedy. 10 Instrument. 11 A religious initiatory ceremony. 12 Obsequies. [d] And 3 A reflected image. 4 Shade. [e] Or 2 The gate of such an inclosure. 3 A string of bells, worn by women. 4 A rope round an elephant's body. 5 Effort, exertion. m. 6 The armpit. [f] To whom sacrifices are offered for destructive and magical purposes. Or 3 Pestilence m. f. n. 4 Seduced from an alliance. 5 Any thing to be done. [g] Neuter in the sense exhibited. m. f. n. 2 To be produced. 3 A relation of a bride. 4 Her attendant. 5 The companion of a bridegroom. n. 6 A market. 7 War. 8 A meteor. m. 9 A father. f. 10 A mother. 11 A mother's female companion. [h] Likewise 3 Fit to be said. [i] Also 3 Skilful. m. f. 4 One deaf and dumb. n. 5 Morning. f. 6 Auspicious speech.

1 Intelligent. 2 Wealthy. a — 162. (आत्मवाननपेतोर्थाद्) अर्थ्यः *m f n*

Pleasing. b — पुण्यं (तु चार्वपि) *m f n*

Beautiful. c — रूप्यं (प्रशस्तरूपे ऽपि) *m f n*

Eloquent. d — वदान्यो (वल्गुवागपि) *m f n*

Just, reasonable. e — 163. (न्याय्ये ऽपि) मध्यं *m f n*

1 Handsome, 2 Sacred to the moon. f — सौम्यं (तु सुन्दरे सोमदैवते) *m f n*

SECTION XXI.

1 Multitude. 2 Occasion. g — (निवहावसरौ) वारौ *m* h

1 A bed of grass or bark. 2 A sacrifice. — संस्तरौ (प्रस्तराध्वरौ) *m*

1 VRIHASPATI. 2 A parent. i — 164. गुरू (गीष्पतिपित्राद्यौ) *m*

1 The 3d age. 2 Doubt. — द्वापरौ (युगसंशयौ) *m*

1 Difference. 2 Similitude. — प्रकारौ (भेदसादृश्याव्) *m*

---

[a] Or 3 Right, reasonable. n. 4 Red chalk. [b] Also n. 2 A good action. 3 Virtue, moral or religious merit. [c] Likewise n. 2 Silver. 3 Wrought silver and gold. [d] Also 2 Generous, munificent. [e] Likewise 2 Middle. 3 Low. And n. 4 The middle. [f] Also 3 Mild. m. 4 Patronymic of *Budha*, or Mercury. [g] And 3 A day of the week. n. 4 A vessel for spirituous liquor. [h] वारः or बारः. [i] Or other venerable relative. And 3 A spiritual teacher. m. f. n. 4 Heavy. 5 Great.

[1] m आकाराव् (इङ्गिताकृती)	1 Hint. 2 Form.
165. m किंशारू (धान्यशूकेषु)	1 Beard of corn. 2 An arrow.
m मरू (धन्वधराधरौ)	1 A country void of water. 2 A mountain.
[2] m अद्रयो (द्रुमशैलार्काः)	1 A tree. 2 A mountain. 3 The Sun.
(स्त्रीस्तनाब्दौ) m पयोधरौ	1 A woman's breast. 2 A cloud. a
166. (ध्वान्तारिदानवा) m वृत्रा	1 Darkness. 2 A foe. 3 A demon. b
(बलिहस्तांशवः) m कराः	1 Tax. 2 Hand. 3 Ray of light. c
m प्रदरा (भङ्गनारीरुग् बाणा)	1 Splitting. d
m अस्राः (कचा अपि)	Hair. e
167. (अजातशृङ्गो गौः काले ऽप्यश्मश्रु नरो च) m तूबरः	1 A hornless bull. 2 A beardless man. f
(स्वर्णे ऽपि) [3] m राः	Gold. g
m परिकरः (पर्य्यङ्कपरिवारयोः)	1 A bed. 2 A dependent. h
168. (मुक्ताशुद्धौ च) m तारः (स्याच्)	1 Elegance of a pearl. i

1—र. 2—द्रि. 3 रै.

a Also 3 Coconut. b Who was slain by INDRA. c Likewise 4 An elephant's trunk. 5 Hair. d Or 2 Fracture. 3 A feminine disease (excess of menstruation). 4 An arrow. e Also 2 A corner. n. 3 A tear. 4 Blood. f Although of an age to have a beard; and, in the instance of the bull, of an age to have horns. 3 Astringent taste. g Likewise 2 Wealth. 3 A cloud. h Also 3 Commencement. 4 Multitude. 5 Girding (as for battle). i Or 2 A beautiful pearl. 3 The pupil of the eye. 4 A high note. m. f. n. 5 High, as a note in music. n. 6 Silver. f. n. 7 A star. f. 8 The wife of VRIHASPATI. 9—of SUGRÍVA. 10 A goddess of the *Baudd'has*.

1 Air. a	1 m शारो (वायौ स तु त्रिषु कर्बुरे)
1 Promise. 2 War. 3 Bargain. b	m (ऽथ प्रतिज्ञाजिसंविदापत्सु) सङ्गरः
1 The prayers of the *Védas*. c	m 169. (वेदभेदे गुप्तिवादे) मन्त्रो
The sun. d	m मित्रो (रवावपि)
1 A sacrifice. 2 An arrow. e	m f (मखेषु यूपखण्डे ऽपि) स्वरुः
Part to be concealed. g	m (गुह्ये ऽप्य) ऽवस्करः
1 Charge sounded by trumpets. h	m 170. आडम्बर (स्तूर्य्यरवे गजेन्द्राणां च गर्जिते)
1 A brisk assault. 2 Robbery. i	m अभिहारो (ऽभियोगे च चौर्य्ये सन्नहने ऽपि च)
1 An attendant 2 A scabbard. j	k 171. (स्याज्जङ्गमे) परीवारः (खड्गकोशे परिच्छदे)
1 A tree. 2 A handful of sacred grass. l	m विष्टरो (विटपीदर्भमुष्टिः पीठाद्यमासनं)
1 A door. 2 A porter.	m 172. (द्वारिद्वाःस्थे) प्रतीहारः
A female porter.	2 f प्रतीहार्य्य (ऽप्यनन्तरे)

1 शार. 2—री (नृ).

[a] And m. f. n. 2 Variegated. Also m. 3 Tables for playing. [b] And 4 Calamity, distress. [c] And 2 Secret consultation; private advice. 3 Incantation or charm. [d] Also n. 2 A friend. [e] And 3 Shavings of the wood of which a sacrificial post is made. [f] स्वरुः (स्व or स्वस्). [g] And 2 Ordure, excrement. 3 Sweepings. [h] And 2 Roaring of large elephants. 3 Beginning. 4 Making a show. [i] And 3 Arming; taking arms. [j] And 3 The insignia of dignity. [k] Or परिवार. [l] And 3 A stool or cushion.

m

(विपुले नकुले विष्णौ) बभ्रुः (स्यात्पिङ्गले त्रिषु) — 1 A large ichneumon. 2 VISHNU. a

m

173. सारो (बले स्थिरांशे च न्याय्ये क्लीबं वरे त्रिषु) — 1 Strength. 2 Essence. b

m *n* d

दुरोदरो (द्यूतकारे पणे द्यूते) दुरोदरम् — 1 A gamester. 2 A stake. c

m n

174. (महारण्ये दुर्गपथे) कान्तारः (पुन्नपुंसकम्) — 1 A forest. 2 A difficult road. e

m

मत्सरो (ऽन्यशुभद्वेषे तद्वत्कृपणयोस्त्रिषु) — 1 Envy. f

m h

175. (देवाद्वृते) वरः (श्रेष्ठे त्रिषु क्लीबे मनाक् प्रिये) — 1 A boon. g

m n

(वंशाङ्कुरे) करीरो (ऽस्त्री तरुभेदे घटे च ना) — 1 Shoot of a bambu. i

m

176. (ना चमूजघने हस्तसूत्रे) प्रतिसरो (ऽस्त्रियाम्) — 1 Rear-guard j

(यमानिलेन्द्रचन्द्रार्कविष्णुसिंहांशुवाजिषु — 1 YAMA. 2 Wind. 3 INDRA. k

---

[a] Also 3 SIVA. 4 Fire 5 Proper name ; a sage m. f. n. 6 Tawny. 7 Large. [b] Likewise 3 Marrow. n. 4 Propriety. 5 Water. 6 Wealth. m. f. n. 7 Excellent. [c] And n. 3 Play, gaming. [d] Or दुरोदरः—रं. [e] Also m. 3 A sort of sugarcane. [f] And m. f. n. 2 Envious. 3 Avaricious, niggardly. f. 4 A gnat. [g] And m. f. n. 2 Excellent n. (some say indecl.) 3 A little approved. Likewise m. 4 A son-in-law. 5 Appointment. n. 6 Saffron. f. 7—रा. The three myrobalans.—री. 8 Asparagus racemosus. [h] Or वरः. [i] And m. 2 Sort of plant (common in dry deserts). 3 A jar. [j] And m. n. 2 A string worn on the wrist at nuptials, &c. Also m. 3 Counsel. 4 A bracelet. 5 A wreath. m. n. 6 Territory. m. f. n. 7 Fit to be employed. [k] And 4 the Moon. 5 The sun. 6 VISHNU. 7 A lion. 8 A ray of light. 9 A horse. 10 A parrot. 11 A serpent. 12 An ape. 13 A frog. m. f. n. 14 Tawny. 15 Green. Or 16 Yellow.

m

177. शुकाहिकपिभेकेषु) हरि (र्ना कपिले त्रिषु)

f

A potsherd. a — शर्करा (कर्परांशे ऽपि)

f

1 Passing away time. b — यात्रा (स्याद्यापने गतौ)

f

1 The earth. 2 Speech. 3 Ardent spirit. c — 178. इरा (भूवाक्सुराप्सु स्यात्)

f d

1 Drowsiness. 2 Lassitude. — तन्द्री (निद्राप्रमीलयोः)

f

1 A nurse. 2 The earth. e — धात्री (स्यादुपमाताऽपि क्षितिरप्यामलक्यपि)

f

1 Wanting a limb. 2 A dancing girl. f — 179. क्षुद्रा (व्यङ्गा नटी वेश्या सरघा कण्टकारिका

m f n

त्रिषु क्रूरे ऽधमे ऽल्पे ऽपि) क्षुद्रं।

f

1 Requisites, materials. 2 A little. g — मात्रा (परिच्छदे

n

180. अल्पे च परिमाणे सा) मात्रं (कार्त्स्न्ये ऽवधारणे)

n

1 Painting, delineation. 2 Wonder. h — (आलेख्याश्चर्ययोश्) चित्रं

---

[a] Also 2 A stony nodule. 3 A country abounding in such. 4 A disease (the gravel). 5 Clayed sugar. [b] Or 2 Livelihood. And 3 Travelling. 4 Festival; procession. [c] And 4 Water. [d] Or तन्द्रा or तन्द्रिः. [e] Also 3 A mother. 4 An emblic myrobalan. [f] And 3 A courtesan. 4 A bee. 5 An egg-plant. m. f. n. 6 Cruel. 7 Low. 8 Small. Also 9 Miserly. 10 Poor. And f. A fly. [g] And 3 Quantity. n. 4 The whole. 5 Only; (exclusive and identical). Also f. 6 An earring. 7 An instant. 8 Half a short syllable. [h] Also 3 A circlet or mark. 4 Variegated colour. m. f. n. 5 Variegated. 6 Wonderful. f. चित्रा. 7 A star in the Virgin's spike. 8 Title of Subhadra´.

n कलत्रं (श्रोणिभार्य्ययोः)	1 The hip and loins. 2 A wife. a
181. (योग्यभाजनयोः) *n* पात्रं	1 Fit. capable. 2 A vessel. b
n पत्रं (वाहनपक्षयोः)	1 A vehicle. 2 A wing. c
(निदेशग्रन्थयोः) *n* शास्त्रं	1 Command. 2 Institutes of a science.
n शस्त्रम् (आयुधलोहयोः)	1 A weapon. 2 Iron. d
182. (स्याज्जटांशुकयोर्) *n* नेत्रं	1 Root of a tree. 2 Wove silk bleached. e
n क्षेत्रं (पत्नीशरीरयोः)	1 A wife. 2 Body. f
(मुखाग्रे क्रोडहलयोः) *n* पोत्रं	1 Snout of a hog. 2 Fore-part of a plough. g
n गोत्रं (तु नाम्नि च)	Name. h
183. *n* सत्रम् (आच्छादने यज्ञे सदादाने वने ऽपि च)	1 Vesture. 2 A sacrifice. 3 Constant alms. i
n अजिरम् (विषये काये ऽप्य्)	1 Object of perception. 2 A body. j
n ऽम्बरं (व्योम्नि वाससि)	1 Ether ; the sky. 2 Apparel. k

---

[a] Likewise 3 A fastness or strong hold. [b] Also 3 A king's minister. 4 The channel of a river, or space between the banks. 5 A vessel used in sacrifice ; as a ladle, &c. 6 A leaf. 7 A person of a drama. [c] Likewise 3 A leaf. 4 The feather of an arrow. [d] Also f. शस्त्री. 3 A knife. [e] Likewise 3 An eye. 4 The rope of a churn. 5 A car. m. f. n. 6 A guide. [f] Also 3 A field. 4 A holy spot. 5 A geometrical figure. [g] Likewise 3 Sort of cloth. [h] Also 2 Family, race, line. 3 Wealth. m. 4 A mountain. f. 5 The earth. 6 A herd of kine. [i] And 4 A forest, or 5 Wealth. [j] Likewise 3 A court-yard. 4 Wind. [k] Also 3 Ambergris.

A realm. a — 184. चक्रं[m] (राष्ट्रे ऽप्य्)

Exemption from transmigration. b — ऽक्षरं[n] (तु मोक्षे ऽपि)

Water. c — क्षीरम्[n] (अप्सु च)

Gold. d — (स्वर्णे ऽपि) भूरि[m]चन्द्रौ[m] (द्वौ)

A door. e — (द्वारमात्रे ऽपि) गोपुरम्[n]

1 A cavern. 2 Pride. f — 185. (गुहादम्भौ) गह्वरे[n] (द्वे)

1 Solitude. 2 Near. — (रहो ऽन्तिकम्) उपह्वरे[n]

1 Front, forepart. g — (पुरोधिकमुपर्य्) ऽग्राण्य्[1 n]

1 A house. 2 A town. h — (आगारे नगरे) पुरम्[n]

186. मन्दिरं[n] (च।)

1 A country, or realm. 2 Calamity. — (ऽथ) राष्ट्रो[m n] (ऽस्त्री विषये स्यादुपद्रवे)

---

1 अग्र.

[a] Likewise 2 A wheel. 3 A circular missile weapon : a sharp discus. 4 A potter's wheel. 5 A mill. 6 A multitude. 7 An army. 8 A whirlpool. 9 Pride. m. 10 A ruddy goose, (Anas Casarca). [b] Also 2 A letter, or written character. 3 BRAHMA, m. 4 SIVA. m. f. n. 5 Unalterable. [c] Likewise 2 Milk. [d] Also भूरिः m. f. n. 2 Frequent, numerous. m. 3 BRAHMA. 4 VISHNU. 5 SIVA, And चन्द्रः. 2 The Moon, 3 Camphor. 4 Water. m. f. n. 5 Pleasing. [e] Also 2 A town gate. 3 Sort of grass : Cyperus ? [f] Likewise 3 A forest. m. 4 An arbour. [g] And m. f. n. 2 More, much. n. 3 Top, summit. 4 Point, extremity. 5 Assemblage, multitude. 6 Resting place, end of a journey. 7 Quantity of a *pala*. 8 Limited alms (four mouthfuls) m. f. n. 9 Chief, principal. 10 First, prior. [h] Also पुरं. 3 A body. 4 City of Patna. m. 5 Bdellium. And मन्दिरः m. 3 The sea.

दरो (ऽस्त्रियां भये श्वभ्रे) [m]	1 Fear, dread 2 A hole in the ground. a.
वज्रो (ऽस्त्री हीरके पवौ) [m n]	1 A diamond. 2 The thunderbolt. b
187. तन्त्रं (प्रधाने सिद्धान्ते सूत्रवाये परिच्छदे)	1 Chief. 2 Right conclusion. c
औशीर (श्चामरे दण्डे ऽप्यौ) शीरं (शयनासने) [m] [1 n]	1 Handle of a fan of cow's hair. d
188. पुष्करं (करिहस्ताग्रे वाद्यभाण्डमुखे जले व्योम्नि खड्गफले पद्मे तीर्थौषधिविशेषयोः) [n]	1 Tip of an elephant's trunk. e
189. अन्तरम् (अवकाशावधिपरिधानान्तर्धिभेदतादर्थ्ये छिद्रात्मीयविनाबहिरवसरमध्ये ऽन्तरात्मनि च) [n]	1 Interval. 2 Period. 3 Clothing. 4 Covering. f
190. (मुस्ते ऽपि) पिठरं [n]	Fragrant root of grass. g

---

1 औ—.

[a] Likewise indec. 3 A little. And f. दरि. 4 A cavern. [b] Also m. 3 One of the 28 astrological *yógas*. [c] And 3 A weaver's lay or batten. 4 Raiment. 5 Care of a realm. 6 Dependence. 7 A sacred book. 8 An excellent medicament. [d] And n. 2 A bed. 3 A chair or stool. Likewise 4 Fragrant root of grass (Andropogon muricatum.) [e] And 2 Head of a drum, or place where any musical instrument is struck. 3 Water. 4 The sky. 5 Edge of a scimitar, or 6 A scabbard. 7 A lotos. 8 Name of a place. 9 A drug (Costus Arabicus.) 10 One of the *Dwipas* or continents. m. 11 The Indian Crane. [f] And 5 Difference. 6 Sake. 7 A hole or rent. 8 Own. 9 Without, except. 10 Outside. 11 Opportune time. 12 Midst. 13 Supreme soul. 14 Similar. 15 Other. *This term is a pronoun in the 3d and 10th acceptations.* [g] Cyperus rotundus. Also 2 A churning stick. m. 3 A seether or boiler.

Another sort, a — (राजकशेरुण्यपि) नागरम् *n*

1 Very dark. 2 Mischievous, destructive. b — शार्वरं (त्वन्धतमसे घातुके भेद्यलिङ्गकः) *m f n*

1 Pale red. 2 White. 3 Yellow. c — 191. गौरो (ऽरुणे सिते पीते) *m f n*

Sharp, corrosive. d — (व्रणकार्य्यप्य) रुष्करः *m f n*

Hard, e — जठरः (कठिनेऽपि स्यात्) *m f n*

Inferior, low. f — (अधस्तादप्यधरः) *m f n*

Unperplexed. g — 192. (अनाकुलेऽपि चै) काग्रः [1] *m f n*

1 Distracted. 2 Perplexed. h — व्यग्रो (व्यासक्त आकुले) *m f n*

1 Superior, high. 2 Northern. i — (उपर्युदीच्यश्रेष्ठेष्वप्य) त्तरः (स्यात्) [2] *m f n*

1 Inferior. 2 Southern. j — अनुत्तरः *m f n*

---

1 ए—. 2 च—.

[a] Cyperus pertenuis. Likewise 2 Ginger. m. f. n. 3 Of or belonging to a city. 4 Sagacious. [b] According to another reading. m. 3 A vicious elephant. [c] Likewise 4 Clean. m. 5 White mustard. 6 The moon. n. 7 Filament of a lotos. f. 8 The goddess, wife of Siva. 9—of Varun'a. 10 The earth. 11 Name of a river. 12 A young girl. 13 Turmeric. [d] Also m. 2 Semecarpus Anacardium. [e] Likewise 2 Old. m. n. 3 The belly. [f] Also 2 Less, worse. m. 3 The lip. 4 The nether lip. [g] Likewise 2 Intent, attentive. [h] Or 3 Frightened. [i] And 3 Excellent. Also n. 4 An answer. m. 5 Proper name, the son of Vira'ta. f. 6 The wife of Abhimanyu. 7 The north. [j] And 3 Worse. Likewise 4 Excellent. 5 Silent, unable to answer.

193. (एषां विपर्यये श्रेष्ठे)

m f n

(दूरानात्मोत्तमाः) पराः — 1 Distant, remote. 2 Other. [a]

m f n

(स्वादुप्रियौ तु) मधुरौ — 1 Sweet. 2 Pleasing. [b]

m

क्रूरौ (कठिननिर्दयौ) — 1 Hard. 2 Pitiless; cruel. [c]

m f n e

194. उदारो (दातृमहतोः) — 1 Generous. 2 Great. [d]

m f n

इतर (अन्यनीचयोः) — 1 Other. 2 Low, vile.

m f n

(मन्दस्वच्छन्दयोः) स्वैरः — 1 Indolent. 2 Independent, uncontrolled.

m f n

शुभ्रम् (उद्दीप्तशुक्लयोः) — 1 Splendid. 2 White. [f]

SECTION XXII.

1 m f

195. (चूडाकिरीटं केशाश्च संयता) मौलयस् (त्रयः) — 1 Lock on the crown of the head. [g]

2 m

(द्रुमप्रभेदमातङ्ग काण्डपुष्पाणि) पीलवः — 1 The tree *Pilu*. 2 An elephant. [h]

1—त्रि. 2—द्रु.

[a] And 3 Pre-eminent. Or 4 Subsequent. 5 Inimical, enemy. n. (some say indec.) 6 Only. [b] Also m. 3 A sweet taste. n. 4 Poison. f. 5 Anise. [c] Likewise 3 Terrible. 4 Destructive. [d] Also 3 Gentle. 4 Unperplexed. [e] Fem. उदारा,—री. [f] And n. Talc. [g] And 2 A diadem. 3 Hair tied on the head. 4 Head. m. 5 Jonesia Asoca. 6 The earth. [h] And 3 An arrow. 4 A flower (Or 5 Blossom of the Saccharum Sara). Also 7 An atom.

1 YAMA. 2 Measured time. a — 196. (कृतान्तानेहसोः) कालश्[1 m]

The fourth age. b — (चतुर्थेऽपि युगे) कलिः[m]

A deer. c — (स्यात्कुरङ्गेऽपि) कमलः[m]

A blanket. d — (प्रावारेऽपि च) कम्बलः[m]

1 Tax, revenue. 2 An oblation. e — 197. (करोपहारयोः पुंसि) बलिः[m] (प्राण्यङ्गजे स्त्रियाम्)

1 Bulkiness. 2 Strength. 3 Army, forces. f — (स्थौल्यसामर्थ्यसैन्येषु) बलं[n] (ना काकसीरिणोः)

1 A whirlwind. g — 198, वातूलः[m h] (पुंसि वात्यायामपि वातसहे त्रिषु)

1 Wicked. — (भेद्यलिङ्गः शठे) व्यालः[m/f/n j] (पुंसि श्वापदसर्पयोः)

---

1 काल.

[a] Likewise 3 Death. 4 Time (infinite). 5 Black colour. f. काला 6 Madder. 7 Indigo. काली. 8 The goddess GAURI'. 9 One of the MA'TRIS. 10 Heavy clouds. [b] Likewise 2 Quarrel, strife. 3 War, battle. 4 Bellerick myrobalan. 5 An unblown flower. [c] Also n. 2 A Lotos. 3 Water. 4 Copper. f. 5 The goddess LAKSHMI'. 6 An excellent woman. [d] Also 2 A dewlap. 3 A fabulous chief of serpents. n. 4 Water. [e] And f. बलिः—ली (or बलीः). 3 A wrinkle. Also m. 4 Proper name; a giant. 5 Handle of a flyflapper. f. 6 Ridge of a roof. [f] And m. 4 A crow. 5 Proper name; BALARA'MA. Also 6 Name of a demon slain by INDRA. m. f. n. 7 Strong. f. 8 Sida cordifolia, &c. [g] And 2 Gouty, Rheumatic. 3 Insane. [h] Or वातुलः. [i] And m. 2 A beast of prey; tiger, &c. 3 A serpent. 4 A vicious elephant. 5 A king. [j] Fem. व्याली.

199. मलो (ऽस्त्री पापविट्किट्टान्य) [m n] — 1 Sin. 2 Filth. 3 Excretion. [a]

(ऽस्त्री) शूलं (रुगायुधम्) [m n] — 1 Colic. 2 A weapon. [b]

(शङ्कावपि द्वयोः) कीलः [m f] — A lance. [c]

पालिः (स्त्र्यश्र्यङ्कपङ्क्तिषु) [f] — 1 A corner. 2 The hollow above the hip. [d]

200. कला (शिल्पे कालभेदे ऽप्य्) [f] — 1 A mechanical art. 2 A measure of time. [e]

आली (सख्यावली अपि) [1 f] — 1 A companion. 2 A row. [f]

(अब्ध्यम्बुविकृतौ) वेला (कालमर्यादयोरपि) [f h] — 1 Tide. 2 Time. 3 Limit. [g]

201. बहुलाः (कृत्तिकागावो) [f j] बहुलो (ऽग्नौ शितौ त्रिषु) [m] — 1 The Pleiades. 2 A cow. [i]

लीला (विलासक्रिययोर्) [f] — 1 Sport. 2 Gesture.

उपला (शर्करापि च) [f] — A stony nodule. [k]

1—लि or —ली.

[a] As sweat, snot, earwax, &c. 4 Dregs. 5 Rust. m. f. n. 6 Niggardly. [b] A trident or a pike. Also f. 3 A courtesan. [c] Likewise 2 A gnomon. 3 A stake. 4 A post. 5 Flame. 6 The elbow. 7 A thump on the breast. 8 A punch with the elbow. f. 9 A blow. [d] Or 3 Sharp edge. 4 A mark. 5 A row or string. Also 6 Delineation with sandal, &c. on the ear. 7 Contiguity. 8 Allowance to a dependant. 9 A masculine woman (who has a beard). 10 A handful. 11 Praise. [e] Likewise 3 A digit of the moon. 4 Interest on a capital sum. 5 A part. 6 Collection. [f] Also 3 A bridge. m. f. n. 4 Intelligent, wise. [g] Likewise 4 Seashore. 5 Easy and sudden death. [h] Or बेला. [i] In the first acceptation, invariably plural. And m. 3 Fire. m. f. n. 4 Black. Also 5 Cardamum. m. 6 The dark half of the month. n. The sky. [j] Or बहुलाः. [k] Also 2 Manufactured sugar. m. 3 A stone. 4 A gem.

1 Blood. 2 Water. — 202. (शोणिते ऽम्भसि) कीलालं [f]

1 Origin. 2 Root. a — मूलम् [n] (आद्ये शिफाकयोः)

1 A multitude. 2 A net. b — जालं [n] (समूह आनायो गवाक्षक्षारकेष्वपि)

1 Disposition. 2 Good conduct. — 203. शीलं [n] (स्वभावे सद्वृत्ते)

1 Fruit. 2 Result. c — (सस्ये हेतुकृते) फलम् [n]

1 A roof. 2 A film over the eye. d — (छदिर्नेत्ररुजोः क्लीबं समूहे) पटलं [n] (न ना)

1 Bottom. 2 Essential character. e — 204. (अधःस्वरूपयोरस्त्री) तलं [n]

Flesh. f — (स्याच्चामिषे) पलम् [n]

Submarine fire. g — (और्वानलेऽपि) पातालं [n]

1 Clothes, vesture. h — चेलं [n] (वस्त्रे ऽधमे त्रिषु)

1 A hole filled with stakes. i — 205. कुकूलं [n] (शङ्कुभिः कीर्णे श्वभ्रे ना तु तुषानले)

---

[a] And m. n. 3 An asterism (the Scorpion's tail). Or n. 4 Principal, capital. [b] And 3 A window, a lattice. 4 An unblown flower. 5 Magic, illusion. 6 Pride. f. जाली. 7 Trichosanthes dioica. [c] Likewise 3 Edge of a weapon. 4 A nutmeg. 5 A Pearl. 6 Profit. 7 A shield. [d] And f. n. (—ली, ला or लं.). 3 A multitude. n. 4 Retinue. [e] Likewise f. n. 3 A guard for an archer's arm. m. 4 A span. 5 The palm with extended fingers. [f] Also 2 A measure, consisting of four *Karshas*. [g] Likewise 2 The infernal regions. 3 A hole. [h] And m. f. n. 2 Inferior; low in situation. Fem. चेली. [i] And m. 2 Conflagration of chaff.

n
(निर्णीते) केवलम् (इति त्रिलिङ्गं त्वेककृत्स्नयोः) — 1 Absolute, certain. a

n
206. (पर्याप्तिक्षेमपुण्येषु) कुशलं (शिक्षिते त्रिषु) — 1 Adequacy. 2 Safety. 3 Virtue. b

m n
प्रवालम् (अङ्कुरे ऽप्यस्त्री) — 1 A shoot or sprout. c

m f n
(त्रिषु) स्थूलं (जडे ऽपि च) — Stupid. d

m f n
207. करालो (दन्तुरे तुङ्गे) — 1 Having projecting teeth. 2 High. e

m f n g
(चारौ दक्षे च) पेशलः — 1 Beautiful. 2 Expert. f

m f n
(मूर्खे ऽर्भके ऽपि) बालः (स्याल्) — 1 Ignorant. 2 Young, a child. h

m f n
लोल (श्चलसतृष्णयोः) — 1 Tremulous. 2 Thirsty. i

SECTION XXIII.

m *m*
208. दवदावौ (वनारण्यवह्नी) — 1 A forest. 2 Fire in a forest. j

m
(जन्महरौ) भवौ — 1 Birth. 2 SIVA. k

---

[a] And m. f. n. 2 Alone, sole. 3 Entire, all. Fem.—ला, ली. [b] And m. f. n. 4 Skilfuil, expert. [c] Or 2 A new leaf. Also 3 Coral. 4 The neck of a lute. [d] Likewise 2 Bulky. [e] Likewise 3 Terrible. [f] Also 3 Soft. [g] Or पेषलः [h] Likewise m. 3 Hair. 4 Tail of a horse. 5—of an elephant. m. n. 6 Andropogon Schœnanthus. [i] Also f.—ला. 3 The tongue. 4 The goddess LAKSHMI′. Likewise 3 Fire in general. [k] Also 3 Existence. 4 Acquisition. 5 This world. 6 Safety, well being.

1 A counsellor. 2 A companion. — (मन्त्री सहायः) सचिवौ [m]

1 A husband. 2 Lythrum fruticosum. a — (पतिशाखिनराः) धवाः [m]

1 A mountain. 2 A sheep. 3 The sun. b — 209. अवयः [1 m] (शैलमेषार्काः)

1 Command. 2 Call. 3 Sacrifice. — (आज्ञाह्वानाध्वराः) हवाः [m]

1 A living being. c — भावः [m] (सत्तास्वभावाभिप्रायचेष्टात्मजन्मसु)

1 Production. 2 Fruit. 3 Blossom. d — 210. (स्यादुत्पादे फले पुष्पे) प्रसवो [m] (गर्भमोचने)

1 Distrust. 2 Denial. 3 Concealment. — (अविश्वासेऽपह्नवेऽपि निकृतावपि) निह्नवः [m]

1 Elevation. 2 Impatience. e — 211. (उत्सेकामर्षयोरिच्छाप्रसरे मह) उत्सवः [m]

1 Dignity, authority. 2 Firm opinion. f — अनुभावः [m] (प्रभावे स्यात्सतां च मतिनिश्चये)

1 Generative cause. 2 Origin. g — 212. (स्याज्जन्महेतुः) प्रभवः [m] (स्थानं चाद्योपलब्धये)

1 Son of a *Bra hmana* by a *Sudra* woman. h — (शूद्रायां विप्रतनये शस्त्रे) पारशवः [m] (पुमान्)

---

1 अवि.

[a] And 3 A man. 4 A cheater. [b] Also 4 The shawl goat. [c] Or (varying the reading.) 2 Existence, state. 3 Nature, disposition. 4 Meaning, intention. 5 Gesture, movement. 6 Soul. 7 Birth. 8 Thing. 9 Venerable. 10 (in dramatic language.) Learned. 11 State, condition. [d] And 4 Bringing forth. 5 Offspring. [e] And 3 Formation of a wish. 4 Festival, jubilee. [f] Or 3 Certainty. 4 Indication, hint. [g] Or 3 Source. 4 Place where a thing is first perceived. 5 Strength. [h] And 2 Battle-axe. 3 A son born in adultery.

213. ध्रुवो[m] (ऽभेदे क्लीबं तु निश्चिते शाश्वते त्रिषु)	1 The polar star. a
स्वो[m] (ज्ञातावात्मनि) स्वं[mfn] (त्रिष्वात्मीये) स्वो[mn] (ऽस्त्रियां धने)	1 A kinsman. 2 The soul. b
214. (स्त्रीकटीवस्त्रबन्धेऽपि) नीवी[f d] (परिपणेऽपि च)	Cloth round a woman's waist. c
शिवा[f] (गौरीफेरवयोर्)	1 GAURI´. 2 A jackal. e
द्वन्द्वं[n] (कलहयुग्मयोः)	1 Dispute, quarrel. 2 A pair. f
215. (द्रव्यासुव्यवसायेषु) सत्त्वम्[n h] (अस्त्री तु जन्तुषु)	1 Substance. 2 Breath. g
क्लीबं[n j] (नपुंसके षण्ढे वाच्यलिङ्गमविक्रमे)	1 Neuter gender. 2 An eunuch. i

SECTION XXIV.

216. (द्वौ) विशौ[1 m] (वैश्यमनुजौ)	1 Man of the commercial tribe. k

---

1 श्—.

[a] And n. 2 Certainty. m. f. n. 3 Perpetual, constant. Also m. 4 A stake. 5 An axis, or pole. 6 S´IVA. f.—वा. 7 Burden of a song. 8 A ladle or spoon. n. 9 Reasoning. m. f. n. 10 Immovable. [b] And m. f. n. 3 Own. m. n. 4 Wealth. *It is a pronoun in the 3d acceptation.* [c] And 2 Mercantile stock. 3 A stake at play. [d] Or नीविः. [e] Also m. 3 MAHA´DE´VA. 4 One of the astrological *Yógas.* 5 The *Védas.* n. 6 Pleasure, ease. 7 Auspiciousness; well being. 3 Water. f. 9 The yellow myrobalan. [f] Likewise 3 Union of the sexes. [g] Or other unconscious function. 3 Vigour. m. n. 4 An animal. Also n. 5 A quality. 6 Nature. 7 Strength. 8 A demon. 9 Existence. 10 Essence. 11 Self-command. [h] सत्वं or सत्त्वं. [i] And m. f. n. 3 Weak. 4 Idle. [j] Or क्लीवं. [k] And 2 Man in general. f. 3 Entrance, Sing. विश्.

1 A spy. 2 War.[a]	(द्वौ चराभिसरौ) स्पशौ [m]
1 A heap. 2 A sign of the zodiac.	(द्वौ) राशी [1 m] (पुञ्जमेषाद्यौ)
1 Family, race. 2 A bambu.[b]	(द्वौ) वंशौ [m] (कुलमस्करौ)
1 Solitude. 2 Display.	217. (रहः प्रकाशौ) वीकाशौ [m c]
1 Wages, hire 2 Enjoyment.[d]	निर्वेशो [m] (भृतिभोगयोः)
1 YAMA.[e]	(कृतान्ते पुंसि) कीनाशः [m] (क्षुद्रकर्षकयोस्त्रिषु)
1 A place or spot. 2 A butt. 3 A cause.	218. (पदे लक्ष्ये निमित्ते) ऽपदेशः [m]
water.[f]	(स्यात्) कुशम् [n] (अप्सु च)
Age, as youth, &c.[g]	दशा [f] (वस्थानेक विधाप्य्)
1 Hope, desire. 2 Breadth.[h]	आशा [f] (तृष्णापि चायता)
1 A woman. 2 A female elephant.[i]	219. वशा [f] (स्त्री करिणी च स्याद्)
1 Knowledge.	दृग् [2 f] (ज्ञाने ज्ञातरि त्रिषु)

1—त्रि. 2—पु.

[a] Also. 3 Conflict with a dangerous animal in hopes of reward. [b] Likewise 3 The back bone. 4 A multitude. [c] Or विकाशः. [d] Or 3 Eating. [e] And m. f. n. 2 Small. Or 3 Niggardly. 4 A cultivator. Also 5 slayer of cattle. m. 6 An ape. [f] Also m. 2 Proper name: Son of RÁMA. 3 Sacrificial grass (Poa Cynosuroides). 4 One of the continents. 5 A yoke. f.—शी. 6 Share of a plough. [g] Likewise 2 Wick of a lamp. 3 (Invariably pl.) Border or edge of cloth. [h] Also 3 Region; quarter. [i] Likewise 3 A barren cow. 4 A daughter. n. 5 Subjection. 6 Desire, wish. m. f. n. 7 Subject, dependent. And m. f. n. 2 One who sees or knows. Also f. 3 Sight. 4 An eye.

	(स्यात्) कर्कशः (साहसिकः कठोरामसृणावपि) *m f n*	1 Violent. 2 Hard. 3 Intangible. a
220.	प्रकाशोऽ (ऽतिप्रसिद्धेऽपि) *m f n*	Notorious. b
	(शिशावज्ञे च) बालिशः *m f n*	1 Young. 2 Ignorant.

SECTION XXV.

	(सुरमत्स्याव्) अनिमिषौ *m*	1 A god. 2 A fish.
	पुरुषाव् (आत्ममानवौ) *m*	1 The soul. 2 A man.
221.	(काकमत्स्यात्खगौ) ध्वांक्षौ *m*	1 A crow. 2 Any bird which preys on fish. c
	कक्षौ (तु तृणवीरुधौ) *m*	1 Grass. 2 A climbing plant. d
	अभीषुः (प्रग्रहे रश्मौ) *m e*	1 A halter or rein. 2 A ray of light.
	प्रैषः (प्रेषणमर्दने)	1 Despatch, sending. 2 Paining. f

---

[a] Or 4 Harsh. 5 Cruel. 6 Unmerciful. 7 Miserly. [b] Also 2 Light. 3 Display. 4 Loud laugh. [c] Likewise 3 A beggar. [d] Also 3 The armpit. 4 A forest of dead trees. 5 A wall. 6 The side. m. f. n. 7 End of a cloth fixed in the waistband. f. 8 The string round an elephant's neck. 9 Objection in argument. 10 Emulation. [e] Or अभीषु. [f] Likewise 3 Fatigue.

Partisan. a — 222. पक्षः[m] (सहाये ऽप्य्)

1 A turban. 2 A diadem. — उष्णीषः[m n] (शिरोवेष्टकिरीटयोः)

1 Lustful. 2 A rat. b — (शुक्ले मूषिके श्रेष्ठे सुकृते वृषभे) वृषः[m]

1 A bud. 2 A sheath. 3 Treasure. c — 223. कोषो[m n d] (ऽस्त्री कुड्मले खड्गपिधाने ऽर्थौघदिव्ययोः)

1 Gaming with dice. 2 A die. e — (द्यूते ऽक्षे सारिफलके ऽप्य्) आकर्षो[m]

(ऽथा) ऽक्षम्[n] (इन्द्रिये)

1 An organ of sense. f — 224. (ना द्यूताङ्गे कर्षचक्रे व्यवहारे कलिद्रुमे)

1 Agriculture. 2 Fire with cowdung. g — कर्षू[m] (र्स्त्री करीषाग्निः) कर्षूः[f] (कुल्याभिधायिनी)

---

[a] Also 2 Side. 3 Alternative. 4 Half of the lunar month. 5 Army, forces. 6 Friends. 7 Wing. 8 Thesis, doctrine to be maintained. 9 Contradiction. 10 Subject of an inference. 11 (In composition with केश) Great quantity. [b] In composition. 3 Chief, pre-eminent. 4 Virtue, personified in the shape of a bull. 5 A bull. 6 The sign of the Zodiac (Taurus). 7 Proper name; title of KARN'A. f.—षा. 8 Cowich (Dolichos or Carpopogon pruriers)—षी. 9 Cushion used by ascetics. [c] And 4 Oath or ordeal. 5 A vessel used at sacrifices. 6 A cocoon of silk. 7 Eye ball. 8 Testicle. 9 Dictionary. [d] Or कोशः. [e] And 3 A board for playing. 4 An organ of sense. 5 Attraction. 6 Drawing the bow. [f] And m. 2 A die. 3 A measure (a *Karsha* or 16 *máshas*). 4 A wheel. 5 A lawsuit. 6 The belleric myrobalan. Also 7 Wood of a car. 8 Business, transaction. 9 Proper name, son of RA'VANA. n. 10 Kind of salt. [g] And f. 3 A river. 4 A canal.

225. (पुंभावे तत् क्रियायां च) पौरुषं *n* — 1 Virility. 2 Manly act. a

विषम् *n* (अप्सु च) — Water. b

(उपदाने ऽप्य्) आमिषं *m n* (स्याद्) — A bribe. c

(अपराधे ऽपि) किल्बिषम् *n* — An offence. d

226. (स्याद्वृष्टौ लोकधात्वंशे वत्सरे) वर्षम् *m n* (अस्त्रियाम्) — 1 Rain. 2 A country. 3 A year. e

प्रेक्षा *f* (नृत्येक्षणं प्रज्ञा) — 1 Dancing. 2 View. f

भिक्षा *f* (सेवा ऽर्थना भृतिः) — 1 Service. 2 Begging. 3 Hire, wages. g

227. त्विट् [1] *f* (शोभा ऽपि) — Splendour. h

(त्रिषु परे) i

न्यक्षं *m f n* (कार्त्स्न्येऽनिकृष्टयोः) — 1 Entire. 2 Inferior.

(प्रत्यक्षे ऽधिकृते) ऽध्यक्षो *m f n* — 1 Perceptible. 2 Superintendent.

रूक्ष *m f n* (स्त्वप्रेम्ण्यचिक्कणे) — 1 Unfriendly. 2 Rough.

1—षृ.

a Also 3 Semen. m. f. n. 4 Measured by the human stature, or by the height to which a man reaches. b Likewise 2 Poison. f.—षा. 3 A plant (sort of Betula ?) c Also 2 Flesh. 3 Food. d Likewise 2 Disease. e Also 4 A cloud. f. pl. वर्षाः. 5 Rainy season. f Or 3 Viewing an exhibition of dancing. 4 Intellect. g Likewise 4 Alms. h Also 2 Ray of light. i The following admit the three genders.

SECTION XXVI.

1 The sun. 2 A goose. a — 228. (रविश्वेतच्छदौ) हंसौ [m]

1 The sun. 2 Fire. — (सूर्यवह्नी) विभावसू [1 m]

1 A calf. 2 A year. b — वत्सौ [m] (तर्णकवर्षौ द्वौ)

A bird: Cuculus. c — (सारङ्गाश्च) दिवौकसः [2 m d]

1 Taste or sentiment in dramas. e — 229. (शृङ्गारादौ विषे वीर्ये गुणे रागे द्रवे) रसः [m]

1 An earring. 2 A crest. — (पुंस्युत्तंसा) उत्तंसा [m n] ऽवतंसौ [m n f] (द्वौ कर्णपूरे ऽपि शेखरे)

1 A class of deities. 2 Fire. g — 230. (देवभेदे ऽनले रश्मौ) वसू [3 m] (रत्ने धने) वसु [n]

1—सु. 2—सृ. 3—सु.

[a] Likewise 3 VISHNU. 4 The Supreme Being. 5 The soul. 6 Breath. 7 A sort of ascetic life. 8 A person devoid of covetousness. 9 Unenvious. 10 A king. 11 The horse sacrificed by YUD'HISH'THIRA. [b] Also 3 An endearing appellation of a son or grand-child. n. 4 The breast. [c] Likewise 2 A god. 3 A bee. 4 An antilope. [d] दिवोकाः: or दिवौकाः. [e] Amatory, heroic, tender, pathetic, &c. And 2 Poison, or 3 Water. 4 Semen virile, or 5 Quicksilver. 6 Quality of taste; savour, as sweet, sour, &c. 7 Zeal, ardour, passion. 8 Juice, a liquid. 9 Juices of the body. 10 Myrrh. f. 11 The tongue. 12 The earth. [f] Or वतंस. [g] And 3 A ray of light. Or 4 A rein, or halter. n. 5 A gem. 6 Wealth. Also 7 Gold. m. 8 Tie of the yoke. 9 A plant (*Bakapushpa*).

(विष्णौ च) वेधाः [1 *m*]	VISHNU. a
(स्त्रीत्वा) शी (र्हिताशंसा ऽहिदंष्ट्रयोः) [2 *f*]	1 Benediction. 2 Fang of a serpent.
231. लालसे (प्रार्थनौत्सुक्ये) [3 *f*]	1 Request. b
हिंसा (चौर्य्यादिकर्म्म च) [*f*]	Injury, mischief, as robbery, &c. c
प्रसू (रश्वापि) [*f*]	A mare. d
(भूद्यावौ) रोदस्यौ रोदसी (च ते) [4 *f*, 5 *n*]	Earth and sky. e
232. (ज्वालाभासोर्नपुंस्य) ऽर्चिर् [6 *fn*]	1 Flame. 2 Light.
ज्योतिर् (भद्योतदृष्टिषु) [7 *n*]	1 A star. 2 Light. 3 Pupil of the eye. f
(पापापराधयोर्) आगः [8 *n*]	1 Sin. 2 An offence.
(खगबाल्यादिनोर्) वयः [9 *n*]	1 A bird. 2 Age. g
233. (तेजः पुरीषयोर्) वर्चो [10 *n*]	1 Splendour. 2 Ordure. h
महस् (तूत्सवतेजसोः) [*n* i]	1 A festival. 2 Light.
रजो (गुणे स्त्रीपुष्पे च) [11 *n* k]	1 Quality of passion. 2 Woman's menses. j

1—स्. 2 आशीस्. 3—सा. 4—सी. 5—स्. 6—स्. 7—स्. 8—स्. 9—स्. 10—स् 11—स्.

[a] Also 2 BRAMHA. 3 Intelligent, wise. [b] Likewise 3 Thirst, desire. [c] Also 2 Slaughter. [d] Likewise 2 A mother. [e] And 2 The earth. 3 The sky. Collectively, dual; severally, singular. Ex. रोदः. [f] Also m. 4 The sun. 5 Fire. [g] Likewise 3 Youth. [h] Also 3 Colour. [i] Or m. महः (ह). Likewise 3 Dust. 4 Farina of flowers, pollen. [k] Or m. रजः (ज).

1 Moon's ascending node. 2 Darkness. [a] — (राहौ ध्वान्ते गुणे) तमः [n]

1 Poetical metre. 2 Desire. [b] — 234. छन्दः [n] (पद्ये ऽभिलाषे च)

Austerity, penance. [c] — तपः [n] (कृच्छ्रादिकर्म च)

1 Strength. 2 Month of *Agrahá'yana*. [d] — सहो [1 n] (बलं) सहा [1 m] (मार्गो)

1 The sky. [e] — नभः [2 n] (खं श्रावणो) नभाः [2 m]

1 A house. [f] — 235. ओकः [n g] (सद्माऽश्रयश्चौ) काः [3 m]

1 Milk. 2 Water. — पयः [n] (क्षीरं) पयो [n] (ऽम्बु च)

1 Splendour. 2 Strength. — ओजो [n h] (दीप्तौ बले)

1 Organ of sense. 2 Stream of a river. — स्रोत [4 n i] (इन्द्रिये निम्नगारये)

1 Dignity. 2 Splendour. 3 Strength. [j] — 236. तेजः [n] (प्रभावे दीप्तौ च बले शुक्रे ऽप्य)

(ऽतस्त्रिषु) [k]

1—स्. 2—स्. 3—ओकस्. 4—स्.

[a] And 3 The third quality, according to the *Sán'khya* system of philosophy : darkness or illusion, contrasted to truth and passion. 4 Grief. [b] Also 3 The *Véda*. 4 Uncontrolled conduct. Likewise, in the second acceptation, छन्दं(न्द्). [c] Also 2 Virtue, moral merit. 3 One of the superior worlds. m. तपाः (स्). 4 The month of *Mágha*. 5 The cold season. [d] सहः (—स्) or सहं (ह्). 1 Strength. And m. सहाः (स्) or सहः (ह्). 2 The month of *Agrahàyana*. Also 3 The winter. n. 4 A luminary. [e] And m. 2 The month of *Srávan'a*. 3 Rain. 4 A cloud. [f] And m. 2 An asylum. [g] Or ओकं. [h] Or ओजं. [i] Or स्रोतं. [j] And 4 Semen virile. [k] The following admit the three genders.

1 *m f n* विद्वान् (विद्दंश्च)	Intelligent. [a]
m f n बीभत्सो (हिंस्रो ऽप्य्) (अतिशये त्वमी)	Mischievous, cruel. [b]
2 *m f n* [c] (वृद्धप्रशस्यवोर्) ज्यायान्	1 Very old. 2 Very excellent.
3 *m f n* [d] कनीयाँश्च (युवाल्पयो:)	1 Very young. 2 Very small.
4 *m f n* [e] वरीयाँ (स्थूलवरयो:)	1 Very great. 2 Very excellent.
5 *m f n* [f] साधीयान् (साधुबाढयो:)	1 Very right. 2 Very firm.

SECTION XXVII.

238. (दले ऽपि) *m n* बर्हं	A leaf. [g]
(निर्बन्धोपरागार्कादयो) *m* ग्रहा:	1 Seizure. 2 An eclipse. 3 A planet. [h]

---

1 विद्वस. 2 ज्यायस्. 3—यस्. 4—यस्. 5—यस्.

[a] Also 2 Learned. 3 Having a true knowledge of the soul. [b] Likewise 2 Envious. n. 3 Arjuna. Fem. बीभत्सा. [c] Fem. ज्यायसी. [d] Fem. कनीयसी. [e] Fem. वरीयसी. [f] Fem. साधीयसी. [g] Or 2 Retinue. 3 A peacock's tail. [h] Also 4 The moon's node. 5 Seizure, caption. 6 Effort in battle 7 A class of imps.

1 A door. 2 A chaplet. a — (द्वार्यापीडे क्वाथरसे) निर्यूहो (नागदन्तके) *m*

1 The string suspending a balance. b — 239. (तुलासूत्रे ऽश्वादिरश्मौ) प्रग्राहः *m* प्रग्रहो *m* (ऽपि च)

1 A wife. 2 Family; dependent. c — (पत्नीपरिजनादानमूलशापाः) परिग्रहाः *m*

A wife. d — 240. (दारेष्वपि) गृहाः *m pl.*

A woman's waist. e — (श्रोण्यामप्या) रोहो *1 m* (वरस्त्रियाः)

A multitude. f — व्यूहो *m* (वृन्दे ऽप्य्)

The demon *Vritra*. g — अहि *m* (र्वृत्रे ऽप्य्)

1 Fire. 2 The moon. 3 The sun. h — (अग्नीन्द्वर्कास्) तमोपहाः *m*

1 Retinue. 2 Insignia of Royalty. i — 241. (परिच्छदे नृपार्हे ऽर्थे) परिबर्हो *m*

(ऽव्ययाः परे) j

---

1 वा—.

a Or 3 A piece of wood jutting out of a wall. 4 Extracted juice. 5 Wood placed in a wall (for doves to build nests on). b And 2 A rein or halter for horses, &c. 3 Prisoners. 4 Restraint. 5 An arm. 6 A ray of light. c And 3 Acceptance. 4 Origin; or 5 Root. 6 Oath; or 7 Quarrel. Also 8 The sun near the moon's node. d And 2 A house. Invariably plural; but in the 2d acceptation also neuter sing. e Likewise 2 Ascent as a climbing plant. 3 Rider of an elephant or horse. 4 Length. 5 Height. f Likewise 2 Array of troops. 3 Fabrication. 4 Reasoning. g Also 2 A serpent. h Likewise 4 A deified saint or prophet. i Or 3 A thing. j The following are indeclinable.

SECTION XXXIII.

INDECLINABLES.

1. आङ्[b] (ईषदर्थेऽभिव्याप्तौ सीमार्थे धातुयोगजे) — 1 A little. 2 Untill. a

आ[d] (प्रगृह्यः स्मृतौ वाक्येऽप्य्) — 1 Oh (remembering). c

आस्(तु स्यात्कोपपीडयोः) — 1 Ah! (angrily). 2 Alas (sorrowfully).

2. (पापकुत्सेषदर्थे) कु — 1 Sinful. 2 Bad. 3 A little.

धिङ्[1] (निर्भर्त्सननिन्दयोः) — 1 Fy! (menacingly). 2 Fy! (reproachfully.)

च[2] (ऽन्वाचये समाहारेतरेतरसमुच्चये) — 1 Moreover. 2 And. 3 Mutually. 4 Also. e

3. स्वस्त्या[3] (शीः क्षेमपुण्यादौ) — 1 Well (a benidiction.) 2 Safe. f

---

1 धिक्. 2 च. 3 स्वस्ति:

[a] Including the limit. Or 3 Exclusive of the bound or limit. 4 Preposition joined to verbs, and altering their sense, or giving intensity to it. [b] आ (for the final consonant is expunged). [c] And 2 But (indicating a change). 3 And (collective). [d] Unalterable in orthography even before vowels. [e] In the first acceptation, the particle connects a secondary with a primary object; in the second it conjoins equal objects; in the third it indicates reciprocation: in the fourth it connects different acts with the same subject. It has other acceptations, as 5 But, (indicating a converse proposition). 6 But (excusingly). 7 Forthwith. 8 Expletive. [f] And 3 Right. 4 Auspicious.

1 Very.
2 Surpassing.

(प्रकर्षे लंघने ऽप्यु) ऽति

1 What ? (interrogative).
2 (Doubtingly).

स्वित् (प्रश्ने च वितर्के च)

1 But (indicating difference).
2 Indeed. a

तु (स्याद्भेदे ऽवधारणे)

1 Together.
2 Once. b

4. सकृत् (सहैकवारे स्याद्)

1 Far.
2 Near.

आराद्[1] (दूरसमीपयोः)

1 Westward.
2 Behind.

(प्रतीच्यां चरमे) पश्चाद्[2]

1 Also.
2 What ? c

उता[3] (प्यर्थविकल्पयोः)

1 Again, often.
2 Always. d

5. (पुनः सदार्थयोः) शश्वत्[e]

1 In presence, before.
2 As, like.

साक्षात् (प्रत्यक्षतुल्ययोः)

1 Also !
(Sorrow).
2 (Compassion). f

(खेदानुकम्पासन्तोषविस्मयामन्त्रणे) बत

1 Oh (joy).
2 (Pity).
3 (Inceptive).
4 Alas ! g

6. हन्त (हर्षे ऽनुकम्पायां वाक्यारम्भविषादयोः)

1 Instead.
2 Each, respectively.
3 Towards. b

प्रति (प्रतिनिधौ वीप्सालक्षणादौ प्रयोगतः)

1—द्. 2—द्. 3 उत or उत्.

a Also 3 And. 4 Again. 5 Expletive. b Likewise. 3 Always. c Interrogatively. 3 What ! doubtingly. 4 Either, or 5 Expletive. d Or 3 Together. 4 Perpetually. e Or सश्वत्. f And 3 Indicating joy. 4 Indicating surprise. 5 Oh ! (vocative). g Also 5 Certainly ; indeed. 6 Gift. Ex. हन्तकारः, generous. h Likewise 4 For. 5 Belonging to (as a portion). 6 In exchange. 7 A little.

7. इति (हेतुप्रकरणप्रकर्षादिसमाप्तिषु)	1 Therefore. 2 Thus. [a]
(प्राच्यां) पुरस्तात्[b] (प्रथमे पुरार्थे ऽग्रत इत्यपि)	1 Eastward. 2 Prior, first. 3 Formerly. 4 In front.
8. यावत्[1] तावत् (च साकल्ये ऽवधौ माने ऽवधारणे)	1 As much as (the whole). 2 Until. [c]
(मङ्गलानन्तरारम्भप्रश्नकार्त्स्न्येष्व्) अथो अथ	1 Auspicious particle. 2 After. [d]
9. वृथा (निरर्थकाविध्योर्)	1 In vain. 2 Wrong.
नाना (ऽनेकोभयार्थयोः)	1 Many. 2 Both. [e]
नु (पृच्छायां विकल्पे च)	1 What? (interrogative). 2 Or. [f]
(पश्चात्सादृश्ययोर्) अनु	1 After. 2 Like. [g]
10. (प्रश्नावधारणानुज्ञा ऽनुनयामन्त्रणे) ननु	1 Interrogative particle. [h]

1—षु.

[a] Indicating a sort or set. 3 So : well known as such. 4 Etcœtera. 5 Even so : exactly thus. 6 Indicating the preceding sound to be meant. 7 Indicating the sense to be intended. 8 So ; of this opinion. 9 Finis : marking a close. 10 So ; of this form. [b] Or पुरः (स). [c] And 3 As many as (number). 4 As many as there are. 5 So much (affirmative). [d] And 3 Now (inceptive). 4 What ? (interrogatively). 5 All (comprehensively). 6 Now (premising). 7 Imperative particle. 8 And. [e] Also 3 Without, except. [f] Likewise 3 An indication of doubt. [g] Also 3 Along. 4 Under, inferior to. 5 With. 6 Near. 7 Towards. 8 In regard to. 9 A share. 10 Severally, respectively. [h] And 2 Certainly. 3 Indicating assent. 4 A consolatory and kind expression. 5 Vocative particle. 6 A conciliatory vocative particle. 7 Inceptive. 8 Reproachful. 9 Responsive.

1 Reprehensive particle. a	(गर्हासमुच्चयप्रश्नशङ्कासम्भावनास्व्) ऽपि
1 As, like. 2 Or, either. b	11. (उपमायां विकल्पे) वा c
1 Half. 2 Blamably.	सामि (त्वर्द्धे जुगुप्सने)
1 With, together. 2 Near.	अमा (सह समीपे च)
1 Water. 2 Head. d	कम् (वारिणी च मूर्द्धि च)
1 Like, as. 2 Thus. e	12. (इवेत्थमर्थयोर्) एवं
1 Perhaps. 2 Certainly. f	नूनं (तर्के ऽर्थनिश्चये)
1 Silently. 2 At ease.	(तूष्णीमर्थे सुखे) जोषं
1 What ? (interrogative). Bad ; ill. g	(किम् पृच्छायां जुगुप्सने)
1 Evidently. 2 Possibly. h	13. नाम (प्रकाश्यसम्भाव्यक्रोधोपगमकुत्सने)
1 Ornament. 2 Enough. 3 Able. i	अलम् (भूषणपर्य्याप्तिशक्तिवारणवाचकम्)

---

[a] And 3 Interrogative particle. 4 Earnest inquiry. 5 Doubt, or suspicion. 6 Possibility and likelihood. 7 Pursuit or seeking. 8 Corroborative of an affirmation. 9 Even. 10 Although. [b] Likewise 3 And. 4 Expletive. 5 Only ; no other. 6 Indication of doubt and consideration. [c] More properly वा. [d] Also 3 Ill ; bad. 4 Ease, pleasure. 5 Expletive. [e] Also 3 Indicative of consent. 4 Certainly. 5 Command. [f] Likewise 3 Indicating recollection. 4 Expletive. [g] Also 3 Indicating doubt or consideration. 4 Prohibition. [h] Or 3 Indicating recollection. 4 Wrath. 5 Indignant consent. 6 Reproach. 7 Pretence. 8 Surprise. [i] And 4 Prohibition. Also 5 Uselessness.

14. हुम् (वितर्के परिप्रश्ने) — 1 Indicative of doubt and reflection. a

समया (ऽन्तिकमध्ययोः) — 1 Near. 2 Within, midst.

पुनर् (अप्रथमे भेदे) — 1 Again. 2 But, on the contrary. b

निर् (निश्चयनिषेधयोः) — 1 Certainly. 2 Negation.

15. (स्यात्प्रबन्धे चिरातीते निकटागामिके) पुरा — 1 Ancient story. 2 Old. 3 Past. c

ऊरर्य्युरी[1 2d] (चो) ररी[3] (च विस्तारे ऽङ्गीकृतौ त्रयम्) — 1 Expansion. 2 Assent.

16. (स्वर्गे परे च लोके) स्वर् — 1 Heaven. 2 The next world. e

(वार्त्तासम्भाव्ययोः) किल — 1 News : so reported. 2 Probably. f

(निषेधवाक्यालङ्कारजिज्ञासानुनये) खलु — 1 Prohibition. 2 Expletive. g

17. (समीपोभयतः शीघ्रसाकल्याभिमुखे) ऽभितः[4] — 1 Near. 2 Both. 3 Quickly. 4 Entirely. 5 In front.

(नामप्रकाशयोः) प्रादुर्[5] — 1 Name. 2 Appearance.

मिथो[6] (ऽन्योऽन्यं रहस्यपि) — 1 Mutually. 2 In private.

18. तिरो[7] (ऽन्तर्द्धौ तिर्य्यगर्थे) — 1 Concealment. 2 Awry. h

---

1 ऊररी. 2 उरी. 3 उररी. 4 —तस्. 5 —स्.
6 मिथस्. 7 तिरस्.

a And 2 Interrogative particle. 3 Yes. 4 Indicating fear. 5 Wrath 6 Aversion, dislike. 7 Reaproach. b Also 3 Indicating change of subject. c Or 4 Long since past. 5 Near. 6 Future. Or 7 Proximate future. d Or उरी. Also उररी. e Also the sky or atmosphere. f Likewise 3 Conciliatory expression. 4 Indeed. 5 Falsely indicating displeasure. g And 3 Indicating inquiry. 4 A conciliatory expression. 5 Indeed, certainly. h Also 3 Contempt, disregard.

1 Alas ! (sorrow). 2 (Regret).

हा (विषादशुगर्त्तिषु)

1 Indication of wonder. 2 Of pain or fatigue.

1

अहहे (त्यद्भुते खेदे)

1 Because, for. 2 Indeed. a

हि (हेतावधारणे)

CHAPTER V.

Long time.

i b *i* 2 *i*

1. चिराय चिररात्राय चिरस्या (द्याश्चिरार्थकाः)

Again and again ; frequently.

3 *i* 4 *i* 5 *i* 6 *i* c 7 *i*

मुहुः पुनःपुनः शश्वदभीक्ष्णमसकृत् (समाः)

Soon ; instantly.

8 *i* 9 *i* 10 *i* *i* *i* 11 *i* *i* d

2. स्रागझटित्यञ्जसा ऽह्नाय सपदि द्राङ्मंक्षु (च द्रुते)

Much ; very.

i *i* 12 *i* 13 *i* 14 *i*

बलवत् सुष्ठु किमुत सु ऽत्यतीव (च निर्भरे)

Without ; except.

15 *i* 16 *i* *i* e 17 *i* 18 *i* 19 *i*

3. पृथग्विना ऽन्तरेणर्त्ते हिरुङ्नाना (च वर्ज्जने)

1—ह or —हा. 2—स्या. 3—मु. 4—र्. 5—श्.
6 अ—. 7 अ—. 8—क्. 9—ति. 10 अ—.
11—क्. 12 सु. 13 अति. 14 अ—. 15—क्.
16 विना. 17 ऋते. 18—क् 19 नाना.

[a] Likewise 3 Interrogative. 4 Expletive. 5 Indicating difference. [b] Also चिरं, चिरेण, चिरात्, चिरे. [c] This term is also declinable. [d] One adds, but erroneously, मंक्षु. [e] Also अन्तरा.

i i i i यत्तद्यतस्ततो (हेतौ)	Because; therefore. a
1 i 2 i (असाकल्ये तु) चिच्चन	Some. b
3 i 4 i 4. कदाचिज्जातु	Sometimes.
i ic i i id सार्धं (तु) साकं सत्रा समं सह	Together with.
i (आनुकूल्यार्थकं) प्राध्वं	Conformity.
i ie (व्यर्थके तु) वृथा मुधा	In vain.
if i i i 5i 6i 5. आहो उताहो किमुत (विकल्पे) किं किमूत च	Either, or (indicating deliberation).
i i i i i i तु हि च स्म ह वै (पादपूरणे)	Expletives.
7i 8i (पूजने) स्वति	Particles of praise and reverence.
i 6. दिवा (ऽह्नीत्य्)	By day. g
i i (ऽथ) दोषा (च) नक्तं (च रजनाविति)	By night.
ih 9i (तिर्यगर्थे) साचि तिरो (ऽप्य्)	Crooked, bent; awry.
(ऽथसम्बोधनार्थकाः	Vocative particles.

1—त्. 2 च—. 3—त्. 4 जा—. 5 किम्. 6 उत. 7 सु. 8 अति. 9 तिरस्.

a Correlatives; यत्, यतः or येन, because, तत्, ततः, तेन, therefore. b In composition with the pronoun किम् and its derivatives. Ex. किञ्चित्, something; कश्चन, somebody; a certain person. c One commentator adds साकं; but erroneously. d Also सजूः (—जुष्). e Some read बृथा. f Or अहो. Also आहोस्वित् and उताहोस्वित्. g Likewise the day, generally. h This term is also declinable and is fem.

i 1i 2i i i i

7. स्युः) प्याट् पाडङ्ग हे है भोः

i i i

1 Near. 2 Midst. a — समया निकषा हिरुक्

i

Inconsiderately, suddenly. — (अतर्किते तु) सहसा

3i 3i 3i

Before, in front. — (स्यात्) पुरः पुरतो ऽग्रतः

ic 4i i i

Oblations to the gods or manes. b — 8. स्वाहा (देवहविर्दाने) श्रौषट् वौषट् वषट् स्वधा

5i 6i 7i

A little. — किञ्चिदीषन्मनाक् (अल्पे)

8i i

In the next life. — प्रेत्या ऽमुत्र (भवान्तरे)

9id i i 10i 11i12i e

As, like. — 9. वद्वा यथातथैवैवं (साम्ये)

i i

Ah! (indicating surprise). — ऽहो ही (च विस्मये)

i i

Silently. — (मौने तु) तूष्णीं तूष्णीकां

i i

Instantly. — सद्यस् सपदि (तत्क्षणे)

i 13i if

Indication of joy. — 10. दिष्ट्याथमुपजोषं (चेत्यानन्दे)

i i

Between; amidst. — (स्यात्) ऽन्तरे ऽन्तरा

---

1 पाट्. 2 वङ्ग. 3—स्. 4—ट्. 5—त्. 6 इषत्.
7—क्. 8—म्. 9 वा. 10 तथा. 11 इव. 12 एवं. 13 स.

a The terms are synonymous in both acceptations. b The terms are used as invocations with such offerings: the first peculiar to an oblation presented to a god; the last to one offered to the manes. Ex. इन्द्राय स्वाहा, this oblation to Indra. पितृभ्यःस्वधा, this oblation to the manes. c In a different acceptation this term is declinable and fem. B. II. Ch. 7. v. 21. d वत. One commentator reads व. e Also एव. f Also समुपजोषं. Some read जपयोषं.

i

अन्तरेण (च मध्ये स्युः)

i

प्रसह्य (तु हठार्थकम्) Forcibly, violently.

i i

11. (युक्ते द्वे) साम्प्रतं स्थाने Properly.

i 1 i

ऽभीक्ष्णं शश्वद् (अनारते) Continually, perpetually.

2 i 3 i i a 4 i

(अभावे) नह्यनो ना (ऽपि) No, not.

i i i

मास्म मा ऽलं (च वारणे) Negative and prohibitive.

5 i 6 i

12. (पक्षान्तरे) चेद्यदि (च) If.

i i

(तत्त्वे त्व) ऽद्धा ऽञ्जसा (द्वयम्) Truly.

7 i 8 i

(प्राकाश्ये) प्रादुराविः (स्यात्) Apparent.

9 i 10 i i b

ओमेवं परमं (मते) Yes.

i i i 11 i c

13. समन्ततस् (तु) परितः सर्व्वतो विष्वग् (इत्यपि) Every way; all around.

(अकामानुमतौ) कामम् Willingly. d

i

(अस्तूयोपगमे) ऽस्तु (च) Be it so. e

1—द्. 2 नहि. 3 अ. 4 न, or ना. 5 चेत्. 6 यदि.
7—स्. 8 आविस्. 9—म्. 10 एवं. 11 क्. (ष्.)

a नो or अनो Also अन. b Likewise आं. c Also विश्वतः, समन्तात्, &c.
d Implying previous disinclination, but ultimate acquiescence. Also, according to a different reading, 2 Willing compliance; and (synonymous with the next.) 3 Acquiescing with reluctance. e Implying regret in the acknowledgment or acquiescence.

Indicating contradiction. — 14. ननु[i a] च (स्याद्विरोधोक्तौ)

Introductory of a kind question.[b] — कच्चित्[i] (कामप्रवेदने)

Improperly; unseasonably. — निःषमन्[i] दुःषमं[i] (गर्ह्ये)

As thereto appertaining. — यथास्वं[i] (तु) यथायथम्[i]

Falsely. — 15. मृषा[i] मिथ्या[i] (च वितथे)

Properly, suitably. — यथार्थं[i] (तु) यथायथम्[i]

Indeed. — (स्युर्) एवं[i] तु[i] पुनर्[1 i] वै[2 i] वे[3 i c] (त्यवधारणवाचकाः)

Before; anterior. — 16 प्राग्[4 i] (अतीतार्थकं)

Certainly; necessarily. — नूनम्[i] अवश्यं[5 i] (निश्चये द्वयम्)

A year. — सम्वद्[6 i] (वर्षे)

Former, prior. — (ऽवरे त्व) ऽर्वाग्[7 i]

Assent, consent, promise. — आम्[8 i] एवं[9 i]

Self; of himself. — स्वयम्[i] (आत्मना)

Little; low. — 17. (अल्पे) नीचैः[10 i]

Great; high, load. — (महत्यु) च्चैः[11 i]

Frequently; generally. — प्रायो[12 i] (भूम्नि)

Slowly. — (अद्रुते) शनैः[i]

1—र्. 2 वै. 3 वा. 4—क्. (च). 5 अ—. 6—द्. 7—क् (च). 8 आं. 9 एवं. 10—स्. 11 उच्चैस्. 12—स्.

[a] Or ननु. [b] Wishing that it may be so. [c] Or, according to another reading, एव and च.

सना[i a] (नित्ये)	Perpetually, ever.
बहिर्[1 i] (बाह्ये)	External; out.
स्म[2] (ऽतीते)	Formerly.[b]
ऽस्तम्[i] (अदर्शने)	Disappearance.
18. अस्ति[i] (सत्त्वे)	Present; now, being.
(रुषोक्ताव्) उम्[i]	Interjection, expressive of wrath.
उं[i] (प्रश्ने)	Interrogative particle.
(ऽनुनयेत्व्) ऽयि[i]	Encouraging vocative.[c]
हुं[i d] (तर्के स्यात्)	Particle indicating reflection.
उषा[i e] (रात्रेरवसाने)	Close of the night; morn, break of day.
नमो[3 i] (नतौ)	Hail! salutation; bow.
19. (पुनरर्थे) ऽङ्ग[i]	Again.[f]
(निन्दायां) दुष्टु[i]	Ill.
सुष्टु[i] (प्रशंसने)	Well.
सायं[4 i] (साये)	Evening, close of the day.
प्रगे[i] प्रातः[5 i] (प्रभाते)	Morning.
निकषा[i] (ऽन्तिके)	Near.

1—स्. 2 स्. 3—स्. 4—स्. 5—र्.

[a] Also सनात्. and सनत्. [b] This particle, indicating past time, converts the present tense into the preterite. [c] Some say, indicating anger also. [d] Also हूं. Some read हु. [e] Likewise उषः (स्). [f] Implying, however, a difference: "the rather."

Last year; penult. and present years. a	20. परुत्[i] परार्य्य[i] ऐषमो[i] (ऽब्दे पूर्व्वे पूर्व्वतरे यति)
To-day.	अद्य[1 i] (ऽत्राह्नि)
A former day, &c. b	(ऽथ पूर्व्वे ऽह्नीत्यादौ पूर्व्वोत्तरापरात्
	21. तथा ऽधरा ऽन्या ऽन्यतरे ऽतरात्) पूर्व्वेद्युर्[i] (आदयः)
Both days. c	उभयद्यु[2 i] (श्चो) भयेद्युः[3 i]
Next day.	(परे त्वह्नि) परेद्यवि
Yesterday.	22. ह्यो[4 i] (गते)
To-morrow.	(ऽनागते ऽह्नि) श्वः[5 i]
The day after to-morrow.	परश्वस्[i d] (तत्परे ऽहनि)
Then, at that time.	तदा[i] तदानीं[i]
At once; at the same time.	युगपद्[6 i] एकदा[7 i]
Always; at all times.	सर्व्वदा सदा[i]

1 अद्य. 2 उ—स्. 3—स्. 4—स्. 5—स्. 6—त्. 7—त्.

[a] परुत्, last year; परारि, year before the last; ऐषमः (स्), current year. [b] पूर्व्वेद्युः, a former day; yesterday. उत्तरेद्युः, a subsequent day; to-morrow. अपरेद्युः, another day; the day after to-morrow. अधरेद्युः, a past day; the day before yesterday. अन्येद्युः, another day. अन्यतरेद्युः, either day; one of two days. इतरेद्युः, a different day. [c] The past day and the day to come. [d] परश्वः or परःश्वः (—स्).

i 1i i 2i i
23. एतर्हि सम्प्रतीदानीमधुना साम्प्रतं (तथा) — Now; at this time.
3i 4i 5i
(दिग्देशकाले पूर्वादौ) प्रागुदक्प्रत्यग् (आदय:) — East, North, West, &c. [a]

CHAPTER VI.

SECTION I.

1. सलिङ्गशास्त्रैः सन्नादिकृत्तद्धितसमासजैः
अनुक्तैः संग्रहे लिङ्गं सङ्कीर्णवदिहोन्नयेत्

1—र्ति. इ—म्. 2 श—. 3—क् (च्). 4 उ—च्. 5—क् (च).

[a] प्राक् (च्) the east; from or in the east: or eastern (country). or prior time. उदक् (च्), North; northern, or subsequent. प्रत्यक् (च्,) West, western, or subsequent. Besides other terms, as अपाक् (च्) South: Southern or former. दक्षिणात्—णतः—णेन, Southward. उत्तरात्—रतः—रेण, Northward. अधरात्—रतः—रेण—स्तात्, underneath. पुरस्तात्, before. उपरि उपरिष्टात्, above. पश्चात्, behind.

The following are feminine, viz. Monosyllables in ई or ऊ. a

2. लिङ्गशेषविधिर्व्यापी विशेषैर्यद्यबाधितः

स्त्रियामीदूद्विरामैकाच्

Names of female beings. b

सयोनिप्राणिनाम च

Terms signifying lightning. c

3. नाम विद्युन्निशावल्लीवीणादिग्भूनदीह्रियां

A compound in अ with a numeral. d

अदन्तैर्द्विगुरेकार्थो न स पात्रयुगादिभिः

A noun ending in the affixes तल्, &c.

4. तल्वृन्दे ये निकव्यता वैरमैथुनकादिवुन्

---

[a] Example, श्रीः, prosperity. भ्रूः, eyebrow. [b] Except कलत्रं and क्षत्रं, neut. and दाराः masc. pl. signifying a wife. [c] Viz. lightning; night; any creeping plant; a lute; (some read वाणी, speech;) space, quarter; earth; river; modesty (some read धी intellect). [d] Provided the sense be singular (Ex. त्रिलोकी, the aggregate of three worlds;) except such compound term, formed with the words पात्रं, युगः, &c. (Ex. चतुर्युगं, Total of four ages). [e] Viz. तल्, which imports state of being, and multitude, or is pleonastic, (Ex. देवता, God, deity): य, इनि, काच्य् and त्र signifying multitude, as पाश्या assemblage of chains or bonds; पद्मिनी, a pond (abounding in lotuses); रथकड्या, a crowd of carriages; गोत्रा, a herd of kine: वुन्, (or वु with वुञ् or वुच्, all convertible into अक, and finally into इका;) signifying enmity, nuptial union, &c. (including the distributive import, and gift and amercement). Ex. काकोलूकिका, enmity of crows and owls.

स्त्रीभावादावनिक्तिन्ण्वुज्ण्यच्यप्युजिञक्शयाः । Or in अनि, &c. a

5. उणादिषु निरूरीश् । Or in certain *un'ádi* affixes. b

ङ्याबूङन्तं चरं स्थिरम् । Or in a feminine termination. c

तत्क्रीडायां प्रहरणं चेन्मौष्टा पाल्लवा णदिक् । Or in ण, &c. d

---

[a] Nouns ending in these eleven affixes, which import the state of being, &c. are feminine : viz. अनि, signifying an imprecation. क्तिन् (ति) for the abstract sense (Ex. स्मृतिः, recollection) : ण्वुन् (convertible into इका) denominating a disease ; or implying the import of the verb (as जीविका, livelihood) ; also ण्वुच् ; णच् (आ ई) implying reciprocity ; as व्यावक्रोशी, mutual imprecation : क्यप् (या) conveying the abstract sense ; as ब्रह्महत्या, sacrilege : युच् (अना) with the abstract sense ; as कल्पना, decoration : इञ् (इ) indicating question and reply : अङ् (आ आ) for the abstract sense ; Ex. पचा, cookery : नि with the abstract import ; Ex. ग्लानिः, fatigue : स also in the abstract sense ; as चिकीर्षा, desire to act : (but some omit this affix ; others interpose it after क्यप्, others transpose some of the latter affixes :) श (आ आ) with the same abstract import : Ex. क्रिया, action. [b] Viz. नि ; as श्रेणिः, a string or row. Some read अनिः ; as अवनिः, the earth ; ऊ as चमू, an army. ई as लक्ष्मी, prosperity. [c] Terminated by an affix denoting the feminine gender (ङी, आप् or ऊङ्) whether the noun signify any thing locomotive or fixed, or whether it vary the gender, or be ristricted to the feminine. [d] Indicating play in which the thing is used as a weapon. Ex. मौष्टा, boxing, playing at fisty cuff.

Or in ञ following घञ. a

6\. घञोऽञः सा क्रियास्यां चेद्दाण्डपाता हि फाल्गुनी

श्यैनम्पाता च मृगया तैलम्पाता स्वधेति दिक्

Diminutives. b

7\. स्त्री स्यात्काचिन्मृणाल्यादिर्विवक्षाऽपचये यदि

And the particular nouns here enumerated. b

c d e f g 1h

लङ्का शेफालिका टीका धातकी पञ्जिकाढकी

i j k l 2m n

8\. सिध्मका सारिका हिक्का प्राचिकोल्का पिपीलिका

o p q r s 3t

तिन्दुकी कणिका भङ्गिः सुरङ्गा सूचि माढयः

u v 4w x y z aa

9\. पिच्छावितण्डाकाकिण्यश्चूर्णिः शाणी द्रुणी दरत्

---

[1] धा—. [2] छु—. [3] माढि. [4] णी or नी.

[a] And implying, that such act takes place at such time or in such circumstance. Ex. श्येनपाताऽत्र मृगया. [b] Formed by giving the feminine termination to a masculine noun : as मृणाली, a small fibre of a water lily. [c] The city of the name. [d] Nyctanthes arbortristis. [e] A commentary : annotations. [f] Grislea tomentosa. [g] 1 A perpetual commentary. 2 A book of accounts ; a journal. 3 A calendar or almanac. [h] Cytisus Cajan. [i] The plant. [j] A sort of bird : Turdus Salica, Buch. MS. [k] Hiccough. [l] A sort of bird : others say, a gadfly. [m] A firebrand. [n] An ant. [o] Diospyros melanoxylon. [p] 1 An atom. 2 A spark. [q] 1 Fracture. 2 Deception. 3 Wave. 4 Irony. [r] A winding hole in the ground, a mine ; an opening by sap, such as house-breakers make. [s] A needle. [t] The gem of leaves ; young leaves undisplayed. [u] Gum of the Bombax heptaphyllum. 2 Scum of boiled rice, &c. [v] Criticising. [w] The quarter of a *pana* ; some say of a *máshá*. [x] चूर्णिः or चूर्णी, selection of an unanswerable argument. [y] 1 A grindstone. 2 A curtain made of rushy Crotalaria. [z] A centipede. [aa] A tribe of barbarians.

a b 1c d e
साति कन्था(तथा)सन्दी नाभी राजसभा(ऽपि च)
f g h i j k
10. झल्लरी चर्चरी पारी होरा लट्वा (च) सिध्मला
l m n o p q
लाक्षा लिक्षा (च) गण्डूषा गृध्रसी चमसी मसी

---

1 ष—.

[a] Extreme pain. 2 Destruction. [b] A rug: a quilt of rags. [c] A small bed or couch; a chair, or stool. [d] नाभी or नाभिः, the navel. It is also masculine. [e] The royal court. [f] Cymbals. [g] Rejoicing: celebration by (song,) &c. According to another reading कर्करी, a small jar. [h] A drinking vessel; a cup or goblet. According to another reading, वारी, 1 A vessel for milking. 2 A rope for binding an elephant. [i] 1 Rising of a zodiacal sign. 2 Half a sign. 3 A sign of the zodiac. 4 Astrology. [j] 1 Name of a plant. 2 Name of a bird. 3 Lock of hair on the forehead. 4— on the side of the face. [k] 1 Blotch of the skin. 2 Sort of leprosy. [l] Lac. [m] Nit, egg of a louse. [n] A mouthful of water to rinse the mouth. [o] Gout or rheumatism affecting the thigh. [p] 1 A small ladle or spoon. 2 Lentils ground to meal. [q] Ink. Also masc. मषिः.

SECTION II.

The following are masculine viz. Nouns signifying gods, &c. a

11. पुंस्त्वे सभेदानुचराः सपर्य्यायाः सुरासुराः

स्वर्गयागाद्रिमेघाब्धिद्रुकालासिशरारयः

12. करगण्डौष्ठदोर्दन्त कण्ठकेशनखस्तनाः

Terms ending in अह्न or अह. b
Names of poisons. c
Compound terms in रात्र. d

अह्नाहान्ताः

क्ष्वेडभेदा

रात्रान्ताः प्रागसंख्यकाः

---

[a] Viz. Gods of various orders with their attendants (under some exceptions). Demons with their attendants (under some exceptions). Likewise the following (under certain exceptions), viz. heaven, and particular heavens ; sacrifice, and its varieties ; a mountain, and particular mountains ; a cloud, or particular descriptions of clouds ; a sea, and particular seas ; a tree, and particular species ; time, and the measures of time ; a sword, and sorts of swords ; an arrow, and varieties of arrows ; an enemy, and descriptions of enemies. Also, Revenue or tax. A ray of light. A hand. A cheek. A lip. An arm. A tooth. The throat. Hair. A nail. A pap. [The exceptions are stated in their places.] [b] As पूर्व्वाह्णः, forenoon. द्व्यहः, a couple of days. [c] With certain exceptions. [d] As वर्षारात्रः, a rainy night. Except in composition with a numeral. Ex. पञ्चरात्रं.

13. श्रीवेष्टाद्याश्च[b] निर्यासा — Resins and gums. [a]

असन्नन्ता अबाधिताः — Nouns in अस or अन्. [c]

कशेरु जतुवस्तूनि हित्वा तुरुविरामकाः — Nouns in तु or रु. [d]

14. क ष ण भ म रोपान्ता यद्यदन्ता अमी अथ — In अ with a penult क, &c. [e]

प थ न य स टोपान्ता — Or with a penult प, &c. [f]

गोत्राख्याः — Names of families. [g]

चरणाह्वयाः — Names of portions of the *Véda*.

15. नाम्न्यकर्त्तरि भावे च घञ ज प न ङ ण घा थुचः — Nouns in घञ्, &c. [h]

---

[a] Or other exudations of trees ; and any vegetable extracts. [b] According to another reading श्रीपिष्टः. [c] With many exceptions. Some erroneously read उस् or अस्. [d] Except कशेरु, root of Scirpus maximus ? which is neuter and masc. (some say fem.); जतु, lac ; वस्तु, a thing : both neuter : besides other exceptions. [e] Viz. क, ष, ण, भ, म, र. [f] Viz. प, थ, न, य, स, ट. Some understand this not to be limited to a final अ, but the better opinion so restricts it. Even with that restriction, the rule admits numerous exceptions. [g] Denominated from a patriarch. [h] Viz. Nouns denominative, terminated by the affixes घञ्, अच्, अप्, (all convertible into अ,) नङ् (न), ण, घ, (both convertible into अ,) and अथुच् (अथु), with the abstract sense, or denoting the import of any case except the agent ; or even this import, if the noun be not denominative. The rule admits exceptions.

In ल्यु, &c. [a]

ल्युः कर्त्तरीमनिज्भावे को घोः किः प्रादितोऽन्यतः

The compound term अश्ववडव. [b]

16. द्वन्द्वेऽश्ववडवावश्ववडवा न समाहृते

कान्त in composition [c]

कान्तः सूर्य्येन्दुपर्य्याय पूर्वोऽयः पूर्व्वकोऽपि च

The nouns here enumerated.

17. वटकः [d] (स्या)ऽनुवाक [e] (स्यु) रल्लक [f] (स्यु) कुटङ्गकः [g]

पुङ्खो [h] न्युङ्खः [i] समुद्ग [j] (स्यु) विट [k] पट्ट [l] घटाः [m] खटः [n]

---

[a] Viz. Terminated in ल्यु (convertible into अन) with the active import; in इमनिच् (इमन्) with the abstract sense (some say the passive als›); in क (convertible into अ), with the abstract sense; and in कि (इ) affixed to the verbs termed घु (viz. दा, &c.) with a preposition or noun prefixed. [b] Du. अश्ववडवौ, a horse and mare. pl. अश्ववडवाः, horses and mares: but अश्ववडवं, a stud of horses and mares. [c] With names of the sun and moon, or with the word अयस्. Ex. सूर्य-कान्तः, a crystal lens. [d] Pulse ground and fried with oil and butter. [e] A hymn in the *védas.* [f] 1 Sort of deer. 2 Eyelid. [g] Or कुटङ्ककः. 1 An arbour formed by creeping plants overrunning a tree. 2 A root or thatch. 3 A house or hut. [h] Feathered part of an arrow. [i] Or न्यूङ्खः. 1 Sixfold repetition of the triliteral name of God. 2 The *Sámavéda.* 3 Pleasing. [j] A box with a cover or lid. [k] A sodomite. [l] 1 Cloth. 2 Wove silk. 3 A royal patent. 4 A stone for grinding with a mullar. [m] A balance. [n] 1 Grass. 2 A blind well.

a b c d e f च

18. कोट्टारघट्टहट्टा (श्च) पिण्डगोलण्डविपिण्ड (वत्)

g h i j k l

गडुः करण्डोलगुडोवरण्ड (श्च) किणघुणाः

m n 1o p 2q r

19. इति सीमन्त हरितोरोमन्थोद्गीथबुद्बुदाः

s t u v w x

वासमर्द्दा ऽर्बुदः कुन्दफेनस्तूपौ (स) यूपकौ

1—तु. 2 च—.

a कोट्टः, a fort. According to another interpretation कोट्टारः, 1 The town well. 2 The stairs of a pond. b घरघट्टः, machine for drawing water. According to another interpretation, घट्टः, a wharf: stairs. c हट्टः, a market. d 1 A lump of food. 2 A lump of flesh ? 3 A body. 4 An oblation of food to the manes of ancestors. e 1 A tribe of mountaineers 2 A person having the navel prominent. Some read गोलः, others गोण्डः ; and interpret a lump of flesh on the navel. f The Abdomen. g 1 A goitre. 2 Hump on the back. h 1 A box with a lid or cover. 2 A basket. i 1 A staff. 2 A club armed with iron, or made of it. j 1 A multitude. 2 Pimples on the face. 3 A portico. k 1 A wart. 2 A scar. l An insect which eats wood. m Bellows. n Dressing of hair ; separating the hair, so as to leave a line on the top of the head. o Green colour. p Chewing the cud. q 1 Designation of the triliteral name of God. 2 A portion of the *Sámavéda.* r Bubble of water. s Or कासमर्दः. 1 The plant (Cassia esculenta). 2 An acid preparation of tamarind and mustard. t 1 In numeration ; a hundred millions. 2 In medicine, An indolent swelling. Some read अर्द्दनिः : 1 Fire. 2 Disease. u 1 The plant (Jasminum multiflorum). 2 A turner's lathe. v Froth. w A mound of earth. x यूपः, a sacrificial post to which a victim is bound. According to another reading पूपः, bread.

a b c d e

20. आतपः (क्षत्रिये) नाभि कणप क्षुरकेदराः

f g h i j k

पूरक्षुरप्रचुक्रा (श्च) गोल हिङ्गु,लपुद्गलाः

l m n o p

21. वेताल मल्लभल्ला (श्च) पुरोडाशो (ऽपि) पट्टिशः

q r s t

कुल्माषोऽरभस (श्चैव च) कटाहः पतद्ग्रहः

---

[a] Sunshine. [b] A soldier or man of the military tribe. [c] A spear or lance. According to another reading कुणपः, 1 A dead body. 2 A stink. 3 A spear. [d] Or क्षुरः. 1 A razor. 2 Barleria (or Ruellia) longifolia. [e] Name of a plant. [f] A wave. [g] Or क्षुरप्रः, sort of arrow. [h] चुक्रः, 1 Acid sauce. 2 Sorrel. [i] 1 A globe. 2 A widow's bastard. [j] हिङ्गुः, m. n. or हिङ्गुलः, m. Vermilion. [k] Or पुद्गलः, 1 Soul. 2 Body. [l] A dead body, occupied by an evil spirit. [m] A wrestler or boxer. [n] 1 A bear. m. f. 2 Sort of arrow. [o] Or पुरोडाः (स्). 1 The residue of an oblation. 2 Sort of oblation. [p] Or पट्टिसः, a battle axe. [q] Or कुल्माषः, a dish consisting of half boiled rice with pulse ; or half boiled barley, &c. [r] 1 Joy. 2 Mental exertion. [s] 1 A shallow boiler. 2 A turtle's shell. 3 A young buffalo. [t] A spitting pot.

SECTION III.

22. द्विहीने ऽन्यच्चारण्यपर्णश्वभ्रहिमोदकम्
शीतोष्णमांसरुधिर मुखाक्षिद्रविणम्बलम्

The following are neuter: viz. Nouns signifying sky, &c. [a]

23. फलहेमशुल्वलोह सुखदुःखशुभाशुभम्
जलपुष्पाणि लवणं व्यञ्जनान्यनुलेपनम्

24. कोट्याः शतादिसंख्यान्या वा लक्षा नियुतं च तत्
द्व्यच्कमस्सिसुसन्नन्तं

Dissyllables in अस् इस् उस् or अन्. [b]

यदनान्तमकर्त्तरि

Nouns in अन. [c]

---

[a] Viz. (Under various exceptions). The sky or atmosphere, or the etherial element; an organ of sense; a forest; a leaf; a hole; frost; water; cold; heat; flesh; blood; the face; an eye; wealth, substance; force, strength; forces, army; fruits of various sorts (or according to another reading हल, a plough); gold; copper; iron; metal; pleasure; pain; good luck; ill luck; aquatic flowers; salts of various kinds; sauce or condiment; and various sorts of condiments; perfumes of various kinds; numerals from 100 upwards, except कोटि, ten millions, which is fem. and लक्ष fem. and neut. and नियुत masc. and neut. both signifying a hundred thousand. [b] Example यशः (स्), glory. हविः (स्), oblation of butter. वपुः (स्), body. नाम (न्), name. [c] With that termination bearing any import but that of agent. गमनं, movement, going.

In त्र, ष and ल. a

25. त्रान्तं सलोपधं शिष्टं

In रात्र with a numeral. b

रात्रं प्राक् संख्ययान्वितम्

Compounds in पात्र, &c. c

पात्राद्यदन्तैरेकार्थो द्विगुर्लक्ष्यानुसारतः

Nouns compounded copulatively or adverbially. d

26. द्वन्द्वैकत्वाव्ययीभावौ

पथिन्, with a numeral or particle. e

पथः संख्याव्ययात्परः

छाया, with a word in the 6th case. f

षष्ठ्याश्छाया बहूनां चेद्विच्छायं

सभा in composition with the 6th case. g

संहतौ सभा

---

[a] Ex. मित्रं, a friend, तुषं chaff, कुलं, a family. The rule is subject to many exceptions. Some read त्र for ल, and interpret the rule as restricted to nouns in त्र with स्, or न् prefixed. Ex. वस्त्रं, cloth. यन्त्रं, a machine. [b] Ex. त्रिरात्रं, the duration of three nights. [c] Compound terms in अ formed of पात्र and certain other nouns with numerals; and signifying one whole. Ex. चतुर्युगं, entire period of the four ages. [d] The first implying one whole. Ex. शिरोग्रीवं, head and neck. The second joining a noun with a particle. Ex. यथाशक्ति, as much as able. [e] कापथं, a bad road. [f] Provided such word be plural. Ex. विच्छायं, shadow of a flock of birds. [g] Provided it signify an assembly. Ex. दासीसभं, a multitude of female slaves. Or whether it signify an assembly or a house, if the term to which it is joined signify king, (except the word राजन्), or a demon, or similar being, (neither man nor god). Ex. नृपसभं, a king's palace, or a meeting of kings. रक्षःसभं, a multitude of demons.

27. आबाधापि पराराजा ऽमनुष्यार्थादराजकात्

दासीसभं नृपसभं रक्षःसभमिमा दिशः

28. उपज्ञोपक्रमान्तश्च तदादित्वप्रकाशने — So उपज्ञा, and उपक्रम. a

कोपज्ञं कोपक्रमादि

कन्थोशीनरनामसु — Also कन्था. b

29. भावेनणकचिद्भ्यो ऽन्ये समूहे भावकर्मणोः — Nouns in affixes having an abstract sense. c

अदन्तप्रत्ययाः

पुण्यसुदिनाभ्यां त्वह्नःपरः — In अह्न, with certain terms. d

30. क्रियाव्ययानां भेदकान्येकत्वे ऽप्य् — Adverbs and epithets of indeclinables

उक्थतोटके [e] [f] — The nouns here specified.

---

[a] In composition with the sixth case, provided the import be commencement. Ex. कौपज्ञं, and कौपक्रमं, the creation by *Brahmá*. [b] Provided the compound term be the name of a town in the province of *Us'ínara*. Else it is feminine. Ex. सौशमिकन्थं and दाक्षिकन्था, names of towns; the first situated in *Us'ínara*, the other out of that province. [c] Being terminations in अ, forming verbal derivatives. Except न, (नङ्); ण, क, (as well as णच्,) reducible to अ; and such as are distinguished by an indicatory च. (as चञ्, &c.) Also affixes in अ, with the abstract or the passive import, or with the sense of multitude, forming derivatives from nouns. [d] Viz. With पुण्य, or सुदिन. Ex. पुण्याहं, a holiday. [e] 1 A portion of the *Sámavéda*. 2 A monosyllabic verse. [f] 1 Name of a metre. 2 Species of drama.

a b c d e f
चोचं पिच्छं ग्टहस्थूणं तिरीटं मर्मयोजने

g h i j
31. राजसूयं वाजपेयं गद्यपद्ये (कृतौ कवेः)

k l m n o p
माणिक्यभाष्यसिन्दूरचीरचीवरपञ्जरम्

q r s t u
32. लोकायतं हरितालं विदलं स्थालबाह्लिकम्

---

[a] 1 Half-eaten fruit. 2 Fruit of the palm. 3 A cocoanut. Or मोचं, a plantain. Also, according to another reading, खेटं, chase; hunting. [b] A peacock's tail: some say m. f. a monosyllabic verse. Also, according to different readings, उच्छं (vide उच्छ्रायं); and मुक्तं, released. [c] Pillar of a house. [d] 1 A turban. 2 A diadem. [e] A joint, or place of junction of parts of the body. [f] A long measure: 4 *Krósa.* [g] A grand sacrifice by an emperor attended by tributary kings. It is also masc. [h] Name of a sacrifice. [i] Prose. [j] Verse. [k] A gem. [l] 1 Commentary. 2 Sort of building. [m] Minium. [n] 1 Bark. 2 Rag. 3 Dress of a priest of the sect of *Budd'ha.* [o] Dress of a mendicant. 2 Dress of priest of the sect of *Budd'ha.* [p] Or पिञ्जरं, 1 A cage. 2 The ribs. It is also masc. [q] System of atheistical philosophy taught by CHARVA'CA. [r] Yellow orpiment. [s] A basket made of split bambus. 2 Bark of pomegranate. 3 Split peas. [t] A caldron. [u] 1 Name of a country. 2 Production of that country. Also बाह्लीकं, sort of saffron.

SECTION IV.

(पुंनपुंसकयोः) शेषो[a]ऽर्धर्च[b]पिण्याक[c]कण्टकाः[d]

33. मोदक[e]स्तण्डक[1f]ष्टङ्क[g]श्शाटकः[h] कर्वटो[i]ऽर्बुदः[j]

पातको[k]द्योग[2l]चरक[m]तमाला[n]मलका[o] नडः[p]

The nouns here specified are masculine and neuter.

---

1 स—. 2 ख—.

[a] Some include this among the terms exhibited : m. n. in the sense of remainder ; but masc. as a name of the eternal serpent *Séshanága*. [b] Half a verse of the *ve'das*. [c] An oil cake. [d] 1 A thorn or prickle. 2 A fault or defect. 3 Horripilation. [e] Sort of sweetmeat. [f] Performance. Right preparation. According to another reading दण्डकः, sort of metre. [g] टङ्कः, a hatchet, or a stone-cutter's chisel. Or, according to another reading, शङ्कः. 1 Grief at separation from a beloved object. 2 Terror. [h] A petticoat. [i] Capital of a district (of two or four hundred villages): not a city nor a village ; but partaking of both. Some write खर्वटः. But, according to another reading, कर्पटः, cloth. [j] 1 In numeration, a million. 2 In medicine, Ophthalmia. [k] Sin. [l] Exertion, endeavour. [m] Name of a book on medicine : (so dinominated from its author). Or वरकः, sewn cloth. [n] 1 Name of a tree. 2 Bark of bambu. [o] Emblic myrobalan. Or आमालकः, an inhabited place on a hill or mountain. [p] A hollow reed.

34. कुष्ठं^a मुण्डं^b सीधु^c बुस्तं^d क्ष्वेडितं^e क्षेमकुट्टिमम्^f ^g

सङ्गमं^h शतमाना^i ऽर्म^j शम्बला^k ऽव्यय^l ताण्डवम्^m

35. कवियं^n कन्द^o कार्पासं^p पारा^q ऽवारं^r युगन्धरम्^s

यूपं^t प्रग्रीव^u पात्रीवे^v यूषं^w चमस^x चिक्कसौ^y

---

[a] 1 Leprosy. 2 Costus. [b] 1 The head, m. f. n. 2 Shaved or shorn. [c] Rum. [d] 1 Forcemeat. 2 Fried meat. Some read बुक्कं. Also, according to various readings, पुस्तं plaster. धुस्तं, dust. मस्तं, excellence. [e] Warwhoop. [f] Well-being. [g] 1 A mine of gems. 2 Ground smoothed and plastered. 3 A poor man's abode, a cottage. [h] Confluence of rivers, &c. [i] 1 A *pala* of silver. 2 An *ád'haca.* [j] A disease of the eye. [k] शम्बलं or सम्बलं, stock for travelling expenses. [l] An indeclinable word. [m] Dancing with violent gesticulation. [n] A bridle. [o] A bulbous or tuberous root. Or कर्म, act. [p] Cotton cloth. Or कर्पासं, cotton. [q] The opposite bank or shore. [r] The near bank or shore. According to another reading, वारं, 1 Multitude. 2 Opportunity. 3 Succession. 4 Going forth to spy. [s] 1 A yoke. 2 Name of a mountain. [t] A post to which a victim is tied at a sacrifice. Or पूयं, Pus. [u] 1 A window. 2 A house for recreation. 3 Top of a tree. [v] पात्रीवं or पात्रीरं, sort of vessel used at religious ceremonies. [w] Or जूषं, Peas-porridge : the water of boiled pulse (Phaseolus mungo, &c.) [x] A spoon ; a vessel for drinking the extract of acid asclepias. [y] Barley meal.

36. अर्द्धर्चादौ घृतादीनां पुंस्त्वाद्यं वैदिकं ध्रुवम्[a]

तन्नोक्तमिह लोके ऽपि तच्चेदस्त्यस्तु शेषवत्

SECTION V.

37. स्त्रीपुंसयोरपत्यान्ता — The following are masculine and feminine, viz. Patronymics.

द्विचतुःषट्पदोरगाः

जातिभेदाः — Generic names of animals. [b]

पुमाख्याश्च स्त्रीयोगैः सह — Names of males, and by association, of females. [c]

मल्लकः[d] — The terms here specified.

---

[a] Certain other terms, as घृतं, &c. which are m. and n. in the *Védas*, are exclusively neuter in popular speech. Other terms, employed in both genders, must be learnt from practice. [b] As bipeds, quadrupeds, insects, reptiles; also fish, &c. This rule is however subject to exceptions. Ex मक्षिका, a fly. शिवा, a jackal. लूता, a spider. पिपीलिका, an ant. All which are feminine whatever sex be intended. [c] Ex. गोपः, a cowherd गोपी, a cowherd's wife. [d] A vessel holding oil: a cruet.

a b c 1d e f

38. मुनिर्वराटकः स्वातिर्वर्णको आटलिर्मनुः

g h i 2j k l m

मूषा त्वपाटी कर्कन्धुर्यष्टिः शाटी कटी कुटिः

SECTION VI.

The following are feminine and neuter, viz. Nouns in ष्यञ् or वुञ्, sometimes. n Compounds in सेना, &c. o

39. स्त्रीनपुंसकयोर्भावक्रिययोः ष्यञ् कचिच्च वुञ्

औचित्यमौचिती मैत्री मैत्रं वुञ् प्रागुदाहृतः

40. षष्ठ्यन्त प्राक्पदाः सेना छायाशालासुरानिशाः

स्याद्वा नृसेनं श्वनिशं गोशालमितरे च दिक्

---

1 व—. 2 व—.

[a] A devotee or ascetic. [b] A cowry. [c] The star: Arcturus. [d] A pigment, as indigo, orpiment, &c. But m. f. n. a perfume, as sandal wood. [e] Name of a tree. Some read पाटलिः, Bignonia chelonoides. [f] Name of Manu, or of his wife. [g] A crucible. [h] A measure: masc. त्वपाटः, fem. त्वपाटी. Also वसुपाटी,—टः, A stream of blood. [i] A jujube. [j] A staff. [k] A petticoat. [l] M. कटिः, and f. कटिः, कटी. The hollow above the hip. Or m. कटः, f. कटी, a mat. [m] A hut. [n] Nouns in ष्यञ्, (य), or वुञ् (अक), with the abstract or the passive import, are commonly fem. and neut. but sometimes fem. only; and sometimes neut. Ex. औचित्यं—ती, Propriety. मैत्र्यं, मैत्री, Friendship. वार्धकं,—का, Old age. [o] With a term in the sixth case. As नृसेनं, an army of men. श्वनिशं, a night during which dogs bark and howl. गोशालं, a cowpen.

41. आबन्तोत्तरपदो द्विगुश्चापुंसि नश्च लुप्

त्रिखट्वञ्च त्रिखट्वी च त्रितक्षञ्च त्रितक्ष्यपि

> Numerals with nouns in आप् or अन्.[a]

SECTION VII.

42. (त्रिषु) पात्री[b] पुटी[c] वाटी[d] पेटी[e] कुवलदाडिमौ

> The nouns here specified admit the three genders.

---

[a] Compound terms ending in nouns terminated by आप्, (आ, denoting the feminine) or by अन्; joined with numerals and denoting a single whole. The final न् is in such compounds expunged. Ex. त्रिखट्वं, or—ट्वी, aggregate of three beds. त्रितक्षं, or—क्षी, a party of three carpenters. [b] पात्रः,—त्री,—त्रं, a vessel. [c] पुटः, टी, टं; 1 A lid or cover. 2 A plate made of leaves. Or पटः,—टी,—टं, covering; cloth [d] वाटः, टी, टं, 1 An enclos^ed piece of ground: a yard. 2 An orchard, or place for planting Arecas, &c. 3 A road. [e] पेटः, टी or टा, टं; 1 A multitude: an assembly. 2 A basket. 3 Retinue. [f] कुवलं, —ली,—लं; 1 Jujube. 2 The jujube tree (some distribute the genders, m. f. the tree; n. the fruit). [g] दाडिमः,—मी, मं, pomegranate: (or else m. f. the tree; n. the fruit.)

SECTION VIII.

The gender of the final is retained. a That of another term is followed in certain compounds. b

परलिङ्गं स्वप्रधाने द्वन्द्वे तत्पुरुषे ऽपि तत्

43. अर्थान्ताः प्राद्यलं प्राप्तापन्नपूर्वाः परोपगाः

तद्धितार्थो द्विगुः

Numerals and pronouns. c Compound epithets. d Epithets expressing a quality, thing, or action. e

संख्या सर्वनाम तदन्तकाः

44. बहुव्रीहिरदिङ्नाम्ना मुन्नेया तदुदाहृतिः

गुणद्रव्यक्रियायोगोपाधयः परगामिनः

---

[a] In certain compound terms, viz. Conjunctive compounds in which the several terms are principal; and compound terms formed of a principal one with a modification of it. Ex. (fem.) कुक्कुटमयूर्यौ, a dunghill cock and a peahen. (masc.) मयूरीकुक्कुटौ, a peahen and a dunghill cock. (m.) कुलविप्रः, the priest of the family. (n.) विप्रकुलं, the family of the priest. [b] Viz. Those ending in the word अर्थं (as ब्राह्मणार्थः,—र्था,—र्थं, intended for a *Bráhman'a*): and compound terms beginning with प्र and certain other terms. (Ex. अलञ्जीविकः,—का,—कं, competent to a livelihood): and compound terms containing a numeral, and terminated by an affix peculiar to derivatives from nouns: (Ex. पञ्चकपालः,—ला,—लं, prepared in five posts). They agree in gender with another term. [c] And terms ending in numerals and pronouns. However, most numerals must be excepted; and the rule applies only to those from one to four, which agree in gender with the subject. [d] As बहुधनः,—ना,—नं, opulent. Except names of regions of space. [e] Example, m. f. n. शुक्लः (पटः) शुक्ला, शुक्लं, white cloth, &c. But शुक्लः, the white colour. दण्डी, दण्डिनी, दण्डि, one who bears a staff. याचक,—काः,—कं, one who begs.

45. कृतः कर्त्तर्य्यसंज्ञायां कृत्याः कर्त्तरि कर्मणि

अणाद्यन्तास्तेन रक्ताद्यर्थे नानार्थभेदकाः

46. षट्संज्ञकास्त्रिषु समा युष्मदस्मत्तिङव्ययम्

[d] परं विरोधे शेषं तु ज्ञेयं शिष्टप्रयोगतः

47. इत्यमरसिंहकृतौ नामलिङ्गानुशासने

सामान्यस्तृतीयः काण्डः साङ्ग एव समर्थितः ।

Verbal active nouns. a

Adjectives derived from nouns. b

Some numerals, &c. do not vary. c

---

[a] Derivatives from verbs, terminated by affixes named कृत्, and denoting the agent, but not forming denominatives. Ex. कर्त्ता,—र्त्री, र्त्तृ, agent. कुर्वन्, ती, त्, acting. Or terminated by affixes named कृत्य, with the active or passive, (not the neuter and abstract sense.) Ex. भव्यः (तरुः)—व्या,—व्यं, a tree, that is to be. गन्तव्यः (ग्रामः),—व्या, —व्यं, a village which may be approached or travelled to. [b] That is, according to the literal sense of this rule, Derivatives from nouns with the termination अण्, &c. (among the affixes named तद्धित), and which are epithets of various subjects, or of which the subjects are various. Ex. कौसुम्भः,—म्भी,—म्भं, dyed with safflower. हैमः, मी, मं, made of gold. ऐन्द्रः,—न्द्री,—न्द्रं, sacred to INDRA. [c] The numerals denominated षट्, viz. from 5 to 10, do not vary in gender: nor the personal pronouns; nor inflected verbs; nor indeclinable particles. [d] In instances where any of the preceding rules are at variance, the last is an exception to the first: and what has been left unsaid, must be learnt from the practice of good writers.

ALPHABETICAL INDEX.

N. B. p *stands for page. And* n. *for note. The English figures point out the couplets in which the word is to be found.*

एका—ऐका.

ऐका—ओज.

ओड़—औष्ठ.

कोठ—कोवि.

कोवि—कौल.

कौल—क्रन्दि.

चिन्ता—चिह्न.

चिवि—चेट.

चेट—चौरी.

निर्जि—निर्वा.

निर्वा—निशि.

निशी—निष्ठी.

नेमि—न्याय्य.

न्यास—पंक्ति.

पंक्ती—पटी.

प्रमा—प्रव.

प्रव—प्रस.

प्रस—प्रसू.

प्रसू—प्राक्.

प्रसूतिज, p 59, 3.
प्रसून, p90, 17. p336, 125.
प्रसृत, p 220, n. p 280, 38. p 160, 36.
प्रसृता, p 156, 23.
प्रसृति, p 160, n.
प्रसेव, p 227, 26. p46, n.
प्रसेवक, p 46, 7.
प्रस्तर, p 84, 4.
प्रस्ताव, p 293, 24.
प्रस्थ, p 242, 89. p85, 5. p 325, n.
प्रस्थपुष्प, p 105, 59.
प्रस्थान, p 214, 63.
प्रस्फोटन, p 227, 26.
प्रस्रवण, p 85, 5.
प्रस्राव, p 155, 18.
प्रस्वेद, p 54, n.
प्रहर, p 25, 6.
प्रहरण, p 204, n. p211, 50.
प्रहस्त, p 160, 35.
प्रहि, p 68, 26.
प्रहेलि, p 40, n.
प्रहेलिका, p 40; 6.
प्रह्लन, p 284, 52.
प्रांशु, p 275, 19.
प्राक्, p 380, 16.

प्राका—प्राथ.

प्राकार, p 78 3.
प्राक्तन, p 251, 16.
प्राग्वंश, p 178, 15.
प्राघ्वर, p 273, 7.
प्राचार, p 289, 10.
प्राच्, p 383, n.
प्राचिका, p 386, 8.
प्राची, p 16, 3.
प्राचीन, p 78, n
प्राचीना, p 106, 3.
प्राचीनावीत, p 188, 49.
प्राचीर, p 78, 3.
प्राच्य, p 74, 7.
प्राजन, p 222, 12.
प्राजितृ, p 206, 27.
प्राज्ञ, p 176, 5.
प्राज्ञा, p 140, 12. p33, n.
प्राज्ञी, p 140, 12. p 176, n.
प्राज्य, p 274, 12.
प्राड्विवाक, p 192, 5.
प्राण, p 12, 59.
प्राणिन्, p 33, 8.
प्रातर्, p 381, 19.
प्रातिहार, p 250, n.
प्रातिहारक, p 250, n.
प्रातिहारिक, p 250, 11.
प्राथमकल्पिक, p 177, 10.

प्रादु—प्रास.

प्रादुस्, p 375, 17. p 379, 12.
प्रादेश, p 159, 34.
प्रादेशन, p 182, 29.
प्राध्वन्, p 377, 4.
प्रान्तर, p 77, 17.
प्राप्त, p 280, 36. p 284, 54.
प्राप्तपञ्चत्व, p 218, 85.
प्राप्तरूप, p 338, 134.
प्राप्ति, p 320, 71.
प्राप्य, p 281, 42.
प्राभृत, p 197, 27.
प्राय, p 189, 52. p 344, 155. p 380, 17.
प्रायस्, p 410, 17.
प्रायश्चित्त, p 283, 47.
प्रारब्ध, p 173, 37.
प्रालम्बिका, p 165, 6.
प्रालेय, p 19, 20.
प्रावरण, p 169, 20.
प्रावार, p 169, 19.
प्रावृत, p 168, 15. n.
प्रावृता, p 168, n.
प्रावृष्, p 30, 19.
प्रावृषा, p 30, n.
प्रावृषायणी, p 106, 5.
प्रास, p 214, n.

मह—महि.

मही—माग.

माघ—मातृ.

मातृ—मायि.

मायु—माला.

मालि—मिथ्या.

रुत—रेप.

रेप—रोम.

रोमा—लक्ष.

लिप्सा—लेख.

लेख—लोल.

लोला—वंश.

वारि—वाल्क.

वाल्की—वासू.

वास्तु—वाह्लि.

वित—विद्रु.

विद्रु—विना.

विना—विपु.

सर—सर्ज्ज.

सर्ज्ज—सर्व्वा.

सर्व्वा—सह.

सुक—सुन्द.

सुन्द—सुर.

सुर—सुषे.

स्रोत—स्वर्ण.

स्वर्ण—स्वेद.

स्वैर—हरि.